UNI

Programmer's Guide: ANSI C and Programming Support Tools

UNIX
SYSTEM LABORATORIES

P R E N T I C E   H A L L

ORDERING INFORMATION

UNIX® SYSTEM V RELEASE 4.2 DOCUMENTATION

To order single copies of UNIX® SYSTEM V Release 4.2 documentation, please call (515) 284-6761.

ATTENTION DOCUMENTATION MANAGERS AND TRAINING DIRECTORS:
For bulk purchases in excess of 30 copies, please write to:

Corporate Sales Department
PTR Prentice Hall
113 Sylvan Avenue
Englewood Cliffs, N.J. 07632

or

Phone: (201) 592-2863
FAX: (201) 592-2249

ATTENTION GOVERNMENT CUSTOMERS:

For GSA and other pricing information, please call (201) 461-7107.

Prentice-Hall International (UK) Limited, *London*
Prentice-Hall of Australia Pty. Limited, *Sydney*
Prentice-Hall Canada Inc., *Toronto*
Prentice-Hall Hispanoamericana, S.A., *Mexico*
Prentice-Hall of India Private Limited, *New Delhi*
Prentice-Hall of Japan, Inc., *Tokyo*
Simon & Schuster Asia Pte. Ltd., *Singapore*
Editora Prentice-Hall do Brasil, Ltda., *Rio de Janeiro*

AT&T UNIX® System V Release 4

General Use and System Administration

UNIX® System V Release 4 Network User's and Administrator's Guide
UNIX® System V Release 4 Product Overview and Master Index
UNIX® System V Release 4 System Administrator's Guide
UNIX® System V Release 4 System Administrator's Reference Manual
UNIX® System V Release 4 User's Guide
UNIX® System V Release 4 User's Reference Manual

General Programmer's Series

UNIX® System V Release 4 Programmer's Guide: ANSI C
  and Programming Support Tools
UNIX® System V Release 4 Programmer's Guide: Character User Interface
  (FMLI and ETI)
UNIX® System V Release 4 Programmer's Guide: Networking Interfaces
UNIX® System V Release 4 Programmer's Guide: POSIX Conformance
UNIX® System V Release 4 Programmer's Guide: System Services
  and Application Packaging Tools
UNIX® System V Release 4 Programmer's Reference Manual

System Programmer's Series

UNIX® System V Release 4 ANSI C Transition Guide
UNIX® System V Release 4 BSD / XENIX® Compatibility Guide
UNIX® System V Release 4 Device Driver Interface / Driver–Kernel
  Interface (DDI / DKI) Reference Manual
UNIX® System V Release 4 Migration Guide
UNIX® System V Release 4 Programmer's Guide: STREAMS

Available from Prentice Hall

Contents

A   Appendix A: Enhanced asm Facility

B   Appendix B: Mapfile Option

Glossary

I   Index

Figures and Tables

Purpose

The *Programmer's Guide: ANSI C and Programming Support Tools* describes UNIX system tools supplied with the C compilation system for AT&T 3B2 and 6386 computers. We do not attempt to teach you how to program in C, nor do we cover every UNIX system tool you might conceivably use in creating a C program. The UNIX system text editor vi, for example, which you might use to create the source files for a C program, and the file system itself, are described in the *User's Guide*. UNIX system calls are described in the *Programmer's Guide: System Services and Application Packaging Tools*, networking services in the *Programmer's Guide: Networking Interfaces*, and so on. The guides themselves elaborate on two foundation documents of the UNIX system, the *User's Reference Manual* and the *Programmer's Reference Manual*. The manuals are foundation documents in the sense that they describe formally and comprehensively every feature of the UNIX system. Because their formality takes some getting used to, the guides are provided to help you get started.

This book concentrates on tools described in Section 1 of the *Programmer's Reference Manual*:

- the compilation system

- the program analysis tools lint, sdb, lprof, and cscope

- the program maintenance tools make and SCCS

- the program development tools lex, yacc, and m4

See Chapter 1 for a complete summary of contents. Of course, we refer you to other documents wherever appropriate.

We recommend two texts for programmers new to the C language: Kernighan and Ritchie, *The C Language*, Second Edition, 1988, Prentice-Hall; Harbison and Steele, *C: A Reference Manual*, Second Edition, 1987, Prentice-Hall. For implementation-specific details not covered in this book, refer to the *Application Binary Interface* for your machine. For tutorial discussions of the transition to ANSI C, consult the *ANSI C Transition Guide*.

Notation Conventions

The following conventions are observed in this book:

- Computer input and output appear in constant width type, substitutable values in *italic* type:

    $ cc *file.c file.c file.c*

    The dollar sign is the default system prompt for the ordinary user. There is an implied carriage return at the end of each command. When a command extends beyond the width of our page, we mark the break with a backslash and an indented second line:

    $ cc -L../archives -L../mylibs file1.c file2.c file3.c \
        file4.c -lfoo

    Of course, a command that extends beyond the width of your terminal screen will wrap around. You should use the backslash only if you enter the command exactly as we show it.

- In cases where you are expected to enter a control character, the character is shown as, for example, control_d or ^d. Either form means that you press the d key while holding down the CTRL key.

- A number in parentheses following a command or function name refers to the section of the *Programmer's Reference Manual* in which the command or function is described. ld(1), for example, means that the ld command is described in Section 1 of the *Programmer's Reference Manual*.

1 Overview

Introduction

This volume of the *Programmer's Guide* is about UNIX system tools that are used to create, maintain, and extend C programs. As we noted in the "Purpose" section in the beginning of this book, we do not attempt to teach you how to program in C. We assume you know how to do that, or are learning how to do it concurrently.

Nor could we possibly cover every tool that is supplied with the C compilation system, or every facet of the tools that we do cover. The *Programmer's Reference Manual* exists to do both those things. The idea, instead, is to explain and provide examples of how you use the most important of these tools, and to present a coherent picture of how they fit together. In addition, we have included material that we think most C programmers will find invaluable, but that does not lend itself to the reference manual format. The C compiler diagnostics chapter is a good example of what we mean.

So how should you read the *Guide*? If you are not experienced in writing C programs, you will probably want to read it sequentially, since, as far as possible, we've organized the tools in functional groupings. At the same time, you will also want to read it selectively. We don't expect anyone to read through all four hundred or so compiler diagnostics, or casual programmers to read the entire chapter on object files. The information you will need to make decisions about what to read is contained in the "Summary of Contents" section below, which introduces the programming support tools covered in the *Guide* and sketches their relationship. Before we turn to it, there's some background we want to give on C compilation and the C language.

C Compilation

The most important of the tools we discuss in these pages is the C compilation system, which translates your C source code into the machine instructions of the computer your program is to run on — compiles it, in other words. On the UNIX operating system, the command to do this is cc:

```
$ cc mycode.c
```

If your program is in multiple source files, then the command is

```
$ cc file1.c file2.c file3.c
```

and so on. As the examples suggest, the source files to be compiled must have names that end in the characters .c.

There are other things going on invisibly in these command lines that you will want to read about in Chapter 2, which describes the C compilation system. For now it's enough to note that either of these commands will create an executable program in a file called a.out in your current directory. The second command will also create in your current directory object files that correspond to each of your source files:

```
$ ls -1
a.out
file1.c
file1.o
file2.c
file2.o
file3.c
file3.o
```

Each .o file contains a binary representation of the C language code in the corresponding source file. The cc command creates and then links these object files to produce the executable object file a.out. The standard C library functions that you have called in your program — printf(), for example — are automatically linked with the executable at run time. You can, of course, avoid these default arrangements by using the command line options to cc that we describe in Chapter 2. We'll talk a bit more formally about link editing in the "Summary of Contents" section below. We'll look at libraries in the next section.

You execute the program by entering its name after the system prompt:

```
$ a.out
```

Since the name a.out is only of temporary usefulness, you will probably want to rename your executable:

```
$ mv a.out myprog
```

You can also give your program a different name when you compile it — with a cc command line option:

```
$ cc -o myprog file1.c file2.c file3.c
```

Here, too, you execute the program by entering its name after the prompt:

```
$ myprog
```

C Language

The UNIX system supports many programming languages, and C compilers are available on many different operating systems. All the same, the relationship between the UNIX system and the C language has been and remains very close. The language was developed on the UNIX operating system, and is used to code the UNIX system kernel. Most UNIX application programs are written in C.

Chapter 3 provides a complete reference guide to the C language. Here are some features of the language:

- basic data types: characters, integers of various sizes, and floating point numbers;

- derived data types: functions, arrays, pointers, structures, and unions;

- a rich set of operators, including bit-wise operators;

- flow of control: if, if–else, switch, while, do–while, and for statements.

Application programs written in C usually can be transported to other machines without difficulty. Programs written in ANSI standard C (conforming to standards set down by the American National Standards Institute) enjoy an even higher degree of portability.

Programs that require direct interaction with the UNIX system kernel — for low-level I/O, memory management, interprocess communication, and the like — can be written efficiently in C using the calls to system functions contained in the standard C library, and described in Section 2 of the *Programmer's Reference Manual*.

Modular Programming in C

C is a language that lends itself readily to modular programming. It is natural in C to think in terms of functions. And since the functions of a C program can be compiled separately, the next logical step is to put each function, or group of related functions, in its own file. Each file can then be treated as a component, or a module, of your program.

Chapter 3 describes how you write C code so that the modules of your program can communicate with each other. What we want to stress here is that coding a program in small pieces eases the job of making changes: you need only recompile the revised modules. It also makes it easier to build programs from code you have written already: as you write functions for one program, you will surely find that many can be picked up for another.

Libraries and Header Files

The standard libraries supplied by the C compilation system contain functions that you can use in your program to perform input/output, string handling, and other high-level operations that are not explicitly provided by the C language. Header files contain definitions and declarations that your program will need if it calls a library function. The functions that perform standard I/O, for example, use the definitions and declarations in the header file stdio.h. When you use the line

```
#include <stdio.h>
```

in your program, you assure that the interface between your program and the standard I/O library agrees with the interface that was used to build the library.

Chapter 2 describes some of the more important standard libraries and lists the header files that you need to include in your program if you call a function in those libraries. It also shows you how to use library functions in your program and how to include a header file. You can, of course, create your own libraries and header files, following the examples of modular programming described in Chapter 2.

How C Programs Communicate with the Shell

Information or control data can be passed to a C program as an argument on the command line, which is to say, by the shell. We have already seen, for instance, how you invoke the cc command with the names of your source files as arguments:

```
$ cc file1.c file2.c file3.c
```

When you execute a C program, command line arguments are made available to the function main() in two parameters, an argument count, conventionally called argc, and an argument vector, conventionally called argv. (Every C program is required to have an entry point named main.) argc is the number of arguments with which the program was invoked. argv is an array of pointers to character strings that contain the arguments, one per string. Since the command name itself is considered to be the first argument, or argv[0], the count is always at least one. Here is the declaration for main():

```
int
main(int argc, char *argv[])
```

For two examples of how you might use run-time parameters in your program, see the last subsection of Chapter 2.

The shell, which makes arguments available to your program, considers an argument to be any sequence of non-blank characters. Characters enclosed in single quotes ('abc def') or double quotes ("abc def") are passed to the program as one argument even if blanks or tabs are among the characters. You are responsible for error checking and otherwise making sure that the argument received is what your program expects it to be.

In addition to argc and argv, you can use a third argument: envp is an array of pointers to environment variables. You can find more information on envp in the *Programmer's Reference Manual* under exec in Section 2 and environ in Section 5.

C programs exit voluntarily, returning control to the operating system, by returning from main() or by calling the exit() function. That is, a return(n) from main() is equivalent to the call exit(n). (Remember that main() has type "function returning int.")

Your program should return a value to the operating system to say whether it completed successfully or not. The value gets passed to the shell, where it becomes the value of the $? shell variable if you executed your program in the foreground. By convention, a return value of zero denotes success, a non-zero return value means some sort of error occurred. You can use the macros EXIT_SUCCESS and EXIT_FAILURE, defined in the header file stdlib.h, as return values from main() or argument values for exit().

Summary of Contents

This section sketches the programming support tools covered by the *Guide* in five functional groupings:

- creating an executable

- program analysis

- program management

- program development

- advanced programming utilities

Italicized notes suggest typical ways in which the tools are used.

In addition to the chapters discussed here, the *Guide* includes appendices on assembly language escapes that use the keyword asm, and on mapfiles, a facility for mapping object file input sections to executable file output segments. It also includes a glossary and an index.

Creating an Executable

Chapter 2 describes the C compilation system, the set of software tools that you use to generate an executable program from C language source files. It contains material that will be of interest to the novice and expert programmer alike.

The first section, "Compiling and Linking," details the command line syntax that is used to produce a binary representation of a program — an executable object file. We mentioned earlier that the modules of a C program can communicate with each other. A symbol declared in one source file can be defined in another, for example. Link editing refers to the process whereby the symbol referenced in the first file is connected with the definition in the second. By means of command line options to the cc command, you can select either of two link editing models:

- static linking, in which external references are resolved before execution;

- dynamic linking, in which external references are resolved during execution.

"Compiling and Linking" describes, among many other things, the options that let you tailor the link editor's behavior to your needs. It also includes a discussion of the advantages and disadvantages of each model. One major difference is that dynamic linking permits library code to be shared — used simultaneously — by different programs at run time. Another is that dynamically linked code can be fixed or enhanced without having to relink applications that depend on it.

The second section of the chapter, "Libraries and Header Files," focuses on the standard C library, in particular, the functions you use for standard I/O. It also describes the math library and libgen. The header files that you need to include in your program if you call a function in these libraries are listed in this section.

Use the cc *command and its options to control the process in which object files are created from source files, then linked with each other and with the library functions called in your program.*

As noted, Chapter 3 provides a reference guide to the C language, which is to say, the language accepted by the C compilation system. Chapter 4 lists the warning and error messages produced by the C compiler. Check the code examples given in the compiler diagnostics chapter when you need to clarify your understanding of the rules of syntax and semantics summarized in the language chapter. In many cases they'll prove helpful.

Program Analysis

The lint program, described in Chapter 5, checks for code constructs that may cause your C program not to compile, or to execute with unexpected results. lint issues every error and warning message produced by the C compiler. It also issues "lint-specific" warnings about inconsistencies in definition and use across files and about potential portability problems. The chapter includes a list of these warnings, with examples of source code that would elicit them.

sdb stands for "symbolic debugger," which means that you can use the symbolic names in your program to pinpoint where a problem has occurred. You can run your program under control of sdb to see what the program is doing up to the point at which it fails. Alternatively, you can use it to rummage through a core image file left by a program that failed. That lets you check the status of the program at the moment of failure, which may disclose the underlying problem. Chapter 6 is a tutorial on sdb.

Use lint *to check your program for portability and cross-file consistency, and to assure it will compile. Use* sdb *to locate a bug.*

Profilers are tools that analyze the dynamic behavior of your program: how fast and how often the parts of its code are executed.

- prof is a time profiler. It reports the amount of time and the percentage of time that was spent executing the parts of a program. It also reports the number of calls to each function and the average execution time of the calls.

- lprof is a line-by-line frequency profiler. It reports how many times each line of C source code was executed. In that way, it lets you identify the unexecuted and most frequently executed parts of your code.

Chapter 7 of the *Guide* discusses the lprof program in greater detail. It includes an overview of the C profiling utilities that describes the procedure you must follow to profile a program with either of these tools.

The cscope browser is an interactive program that locates specified elements of code in C, lex, or yacc source files. It lets you search and, if you want, edit your source files more efficiently than you could with a typical editor. That's because cscope knows about function calls — when a function is being called, when it is doing the calling — and C language identifiers and keywords. Chapter 8 is a tutorial on the cscope browser.

Use prof *and* lprof *to identify, and* cscope *to rewrite, inefficient lines of code. Use* cscope *for any other program-editing task.*

Program Management

A number of UNIX system tools were designed to make it easier to manage C programs. make, Chapter 9, is used to keep track of the dependencies between modules of a program, so that when one module is changed, dependent ones are brought up to date. make reads a specification of how the modules of your program depend on each other, and what to do when one of them is modified. When make finds a component that has been changed more recently than modules that depend on it, the specified commands — typically to recompile the dependent modules — are passed to the shell for execution.

The Source Code Control System, SCCS, is a set of programs that you can use to track evolving versions of files, ordinary text files as well as source files. When a file has been put under control of SCCS, you can specify that only a single copy of any version of it can be retrieved for editing at a time. When the edited file is returned to SCCS, the changes are recorded. That makes it possible to audit the changes and reconstruct the file's earlier versions. Chapter 10 describes SCCS.

Use make *for any program with multiple files. Use SCCS to keep track of program versions.*

Program Development

Two UNIX system tools were designed to make it easier to build C programs. lex, Chapter 11, and yacc, Chapter 12, generate C language modules that can be useful components of a larger application, in fact, any kind of application that needs to recognize and act on a systematic input.

lex generates a C language module that performs lexical analysis of an input stream. The lexical analyzer scans the input stream for sequences of characters — tokens — that match regular expressions you specify. When a token is found, an action, which you also specify, is performed.

yacc generates a C language module that parses tokens that have been passed to it by a lexical analyzer. The parser describes the grammatical form of the tokens according to rules you specify. When a particular grammatical form is found, an action, which again you specify, is taken. The lexical analyzer need not have been generated by lex. You could write it in C, with somewhat more effort.

Use lex *to create the lexical analyzer, and* yacc *the parser, of a user interface.*

Advanced Programming Utilities

Chapter 13, "Object Files," describes the executable and linking format (ELF) of the object code produced by the C compilation system. Strictly speaking, the chapter is required reading only for programmers who need to access and manipulate object files. Still, because it provides a larger perspective on the workings of the compilation system, especially the dynamic linking mechanism, it may prove useful to readers who seek to widen their understanding of the material presented in earlier chapters.

Chapter 14, "Floating Point Operations," details the standard single- and double-precision data types, operations, and conversions for floating point arithmetic that are generated by the C compiler. It also describes the low-level library functions that are provided to programmers who need the full range of floating point support. Most users will not need to call low-level functions to employ floating point operations in their programs. Those who do will find the information they need in Chapter 14.

Chapter 15 describes m4, a general purpose macro processor that can be used to preprocess C and assembly language programs.

Other Tools

This section lists programming support tools that do not receive extended treatment in the *Guide*. Consult the index for references to these tools in related contexts, and Section 1 of the *Programmer's Reference Manual* for details of usage.

Tools for analyzing source code:

- cflow produces a chart of the external references in C, lex, yacc, and assembly language files. Use it to check program dependencies.

- ctrace prints out variables as each program statement is executed. Use it to follow the execution of a C program statement by statement.

- cxref analyzes a group of C source files and builds a cross-reference table for the automatic, static, and global symbols in each file. Use it to check program dependencies and to expose program structure.

Tools for reading and manipulating object files:

- cof2elf translates object files in the common object file format (COFF) to the executable and linking format (ELF).

- dis disassembles object files.

- dump dumps selected parts of object files.

- lorder generates an ordered listing of object files.

- mcs manipulates the sections of an object file.

- nm prints the symbol table of an object file.

- size reports the number of bytes in an object file's sections or loadable segments.

- strip removes symbolic debugging information and symbol tables from an object file.

2 C Compilation System

ANSI C and Programming Support Tools

Introduction

This chapter describes the UNIX system tools that you use to generate an executable program from C language source files.

The first section, "Compiling and Linking," details the command line syntax that you use to produce a binary representation of a program — an executable object file. It concentrates on the options to the cc command that control the process in which object files are, first, created from source files, then linked with each other and with the library functions that you have called in your program. As we indicated in Chapter 1, the major focus of the section is on static vs. dynamic linking: how each model is implemented and invoked, and its relative merits.

Standard libraries are the focus of the second section of the chapter, "Libraries and Header Files." Because the C language contains no intrinsic input/output facility, for example, I/O must be carried out by explicitly called functions. On the UNIX system, the functions that perform these and other high-level tasks have been standardized and grouped in libraries; they are convenient, portable, and, in most cases, optimized for your machine. The contents of some important standard libraries are described later in this chapter.

Header files contain definitions and declarations that serve as the interface between your program and the functions in these libraries. They also contain a number of "functions" — getc() and putc(), for example — that actually are defined as macros. (The manual page will generally tell you whether what you are using is a macro or a function. As a practical matter, it makes very little difference: you use them the same way in your program.) The descriptions of standard libraries in this chapter show the header files that you need to include in your program if you call a function in those libraries; the manual page for each function also lists the required header files. In a later section of this chapter, we'll show you how to use library functions in your program and how to include header files. We'll pay particular attention to standard I/O.

Compiling and Linking

The C compilation system consists of a compiler, assembler, and link editor. The cc command invokes each of these components automatically unless you use command line options to specify otherwise. Before we turn to the cc command line syntax, let's look briefly at the four steps in which an executable C program is created:

1. The preprocessor component of the compiler reads lines in your source files that direct it to replace a name with a token string (#define), perhaps conditionally (#if, for example). It also accepts directives in your source files to include the contents of a named file in your program (#include). As we'll see in the second part of this chapter, included header files for the most part consist of #define directives and declarations of external symbols, definitions and declarations that you want to make available to more than one source file.

2. The compiler proper translates the C language code in your source files, which now contain the preprocessed contents of any included header files, into assembly language code.

3. The assembler translates the assembly language code into the machine instructions of the computer your program is to run on. As we indicated in Chapter 1, these instructions are stored in object files that correspond to each of your source files. In other words, each object file contains a binary representation of the C language code in the corresponding source file. Object files are made up of sections, of which there are usually at least two. The text section consists mainly of program instructions; text sections normally have read and execute, but not write, permissions. Data sections normally have read, write, and execute permissions. See Chapter 13 for the details of the object file format.

4. The link editor links these object files with each other and with any library functions that you have called in your program, although when it links with the library functions depends on the link editing model you have chosen:

   - An archive, or *statically* linked library, is a collection of object files each of which contains the code for a function or a group of related functions in the library. When you use a library function in your program, and specify a static linking option on the cc command line, a copy of the object file that contains the function is incorporated in your executable at link time.

■ A shared object, or *dynamically* linked library, is a single object
file that contains the code for every function in the library.
When you call a library function in your program, and specify a
dynamic linking option on the cc command line, the entire contents of the shared object are mapped into the virtual address
space of your process at run time. As its name implies, a shared
object contains code that can be used simultaneously by different
programs at run time.

We'll discuss these two ways in which libraries are implemented in the "Link
Editing" section below. We'll also show you how to combine the static and
dynamic linking approaches in different ways according to your needs.

Figure 2-1 shows the organization of the C compilation system. Note that we
have omitted discussing the optimizer here because it is optional. We'll show
you how to invoke it in "Commonly Used cc Command Line Options" below.

Figure 2-1: Organization of C Compilation System

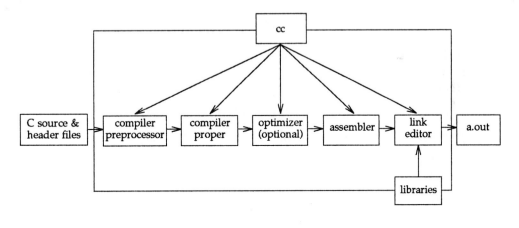

Basic cc Command Line Syntax

Now let's look at how this process works for a C language program to print the words hello, world. Here is the source code for the program, which we have written in the file hello.c:

```
#include <stdio.h>
main()
{
        printf("hello, world\n");
}
```

As we noted in Chapter 1, the UNIX system command to create an executable program from C language source files is cc:

```
$ cc hello.c
```

As we also noted there, the source files to be compiled must have names that end in the characters .c. Otherwise you can name them anything you want.

Since we haven't committed any syntactic or semantic errors in our source code, the above command will create an executable program in the file a.out in our current directory:

```
$ ls -1
a.out
hello.c
```

Note that a .o file is not created when you compile a single source file.

We can execute the program by entering its name after the system prompt:

```
$ a.out
hello, world
```

Since the name a.out is only of temporary usefulness, we'll rename the executable:

```
$ mv a.out hello
```

We could also have given the program the name hello when we compiled it, with the -o option to the cc command:

```
$ cc -o hello hello.c
```

In either case, we execute the program by entering its name after the system prompt:

```
$ hello
hello, world
```

Now let's look at how the cc command controls the four-step process that we described in the previous section. When we specify the −P option to cc, only the preprocessor component of the compiler is invoked:

```
$ cc -P hello.c
```

The preprocessor's output — the source code plus the preprocessed contents of stdio.h — is left in the file hello.i in our current directory:

```
$ ls -1
hello.c
hello.i
```

That output could be useful if, for example, you received a compiler error message for the undefined symbol a in the following fragment of source code:

```
if (i > 4)
{
        /* declaration follows
        int a; /* end of declaration */
        a = 4;
}
```

The unterminated comment on the third line will cause the compiler to treat the declaration that follows it as part of a comment. Because the preprocessor removes comments, its output

```
if (i > 4)
{


        a = 4;
}
```

will clearly show the effect of the unterminated comment on the declaration. You can also use the preprocessed output to examine the results of conditional compilation and macro expansion.

If we specify the -S option to the cc command, only the preprocessor and compiler phases are invoked:

```
$ cc -S hello.c
```

The output — the assembly language code for the compiled source — is left in the file hello.s in our current directory. That output could be useful if you were writing an assembly language routine and wanted to see how the compiler went about a similar task.

If, finally, we specify the -c option to cc, all the components but the link editor are invoked:

```
$ cc -c hello.c
```

The output — the assembled object code for the program — is left in the object file hello.o in our current directory. You would typically want this output when using make (Chapter 9).

Now we need only enter the command

```
$ cc hello.o
```

to create the executable object file a.out. By default, the link editor arranges for the standard C library function that we have called in our program — printf() — to be linked with the executable at run time. In other words, the standard C library is a shared object, at least in the default arrangement we are describing here.

The outputs we have described above are, of course, inputs to the components of the compilation system. They are not the only inputs, however. The link editor, for example, will supply code that runs just before and just after your program to do startup and cleanup tasks. This code is automatically linked with your program only when the link editor is invoked through cc. That's why we specified cc hello.o in the previous example rather than ld hello.o. For similar reasons, you should invoke the assembler through cc rather than as:

```
$ cc hello.s
```

As we noted in Chapter 1, the compilation process is largely identical if your program is in multiple source files. The only difference is that the default cc command line will create object files, as well as the executable object file a.out, in your current directory:

```
$ cc file1.c file2.c file3.c
$ ls -1
a.out
file1.c
file1.o
file2.c
file2.o
file3.c
file3.o
```

What this means is that if one of your source files fails to compile, you need not recompile the others. Suppose, for example, you receive a compiler error diagnostic for file1.c in the above command line. Your current directory will look like this:

```
$ ls -1
file1.c
file2.c
file2.o
file3.c
file3.o
```

That is, compilation proceeds but linking is suppressed. Assuming you have fixed the error, the following command

```
$ cc file1.c file2.o file3.o
```

will create the object file file1.o and link it with file2.o and file3.o to produce the executable program a.out. As the example suggests, C source files are compiled separately and independently. To create an executable program, the link editor must connect the definition of a symbol in one source file with external references to it in another.

Note, finally, that not all the cc command line options that we have discussed are compiler options. Because, for example, it is the link editor that creates an executable program, the −o option — the one you use to give your program a name other than a.out — is actually an ld option that is accepted by the cc command and passed to the link editor. We'll see further examples of this below. The main reason we mention it is so that you can read about these options on the appropriate manual page.

Commonly Used cc Command Line Options

In this section we'll talk about cc command line options that let you

- specify the order in which directories are searched for included header files;
- prepare your program for symbolic debugging or profiling;
- optimize your program.

We'll postpone until the next section a discussion of the cc command line options that you use to link your program with the library functions you have called in it.

Searching for a Header File

Recall that the first line of our sample program was

```
#include <stdio.h>
```

The format of that directive is the one you should use to include any of the standard header files that are supplied with the C compilation system. The angle brackets (< >) tell the preprocessor to search for the header file in the standard place for header files on your system, usually the /usr/include directory.

The format is different for header files that you have stored in your own directories:

```
#include "header.h"
```

The quotation marks (" ") tell the preprocessor to search for header.h first in the directory of the file containing the #include line, which will usually be your current directory, then in the standard place.

If your header file is not in the current directory, you specify the path of the directory in which it is stored with the −I option to cc. Suppose, for instance, that you have included both stdio.h and header.h in the source file mycode.c:

```
#include <stdio.h>
#include "header.h"
```

Suppose further that `header.h` is stored in the directory `../defs`. The command

```
$ cc -I../defs mycode.c
```

will direct the preprocessor to search for `header.h` first in the current directory, then in the directory `../defs`, and finally in the standard place. It will also direct the preprocessor to search for `stdio.h` first in `../defs`, then in the standard place — the difference being that the current directory is searched only for header files whose name you have enclosed in quotation marks.

You can specify the `-I` option more than once on the `cc` command line. The preprocessor will search the specified directories in the order they appear on the command line. Needless to say, you can specify multiple options to `cc` on the same command line:

```
$ cc -o prog -I../defs mycode.c
```

Preparing Your Program for Symbolic Debugging

When you specify the `-g` option to `cc`

```
$ cc -g mycode.c
```

you arrange for the compiler to generate information about program variables and statements that will be used by the symbolic debugger `sdb` (Chapter 6). The information supplied to `sdb` will allow you to use the symbolic debugger to trace function calls, display the values of variables, set breakpoints, and so on.

Preparing Your Program for Profiling

To use either of the profilers (Chapter 7) that are supplied with the C compilation system, you must do two things:

1. Compile and link your program with a profiling option:

    ```
    for prof:   $ cc -qp mycode.c
    for lprof:  $ cc -ql mycode.c
    ```

2. Run the profiled program:

    ```
    $ a.out
    ```

At the end of execution, data about your program's run-time behavior are written to a file in your current directory:

for prof: mon.out
for lprof: *prog*.cnt

where *prog* is the name of the profiled program. The files are inputs to the profilers.

Optimizing Your Program

The −O option to cc invokes the optimizer:

```
$ cc -O mycode.c
```

The optimizer improves the efficiency of the assembly language code generated by the compiler. That, in turn, will speed the execution time of your object code. Use the optimizer when you have finished debugging and profiling your program.

Link Editing

NOTE Because we try to cover the widest possible audience in this section, it may provide more background than many users will need to link their programs with a C language library. If you are interested only in the how-to, and are comfortable with a purely formal presentation that scants motivation and background alike, you may want to skip to the quick-reference guide in the last subsection.

Link editing refers to the process in which a symbol referenced in one module of your program is connected with its definition in another — more concretely, the process by which the symbol printf() in our sample source file hello.c is connected with its definition in the standard C library. Whichever link editing model you choose, static or dynamic, the link editor will search each module of your program, including any libraries you have used, for definitions of undefined external symbols in the other modules. If it does not find a definition for a symbol, the link editor will report an error by default, and fail to create an executable program. (Multiply defined symbols are treated differently, however, under each approach. For details, see the section "Multiply Defined Symbols" below.) The principal difference between static and dynamic linking lies in what happens after this search is completed:

- Under static linking, copies of the archive library object files that satisfy still unresolved external references in your program are incorporated in your executable at link time. External references in your program are connected with their definitions — assigned addresses in memory — when the executable is created.

- Under dynamic linking, the contents of a shared object are mapped into the virtual address space of your process at run time. External references in your program are connected with their definitions when the program is executed.

In this section, we'll examine the link editing process in detail. We'll start with the default arrangement, and with the basics of linking your program with the standard libraries supplied by the C compilation system. Later, we'll discuss the implementation of the dynamic linking mechanism, and look at some coding guidelines and maintenance tips for shared library development. Throughout the discussion, we'll consider the reasons why you might prefer dynamic to static linking. These are, briefly:

- Dynamically linked programs save disk storage and system process memory by sharing library code at run time.

- Dynamically linked code can be fixed or enhanced without having to relink applications that depend on it.

Default Arrangement

We stated earlier that the default cc command line

```
$ cc file1.c file2.c file3.c
```

would create object files corresponding to each of your source files, and link them with each other to create an executable program. These object files are called relocatable object files because they contain references to symbols that have not yet been connected with their definitions — have not yet been assigned addresses in memory.

We also suggested that this command line would arrange for the standard C library functions that you have called in your program to be linked with your executable automatically. The standard C library is, in this default arrangement, a shared object called libc.so, which means that the functions you have called will be linked with your program at run time. (There are some exceptions. A number of C library functions have been left out of libc.so by design. If you use one of these functions in your program, the code for the function will be incorporated in your executable at link time. That is, the function will still be automatically linked with your program, only statically rather than dynamically.) The standard C library contains the system calls described in Section 2 of the *Programmer's Reference Manual*, and the C language functions described in Section 3, Subsections 3C and 3S. See the second part of this chapter for details.

Now let's look at the formal basis for this arrangement:

1. By convention, shared objects, or dynamically linked libraries, are designated by the prefix lib and the suffix .so; archives, or statically linked libraries, are designated by the prefix lib and the suffix .a. libc.so, then, is the shared object version of the standard C library; libc.a is the archive version.

2. These conventions are recognized, in turn, by the −l option to the cc command. That is,

   ```
   $ cc file1.c file2.c file3.c −lx
   ```

   directs the link editor to search the shared object libx.so or the archive library libx.a. The cc command automatically passes −lc to the link editor.

3. By default, the link editor chooses the shared object implementation of a library, libx.so, in preference to the archive library implementation, libx.a, in the same directory.

4. By default, the link editor searches for libraries in the standard places on your system, /usr/ccs/lib and /usr/lib, in that order. The standard libraries supplied by the compilation system normally are kept in /usr/ccs/lib.

Adding it up, we can say, more exactly than before, that the default cc command line will direct the link editor to search /usr/ccs/lib/libc.so rather than its archive library counterpart. We'll look at each of the items that make up the default in more detail below.

libc.so is, with one exception, the only shared object library supplied by the C compilation system. (The exception, libdl.so, is used with the programming interface to the dynamic linking mechanism described later. Other shared object libraries are supplied with the operating system, and usually are kept in the standard places.) In the next section, we'll show you how to link your program with the archive version of `libc` to avoid the dynamic linking default. Of course, you can link your program with libraries that perform other tasks as well. Finally, you can create your own shared objects and archive libraries. We'll show you the mechanics of doing that below.

The default arrangement, then, is this: the `cc` command creates and then links relocatable object files to generate an executable program, then arranges for the executable to be linked with the shared C library at run time. If you are satisfied with this arrangement, you need make no other provision for link editing on the `cc` command line.

Linking with Standard Libraries

`libc.so` is a single object file that contains the code for every function in the shared C library. When you call a function in that library, and dynamically link your program with it, the entire contents of `libc.so` are mapped into the virtual address space of your process at run time.

Archive libraries are configured differently. Each function, or small group of related functions (typically, the related functions that you will sometimes find on the same manual page), is stored in its own object file. These object files are then collected in archives that are searched by the link editor when you specify the necessary options on the `cc` command line. The link editor makes available to your program only the object files in these archives that contain a function you have called in your program.

As noted, `libc.a` is the archive version of the standard C library. The `cc` command will automatically direct the link editor to search `libc.a` if you turn off the dynamic linking default with the −dn option:

```
$ cc -dn file1.c file2.c file3.c
```

Copies of the object files in `libc.a` that resolve still unresolved external references in your program will be incorporated in your executable at link time.

If you need to point the link editor to standard libraries that are not searched automatically, you specify the −l option explicitly on the `cc` command line. As we have seen, −lx directs the link editor to search the shared object `lib$x$.so` or the archive library `lib$x$.a`. So if your program calls the function `sin()`, for example, in the standard math library `libm`, the command

```
$ cc file1.c file2.c file3.c -lm
```

will direct the link editor to search for `/usr/ccs/lib/libm.so`, and if it does not find it, /usr/ccs/lib/libm.a, to satisfy references to sin() in your program. Because the compilation system supplies shared object versions only of libc and libdl, the above command will direct the link editor to search libm.a unless you have installed a shared object version of libm in the standard place. Note that because we did not turn off the dynamic linking default with the −dn option, the above command will direct the link editor to search libc.so rather than libc.a. You would use the same command with the −dn option to link your program statically with libm.a and libc.a. The contents of libm are described in the second part of this chapter.

Note, finally, that because the link editor searches an archive library only to resolve undefined external references it has previously seen, the placement of the −l option on the cc command line is important. That is, the command

```
$ cc −dn file1.c −lm file2.c file3.c
```

will direct the link editor to search libm.a only for definitions that satisfy still unresolved external references in file1.c. As a rule, then, it's best to put −l at the end of the command line.

Creating and Linking with Archive and Shared Object Libraries

In this section we describe the basic mechanisms by which archives and shared objects are built. The idea is to give you some sense of where these libraries come from, as a basis for understanding how they are implemented and linked with your programs. Of course, if you are developing a library, you will need to know the material in this section. Even if you are not, it should prove a useful introduction to the subsequent discussion.

The following commands

```
$ cc −c function1.c function2.c function3.c
$ ar −r libfoo.a function1.o function2.o function3.o
```

will create an archive library, libfoo.a, that consists of the named object files. (Check the ar(1) manual page for details of usage.) When you use the −l option to link your program with libfoo.a

```
$ cc −Ldir file1.c file2.c file3.c −lfoo
```

the link editor will incorporate in your executable only the object files in this archive that contain a function you have called in your program. Note, again, that because we did not turn off the dynamic linking default with the −dn option, the above command will direct the link editor to search libc.so as well as libfoo.a. We'll look at the directory search option — represented in the above command line by -L*dir* — in the next section. For now it's enough to note that you use it to point the link editor to the directory in which your library is stored.

You create a shared object library by specifying the -G option to the link editor:

```
$ cc -G -o libfoo.so function1.o function2.o function3.o
```

That command will create the shared object libfoo.so consisting of the object code for the functions contained in the named files. (We are deferring for the moment a discussion of a compiler option, -K PIC, that you should use in creating a shared object. For that discussion, see the "Implementation" section below.) When you use the -l option to link your program with libfoo.so

```
$ cc -Ldir file1.c file2.c file3.c -lfoo
```

the link editor will record in your executable the name of the shared object and a small amount of bookkeeping information for use by the system at run time. Another component of the system — the dynamic linker — does the actual linking.

A number of things are worth pointing out here. First, because shared object code is not copied into your executable object file at link time, a dynamically linked executable normally will use less disk space than a statically linked executable. For the same reason, shared object code can be changed without breaking executables that depend on it. In other words, even if the shared C library were enhanced in the future, you would not have to relink programs that depended on it (as long as the enhancements were compatible with your code; see "Checking for Run-Time Compatibility" below). The dynamic linker would simply use the definitions in the new version of the library to resolve external references in your executables at run time.

Second, we specified the name of the shared object that we wanted to be created under the -G option. Of course, you don't have to do it the way we did. The following command, for example, will create a shared object called a.out:

```
$ cc -G function1.o function2.o function3.o
```

You can then rename the shared object:

```
$ mv a.out libfoo.so
```

As noted, you use the lib prefix and the .so suffix because they are conventions recognized by -l, just as are lib and .a for archive libraries. So while it

is legitimate to create a shared object that does not follow the naming convention, and to link it with your program

```
$ cc -G -o sharedob function1.o function2.o function3.o
$ cc file1.c file2.c file3.c /path/sharedob
```

we recommend against it. Not only will you have to enter a path name on the
cc command line every time you use sharedob in a program, that path name
will be hard-coded in your executables. The reason why you want to avoid this
is related to our next point.

We said that the command line

```
$ cc -Ldir file1.c file2.c file3.c -lfoo
```

would direct the link editor to record in your executable the name of the shared
object with which it is to be linked at run time. Note: the *name* of the shared
object, not its path name. What this means is that when you use the −l option
to link your program with a shared object library, not only must the link editor
be told which directory to search for that library, so must the dynamic linker
(unless the directory is the standard place, which the dynamic linker searches by
default). We'll show you how to point the dynamic linker to directories in the
section "Specifying Directories to Be Searched by the Dynamic Linker" below.
What we want to stress here is that as long as the path name of a shared object
is not hard-coded in your executable, you can move the shared object to a different directory without breaking your program. That's the main reason why
you should avoid using path names of shared objects on the cc command line.
Those path names will be hard-coded in your executable. They won't be if you
use −l.

Finally, the cc −G command will not only create a shared object, it will accept
a shared object or archive library as input. In other words, when you create
libfoo.so, you can link it with a library you have already created, say,
libsharedob.so:

```
$ cc -G -o libfoo.so -Ldir function1.o function2.o \
    function3.o -lsharedob
```

That command will arrange for libsharedob.so to be linked with libfoo.so
when, at run time, libfoo.so is linked with your program. Note that here
you will have to point the dynamic linker to the directories in which both
libfoo.so and libsharedob.so are stored.

Specifying Directories to Be Searched by the Link Editor

In the previous section we created the archive library libfoo.a and the shared object libfoo.so. For the sake of discussion, we'll now say that both these libraries are stored in the directory /home/mylibs. We'll also assume that you are creating your executable in a different directory. In fact, these assumptions are not academic. They reflect the way most programmers organize their work on the UNIX system.

The first thing you must do if you want to link your program with either of these libraries is point the link editor to the /home/mylibs directory by specifying its path name with the −L option:

```
$ cc −L/home/mylibs file1.c file2.c file3.c −lfoo
```

The −L option directs the link editor to search for the libraries named with −l first in the specified directory, then in the standard places. In this case, having found the directory /home/mylibs, the link editor will search libfoo.so rather than libfoo.a. As we saw earlier, when the link editor encounters otherwise identically named shared object and archive libraries in the same directory, it searches the library with the .so suffix by default. For the same reason, it will search libc.so here rather than libc.a. Note that you must specify −L if you want the link editor to search for libraries in your current directory. You can use a period (.) to represent the current directory.

To direct the link editor to search libfoo.a, you can turn off the dynamic linking default:

```
$ cc −dn −L/home/mylibs file1.c file2.c file3.c −lfoo
```

Under −dn, the link editor will not accept shared objects as input. Here, then, it will search libfoo.a rather than libfoo.so, and libc.a rather than libc.so.

To link your program statically with libfoo.a and dynamically with libc.so, you can do either of two things. First, you can move libfoo.a to a different directory — /home/archives, for example — then specify /home/archives with the −L option:

```
$ cc −L/home/archives −L/home/mylibs file1.c file2.c \
    file3.c −lfoo
```

As long as the link editor encounters the /home/archives directory before it encounters the /home/mylibs directory, it will search libfoo.a rather than libfoo.so. That is, when otherwise identically named .so and .a libraries exist in your directories, the link editor will search the first one it finds. The same thing is true, by the way, for identically named libraries of either type. If you have different versions of libfoo.a in your directories, the link editor will search the first one it finds.

A better alternative might be to leave libfoo.a where you had it in the first place and use the −Bstatic and −Bdynamic options to turn dynamic linking off and on. The following command will link your program statically with libfoo.a and dynamically with libc.so:

```
$ cc −L/home/mylibs file1.c file2.c file3.c −Bstatic \
    −lfoo −Bdynamic
```

When you specify −Bstatic, the link editor will not accept a shared object as input until you specify −Bdynamic. In other words, you can use these options as toggles — any number of times — on the cc command line:

```
$ cc −L/home/mylibs file1.c file2.c −Bstatic −lfoo \
    file3.c −Bdynamic −lsharedob
```

That command will direct the link editor to search

- first, libfoo.a to resolve still unresolved external references in file1.c and file2.c;

- second, libsharedob.so to resolve still unresolved external references in all three files and in libfoo.a;

- last, libc.so to resolve still unresolved external references in all three files and the preceding libraries.

Files, including libraries, are searched for definitions in the order they are listed on the cc command line. The standard C library is always searched last.

You can add to the list of directories to be searched by the link editor by using the environment variable LD_LIBRARY_PATH. LD_LIBRARY_PATH must be a list of colon-separated directory names; an optional second list is separated from the first by a semicolon:

```
$ LD_LIBRARY_PATH=dir:dir;dir:dir export LD_LIBRARY_PATH
```

The directories specified before the semicolon are searched, in order, before the directories specified with −L; the directories specified after the semicolon are searched, in order, after the directories specified with −L. Note that you can use LD_LIBRARY_PATH in place of −L altogether. In that case the link editor will search for libraries named with −l first in the directories specified before the semicolon, next in the directories specified after the semicolon, and last in the standard places. You should use absolute path names when you set this environment variable.

> **NOTE** As we explain in the next section, LD_LIBRARY_PATH is also used by the dynamic linker. That is, if LD_LIBRARY_PATH exists in your environment, the dynamic linker will search the directories named in it for shared objects to be linked with your program at execution. In using LD_LIBRARY_PATH with the link editor or the dynamic linker, then, you should keep in mind that any directories you give to one you are also giving to the other.

Specifying Directories to Be Searched by the Dynamic Linker

Earlier we said that when you use the −l option, you must point the dynamic linker to the directories of the shared objects that are to be linked with your program at execution. The environment variable LD_RUN_PATH lets you do that at link time. To set LD_RUN_PATH, list the absolute path names of the directories you want searched in the order you want them searched. Separate path names with a colon. Since we are concerned only with the directory /home/mylibs here, the following will do:

    $ LD_RUN_PATH=/home/mylibs export LD_RUN_PATH

Now the command

    $ cc −o prog −L/home/mylibs file1.c file2.c file3.c −lfoo

will direct the dynamic linker to search for libfoo.so in /home/mylibs when you execute your program:

    $ prog

The dynamic linker searches the standard place by default, after the directories you have assigned to LD_RUN_PATH. Note that as far as the dynamic linker is concerned, the standard place for libraries is /usr/lib. Any executable versions of libraries supplied by the compilation system are kept in /usr/lib.

The environment variable LD_LIBRARY_PATH lets you do the same thing at run time. Suppose you have moved libfoo.so to /home/sharedobs. It is too late to replace /home/mylibs with /home/sharedobs in LD_RUN_PATH, at least without link editing your program again. You can, however, assign the new directory to LD_LIBRARY_PATH, as follows:

    $ LD_LIBRARY_PATH=/home/sharedobs export LD_LIBRARY_PATH

Now when you execute your program

```
$ prog
```

the dynamic linker will search for libfoo.so first in /home/mylibs and, not finding it there, in /home/sharedobs. That is, the directory assigned to LD_RUN_PATH is searched before the directory assigned to LD_LIBRARY_PATH. The important point is that because the path name of libfoo.so is not hard-coded in prog, you can direct the dynamic linker to search a different directory when you execute your program. In other words, you can move a shared object without breaking your application.

You can set LD_LIBRARY_PATH without first having set LD_RUN_PATH. The main difference between them is that once you have used LD_RUN_PATH for an application, the dynamic linker will search the specified directories every time the application is executed (unless you have relinked the application in a different environment). In contrast, you can assign different directories to LD_LIBRARY_PATH each time you execute the application. LD_LIBRARY_PATH directs the dynamic linker to search the assigned directories before it searches the standard place. Directories, including those in the optional second list, are searched in the order listed. See the previous section for the syntax.

Note, finally, that when linking a set-user or set-group ID program, the dynamic linker will ignore any directories specified by LD_LIBRARY_PATH that are not "trusted." Trusted directories are built into the dynamic linker and cannot be modified by the application. Currently, the only trusted directory is /usr/lib.

Checking for Run-Time Compatibility

Suppose you have been supplied with an updated version of a shared object. You have already compiled your program with the previous version; the link editor has checked it for undefined symbols, found none, and created an executable. According to everything we have said, you should not have to link your program again. The dynamic linker will simply use the definitions in the new version of the shared object to satisfy unresolved external references in the executable.

Suppose further that this is a database update program that takes several days to run. You want to be sure that your program does not fail in a critical section because a symbol that was defined by the previous version of the shared object is no longer defined by the new version. In other words, you want the information that the link editor gives you — that your executable is compatible with the shared library — without having to link edit it again.

There are two ways you can check for run-time compatibility. The command ldd ("list dynamic dependencies") directs the dynamic linker to print the path names of the shared objects on which your program depends:

    $ ldd *prog*

When you specify the −d option to ldd, the dynamic linker prints a diagnostic message for each unresolved data reference it would encounter if *prog* were executed. When you specify the −r option, it prints a diagnostic message for each unresolved data or function reference it would encounter if *prog* were executed.

You can do the same thing when you execute your program. Whereas the dynamic linker resolves data references immediately at run time, it normally delays resolving function references until a function is invoked for the first time. Normally, then, the lack of a definition for a function will not be apparent until the function is invoked. By setting the environment variable LD_BIND_NOW

    $ LD_BIND_NOW=1 export LD_BIND_NOW

before you execute your program, you direct the dynamic linker to resolve all references immediately. In that way, you can learn before execution of main() begins that the functions invoked by your process actually are defined.

Dynamic Linking Programming Interface

You can use a programming interface to the dynamic linking mechanism to attach a shared object to the address space of your process during execution, look up the address of a function in the library, call that function, and then detach the library when it is no longer needed. The routines for this are stored in libdl.so. Subsection 3X of the *Programmer's Reference Manual* describes its contents.

Implementation

We have already described, in various contexts in this section, the basic implementation of the static and dynamic linking mechanisms:

- When you use an archive library function, a copy of the object file that contains the function is incorporated in your executable at link time. External references to the function are assigned virtual addresses when the executable is created.

■ When you use a shared library function, the entire contents of the library are mapped into the virtual address space of your process at run time. External references to the function are assigned virtual addresses when you execute the program. The link editor records in your executable only the name of the shared object and a small amount of bookkeeping information for use by the dynamic linker at run time.

We'll take a closer look at how dynamic linking is implemented in a moment. First let's consider the one or two cases in which you might not want to use it. Earlier we said that because shared object code is not copied into your executable object file at link time, a dynamically linked executable normally will use less disk space than a statically linked executable. If your program calls only a few small library functions, however, the bookkeeping information to be used by the dynamic linker may take up more space in your executable than the code for those functions. You can use the size command, described in Section 1 of the *Programmer's Reference Manual*, to determine the difference.

In a similar way, using a shared object may occasionally add to the memory requirements of a process. Although a shared object's text is shared by all processes that use it, its data typically are not (at least its writable data; see the section "Guidelines for Building Shared Objects" below for the distinction). Every process that uses a shared object usually gets a private copy of its entire data segment, regardless of how many of the data are needed. If an application uses only a small portion of a shared library's text and data, executing the application might require more memory with a shared object than without one. It would be unwise, for example, to use the standard C shared object library to access only strcmp(). Although sharing strcmp() saves space on your disk and memory on the system, the memory cost to your process of having a private copy of the C library's data segment would make the archive version of strcmp() the more appropriate choice.

Now let's consider dynamic linking in a bit more detail. First, each process that uses a shared object references a single copy of its code in memory. That means that when other users on your system call a function in a shared object library, the entire contents of that library are mapped into the virtual address space of their processes as well. If they have called the same function as you, external references to the function in their programs will, in all likelihood, be assigned different virtual addresses. That is, because the function may be loaded at a different virtual address for each process that uses it, the system cannot calculate absolute addresses in memory until run time.

Second, the memory management scheme underlying dynamic linking shares memory among processes at the granularity of a page. Memory pages can be shared as long as they are not modified at run time. If a process writes to a shared page in the course of relocating a reference to a shared object, it gets a private copy of that page and loses the benefits of code sharing (although without affecting other users of the page).

Third, to create programs that require the least possible amount of page modification at run time, the compiler generates position-independent code under the −K PIC option. Whereas executable code normally must be tied to a fixed address in memory, position-independent code can be loaded anywhere in the address space of a process. Because the code is not tied to specific addresses, it will execute correctly — without page modification — at a different address in each process that uses it. As we have indicated, you should specify −K PIC when you create a shared object:

```
$ cc −K PIC −G −o libfoo.so function1.c function2.c \
function3.c
```

Relocatable references in your object code will be moved from its text segment to tables in the data segment. See Chapter 13, "Object Files," for the details.

In the next section we'll look at some basic guidelines for building shared objects. For now, we'll sum up the reasons why you might want to use one:

- Because library code is not copied into the executables that use it, they require less disk space.

- Because library code is shared at run time, the dynamic memory needs of systems are reduced.

- Because symbol resolution is put off until run time, shared objects can be updated without having to relink applications that depend on them.

- As long as its path name is not hard-coded in an executable, a shared object can be moved to a different directory without breaking an application.

Guidelines for Building Shared Objects

This section gives coding guidelines and maintenance tips for shared library development. Before getting down to specifics, we should emphasize that if you plan to develop a commercial shared library, you ought to consider providing a compatible archive as well. As we have noted, some users may not find a shared library appropriate for their applications. Others may want their applications to run on UNIX system releases without shared object support. Shared object code is completely compatible with archive library code. In other words, you can use the same source files to build archive and shared object versions of a library.

Let's look at some performance issues first. There are two things you want to do to enhance shared library performance:

Minimize the Library's Data Segment. As noted, only a shared object's text segment is shared by all processes that use it; its data segment typically is not. Every process that uses a shared object usually gets a private memory copy of its entire data segment, regardless of how many of the data are needed. You can cut down the size of the data segment a number of ways:

- Try to use automatic (stack) variables. Don't use permanent storage if automatic variables will work.

- Use functional interfaces rather than global variables. Generally speaking, that will make library interfaces and code easier to maintain. Moreover, defining functional interfaces often eliminates global variables entirely, which in turn eliminates global "copy" data. The ANSI C function strerror(), described in Subsection 3C of the *Programmer's Reference Manual*, illustrates these points.

  In previous implementations, system error messages were made available to applications only through two global variables:

  ```
  extern int   sys_nerr;
  extern char  *sys_errlist[];
  ```

  That is, sys_errlist[X] gives a character string for the error X, if X is a nonnegative value less than sys_nerr. Now if the current list of messages were made available to applications only through a lookup table in an archive library, applications that used the table obviously would not be able to access new messages as they were added to the system unless they were relinked with the library. In other words, errors might occur for which these applications could not produce meaningful diagnostics. Something similar happens when you use a global lookup table in a shared library.

First, the compilation system sets aside memory for the table in the address space of each executable that uses it, even though it does not know yet where the table will be loaded. After the table is loaded, the dynamic linker copies it into the space that has been set aside. Each process that uses the table, then, gets a private copy of the library's data segment, including the table, and an additional copy of the table in its own data segment. Moreover, each process pays a performance penalty for the overhead of copying the table at run time. Finally, because the space for the table is allocated when the executable is built, the application will not have enough room to hold any new messages you might want to add in the future. A functional interface overcomes these difficulties. strerror() might be implemented as follows:

```
static const char *msg[] = {
        "Error 0",
        "Not owner",
        "No such file or directory",
        ...
};

char *
strerror(int err)
{
        if (err < 0 || err >= sizeof(msg)/sizeof(msg[0]))
                return 0;
        return (char *)msg[err];
}
```

The message array is static, so no application space is allocated to hold a separate copy. Because no application copy exists, the dynamic linker does not waste time moving the table. New messages can be added, because only the library knows how many messages exist. Finally, note the use of the type qualifier const to identify data as read-only. Whereas writable data are stored in a shared object's data segment, read-only data are stored in its text segment. For more on const, see Chapter 3, "C Language."

In a similar way, you should try to allocate buffers dynamically — at run time — instead of defining them at link time. That will save memory because only the processes that need the buffers will get them. It will also allow the size of the buffers to change from one release of the library to the next without affecting compatibility. Example:

```
char *
buffer()
{
        static char *buf = 0;

        if (buf == 0)
        {
                if ((buf = malloc(BUFSIZE)) == 0)
                        return 0;
        }
        ...
        return buf;
}
```

■ Exclude functions that use large amounts of global data — that is, if you cannot rewrite them in the ways described in the foregoing items. If an infrequently used routine defines a great deal of static data, it probably does not belong in a shared library.

■ Make the library self-contained. If a shared object imports definitions from another shared object, each process that uses it will get a private copy not only of its data segment, but of the data segment of the shared object from which the definitions were imported. In cases of conflict, this guideline should probably take precedence over the preceding one.

Minimize Paging Activity. Although processes that use shared libraries will not write to shared pages, they still may incur page faults. To the extent they do, their performance will degrade. You can minimize paging activity in the following ways:

■ Organize to improve locality of reference. First, exclude infrequently used routines on which the library itself does not depend. Traditional a.out files contain all the code they need at run time. So if a process calls a function, it may already be in memory because of its proximity to other text in the process. If the function is in a shared library, however, the surrounding library code may be unrelated to the calling process. Only rarely, for example, will any single executable use everything in the shared C library. If a shared library has unrelated functions, and if unrelated processes make random calls to those functions, locality of reference may be decreased, leading to more paging activity. The point is that functions used by only a few a.out files do not save much disk space by being in a shared library, and can degrade performance.

Second, try to improve locality of reference by grouping dynamically related functions. If every call to funcA() generates calls to funcB() and funcC(), try to put them in the same page. cflow, described in Section 1 of the *Programmer's Reference Manual*, generates this kind of static dependency information. Combine it with profiling (Chapter 7) to see what things actually are called, as opposed to what things might be called.

- Align for paging. Try to arrange the shared library's object files so that frequently used functions do not unnecessarily cross page boundaries. First, determine where the page boundaries fall. Page size on the 3B2 is typically 2K; on the 6386 it is 4K. You can use the nm command, described in Section 1 of the *Programmer's Reference Manual*, to determine how symbol values relate to page boundaries. After grouping related functions, break them up into page-sized chunks. Although some object files and functions are larger than a page, many are not. Then use the less frequently called functions as glue between the chunks. Because the glue between pages is referenced less frequently than the page contents, the probability of a page fault is decreased. You can put frequently used, unrelated functions together because they will probably be called randomly enough to keep the pages in memory.

- Avoid hardware thrashing. The 3B2, for example, uses memory management hardware with an eight-entry cache for translating virtual to physical addresses. Each segment (128 KB) is mapped to one of the eight entries. So segments 0, 8, 16, ... use entry 0; segments 1, 9, 17, ... use entry 1; and so forth. You get better performance by arranging the typical process to avoid cache entry conflicts. If a heavily used library had both its text and its data segments mapped to the same cache entry, the performance penalty would be particularly severe. Every library instruction would bring the text segment information into the cache. Instructions that referenced data would flush the entry to load the data segment. Of course, the next instruction would reference text and flush the cache entry

again. At least on the 3B2, a library's text and data segment numbers
should differ by something other than eight.

Now let's look at some maintenance issues. We have already seen how allocat-
ing buffers dynamically can ease the job of library maintenance. As a general
rule, you want to be sure that updated versions of a shared object are compatible with its previous versions so that users will not have to recompile their
applications. At the very least, you should avoid changing the names of library
symbols from one release to the next.

All the same, there may be instances in which you need to release a library version that is incompatible with its predecessor. On the one hand, you will want
to maintain the older version for dynamically linked executables that depend on
it. On the other hand, you will want newly created executables to be linked
with the updated version. Moreover, you will probably want both versions to
be stored in the same directory. In this situation, you could give the new
release a different name, rewrite your documentation, and so forth. A better
alternative would be to plan for the contingency in the very first instance by
using the following sequence of commands when you create the original version
of the shared object:

```
$ cc -K PIC -G -h libfoo.1 -o libfoo.1 function1.c \
    function2.c function3.c
$ ln libfoo.1 libfoo.so
```

In the first command -h stores the name given to it, libfoo.1, in the shared
object itself. You then use the UNIX system command ln, described in Section 1
of the *User's Reference Manual,* to create a link between the name libfoo.1 and
the name libfoo.so. The latter, of course, is the name the link editor will look
for when users of your library specify

```
$ cc -Ldir file1.c file2.c file3.c -lfoo
```

In this case, however, the link editor will record in the user's executable the
name you gave to -h, libfoo.1, rather than the name libfoo.so. That
means that when you release a subsequent, incompatible version of the library,
libfoo.2, executables that depend on libfoo.1 will continue to be linked with
it at run time. As we saw earlier, the dynamic linker uses the shared object
name that is stored in the executable to satisfy unresolved external references at
run time.

You use the same sequence of commands when you create `libfoo.2`:

```
$ cc -K PIC -G -h libfoo.2 -o libfoo.2 function1.c \
    function2.c function4.c
$ ln libfoo.2 libfoo.so
```

Now when users specify

```
$ cc -Ldir file1.c file2.c file3.c -lfoo
```

the name `libfoo.2` will be stored in their executables, and their programs will be linked with the new library version at run time.

Multiply Defined Symbols

Multiply defined symbols — except for different-sized initialized data objects — are not reported as errors under dynamic linking. To put that more formally, the link editor will not report an error for multiple definitions of a function or a same-sized data object when each such definition resides within a different shared object or within a dynamically linked executable and different shared objects. The dynamic linker will use the definition in whichever object occurs first on the `cc` command line. You can, however, specify -Bsymbolic when you create a shared object

```
$ cc -K PIC -G -Bsymbolic -o libfoo.so function1.c \
    function2.c function3.c
```

to insure that the dynamic linker will use the shared object's definition of one of its own symbols, rather than a definition of the same symbol in an executable or another library.

In contrast, multiply defined symbols are generally reported as errors under static linking. We say "generally" because definitions of so-called weak symbols can be hidden from the link editor by a definition of a global symbol. That is, if a defined global symbol exists, the appearance of a weak symbol with the same name will not cause an error.

To illustrate this, let's look at our own implementation of the standard C library. This library provide services that users are allowed to redefine and replace. At the same time, however, ANSI C defines standard services that must be present on the system and cannot be replaced in a strictly conforming program. `fread()`, for example, is an ANSI C library function; the system function `read()` is not. So a conforming program may redefine `read()` and still use `fread()` in a predictable way.

The problem with this is that read() underlies the fread() implementation in the standard C library. A program that redefines read() could "confuse" the fread() implementation. To guard against this, ANSI C states that an implementation cannot use a name that is not reserved to it. That's why we use _read() — note the leading underscore — to implement fread() in the standard C library.

Now suppose that a program you have written calls read(). If your program is going to work, a definition for read() will have to exist in the C library. One does. It is identical to the definition for _read() and contained in the same object file.

Suppose further that another program you have written redefines read(), as it has every right to do under ANSI C. And that this same program calls fread(). Because you get our definitions of both _read() and read() when you use fread(), we would expect the link editor to report the multiply defined symbol read() as an error, and fail to create an executable program. To prevent that, we used the #pragma directive in our source code for the library as follows:

```
#pragma weak read = _read
```

Because our read() is defined as a weak symbol, your own definition of read() will override the definition in the standard C library. You can use the #pragma directive in the same way in your own library code.

There's a second use for weak symbols that you ought to know about:

```
#pragma weak read
```

tells the link editor not to complain if it does not find a definition for the weak symbol read. References to the symbol use the symbol value if defined, 0 otherwise. The link editor does not extract archive members to resolve undefined weak symbols. The mechanism is intended to be used primarily with functions. Although it will work for most data objects, it should not be used with uninitialized global data ("common" symbols) or with shared library data objects that are exported to executables.

Quick-Reference Guide

1. By convention, shared objects, or dynamically linked libraries, are designated by the prefix `lib` and the suffix `.so`; archives, or statically linked libraries, are designated by the prefix `lib` and the suffix `.a`. `libc.so`, then, is the shared object version of the standard C library; `libc.a` is the archive version.

2. These conventions are recognized, in turn, by the −l option to the `cc` command. That is, −l*x* directs the link editor to search the shared object `libx.so` or the archive library `libx.a`. The `cc` command automatically passes −lc to the link editor. In other words, the compilation system arranges for the standard C library to be linked with your program transparently.

3. By default, the link editor chooses the shared object implementation of a library, `libx.so`, in preference to the archive library implementation, `libx.a`, in the same directory.

4. By default, the link editor searches for libraries in the standard places on your system, `/usr/ccs/lib` and `/usr/lib`, in that order. The standard libraries supplied by the compilation system normally are kept in `/usr/ccs/lib`.

In this arrangement, then, C programs are dynamically linked with `libc.so` automatically:

```
$ cc file1.c file2.c file3.c
```

To link your program statically with `libc.a`, turn off the dynamic linking default with the −dn option:

```
$ cc −dn file1.c file2.c file3.c
```

Specify the −l option explicitly to link your program with any other library. If the library is in the standard place, the command

```
$ cc file1.c file2.c file3.c −lx
```

will direct the link editor to search for `libx.so`, then `libx.a` in the standard place. Note that the compilation system supplies shared object versions only of `libc` and `libdl`. (Other shared object libraries are supplied with the operating system, and usually are kept in the standard places.) Note, too, that, as a rule, it's best to place −l at the end of the command line.

If the library is not in the standard place, specify the path of the directory in which it is stored with the −L option

```
$ cc −Ldir file1.c file2.c file3.c −lx
```

or the environment variable LD_LIBRARY_PATH

```
$ LD_LIBRARY_PATH=dir export LD_LIBRARY_PATH
$ cc file1.c file2.c file3.c −lx
```

If the library is a shared object and is not in the standard place, you must also specify the path of the directory in which it is stored with either the environment variable LD_RUN_PATH at link time, or the environment variable LD_LIBRARY_PATH at run time:

```
$ LD_RUN_PATH=dir export LD_RUN_PATH
$ LD_LIBRARY_PATH=dir export LD_LIBRARY_PATH
```

It's best to use an absolute path when you set these environment variables. Note that LD_LIBRARY_PATH is read both at link time and at run time.

To direct the link editor to search libx.a where libx.so exists in the same directory, turn off the dynamic linking default with the −dn option:

```
$ cc −dn −Ldir file1.c file2.c file3.c −lx
```

That command will direct the link editor to search libc.a well as libx.a. To link your program statically with libx.a and dynamically with libc.so, use the −Bstatic and −Bdynamic options to turn dynamic linking off and on:

```
$ cc −Ldir file1.c file2.c file3.c −Bstatic −lx −Bdynamic
```

Files, including libraries, are searched for definitions in the order they are listed on the cc command line. The standard C library is always searched last.

Libraries and Header Files

As we have noted, the standard libraries supplied by the C compilation system contain functions that you can use in your program to perform input/output, string handling, and other high-level operations that are not explicitly provided by the C language. Header files contain definitions and declarations that your program will need if it calls a library function. They also contain function-like macros that you can use in your program as you would a function.

In the first part of this chapter, we showed you how to link your program with these standard libraries and how to include a header file. In this part, we'll talk a bit more about header files and show you how to use library functions in your program. We'll also describe the contents of some of the more important standard libraries, and tell you where to find them in the *Programmer's Reference Manual*. We'll close with a brief discussion of standard I/O.

Header Files

Header files serve as the interface between your program and the libraries supplied by the C compilation system. Because the functions that perform standard I/O, for example, very often use the same definitions and declarations, the system supplies a common interface to the functions in the header file stdio.h. By the same token, if you have definitions or declarations that you want to make available to several source files, you can create a header file with any editor, store it in a convenient directory, and include it in your program as described in the first part of this chapter.

Header files traditionally are designated by the suffix .h, and are brought into a program at compile time. The preprocessor component of the compiler does this because it interprets the #include statement in your program as a directive. The two most commonly used directives are #include and #define. As we have seen, the #include directive is used to call in and process the contents of the named file. The #define directive is used to define the replacement token string for an identifier. For example,

```
#define NULL    0
```

defines the macro NULL to have the replacement token sequence 0. See Chapter 3, "C Language," for the complete list of preprocessing directives.

Many different .h files are named in the *Programmer's Reference Manual*. Here we are going to list a number of them, to illustrate the range of tasks you can perform with header files and library functions. When you use a library function in your program, the manual page will tell you which header file, if any, needs to be included. If a header file is mentioned, it should be included before you use any of the associated functions or declarations in your program. It's generally best to put the #include right at the top of a source file.

assert.h	assertion checking
ctype.h	character handling
errno.h	error conditions
float.h	floating point limits
limits.h	other data type limits
locale.h	program's locale
math.h	mathematics
setjmp.h	nonlocal jumps
signal.h	signal handling
stdarg.h	variable arguments
stddef.h	common definitions
stdio.h	standard input/output
stdlib.h	general utilities
string.h	string handling
time.h	date and time
unistd.h	system calls

How to Use Library Functions

The manual page for each function describes how you should use the function in your program. As an example, we'll look at the strcmp() routine, which compares character strings. The routine is described on the string manual page in Section 3, Subsection 3S, of the *Programmer's Reference Manual*. Related functions are described there as well, but only the sections relevant to strcmp() are shown in Figure 2-2.

Figure 2-2: Excerpt from string(3S) Manual Page

```
NAME
        string: strcat, strdup, strncat, strcmp, strncmp, strcpy, strncpy, strlen,
        strchr, strrchr, strpbrk, strspn, strcspn, strok - string operations.

SYNOPSIS
        #include <string.h>

        ...

        int strcmp(const char *, const char *);

        ...
DESCRIPTION

        ...

        strcmp compares its arguments and returns an integer less than, equal to, or
        greater than 0, according as the first argument is lexicographically less than,
        equal to, or greater than the second.
        ...
```

As shown, the DESCRIPTION section tells you what the function or macro does. It's the SYNOPSIS section, though, that contains the critical information about how you use the function or macro in your program.

Note that the first line in the SYNOPSIS is

        #include <string.h>

That means that you should include the header file string.h in your program because it contains useful definitions or declarations relating to strcmp(). In fact, string.h contains the line

```
extern int strcmp(const char *, const char *);
```

that describes the kinds of arguments expected and returned by strcmp(). This line is called a function prototype. Function prototypes afford a greater degree of argument type checking than old-style function declarations, so you lessen your chance of using the function incorrectly. By including string.h, you assure that the compiler checks calls to strcmp() against the official interface. You can, of course, examine string.h in the standard place for header files on your system, usually the /usr/include directory.

The next thing in the SYNOPSIS section is the formal declaration of the function. The formal declaration tells you:

- the type of value returned by the function;

- the arguments the function expects to receive when called, if any;

- the argument types.

By way of illustration, let's look at how you might use strcmp() in your own code. Figure 2-3 shows a program fragment that will find the bird of your choice in an array of birds.

Figure 2-3: How strcmp() Is Used in a Program

```
#include <string.h>

/* birds must be in alphabetical order */
char *birds[] = { "albatross",  "canary", "cardinal", "ostrich", "penguin" };

/* Return the index of the bird in the array. */
/* If the bird is not in the array, return -1 */

int is_bird(const char *string)
{
        int low, high, midpoint;
        int cmp_value;

        /* use a binary search to find the bird */
        low = 0;
        high = sizeof(birds)/sizeof(char *) - 1;
        while(low <= high)
        {
                midpoint = (low + high)/2;
                cmp_value = strcmp(string, birds[midpoint]);
                if (cmp_value < 0)
                        high = midpoint - 1;
                else if (cmp_value > 0)
                        low = midpoint + 1;
                else /* found a match */
                        return midpoint;
        }
        return -1;
}
```

C Library (libc)

In this section, we describe some of the more important routines in the standard C library. As we indicated in the first part of this chapter, libc contains the system calls described in Section 2 of the *Programmer's Reference Manual*, and the C language functions described in Section 3, Subsections 3C and 3S. We'll explain what each of these subsections contains below. We'll look at system calls at the end of the section.

Subsection 3S Routines

Subsection 3S of the *Programmer's Reference Manual* contains the so-called standard I/O library for C programs. Frequently, one manual page describes several related functions or macros. In Figure 2-4, the left-hand column contains the name that appears at the top of the manual page; the other names in the same row are related functions or macros described on the same manual page. Programs that use these routines should include the header file stdio.h. We'll talk a bit more about standard I/O in the last subsection of this chapter.

Figure 2-4: Standard I/O Functions and Macros

fclose	fflush			Close or flush a stream.
ferror	feof	clearerr	fileno	Stream status inquiries.
fopen	freopen	fdopen		Open a stream.
fread	fwrite			Input/output.
fseek	rewind	ftell		Reposition a file pointer in a stream.
getc	getchar	fgetc	getw	Get a character or word from a stream.
gets	fgets			Get a string from a stream.
popen	pclose			Begin or end a pipe to/from a process.
printf	fprintf	sprintf		Print formatted output.
putc	putchar	fputc	putw	Put a character or word on a stream.
puts	fputs			Put a string on a stream.
scanf	fscanf	sscanf		Convert formatted input.
setbuf	setvbuf			Assign buffering to a stream.
system				Issue a command through the shell.
tmpfile				Create a temporary file.
tmpnam	tempnam			Create a name for a temporary file.
ungetc				Push character back into input stream.
vprintf	vfprintf	vsprintf		Print formatted output of a varargs argument list.

Subsection 3C Routines

Subsection 3C of the *Programmer's Reference Manual* contains functions and macros that perform a variety of tasks:

- string manipulation
- character classification
- character conversion
- environment management
- memory management.

Here we'll look at functions and macros that perform the first three tasks.

Figure 2-5 lists string-handling functions that appear on the `string` page in Subsection 3C of the *Programmer's Reference Manual.* Programs that use these functions should include the header file `string.h`.

Figure 2-5: String Operations

`strcat`	Append a copy of one string to the end of another.
`strncat`	Append no more than a given number of characters from one string to the end of another.
`strcmp`	Compare two strings. Returns an integer less than, greater than, or equal to 0 to show that one is lexicographically less than, greater than, or equal to the other.
`strncmp`	Compare no more than a given number of characters from the two strings. Results are otherwise identical to `strcmp`.
`strcpy`	Copy a string.
`strncpy`	Copy a given number of characters from one string to another. The destination string will be truncated if it is longer than the given number of characters, or padded with null characters if it is shorter.

Figure 2-5: String Operations (continued)

strdup	Return a pointer to a newly allocated string that is a duplicate of a string pointed to.
strchr	Return a pointer to the first occurrence of a character in a string, or a null pointer if the character is not in the string.
strrchr	Return a pointer to the last occurrence of a character in a string, or a null pointer if the character is not in the string.
strlen	Return the number of characters in a string.
strpbrk	Return a pointer to the first occurrence in one string of any character from the second, or a null pointer if no character from the second occurs in the first.
strspn	Return the length of the initial segment of one string that consists entirely of characters from the second string.
strcspn	Return the length of the initial segment of one string that consists entirely of characters not from the second string.
strstr	Return a pointer to the first occurrence of the second string in the first string, or a null pointer if the second string is not found.
strtok	Break up the first string into a sequence of tokens, each of which is delimited by one or more characters from the second string. Return a pointer to the token, or a null pointer if no token is found.

Figure 2-6 lists functions and macros that classify 8-bit character-coded integer values. These routines appear on the `conv` and `ctype` pages in Subsection 3C of the *Programmer's Reference Manual*. Programs that use these routines should include the header file `ctype.h`.

Figure 2-6: Classifying 8-Bit Character-Coded Integer Values

`isalpha`	Is *c* a letter?
`isupper`	Is *c* an uppercase letter?
`islower`	Is *c* a lowercase letter?
`isdigit`	Is *c* a digit [0-9]?
`isxdigit`	Is *c* a hexadecimal digit [0-9], [A-F], or [a-f]?
`isalnum`	Is *c* alphanumeric (a letter or digit)?
`isspace`	Is *c* a space, horizontal tab, carriage return, new-line, vertical tab, or form-feed?
`ispunct`	Is *c* a punctuation character (neither control nor alphanumeric)?
`isprint`	Is *c* a printing character?
`isgraph`	Same as `isprint` except false for a space.
`iscntrl`	Is *c* a control character or a delete character?
`isascii`	Is *c* an ASCII character?
`toupper`	Change lower case to upper case.
`_toupper`	Macro version of `toupper`.
`tolower`	Change upper case to lower case.
`_tolower`	Macro version of `tolower`.
`toascii`	Turn off all bits that are not part of a standard ASCII character; intended for compatibility with other systems.

Figure 2-7 lists functions and macros in Subsection 3C of the *Programmer's Reference Manual* that are used to convert characters, integers, or strings from one representation to another. The left-hand column contains the name that appears at the top of the manual page; the other names in the same row are related functions or macros described on the same manual page. Programs that use these routines should include the header file `stdlib.h`.

Figure 2-7: Converting Characters, Integers, or Strings

a641	164a		Convert between long integer and base-64 ASCII string.
ecvt	fcvt	gcvt	Convert floating point number to string.
13tol	1tol3		Convert between 3-byte packed integer and long integer.
strtod	atof		Convert string to double-precision number.
strtol	atol	atoi	Convert string to integer.
strtoul			Convert string to unsigned long.

System Calls

UNIX system calls are the interface between the kernel and the user programs that run on top of it. `read()`, `write()`, and the other system calls in Section 2 of the *Programmer's Reference Manual* define what the UNIX system is. Everything else is built on their foundation. Strictly speaking, they are the only way to access such facilities as the file system, interprocess communication primitives, and multitasking mechanisms.

Of course, most programs do not need to invoke system calls directly to gain access to these facilities. If you are performing input/output, for example, you can use the standard I/O functions described earlier. When you use these functions, the details of their implementation on the UNIX system — for example, that the system call `read()` underlies the `fread()` implementation in the standard C library — are transparent to the program. In other words, the program will generally be portable to any system, UNIX or not, with a conforming C implementation.

In contrast, programs that invoke system calls directly are portable only to other UNIX or UNIX-like systems; for that reason, you would not use read() in a program that performed a simple I/O operation. Other operations, however, including most multitasking mechanisms, do require direct interaction with the UNIX system kernel. These operations are discussed in detail in the *Programmer's Guide: System Services and Application Packaging Tools*.

Math Library (libm)

The math library, libm, contains the mathematics functions supplied by the C compilation system. These appear in Subsection 3M of the *Programmer's Reference Manual*. Here we describe some of the major functions, organized by the manual page on which they appear. Note that functions whose names end with the letter f are single-precision versions, which means that their argument and return types are float. The header file math.h should be included in programs that use math functions.

Figure 2-8: Math Functions

exp(3M)

exp	expf	Return e^x.
cbrt		Return cube root of x.
log	logf	Return the natural logarithm of x. The value of x must be positive.
log10	log10f	Return the base-ten logarithm of x. The value of x must be positive.
pow	powf	Return x^y. If x is zero, y must be positive. If x is negative, y must be an integer.

Figure 2-8: Math Functions (continued)

sqrt	sqrtf	Return the non-negative square root of x. The value of x must be non-negative.

hypot(3M)

hypot	Return $sqrt(x * x + y * y)$, taking precautions against overflows.

gamma(3M)

gamma	lgamma	Return $\ln(\mid \Gamma(x) \mid)$, where $\Gamma(x)$ is defined as $\int_0^x e^{-t}t^{x-1}dt$.

trig(3M)

sin cos tan	sinf cosf tanf	Return, respectively, the sine, cosine, and tangent of x, measured in radians.
asin	asinf	Return the arcsine of x, in the range $[-\pi/2, +\pi/2]$.
acos	acosf	Return the arccosine of x, in the range $[0, +\pi]$.
atan	atanf	Return the arctangent of x, in the range $(-\pi/2, +\pi/2)$.
atan2	atan2f	Return the arctangent of y/x, in the range $(-\pi, +\pi]$, using the signs of both arguments to determine the quadrant of the return value.

Figure 2-8: Math Functions (continued)

---

sinh(3M)

---

sinh	sinhf	Return, respectively, the hyperbolic
cosh	coshf	sine, cosine, and tangent of their argu-
tanh	tanhf	ment.
asinh		Return, respectively, the inverse hyper-
acosh		bolic sine, cosine, and tangent of their
atanh		argument.

---

matherr(3M)

---

matherr	Error handling.

---

erf(3M)

---

erf	Returns the error function of x, defined as $\dfrac{2}{\sqrt{\pi}} \int\limits_{0}^{x} e^{-t^2} dt$.
erfc	erfc, which returns $1.0 - erf(x)$, is provided because of the extreme loss of relative accuracy if erf is called for large x and the result subtracted from 1.0 (e.g., for $x = 5$, 12 places are lost).

---

floor(3M)

---

floor	floorf	Return the largest integer not greater than x.
ceil	ceilf	Return the smallest integer not less than x.
copysign		Return x but with the sign of y.

Figure 2-8: Math Functions (continued)

fmod	fmodf	Return the floating point remainder of the division of x by y: x if y is zero, otherwise the number f with same sign as x, such that $x = iy + f$ for some integer i, and $\mid f \mid < \mid y \mid$.
fabs	fabsf	Return the absolute value of x, $\mid x \mid$.
rint		Return the integer value nearest to the double-precision floating point argument x as a double-precision floating point number. The returned value is rounded according to the currently set machine rounding mode. If round-to-nearest (the default mode) is set and the difference between the function argument and the rounded result is exactly 0.5, then the result will be rounded to the nearest even integer.
remainder		Return the floating point remainder of the division of x by y: NaN if y is zero, otherwise the value $r = x - yn$, where n is the integer nearest the exact value of x/y. Whenever $\mid n - x/y \mid = 1/2$, then n is even.

General Purpose Library (libgen)

libgen contains general purpose functions, and functions designed to facilitate internationalization. These appear in Subsection 3G of the *Programmer's Reference Manual*. Figure 2-9 describes functions in libgen. The header files libgen.h and, occasionally, regexp.h should be included in programs that use these functions.

Figure 2-9: libgen Functions

advance	step	Execute a regular expression on a string.
basename		Return a pointer to the last element of a path name.
bgets		Read a specified number of characters into a buffer from a stream until a specified character is reached.
bufsplit		Split the buffer into fields delimited by tabs and new-lines.
compile		Return a pointer to a compiled regular expression that uses the same syntax as ed.
copylist		Copy a file into a block of memory, replacing new-lines with null characters. It returns a pointer to the copy.
dirname		Return a pointer to the parent directory name of the file path name.
eaccess		Determine if the effective user ID has the appropriate permissions on a file.
gmatch		Check if name matches shell file name pattern.
isencrypt		Use heuristics to determine if contents of a character buffer are encrypted.

Figure 2-9: libgen Functions (continued)

`mkdirp`		Create a directory and its parents.
`p2open`	`p2close`	p2open is similar to popen(3S). It establishes a two-way connection between the parent and the child. p2close closes the pipe.
`pathfind`		Search the directories in a given path for a named file with given mode characteristics. If the file is found, a pointer is returned to a string that corresponds to the path name of the file. A null pointer is returned if no file is found.
`regcmp`		Compile a regular expression and return a pointer to the compiled form.
`regex`		Compare a compiled regular expression against a subject string.
`rmdirp`		Remove the directories in the specified path.
`strccpy`	`strcadd`	strccpy copies the input string to the output string, compressing any C-like escape sequences to the real character. strcadd is a similar function that returns the address of the null byte at the end of the output string.
`strecpy`		Copy the input string to the output string, expanding any non-graphic characters with the C escape sequence. Characters in a third argument are not expanded.
`strfind`		Return the offset of the first occurrence of the second string in the first string. −1 is returned if the second string does not occur in the first.

Figure 2-9: libgen Functions (continued)

strrspn	Trim trailing characters from a string. It returns a pointer to the last character in the string not in a list of trailing characters.
strtrns	Return a pointer to the string that results from replacing any character found in two strings with a character from a third string. This function is similar to the tr command.

Standard I/O

As we have seen, the functions in Subsection 3S of the *Programmer's Reference Manual* constitute the standard I/O library for C programs. In this section, we want to discuss standard I/O in a bit more detail. First, let's briefly define what I/O involves. It has to do with

- reading information from a file or device to your program;

- writing information from your program to a file or device;

- opening and closing files that your program reads from or writes to.

Three Files You Always Have

Programs automatically start off with three open files: standard input, standard output, and standard error. These files with their associated buffering are called streams, and are designated stdin, stdout, and stderr, respectively. The shell associates all three files with your terminal by default.

This means that you can use functions and macros that deal with stdin, stdout, or stderr without having to open or close files. gets(), for example, reads a string from stdin; puts() writes a string to stdout. Other functions and macros read from or write to files in different ways: character at a time, getc() and putc(); formatted, scanf() and printf(); and so on. You can specify that output be directed to stderr by using a function such as fprintf(). fprintf() works the same way as printf() except that it delivers its formatted output to a named stream, such as stderr.

Named Files

Any file other than standard input, standard output, and standard error must be explicitly opened by you before your program can read from or write to the file. You open a file with the standard library function fopen(). fopen() takes a path name, asks the system to keep track of the connection between your program and the file, and returns a pointer that you can then use in functions that perform other I/O operations.

The pointer is to a structure called FILE, defined in stdio.h, that contains information about the file: the location of its buffer, the current character position in the buffer, and so on. In your program, then, you need to have a declaration such as

```
FILE *fin;
```

which says that fin is a pointer to a FILE. The statement

```
fin = fopen("filename", "r");
```

associates a FILE structure with filename, the path name of the file to open, and returns a pointer to it. The "r" means that the file is to be opened for reading. This argument is known as the mode. There are modes for reading, writing, and both reading and writing.

In practice, the file open function is often included in an if statement:

```
if ((fin = fopen("filename", "r")) == NULL)
    (void)fprintf(stderr,"Cannot open input file %s\n",
        "filename");
```

which takes advantage of the fact that fopen() returns a NULL pointer if it cannot open the file. To avoid falling into the immediately following code on failure, you can call exit(), which causes your program to quit:

```
if ((fin = fopen("filename", "r")) == NULL) {
    (void)fprintf(stderr,"Cannot open input file %s\n",
        "filename");
    exit(1);
}
```

Once you have opened the file, you use the pointer `fin` in functions or macros to refer to the stream associated with the opened file:

```
int c;
c = getc(fin);
```

brings in one character from the stream into an integer variable called c. The variable c is declared as an integer even though we are reading characters because `getc()` returns an integer. Getting a character is often incorporated in some flow-of-control mechanism such as

```
while ((c = getc(fin)) != EOF)
        .
        .
        .
```

that reads through the file until EOF is returned. EOF, NULL, and the macro `getc()` are all defined in `stdio.h`. `getc()` and other macros in the standard I/O package keep advancing a pointer through the buffer associated with the stream; the UNIX system and the standard I/O functions are responsible for seeing that the buffer is refilled if you are reading the file, or written to the output file if you are producing output, when the pointer reaches the end of the buffer.

Your program may have multiple files open simultaneously, 20 or more depending on system configuration. If, subsequently, your program needs to open more files than it is permitted to have open simultaneously, you can use the standard library function `fclose()` to break the connection between the FILE structure in `stdio.h` and the path names of the files your program has opened. Pointers to FILE may then be associated with other files by subsequent calls to `fopen()`. For output files, an `fclose()` call makes sure that all output has been sent from the output buffer before disconnecting the file. `exit()` closes all open files for you, but it also gets you completely out of your process, so you should use it only when you are sure you are finished.

Passing Command Line Arguments

As we noted in Chapter 1, information or control data can be passed to a C program as an argument on the command line. When you execute the program, command line arguments are made available to the function `main()` in two parameters, an argument count, conventionally called `argc`, and an argument vector, conventionally called `argv`. `argc` is the number of arguments with which the program was invoked. `argv` is an array of pointers to characters strings that contain the arguments, one per string. Since the command name itself is considered to be the first argument, or `argv[0]`, the count is always at least one.

If you plan to accept run-time parameters in your program, you need to include code to deal with the information. Figures 2-10 and 2-11 show program fragments that illustrate two common uses of run-time parameters:

- Figure 2-10 shows how you provide a variable file name to a program, such that a command of the form

      $ prog filename

  will cause `prog` to attempt to open the specified file.

- Figure 2-11 shows how you set internal flags that control the operation of a program, such that a command of the form

      $ prog -opr

  will cause `prog` to set the corresponding variables for each of the options specified. The `getopt()` function used in the example is the most common way to process arguments in UNIX system programs. `getopt()` is described in Subsection 3C of the *Programmer's Reference Manual*.

Figure 2-10: Using argv[1] to Pass a File Name

```
#include <stdio.h>

int
main(int argc, char *argv[])
{
        FILE *fin;
        int ch;

        switch (argc)
        {
        case 2:
                if ((fin = fopen(argv[1], "r")) == NULL)
                {
                        /* First string (%s) is program name (argv[0]). */
                        /* Second string (%s) is name of file that could */
                        /* not be opened (argv[1]). */

                        (void)fprintf(stderr, "%s: Cannot open input file %s\n",
                                argv[0], argv[1]);
                        return(2);
                }
                break;
        case 1:
                fin = stdin;
                break;

        default:
                (void)fprintf(stderr, "Usage: %s [file]\n", argv[0]);
                return(2);
        }

        while ((ch = getc(fin)) != EOF)
                (void)putchar(ch);

        return (0);

}
```

Figure 2-11: Using Command Line Arguments to Set Flags

```
#include <stdio.h>
#include <stdlib.h>

int
main(int argc, char *argv[])
{
        int oflag = 0;
        int pflag = 0;          /* Function flags */
        int rflag = 0;
        int ch;

        while ((ch = getopt(argc, argv, "opr")) != -1)
        {
                /* For options present, set flag to 1.           */
                /* If unknown options present, print error message. */

                switch (ch)
                {
                case 'o':
                        oflag = 1;
                        break;
                case 'p':
                        pflag = 1;
                        break;
                case 'r':
                        rflag = 1;
                        break;
                default:
                        (void)fprintf(stderr, "Usage: %s [-opr]\n", argv[0]);
                        return(2);
                }
        }
        /* Do other processing controlled by oflag, pflag, rflag. */
        return(0);
}
```

3 C Language

Introduction

This chapter is a guide to the C language compilers for the AT&T 3B2 and 6386 computers. The level of presentation assumes some experience with C, and familiarity with fundamental programming concepts.

The compilers are compatible with the C language described in the American National Standards Institute (ANSI) "Draft Proposed American National Standard for Information Systems—Programming Language C," document number X3J11/88-090, dated December 7, 1988. The standard language is referred to as "ANSI C" in this document. The notation CI4 refers to previous issues of the compilation system: C Issue 4.2 for the 3B2, C Issue 4.1.6 for the 6386.

Compilation Modes

The compilation system has three compilation modes that correspond to degrees of compliance with ANSI C. The modes are:

–Xt
:   Transition mode. Yields behavior compatible with the previous issue (CI4). Under this option, the compiler provides new ANSI C features and supports all extensions that were provided in CI4. Where the interpretation of a construct differs between CI4 and the Standard, the compiler issues a warning and follows the CI4 behavior. This is the default compilation mode.

–Xa
:   ANSI C mode. Under this option, the compiler provides ANSI C semantics where the interpretation of a construct differs between CI4 and the Standard, and issues a warning. Extensions provided in CI4, including those that are incompatible with the Standard, are supported.

–Xc
:   Conformance mode. Enforces ANSI C conformance, and allows the use of conforming extensions. Conforming extensions are those that do not interfere with conforming code. Nonconforming extensions are disallowed or cause diagnostic messages.

Global Behavior

A program that depends on unsigned-preserving arithmetic conversions will behave differently. This is considered to be the most serious change made by ANSI C to a widespread current practice.

In the first edition of Kernighan and Ritchie, *The C Programming Language* (Prentice-Hall, 1978), unsigned specified exactly one type; there were no unsigned chars, unsigned shorts, or unsigned longs, but most C compilers added these very soon thereafter.

In previous AT&T C compilers, the *"unsigned* preserving" rule is used for promotions: when an unsigned type needs to be widened, it is widened to an unsigned type; when an unsigned type mixes with a signed type, the result is an unsigned type.

The other rule, specified by ANSI C, came to be called *"value* preserving," in which the result type depends on the relative sizes of the operand types. When an unsigned char or unsigned short is "widened," the result type is int if an int is large enough (as it is on 3B2 and 6386 computers) to represent all the values of the smaller type. Otherwise the result type would be unsigned int. The "value preserving" rule produces the "least surprise" arithmetic result for most expressions.

Only in the transition (-Xt) mode will the compiler use the unsigned preserving promotions; in the other two modes, conformance (-Xc) and ANSI (-Xa), the value preserving promotion rules will be used. No matter what the current mode may be, the compiler will warn about each expression whose behavior might depend on the promotion rules used.

This warning is not optional since this is a serious change in behavior.

How To Use This Chapter

You can use this chapter either as a quick reference guide, or as a comprehensive summary of the language as implemented by the compilation system. Many topics are grouped according to their place in the ANSI-specified phases of translation, which describe the steps by which a source file is translated into an executable program. The phases of translation are explained in the following section.

Phases of Translation

The compiler processes a source file into an executable in eight conceptual steps, which are called *phases of translation*. While some of these phases may in actuality be folded together, the compiler behaves as if they occur separately, in sequence.

1. Trigraph sequences are replaced by their single-character equivalents. (*Trigraph sequences* are explained in the "Preprocessing" section of this chapter).

2. Any source lines that end with a backslash and new-line are spliced together with the next line by deleting the backslash and new-line.

3. The source file is partitioned into preprocessing tokens and sequences of white-space characters. Each comment is, in effect, replaced by one space character. (*Preprocessing tokens* are explained in the "Preprocessing" section of this chapter).

4. Preprocessing directives are executed, and macros are expanded. Any files named in #include statements are processed from phase 1 through phase 4, recursively.

5. Escape sequences in character constants and string literals are converted to their character equivalents.

6. Adjacent character string literals, and wide character string literals, are concatenated.

7. Each preprocessing token is converted into a token. The resulting tokens are syntactically and semantically analyzed and translated. (*Tokens* are explained in the "Source Files and Tokenization" section of this chapter).

8. All external object and function references are resolved. Libraries are linked to satisfy external references not defined in the current translation unit. All translator output is collected into a program image which contains information needed for execution.

Output from certain phases may be saved and examined by specifying option flags on the cc command line.

The preprocessing token sequence resulting from Phase 4 can be saved by using the following options:

1. −P leaves preprocessed output in a file with a .i extension.

2. −E sends preprocessed output to the standard output.

Output from Phase 7 can be saved in a file with a .o extension by using the −c option to cc. The output of Phase 8 is the compilation system's final output (a.out).

Source Files and Tokenization

Tokens

A token is a series of contiguous characters that the compiler treats as a unit. Translation phase 3 partitions a source file into a sequence of tokens. Tokens fall into seven classes:

- Identifiers
- Keywords
- Numeric Constants
- Character Constants
- String literals
- Operators
- Other separators and punctuators

Identifiers

- Identifiers are used to name things such as variables, functions, data types, and macros.
- Identifiers are made up of a combination of letters, digits, or underscore (_) characters.
- First character may not be a digit.

Keywords

The following identifiers are reserved for use as keywords and may not be used otherwise:

asm	default	for	short	union
auto	do	goto	signed	unsigned
break	double	if	sizeof	void
case	else	int	static	volatile
char	enum	long	struct	while
const	extern	register	switch	
continue	float	return	typedef	

The keyword asm is reserved in all compilation modes except -Xc. The keyword _ _asm is a synonym for asm and is available under all compilation modes, although a warning will be issued when it is used under the -Xc mode.

Constants

Integral Constants

- Decimal

    □ Digits 0–9.

    □ First digit may not be 0 (zero).

- Octal

    □ Digits 0–7.

    □ First digit must be 0 (zero).

- Hexadecimal

    □ Digits 0–9 plus letters a–f or A–F. Letters correspond to decimal values 10-15.

    □ Prefixed by 0x or 0X (digit zero).

■ Suffixes

All of the above can be suffixed to indicate type, as follows:

Suffix	Type
u or U	unsigned
l or L	long
both	unsigned long

Floating Point Constants

■ Consist of integer part, decimal point, fraction part, an e or E, an optionally signed integer exponent, and a type suffix, one of f, F, l, or L.
Each of these elements is optional; however one of the following must be
present for the constant to be a floating point constant:

    □ A decimal point (preceded or followed by a number).

    □ An e with an exponent.

    □ Any combination of the above. Examples:

        xxx e *exp*
        xxx.
        .xxx

■ Type determined by suffix; f or F indicates float, l or L indicates
long double, otherwise type is double. The suffix L is only available
under compilation mode –Xc.

Character Constants

■ One or more characters enclosed in single quotes, as in 'x'.

■ All character constants have type int.

■ Value of a character constant is the numeric value of the character in the
ASCII character set.

- A multiple-character constant that is not an escape sequence (see below) has a value derived from the numeric values of each character. For example, the constant '123' has a value of

0	'3'	'2'	'1'

or 0x333231 on the 3B2. On the 6386 the value is

0	'1'	'2'	'3'

or 0x313233.

- Character constants may not contain the character ' or new-line. To represent these characters, and some others that may not be contained in the source character set, the compiler provides the following escape sequences:

Escape Sequences

new-line	NL (LF)	\n	audible alert	BEL	\a
horizontal tab	HT	\t	question mark	?	\?
vertical tab	VT	\v	double quote	"	\"
backspace	BS	\b	octal escape	000	\000
carriage return	CR	\r	hexadecimal escape	hh	\xhh
formfeed	FF	\f	backslash	\	\\
single quote	'	\'			

If the character following a backslash is not one of those specified, the compiler will issue a warning and treat the backslash-character sequence as the character itself. Thus, '\q' will be treated as 'q'. However, if you represent a character this way, you run the risk that the character may be made into an escape sequence in the future, with unpredictable results. An explicit new-line character is invalid in a character constant and will cause an error message.

- The octal escape consists of one to three octal digits.

- The hexadecimal escape consists of one or more hexadecimal digits.

Wide Characters and Multibyte Characters

- A wide character constant is a character constant prefixed by the letter L.

- A wide character has an external encoding as a multibyte character and an internal representation as the integral type wchar_t, defined in stddef.h.

- A wide character constant has the integral value for the multibyte character between single quote characters, as defined by the locale-dependent mapping function mbtowc.

String Literals

- One or more characters surrounded by double quotes, as in "xyz".

- Initialized with the characters contained in the double quotes.

- Have static storage duration and type "array of characters."

- The escape sequences described in "Character Constants" may also be used in string literals. A double quote within the string must be escaped with a backslash. New-line characters are not valid within a string.

- Adjacent string literals are concatenated into a single string. A null character, \0, is appended to the result of the concatenation, if any.

- String literals are also known as "string constants."

Wide String Literals

- A wide-character string literal is a string literal immediately prefixed by the letter L.

- Wide-character string literals have type "array of wchar_t."

- Wide string literals may contain escape sequences, and they may be concatenated, like ordinary string literals.

Comments

Comments begin with the characters /* and end with the next */.

```
/* this is a comment */
```

Comments do not nest.

If a comment appears to begin within a string literal or character constant, it will be taken as part of the literal or constant, as specified by the phases of translation.

```
char *p = "/* this is not a comment */"; /* but this is */
```

Preprocessing

- Preprocessing handles macro substitution, conditional compilation, and file inclusion.

- Lines beginning with # indicate a preprocessing control line. Spaces and tabs may appear before and after the #.

- Lines that end with a backslash character \ and new-line are joined with the next line by deleting the backslash and the new-line characters. This occurs (in translation phase 2) before input is divided into tokens.

- Each preprocessing control line must appear on a line by itself.

Trigraph Sequences

Trigraph sequences are three-character sequences that are replaced by a corresponding single character in Translation Phase 1, as follows:

??=	#	?? (	[	??<	{
??/	\	??)	]	??>	}
??'	^	??!	|	??–	~

No other such sequences are recognized. The trigraph sequences provide a way to specify characters that are missing on some terminals, but that the C language uses.

Preprocessing Tokens

A token is the basic lexical unit of the language. All source input must be formed into valid tokens by translation phase seven. Preprocessing tokens (pp-tokens) are a superset of regular tokens. Preprocessing tokens allow the source file to contain non-token character sequences that constitute valid preprocessing tokens during translation. There are four categories of preprocessing tokens:

- Header file names, meant to be taken as a single token.

- Preprocessing numbers (discussed in the following section).

■ All other single characters that are not otherwise (regular) tokens. See the example in the "Preprocessing Numbers" section of this chapter.

■ Identifiers, numeric constants, character constants, string literals, operators, and punctuators.

Preprocessing Numbers

■ A preprocessing number is made up of a digit, optionally preceded by a period, and may be followed by letters, underscores, digits, periods, and any one of e+ e− E+ E−.

■ Preprocessing numbers include all valid number tokens, plus some that are not valid number tokens. For example, in the macro definition:

```
#define R 2e ## 3
```

the preprocessing number 2e is not a valid number. However, the preprocessing operator ## will "paste" it together with the preprocessing number 3 when R is replaced, resulting in the preprocessing number 2e3, which is a valid number. See the "Preprocessing Operators" section, below for a discussion of the ## operator.

Preprocessing Directives

Preprocessing Operators

The preprocessing operators are evaluated left to right, without any defined precedence.

A macro parameter preceded by the # preprocessing operator has its corresponding unexpanded argument tokens converted into a string literal. (Any double quotes and backslashes contained in character constants or part of string literals are escaped by a backslash). The # character is sometimes referred to as the "stringizing" operator. This rule applies only within function-like macros.

If a replacement token sequence (see "Macro Definition and Expansion" below) contains a ## operator, the ## and any surrounding white space are deleted and adjacent tokens are concatenated, creating a new token. This occurs only when the macro is expanded.

Macro Definition and Expansion

■ An object-like macro is defined with a line of the form:

#define *identifier token-sequence*_{opt}

where *identifier* will be replaced with *token-sequence* wherever *identifier* appears in regular text.

■ A function-like macro is defined with a line of the form:

#define *identifier* (*identifier-list*_{opt})   *token-sequence*_{opt}

where the macro parameters are contained in the comma-separated identifier-list. The token-sequence following the identifier list determines the behavior of the macro, and is referred to as the *replacement list*. There can be no space between the identifier and the (character. For example:

#define FLM(a,b) a+b

The replacement-list a+b determines that the two parameters a and b will be added.

■ A function-like macro is invoked in normal text by using its identifier, followed by a (token, a list of token sequences separated by commas, and a) token. For example:

FLM(3,2)

■ The arguments in the invocation (comma-separated token sequences) may be expanded, and they then replace the corresponding parameters in the replacement token sequence of the macro definition. Macro arguments in the invocation are *not* expanded if they are operands of # or ## operators in the replacement string. Otherwise, expansion does take place. For example:

Assume that M1 is defined as 3:

```
#define M1 3
```

When the function-like macro FLM is used, use of the # or ## operators will affect expansion (and the result), as follows:

Definition	Invocation	Result	Expansion ?
a+b	FLM(M1,2)	3+2	Yes, Yes
#a	FLM(M1,2)	"M1"	No
a##b	FLM(M1,2)	M12	No, No
a+#a	FLM(M1,2)	3+"M1"	Yes, No

In the last example line, the first a in a+#a is expanded, but the second a is not expanded because it is an operand of the # operator.

■ The number of arguments in the invocation must match the number of parameters in the definition.

■ A macro's definition, if any, can be eliminated with a line of the form:

```
#undef identifier
```

There is no effect if the definition doesn't exist.

File Inclusion

■ A line of the form:

```
#include "filename"
```

causes the entire line to be replaced with the contents of *filename*. The following directories are searched, in order.

   □ The current directory (of the file containing the #include line).

   □ Any directories named in −I options to the compiler, in order.

   □ A list of standard places, typically, but not necessarily, /usr/include.

■ A line of the form:

```
#include <filename>
```

causes the entire line to be replaced with contents of *filename*. The angle brackets surrounding *filename* indicate that *filename* is not searched for in the current directory.

■ A third form allows an arbitrary number of preprocessing tokens to follow the #include, as in:

    #include *preprocessing-tokens*

The preprocessing tokens are processed the same way as when they are used in normal text. Any defined macro name is replaced with its replacement list of preprocessing tokens. The preprocessing tokens must expand to match one of the first two forms (< ... > or "...").

■ A file name beginning with a slash / indicates the absolute pathname of a file to include, no matter which form of #include is used.

■ Any #include statements found in an included file cause recursive processing of the named file(s).

Conditional Compilation

Different segments of a program may be compiled conditionally. Conditional compilation statements must observe the following sequence:

1. One of: #if or #ifdef or #ifndef.

2. Any number of optional #elif lines.

3. One optional #else line.

4. One #endif line.

■ #if *integral-constant-expression*

Is true if *integral-constant-expression* evaluates to nonzero.

If true, tokens following the if line are included.

The *integral-constant-expression* following the if is evaluated by following this sequence of steps:

  1. Any preprocessing tokens in the expression are expanded. Any use of the defined operator evaluates to 1 or 0 if its operand is, respectively, defined, or not.

2. If any identifiers remain, they evaluate to 0.

3. The remaining integral constant expression is evaluated. The constant expression must be made up of components that evaluate to an integral constant. In the context of a #if, the integral constant expression may not contain the sizeof operator, casts, or floating point constants.

The following table shows how various types of constant expressions following a #if would be evaluated. Assume that *name* is not defined.

Constant expression	Step 1	Step 2	Step 3
_ _STDC_ _	1	1	1
!defined(_ _STDC_ _)	!1	!1	0
3||*name*	3||*name*	3||0	1
2 + *name*	2 + *name*	2 + 0	2

■ #ifdef *identifier*

Is true if *identifier* is currently defined by #define or by the -D option to the cc command line.

■ #ifndef *identifier*

Is true if *identifier* is not currently defined by #define (or has been undefined).

■ #elif *constant-expression*

Indicates alternate if-condition when all preceding if-conditions are false.

■ #else

Indicates alternate action when no preceding if or elif conditions are true. A comment may follow the else, but a token may not.

■ #endif

Terminates the current conditional. A comment may follow the endif, but a token may not.

Line Control

- Useful for programs that generate C programs.

- A line of the form

    #line *constant* *"filename"*

  causes the compiler to believe, for the purposes of error diagnostics and debugging, that the line number of the next source line is equal to *constant* (which must be a decimal integer) and the current input file is *filename* (enclosed in double quotes). The quoted file name is optional. *constant* must be a decimal integer in the range 1 to MAXINT. MAXINT is defined in limits.h.

Assertions

A line of the form

    #assert *predicate* *(token-sequence)*

associates the *token-sequence* with the predicate in the assertion name space (separate from the space used for macro definitions). The predicate must be an identifier token.

    #assert *predicate*

asserts that *predicate* exists, but does not associate any token sequence with it.

The compiler provides the following predefined predicates by default on the 3B2:

    #assert machine (u3b2)
    #assert system (unix)
    #assert cpu (M32)

The following defaults apply to the 6386:

    #assert machine (i386)
    #assert system (unix)
    #assert cpu (i386)

Any assertion may be removed by using #unassert, which uses the same syntax as assert. Using #unassert with no argument deletes all assertions on the predicate; specifying an assertion deletes only that assertion.

An assertion may be tested in a #if statement with the following syntax:

> #if #*predicate* (*non-empty token-list*)

For example, the predefined predicate system can be tested with the following line:

> #if #system(unix)

which will evaluate true.

Version Control

The #ident directive is used to help administer version control information.

> #ident "*version*"

puts an arbitrary string in the .comment section of the object file. The .comment section is not loaded into memory when the program is executed.

Pragmas

■ Preprocessing lines of the form

> #pragma *pp-tokens*

specify implementation-defined actions.

■ Three #pragmas are recognized by the compilation system:

□ #pragma ident "*version*"

which is identical in function to #ident "*version*".

□ #pragma weak *identifier*

which identifies *identifier* as a weak global symbol,

or

#pragma weak *identifier* = *identifier2*

which identifies *identifier* as a weak global symbol whose value is the same as *identifier2*. *identifier* should otherwise be undefined. See

"Multiply Defined Symbols" in Chapter 2 for more information on weak global symbols.

□ #pragma int_to_unsigned *identifier*

which identifies *identifier* as a function whose type was int in previous releases of the compilation system, but whose type is unsigned int in this release. The declaration for *identifier* must precede the #pragma.

```
unsigned int strlen(const char*);
#pragma int_to_unsigned strlen
```

#pragma int_to_unsigned makes it possible for the compiler to identify expressions in which the function's changed type may affect the evaluation of the expression. In the –Xt mode the compiler treats the function as if it were declared to return int rather than unsigned int.

■ The 6386 has a fourth #pragma:

□ #pragma pack(*n*)

which controls the layout of structure offsets. *n* is a number, 1, 2, or 4, that specifies the strictest alignment desired for any structure member. If *n* is omitted, the alignment reverts to the default, which may have been set by the –Zp option to cc.

A value of 4 is the default. A value of 2 gives structure layouts that match those on an AT&T 6300+ computer.

■ The compiler ignores unrecognized pragmas.

Error Generation

A preprocessing line consisting of

#error *token-sequence*

causes the compiler to produce a diagnostic message containing the *token-sequence*, and stop.

Predefined Names

The following identifiers are predefined as object-like macros:

_ _LINE_ _	The current line number as a decimal constant.
_ _FILE_ _	A string literal representing the name of the file being compiled.
_ _DATE_ _	The date of compilation as a string literal in the form "*Mmm dd yyyy*."
_ _TIME_ _	The time of compilation, as a string literal in the form "*hh:mm:ss*."
_ _STDC_ _	The constant 1 under compilation mode –Xc, otherwise 0.

With the exception of _ _STDC_ _, these predefined names may not be undefined or redefined. Under compilation mode –Xt, _ _STDC_ _ may be undefined (#undef _ _STDC_) to cause a source file to think it is being compiled by a previous version of the compiler.

Declarations and Definitions

Introduction

A declaration describes an identifier in terms of its type and storage duration. The location of a declaration (usually, relative to function blocks) implicitly determines the scope of the identifier.

Types

Basic Types

The basic types and their sizes are:

- char (1 byte)
- short int (2 bytes)
- int (4 bytes)
- long int (4 bytes)

  Each of char, short, int, and long may be prefixed with signed or unsigned. A type specified with signed is the same as the type specified without signed except for signed char on the 3B2. (char on the 3B2 has only non-negative values.)

- float (4 bytes)
- double (8 bytes)
- long double (12 bytes)

  Under compilation mode −Xc, long double will cause a warning that long double is equivalent to double. Using long double under compilation modes −Xa and −Xt will result in an error.

- void

Integral and floating types are collectively referred to as *arithmetic types*. Arithmetic types and pointer types (see "Pointer Declarators") make up the *scalar types*.

Type Qualifiers

- const

  The compiler may place an object declared const in read-only memory. The program may not change its value and no further assignment may be made to it. An explicit attempt to assign to a const object will provoke an error.

- volatile

  volatile advises the compiler that unexpected, asynchronous events may affect the object so declared, and warns it against making assumptions. An object declared volatile is protected from optimization that might otherwise occur.

Structures and Unions

- Structures

  A structure is a type that consists of a sequence of named members. The members of a structure may have different object types (as opposed to an array, whose members are all of the same type). To declare a structure is to declare a new type. A declaration of an object of type struct reserves enough storage space so that all of the member types can be stored simultaneously.

  A structure member may consist of a specified number of bits, called a bit-field. The number of bits (the size of the bit-field) is specified by appending a colon and the size (an integral constant expression, the number of bits) to the declarator that names the bit-field. The declarator name itself is optional; a colon and integer will declare the bit-field. A bit-field must have integral type. The size may be zero, in which case the declaration name must not be specified, and the next member starts on a boundary of the type specified. For example:

      char :0

  means "start the next member (if possible) on a char boundary." A named bit-field number that is not declared with an explicitly signed type holds values in the range

  $$0 - (2^n - 1)$$

where n is the number of bits. A bit-field declared with an explicit signed type holds values in the range

$$-2^{n-1} - (2^{n-1}-1)$$

An optional structure tag identifier may follow the keyword `struct`. The tag names the kind of structure described, and it and `struct` may then be used as a shorthand name for the declarations that make up the body of the structure. For example:

```
struct t {
    int x;
    float y;
} st1, st2;
```

Here, `st1` and `st2` are structures, each made up of `x`, an `int`, and `y`, a `float`. The tag `t` may be used to declare more structures identical to `st1` and `st2`, as in:

```
struct t st3;
```

A structure may include a pointer to itself as a member; this is known as a *self-referential structure*.

```
struct n {
    int x;
    struct n *left;
    struct n *right;
};
```

■ Unions

A union is an object that may contain one of several different possible member types. A union may have bit-field members. Like a structure, declaring a union declares a new type. Unlike a structure, a union stores the value of only one member at a given time. A union does, however, reserve enough storage to hold its largest member.

Enumerations

An enumeration is a unique type that consists of a set of constants called
enumerators. The enumerators are declared as constants of type int, and
optionally may be initialized by an integral constant expression separated from
the identifier by an = character.

Enumerations consist of two parts:

- The set of constants.

- An optional tag.

For example:

```
enum color {red, blue=5, yellow};
```

color is the tag for this enumeration type.   red, blue, and yellow are its
enumeration constants. If the first enumeration constant in the set is not followed by an =, its value is 0. Each subsequent enumeration constant not followed by an = is determined by adding 1 to the value of the previous enumeration constant. Thus yellow has the value 6.

```
enum color car_color;
```

declares car_color to be an object of type enum color.

Scope

The use of an identifier is limited to an area of program text known as the
identifier's scope. The four kinds of scope are function, file, block, and function
prototype.

- The scope of every identifier (other than label names) is determined by
  the placement of its declaration (in a declarator or type specifier).

- The scope of structure, union and enumeration tags begins just after the
  appearance of the tag in a type specifier that declares the tag. Each
  enumeration constant has scope that begins just after the appearance of its
  defining enumerator in an enumerator list. Any other identifier has scope
  that begins just after the completion of its declarator.

- If the declarator or type specifier appears outside a function or parameter list, the identifier has file scope, which terminates at the end of the file (and all included files).

- If the declarator or type specifier appears inside a block or within the list of parameter declarations in a function definition, the identifier has block scope, which ends at the end of the block (at the } that closes that block).

- If the declarator or type specifier appears in the list of parameter declarations in a function prototype declaration, the identifier has function prototype scope, which ends at the end of the function declarator (at the) that ends the list).

- Label names always have function scope. A label name must be unique within a function.

Storage Duration

- Automatic Storage Duration

  Storage is reserved for an automatic object, and is available for the object on each entry (by any means) into the block in which the object is declared. On any kind of exit from the block, storage is no longer reserved.

- Static Storage Duration

  An object declared outside any block, or declared with the keywords static or extern, has storage reserved for it for the duration of the entire program. The object retains its last-stored value throughout program execution.

Storage Class Specifiers

■ auto

An object may be declared auto only within a function. It has block scope and the defined object has automatic storage duration.

■ register

A register declaration is equivalent to an auto declaration. It also advises the compiler that the object will be accessed frequently.

■ static

static gives a declared object static storage duration (see "Storage Duration"). The object may be defined inside or outside functions. An identifier declared static with file scope has internal linkage. A function may be declared or defined with static. If a function is defined to be static, the function has internal linkage. A function may be declared with static at block scope; the function should be defined with static as well.

■ extern

extern gives a declared object static storage duration. An object or function declared with extern has the same linkage as any visible declaration of the identifier at file scope. If no file scope declaration is visible the identifier has external linkage.

■ typedef

Using typedef as a storage class specifier does not reserve storage. Instead, typedef defines an identifier that names a type. See the section on derived types for a discussion of typedef.

Declarators

A brief summary of the syntax of declarators:

> *declarator:*
>> *pointer*_{opt} *direct-declarator*
>
> *direct-declarator:*
>> *identifier*
>> (*declarator*)
>> *direct-declarator* [*constant-expression*_{opt}]
>> *direct-declarator* (*parameter-type-list*)
>> *direct-declarator* (*identifier-list*_{opt})
>
> *pointer:*
>> * *type-qualifier-list*_{opt}
>> * *type-qualifier-list*_{opt} *pointer*

Pointer Declarators

■ Pointer to a type:

```
char *p;
```

p is a pointer to type char. p contains the address of a char object.

Care should be taken when pointer declarations are qualified with const:

```
const int *pci;
```

declares a pointer to a const-qualified ("read-only") int.

```
int *const cpi;
```

declares a pointer-to-int that is itself "read-only."

■ Pointer to a pointer:

```
char **t;
```

t points to a character pointer.

■ Pointer to a function:

```
int (*f) ();
```

f is a pointer to a function that returns an int.

■ Pointer to void:

```
void *
```

A pointer to void may be converted to or from a pointer to any object or incomplete type, without loss of information. This "generic pointer" behavior was previously carried out by `char *`; a pointer to void has the same representation and alignment requirements as a pointer to a character type.

Array Declarators

■ One-dimensional array:

```
int ia[10];
```

ia is an array of 10 integers.

■ Two-dimensional array:

```
char d[4][10];
```

d is an array of 4 arrays of 10 characters each.

■ Array of pointers:

```
char *p[7];
```

p is an array of seven character pointers.

An array type of unknown size is known as an *incomplete type*.

Function Declarators

■ A function declaration includes the return type of the function, the function identifier, and an optional list of parameters.

■ Function prototype declarations include declarations of parameters in the parameter list.

■ If the function takes no arguments, the keyword void may be substituted for the parameter list in a prototype.

■ A parameter type list may end with an ellipsis ", . . . " to indicate that the function may take more arguments than the number described. The comma is necessary only if it is preceded by an argument.

- The parameter list may be omitted, which indicates that no parameter information is being provided.

Examples:

- `void srand(unsigned int seed);`

  The function `srand` returns nothing; it has a single parameter which is an unsigned int. The name `seed` goes out of scope at the) and as such serves solely as documentation.

- `int rand(void);`

  The function `rand` returns an int; it has no parameters.

- `int strcmp(const char *, const char *);`

  The function `strcmp` returns an int; it has two parameters, both of which are pointers to character strings that `strcmp` does not change.

- `void (*signal(int, void (*)(int)))(int);`

  The function `signal` returns a pointer to a function that itself returns nothing and has an int parameter; the function `signal` has two parameters, the first of which has type int and the second has the same type as `signal` returns.

- `int fprintf(FILE *stream, const char *format, ...);`

  The function `fprintf` returns an int; `FILE` is a typedef name declared in `stdio.h`; `format` is a const qualified character pointer; note the use of ellipsis (. . .) to indicate an unknown number of arguments.

Function Definitions

A function definition includes the body of the function after the declaration of the function. As with declarations, a function may be defined as a function prototype definition or defined in the old style. The function prototype style includes type declarations for each parameter in the parameter list. This example shows how `main` would be defined in each style:

Function Prototype Style   Old Style

```
int
main(int argc, char *argv[])
{
    . . .
}
```

```
int
main(argc, argv)
int argc;
    char *argv[];
{
    . . .
}
```

Some important rules that govern function definitions:

■ An old style definition names its parameters in an identifier list, and their declarations appear between the function declarator and the "{" that begins the function body.

■ Under the old style, if the type declaration for a parameter was absent, the type defaulted to `int`. In the new style, all parameters in the parameter list must be type-specified and named. The exception to this rule is the use of ellipsis, explained in the "Function Declarators" section of this chapter.

■ A function definition serves as a declaration.

■ Incomplete types are not allowed in the parameter list or as the return type of a function definition. They are allowed in other function declarations.

Conversions and Expressions

Implicit Conversions

Characters and Integers

Any of the following may be used in an expression where an `int` or `unsigned int` may be used.

- `char`.

- `short int`.

- A `char`, `short`, or `int` bit-field.

- The signed or unsigned varieties of any of the above types.

- An object or bit-field that has enumeration type.

If an int can represent all values of the original type, the value is converted to an int; otherwise it is converted to an unsigned int. This process is called *integral promotion*.

 NOTE The promotion rules for ANSI C are different from previous releases. The compiler warns about expressions where this may lead to different behavior.

Compilation Mode Dependencies That Affect Unsigned Types

- Under compilation mode −Xt, `unsigned char` and `unsigned short` are promoted to `unsigned int`.

- Under compilation modes −Xa and −Xc, `unsigned char` and `unsigned short` are promoted to `int`.

Signed and Unsigned Integers

- When an integer is converted to another integral type, the value is unchanged if the value can be represented by the new type.

- If a negative signed integer is converted to an unsigned integer with greater size, the signed integer is first promoted to the signed integer corresponding to the unsigned integer.

Integral and Floating

When a floating type is converted to any integral type, any fractional part is discarded.

Float and Double

A float is promoted to double or long double, or a double is promoted to long double without a change in value.

The actual rounding behavior that is used when a floating point value is converted to a smaller floating point value depends on the rounding mode in effect at the time of execution. The default rounding mode is "round to nearest." See Chapter 14, "Floating Point Operations," and the *IEEE Standard for Binary Floating-Point Arithmetic* (ANSI/IEEE Std 754-1985) for a more complete discussion of rounding modes.

Usual Arithmetic Conversions

Some binary operators convert the types of their operands in order to yield a common type, which is also the type of the result. These are called the *usual arithmetic conversions:*

- If either operand is type long double, the other operand is converted to long double.

- Otherwise, if either operand has type double, the other operand is converted to double.

- Otherwise, if either operand has type float, the other operand is converted to float.

- Otherwise, the integral promotions are performed on both operands. Then, these rules are applied:

  □ If either operand has type unsigned long int, the other operand is converted to unsigned long int.

  □ Otherwise, if one operand has type long int and the other has type unsigned int, both operands are converted to unsigned long int.

- Otherwise, if either operand has type `long int`, the other operand is converted to `long int`.

- Otherwise if either operand has type `unsigned int`, the other operand is converted to `unsigned int`.

- Otherwise, both operands have type `int`.

Expressions

Objects and lvalues

An object is a manipulatable region of storage. An lvalue is an expression referring to an object. An obvious example of an lvalue expression is an identifier. There are operators that yield lvalues: for example, if `E` is an expression of pointer type, then `*E` is an lvalue expression referring to the object to which `E` points.

An lvalue is *modifiable* if:

- it does not have array type,

- it does not have an incomplete type,

- it does not have a const-qualified type,

and, if it is a structure or union, it does not have any member (including, recursively, any member of all contained structures or unions) with a const-qualified type.

The name "lvalue" comes from the assignment expression `E1 = E2` in which the left operand `E1` must be an lvalue expression.

Primary Expressions

- Identifiers, constants, string literals, and parenthesized expressions are primary expressions.

- An identifier is a primary expression, provided it has been declared as designating an object (which makes it an lvalue) or a function (which makes it a function designator).

- A constant is a primary expression; its type depends on its form and value.

- A string literal is a primary expression; it is an lvalue.

- A parenthesized expression is a primary expression. Its type and value are identical to those of the unparenthesized version. It is an lvalue, a function designator, or a void expression, according to the type of the unparenthesized expression.

Operators

A table of operator associativity and precedence appears in the next section.

Unary Operators

Expressions with unary operators group right to left.

* e	Indirection operator. Returns the object or function pointed to by its operand. If the type of the expression is "pointer to ...," the type of the result is "...".
& e	Address operator. Returns a pointer to the object or function referred to by the operand. Operand must be an lvalue or function type, and not a bit-field or an object declared register. Where the operand has type "*type*," the result has type "pointer to *type*."
− e	Negation operator. The operand must have arithmetic type. Result is the negative of its operand. Integral promotion is performed on the operand, and the result has the promoted type. The negative of an unsigned quantity is computed by subtracting its value from 2^n where n is the number of bits in the result type.

+ *e*	Unary plus operator. The operand must have arithmetic type. Result is the value of its operand. Integral promotion is performed on the operand, and the result has the promoted type.
! *e*	Logical negation operator. The operand must have arithmetic or pointer type. Result is one if the value of its operand is zero, zero if the value of its operand is nonzero. The type of the result is int.
~ *e*	The ~ operator yields the one's complement (all bits inverted) of its operand, which must have integral type. Integral promotion is performed on the operand, and the result has the promoted type.
++*e*	The object referred to by the lvalue operand of prefix ++ is incremented. The value is the new value of the operand but is not an lvalue. The expression ++x is equivalent to x += 1. The type of the result is the type of the operand.
−−*e*	The modifiable lvalue operand of prefix −− is decremented analogously to the prefix ++ operator.
e++	When postfix ++ is applied to a modifiable lvalue, the result is the value of the object referred to by the lvalue. After the result is noted, the object is incremented in the same manner as for the prefix ++ operator. The type of the result is the same as the type of the lvalue.
e−−	When postfix −− is applied to an lvalue, the result is the value of the object referred to by the lvalue. After the result is noted, the object is decremented in the same manner as for the prefix −− operator. The type of the result is the same as the type of the lvalue.

sizeof *e*

The sizeof operator yields the size in bytes of its operand. When applied to an object with array type, the result is the total number of bytes in the array. (The size is determined from the declarations of the objects in the expression.) This expression is semantically an unsigned constant (of type size_t, a typedef) and may be used anywhere a constant is required (except in a #if preprocessing directive line). One major use is in communication with routines like storage allocators and I/O systems.

sizeof (*type*)

The sizeof operator may also be applied to a parenthesized type name. In that case it yields the size in bytes of an object of the indicated type.

Cast Operators - Explicit Conversions

(*type*) *e*

Placing a parenthesized type name before an expression converts the value of the expression to that type. Both the operand and *type* must be pointer type or an arithmetic type.

Multiplicative Operators

The multiplicative operators *, /, and % group left to right. The usual arithmetic conversions are performed, and that is the type of the result.

e * *e*

Multiplication operator. The * operator is commutative.

e / *e*

Division operator. When positive integers are divided, truncation is toward 0. If either operand is negative, the quotient is negative. Operands must be arithmetic types.

e % *e*

Remainder operator. Yields the remainder from the division of the first expression by the second. The operands must have integral type.

The sign of the remainder is that of the first
operand. It is always true that $(a/b) * b + a\%b$
is equal to a (if a/b is representable).

Additive Operators

The additive operators + and − group left to right. The usual arithmetic
conversions are performed. There are some additional type possibilities for each
operator.

$e+e$

Result is the sum of the operands. A pointer to
an object in an array and an integral value may
be added. The latter is in all cases converted to
an address offset by multiplying it by the size of
the object to which the pointer points. The
result is a pointer of the same type as the original pointer that points to another object in the
same array, appropriately offset from the original object. Thus if P is a pointer to an object in
an array, the expression P+1 is a pointer to the
next object in the array. No further type combinations are allowed for pointers.

The + operator is commutative.

The valid operand type combinations for the +
operator are:

$a + a$

$p + i$ or $i + p$

where a is an arithmetic type, i is an integral
type, and p is a pointer.

$e-e$

Result is the difference of the operands. The
operand combinations are the same as for the +
operator, except that a pointer type may not be
subtracted from an integral type.

Also, if two pointers to objects of the same type
are subtracted, the result is converted (by division by the size of the object) to an integer that

represents the number of objects separating the pointed-to objects. This conversion will in general give unexpected results unless the pointers point to objects in the same array, since pointers, even to objects of the same type, do not necessarily differ by a multiple of the object size. The result type is ptrdiff_t (defined in stddef.h). ptrdiff_t is a typedef for int in this implementation. It should be used "as is" to ensure portability. Valid type combinations are

$$a - a$$
$$p - i$$
$$p - p$$

Bitwise Shift Operators

The bitwise shift operators << and >> take integral operands.

e1 << *e2*	Shifts *e1* left by *e2* bit positions. Vacated bits are filled with zeros.
e1 >> *e2*	Shifts *e1* right by *e2* bit positions. Vacated bits are filled with zeros on the 3B2. On the 6386, vacated bits are filled with zeros if the promoted type of *e1* is an unsigned type. Otherwise they are filled with copies of the sign bit of the promoted value of *e1*.

The result types of the bitwise shift operators are compilation-mode dependent, as follows:

-Xt	The result type is unsigned if either operand is unsigned.
-Xa, -Xc	The result type is the promoted type of the left operand. Integral promotion occurs before the shift operation.

Relational Operators

> *a relop a*
> *p relop p*

- The relational operators < (less than) > (greater than) <= (less than or equal to) >= (greater than or equal to) yield 1 if the specified relation is true and 0 if it is false.

- The result has type int.

- Both operands:

  □ have arithmetic type; or

  □ are pointers to qualified or unqualified versions of the same object or incomplete types.

Equality Operators

> *a eqop a*
> *p eqop p*
> *p eqop 0*
> *0 eqop p*

- The == (equal to) and != (not equal to) operators are analogous to the relational operators; however, they have lower precedence.

Bitwise AND Operator

> *ie1 & ie2*

- Bitwise "and" of *ie1* and *ie2*.

- Value contains a 1 in each bit position where both *ie1* and *ie2* contain a 1, and a 0 in every other position.

- Operands must be integral; the usual arithmetic conversions are applied, and that is the type of the result.

Bitwise Exclusive OR Operator

ie1 ^ *ie2*

- Bitwise exclusive "or" of *ie1* and *ie2*.

- Value contains a 1 in each position where there is a 1 in either *ie1* or *ie2*, but not both, and a 0 in every other bit position.

- Operands must be integral; the usual arithmetic conversions are applied, and that is the type of the result.

Bitwise OR Operator

ie1 | *ie2*

- Bitwise inclusive "or" of *ie1* and *ie2*.

- Value contains a 1 in each bit position where there is a 1 in either *ie1* or *ie2*, and a 0 in every other bit position.

- Operands must be integral; the usual arithmetic conversions are applied, and that is the type of the result.

Logical AND Operator

e1 && *e2*

- Logical "and" of *e1* and *e2*.

- *e1* and *e2* must be scalars.

- *e1* is evaluated first, and *e2* is evaluated only if *e1* is nonzero.

- Result is 1 if both *e1* and *e2* are non-zero, otherwise 0.

- Result type is int.

Logical OR Operator

> *e1* || *e2*

- Logical "or" of *e1* and *e2*.

- *e1* and *e2* must be scalars.

- *e1* is evaluated first, and *e2* is evaluated only if *e1* is zero. Result is 0 only if both *e1* and *e2* are false, otherwise 1.

- Result type is int.

Conditional Operator

> *e* ? *e1* : *e2*

- If *e* is nonzero, then *e1* is evaluated; otherwise *e2* is evaluated. The value is *e1* or *e2*.

- The first operand must have scalar type.

- For the second and third operands, one of the following must be true:

  □ Both must be arithmetic types. The usual arithmetic conversions are performed to make them a common type and the result has that type.

  □ Both must have compatible structure or union type; the result is that type.

  □ Both operands have void type; the result has void type.

  □ Both operands are pointers to qualified or unqualified versions of compatible types. The result type is the composite type.

  □ One operand is a pointer and the other is a null pointer constant. The result type is the pointer type.

  □ One operand is a pointer to an object or incomplete type and the other is a pointer to a qualified or unqualified version of void. The result type is a pointer to void.

For the pointer cases (the last three), the result is a pointer to a type qualified by all the qualifiers of the types pointed to by the operands.

Assignment Expressions

- Assignment operators are:

   =   *=   /=   %=   +=   -=   <<=   >>=   &= |=   ^=

- An expression of the form *e1 op= e2* is equivalent to *e1 = e1 op (e2)* except that *e1* is evaluated only once.

- The left operand:

   □ must be a modifiable lvalue.

   □ must have arithmetic type, or, for += and -=, must be a pointer to an object type and the right operand must have integral type.

   □ of an = operator, if the operand is a structure or union, must not have any member or submember qualified with const.

- Result type is the type of the (unpromoted) left operand.

Comma Operator

   e1 , e2

- *e1* is evaluated first, then *e2*.

- The result has the type and value of *e2* and is not an lvalue.

Structure Operators

   su . mem

Indicates member *mem* of structure or union *su*.

   sup -> mem

Indicates member *mem* of structure or union pointed to by *sup*. Equivalent to (*sup) . mem*.

Associativity and Precedence of Operators

Operators	Associativity
() [] -> .	left to right
! ~ ++ -- + - * & (*type*) sizeof	right to left
* / %	left to right
+ -	left to right
<< >>	left to right
< <= > >=	left to right
== !=	left to right
&	left to right
^	left to right
|	left to right
&&	left to right
||	left to right
?:	right to left
= += -= *= /= %= &= ^= |= <<= >>=	right to left
,	left to right

Unary +, −, and * have higher precedence than their binary versions.

Prefix ++ and -- have higher precedence than their postfix versions.

Constant Expressions

- A constant expression is evaluated during compilation (rather than at run time). As a result, a constant expression may be used any place that a constant is required.

- Constant expressions must not contain assignment, ++, --, function-call, or comma operators, except when they appear within the operand of a sizeof operator.

Initialization

- Scalars (all arithmetic types and pointers):

  Scalar types with static or automatic storage duration are initialized with a single expression, optionally enclosed in braces. Example:

  ```
  int i = 1;
  ```

  Additionally, scalar types (with automatic storage duration only) may be initialized with a nonconstant expression.

- Unions:

  An initializer for a union with static storage duration must be enclosed in braces, and initializes the first member in the declaration list of the union. The initializer must have a type that can be converted to the type of the first union member. Example:

  ```
  union {
      int i;
      float f;
  } u = {1};      /* initialize u.i */
  ```

  For a union with automatic storage duration, if the initializer is enclosed in braces, it must consist of constant expressions that initialize the first member of the union. If the initializer is not enclosed in braces, it must be an expression that has the matching union type.

- Structures:

  The members of a structure may be initialized by initializers that can be converted to the type of the corresponding member.

  ```
  struct s {
      int i;
      char c;
      char *s;
  } st = { 3, 'a', "abc" };
  ```

  This example illustrates initialization of all three members of the structure. If initialization values are missing, as in

  ```
  struct s st2 = {5};
  ```

then the first member is initialized (in this case, member i is initialized with a value of 5), and any uninitialized member is initialized with 0 for arithmetic types and a null pointer constant for pointer types.

For a structure with automatic storage duration, if the initializer is enclosed in braces, it must consist of constant expressions that initialize the respective members of the structure. If the initializer is not enclosed in braces, it must be an expression that has the matching structure type.

■ Arrays:

The number of initializers for an array must not exceed the dimension, (i.e., the declared number of elements), but there may be fewer initializers than the number of elements. When the number of initializers is less than the size of the array, the first array elements are initialized with the values given, until the supply of initializers is exhausted. Any remaining array elements are initialized with the value 0 or a null pointer constant, as explained above in the discussion of structures. Example:

```
int ia[5] = { 1, 2 };
```

In this example, an array of five ints is declared, but only the first two members are initialized explicitly. The first member, ia[0], is initialized with a value of 1; the second member, ia[1], is initialized with a value of 2. The remaining members are initialized with a value of 0.

When no dimensions are given, the array is sized to hold exactly the number of initializers supplied.

A character array may be initialized with a string literal, as in:

```
char ca[] = { "abc" }; /*curly braces are optional*/
```

where the size of the array is four (three characters with a null byte appended). The following:

```
char cb[3] = "abc";
```

is valid; however, in this case the null byte is discarded. But:

```
char cc[2] = "abc";
```

is erroneous because there are more initializers than the array can hold.

Arrays may be initialized similarly with wide characters:

```
wchar_t wc[] = L"abc";
```

Initializing subaggregates (for example, arrays of arrays) requires the proper placement of braces. For example,

```
int ia [4] [2] =
{
    1,
    2,
    3,
    4
};
```

initializes the first two rows of ia (ia[0][0], ia[0][1], ia[1][0], and ia[1][1]), and initializes the rest to 0. This is a *minimally bracketed* initialization.

Note that a similar *fully bracketed* initialization yields a different result:

```
int ia [4] [2] =
{
    {1},
    {2},
    {3},
    {4},
};
```

initializes the first column of ia (ia[0][0], ia[1][0], ia[2][0], and ia[3][0]), and initializes the rest to 0.

Mixing the fully and minimally bracketed styles may lead to unexpected results. Use one style or the other consistently.

Statements

Expression Statement

expression;

The *expression* is executed for its side effects, if any (such as assignment or function call).

Compound Statement

> {
>> *declaration-list*_{opt}
>> *statement-list*_{opt}
> }

- Delimited by { and }.
- May have a list of *declarations*.
- May have a list of *statements*.
- May be used wherever *statement* appears below.

Selection Statements

if

> if (*expression*)
>> *statement*

- If *expression* evaluates to nonzero (true), *statement* is executed.
- If *expression* evaluates to zero (false), control passes to the statement following *statement*.
- The *expression* must have scalar type.

else

```
if  (expression1)
     statement1
else if  (expression2)
     statement2
else
     statement3
```

■ If *expression1* is true, *statement1* is executed, and control passes to the statement following *statement3*. Otherwise, *expression2* is evaluated.

■ If *expression2* is true, *statement2* is executed, and control passes to the statement following *statement3*. Otherwise, *statement3* is executed, and control
passes to the statement following *statement3*.

■ An else is associated with the lexically nearest if that has no else and
that is at the same block level.

switch

```
switch  (expression)
        statement
```

■ Control jumps to or past *statement* depending on the value of *expression*.

■ *expression* must have integral type.

■ Any optional case is labeled by an integral constant expression.

■ If a default case is present, it is executed if no other case match is
found.

■ If no case matches, including default, control goes to the statement following *statement*.

■ If the code associated with a case is executed, control falls through to the
next case unless a break statement is included.

■ Each case of a switch must have a unique constant value after conversion
to the type of the controlling expression.

In practice, *statement* is usually a compound statement with multiple cases, and possibly a default; the description above shows the minimum usage. In the following example, flag gets set to 1 if i is 1 or 3, and to 0 otherwise:

```
switch (i) {
case 1:
case 3:
        flag = 1;
        break;
default:
        flag = 0;
}
```

Iteration Statements

while

```
while (expression)
        statement
```

This sequence is followed repetitively:

- *expression* is evaluated.

- If *expression* is non-zero, *statement* is executed.

- If *expression* is zero, *statement* is not executed, and the repetition stops.

expression must have scalar type.

do-while

```
do
        statement
while (expression);
```

This sequence is followed repetitively:

- *statement* is executed.

- *expression* is evaluated.

- If *expression* is zero, repetition stops.

(do–while tests loop at the bottom; while tests loop at the top.)

for

> for (*expression1; expression2; expression3*)
>   *statement*

- *expression1* initializes the loop.

- *expression2* is tested before each iteration.

- If *expression2* is true:

  □ *statement* is executed.

  □ *expression3* is evaluated.

  □ Loop until *expression2* is false (zero).

- Any of *expression1, expression2,* or *expression3* may be omitted, but not the semicolons.

- *expression1* and *expression3* may have any type; *expression2* must have scalar type.

Jump Statements

goto

> goto *identifier;*

- Goes unconditionally to statement labeled with *identifier.*

- Statement is labeled with an identifier followed by a colon, as in:

  > A2: x = 5;

- Useful to break out of nested control flow statements.

- Can only jump within the current function.

break

Terminates nearest enclosing switch, while, do, or for statement. Passes control to the statement following the terminated statement. Example:

```
for (i=0; i<n; i++) {
    if ((a[i] = b[i]) == 0)
        break; /* exit for */
}
```

continue

Goes to top of smallest enclosing while, do, or for statement, causing it to reevaluate the controlling expression. A for loop's *expression3* is evaluated before the controlling expression. Can be thought of as the opposite of the break statement. Example:

```
for (i=0; i<n; i++) {
    if (a[i] != 0)
        continue;
    a[i] = b[i];
    k++;
}
```

return

```
return;
return expression;
```

- return by itself exits a function.

- return *expression* exits a function and returns the value of *expression*. For example,

```
return a + b;
```

Portability Considerations

Certain parts of C are inherently machine dependent. The following list of potential trouble spots is not meant to be all-inclusive but to point out the main ones.

Purely hardware issues like word size and the properties of floating point arithmetic and integer division have proven in practice to be not much of a problem. Other facets of the hardware are reflected in differing implementations. Some of these, particularly sign extension (converting a negative character into a negative integer) and the order in which bytes are placed in a word, are nuisances that must be carefully watched. Most of the others are only minor problems.

The number of variables declared with `register` that can actually be placed in registers varies from machine to machine as does the set of valid types. Nonetheless, the compilers all do things properly for their own machine; excess or invalid `register` declarations are ignored.

The order of evaluation of function arguments is not specified by the language. The order in which side effects take place is also unspecified. For example, in the expression

```
a[i] = b[i++]
```

the value of `i` could be incremented after `b[i]` is fetched, but before `a[i]` is evaluated and assigned to, or it could be incremented after the assignment.

The value of a multi-character character constant may be different for different machines.

Fields are assigned to words, and characters to integers, right to left on some machines and left to right on other machines. These differences are invisible to isolated programs that do not indulge in type punning (e.g., by converting an `int` pointer to a `char` pointer and inspecting the pointed-to storage) but must be accounted for when conforming to externally imposed storage layouts.

The `lint` tool is useful for finding program bugs and non-portable constructs. For information on how to use `lint`, see Chapter 5.

4 C Compiler Diagnostics

Introduction

This chapter contains the text and explanation for all the warning and error messages produced by the AT&T C compiler. The messages are listed in alphanumeric order (special characters are ignored). Numbers precede capital letters and capital letters precede lowercase letters. *n*, when it represents a number, comes at the beginning of the list.

The message entries are formatted as follows:

Entry	Comment
`n extra byte(s) in string literal initializer ignored`	*Text of message.*
Type: Warning *Options:* all	*Type of message and command-line options which must be set for the message to appear (*all *indicates that the message is independent of options).*
A string literal that initializes a character array contains *n* more characters than the array can hold.	*Explanation of message.*
`char ca[3] = "abcd";`	*Example of code that might generate the message.*
`"file", line 1: warning: 1 extra byte(s) in string literal initializer ignored`	*Message output.*

When an error occurs, the error message is preceded by a file name and line number. The line number is usually the line on which a problem has been diagnosed. Occasionally the compiler must read the next token before it can diagnose a problem, in which case the line number in the message may be a higher line number than that of the offending line.

Note that `lint` (Chapter 5) issues all of the messages listed in this chapter, and additional messages about potential bugs and portability problems.

Message Types and Applicable Options

Each message description includes a *Type* and an *Options* field as follows:

Type   indicates whether the message is a warning, an error, a fatal error, or a combination of error types (see below).

Options   indicates which cc command options must be set for the message to appear. "all" implies that the message is independent of cc options.

The following paragraphs explain the differences between warnings, errors, and fatals.

Warning messages, in which the word warning: appears after the file name and line number, provide useful information without interrupting compilation. They may diagnose a programming error, or a violation of C syntax or semantics, for which the compiler will nevertheless generate valid object code.

Error messages, which lack the warning: prefix, will cause the cc command to fail. Errors occur when the compiler has diagnosed a serious problem that makes it unable to understand the program or to continue to generate correct object code. It will attempt to examine the rest of your program for other errors, however. The cc command will not link your program if the compiler diagnoses errors.

Fatal errors cause the compiler to stop immediately and return an error indication to the cc command. A fatal error message is prefixed with the word fatal:. Such messages typically apply to start-up conditions, such as being unable to find a source file.

Operator Names in Messages

Some messages include the name of a compiler operator, as in:

```
operands must have arithmetic type: op "+".
```

Usually the operator in the message is a familiar C operator. At other times the compiler uses its internal name for the operator, like U-. The "Operator Names" section of this document, found after the message list, lists these internal names and describes what they mean.

Messages

n extra byte(s) in string literal initializer ignored

    Type: Warning   *Options:* all

    A string literal that initializes a character array contains *n* more characters than the array can hold.

    `char ca[3] = "abcd";`

    "file", `line 1: warning: 1 extra byte(s) in string literal`
            `initializer ignored`

0 is invalid in # \<number\> directive

    Type: Error   *Options:* all

    The line number in a line number information directive (which the compiler uses for internal communication) must be a positive, non-zero value.

    `# 0 "foo.c"`

    "file", `line 1: 0 is invalid in # <number> directive`

0 is invalid in #line directive

    Type: Error   *Options:* all

    This diagnostic is similar to the preceding one, except the invalid line number appeared in a #line directive.

    `#line 0`

    "file", `line 1: 0 is invalid in #line directive`

ANSI C behavior differs; not modifying typedef with "*modifier*"

    Type: Warning   *Options:* −Xa, −Xc

    A typedefed type may not be modified with the short, long, signed, or unsigned type modifiers, although earlier versions of C compilers permitted it. *modifier* is ignored. A related message is modifying typedef with "*modifier*"; only qualifiers allowed.

    typedef int INT;
    unsigned INT ui;

    "*file*", line 2: warning: ANSI C behavior differs; not
             modifying typedef with "unsigned"

ANSI C predefined macro cannot be redefined

    Type: Warning   *Options:* all

    The source code attempted to define or redefine a macro that is predefined by ANSI C. The predefined macro is unchanged.

    #define __FILE__ "xyz.c"

    "*file*", line 1: warning: ANSI C predefined macro cannot be
             redefined

ANSI C predefined macro cannot be undefined

    Type: Warning   *Options:* all

    The source code contains an attempt to undefine a macro that is predefined by ANSI C.

    #undef __FILE__

    "*file*", line 1: warning: ANSI C predefined macro cannot
             be undefined

ANSI C requires formal parameter before "..."

Type: Warning   *Options:* −Xc, −v

The AT&T C implementation allows you to define a function with a variable number of arguments and no fixed arguments. ANSI C requires at least one fixed argument.

```
f(...){}
```

"file", line 1: warning: ANSI C requires formal parameter
          before "..."

ANSI C treats constant as unsigned: op *"operator"*

Type: Warning   *Options:* all

The type promotion rules for ANSI C are slightly different from those of previous versions of AT&T C. In the current release the default behavior is to duplicate the previous rules. In future releases the default will be to use ANSI C rules. You may obtain the ANSI C interpretation by using the −Xa option for the cc command.

Previous AT&T C type promotion rules were "unsigned-preserving." If one of the operands of an expression was of unsigned type, the operands were promoted to a common unsigned type before the operation was performed.

ANSI C uses "value-preserving" type promotion rules. An unsigned type is promoted to a signed type if all its values may be represented in the signed type.

ANSI C also has a different rule from previous AT&T C versions for the type of an integral constant that implicitly sets the sign bit.

The different type promotion rules may lead to different program behavior for the operators that are affected by the unsigned-ness of their operands:

■ The division operators: /, /=, %, %=.

■ The right shift operators: >>, >>=.

■ The relational operators: <, <=, >, >=.

The warning message tells you that your program contains an expression in which the behavior of *operator* will change in the future. You can guarantee the behavior you want by inserting an explicit cast in the expression.

```
f (void) {
    int i;
    /* constant was integer in AT&T C, unsigned in ANSI C */
    i /= 0xf0000000;
}
```

"*file*", line 4: warning: ANSI C treats constant as unsigned:
　　　　op "/="

You can get the same behavior as in previous versions of AT&T C by adding an explicit cast:

```
f (void) {
    int i;
    /* constant was integer in AT&T C, unsigned in ANSI C */
    i /= (int) 0xf0000000;
}
```

−D option argument not an identifier

Type: Error　　　　　　　　*Options:* all

An identifier must follow the −D cc command line option.

```
cc −D3b2 −c x.c
```

```
command line: −D option argument not an identifier
```

-D option argument not followed by "="

> *Type:* Warning   *Options:* all

> If any tokens follow an identifier in a –D command line option to the cc command, the first such token must be =.

> cc –DTWO+2 –c x.c

> command line: warning: –D option argument not followed by "="

EOF in argument list of macro: *name*

> *Type:* Error   *Options:* all

> The compiler reached end-of-file while reading the arguments for an invocation of function-like macro *name*.

> #define mac(a)
> mac(arg1

> "*file*", line 5: EOF in argument list of macro: mac

EOF in asm function definition

> *Type:* Error   *Options:* all

> The compiler reached end-of-file while reading an enhanced asm function definition.

EOF in character constant

> *Type:* Error   *Options:* all

> The compiler encountered end-of-file inside a character constant.

`EOF in comment`

Type: Warning   *Options:* all

The compiler encountered end-of-file while reading a comment.

`EOF in string literal`

Type: Error   *Options:* all

The compiler encountered end-of-file inside a string literal.

`NUL in asm function definition`

Type: Warning   *Options:* all

The compiler encountered a NUL (zero) character while reading an enhanced asm function definition. The NUL is ignored.

`-U option argument not an identifier`

Type: Error   *Options:* all

An identifier must follow the –U cc command line option.

`cc -U3b2 -c x.c`

`command line: -U option argument not an identifier`

`a cast does not yield an lvalue`

Type: Warning, Error   *Options:* all

You may not apply a cast to the operand that constitutes the object to be changed in an assignment operation. The diagnostic is a warning if the size of the operand type and the size of the type being cast to are the same; otherwise it is an error.

```
f(void){
    int i;
    (long) i = 5;
    (short) i = 4;
}
```

"*file*", line 3: warning: a cast does not yield an lvalue
"*file*", line 4: a cast does not yield an lvalue

\a is ANSI C "alert" character

Type: Warning   *Options:* -Xt

In earlier AT&T C products, '\a' was equivalent to 'a'. However, ANSI C defines '\a' to be an alert character. In the AT&T implementation, the corresponding character code is 07, the BEL character.

```
int c = '\a';
```

"*file*", line 1: warning: \a is ANSI C "alert" character

access through "void" pointer ignored

Type: Warning   *Options:* all

A pointer to void may not be used to access an object. You wrote an expression that does an indirection through a (possibly qualified) pointer to void. The indirection is ignored, although the rest of the expression (if any) is honored.

```
f(){
    volatile void *vp1, *vp2;
    *(vp1 = vp2);           /* assignment does get done */
}
```

"*file*", line 3: warning: access through "void" pointer ignored argument cannot have unknown size: arg #*n*

>   *Type:* Error   *Options:* all

>   An argument in a function call must have a completed type. You
>   passed a struct, union, or enum object whose type is incomplete.

>    ```
>    f () {
>         struct s *st;
>         g (*st);
>    }
>    ```

>   *"file"*, line 3: argument cannot have unknown size: arg #1

argument does not match remembered type: arg #*n*

>   *Type:* Warning   *Options:* −v

>   At a function call, the compiler determined that the type of the *n*-th
>   argument passed to a function disagrees with other information it has
>   about the function. That other information comes from two sources:

>   >   1. An old-style (non-prototype) function definition, or

>   >   2. A function prototype declaration that has gone out of scope,
>   >   but whose type information is still remembered.

>   The argument in question is promoted according to the default argu-
>   ment promotion rules.

>   This diagnostic may be incorrect if the old-style function definition case
>   applies and the function takes a variable number of arguments.

```
void f(i)
int i;
{ }

void g()
{
    f("erroneous");
}
```
"file", line 7: warning: argument does not match remembered
          type: arg #1

argument is incompatible with prototype: arg #*n*

Type: Error   *Options:* all

You called a function with an argument whose type cannot be converted
to the type in the function prototype declaration for the function.

```
struct s {int x;} q;
f(void){
    int g(int,int);
    g(3,q);
}
```

"file", line 4: argument is incompatible with prototype:
          arg #2

argument mismatch

Type: Warning   *Options:* all

The number of arguments passed to a macro was different from the
number in the macro definition.

```
#define twoarg(a,b) a+b
int i = twoarg(4);
```

"file", line 2: warning: argument mismatch

argument mismatch: *n1* arg[s] passed, *n2* expected

> *Type:* Warning   *Options:* –v

At a function call, the compiler determined that the number of arguments passed to a function disagrees with other information it has about
the function. That other information comes from two sources:

> 1. An old-style (non-prototype) function definition, or

> 2. A function prototype declaration that has gone out of scope,
>   but whose type information is still remembered.

This diagnostic may be incorrect if the old-style function definition case
applies and the function takes a variable number of arguments.

```
extern int out_of_scope();
int f()
{                                /* function takes no args */
    extern int out_of_scope(int);
}

int g()
{
    f(1);                        /* f takes no args */
    out_of_scope();              /* out_of_scope expects one arg */
}
```

"*file*", line 9: warning: argument mismatch: 1 arg passed,
          0 expected
"*file*", line 10: warning: argument mismatch: 0 args passed,
          1 expected

array too big

> *Type:* Error   *Options:* all

An array declaration has a combination of dimensions such that the
declared object is too big for the target machine.

```
int bigarray[1000][1000][1000];
```

```
"file", line 1: array too big
```

```
asm() argument must be normal string literal
```

Type: Error   *Options:* all

The argument to an old-style `asm()` must be a normal string literal, not a wide one.

```
asm(L"wide string literal not allowed");
```

```
"file", line 1: asm() argument must be normal string literal
```

```
asm definition cannot have old-style parameters
```

Type: Error   *Options:* all

The definition of an enhanced asm function may use the ANSI C function prototype notation to declare types for parameters. It may not declare parameters by using the old-style C function definition notation of an identifier list, followed by a declaration list that declares parameter types.

```
__asm is an extension of ANSI C
```

Type: Warning   *Options:* -Xc

You declared an enhanced asm function and compiled the code with -Xc. This warning informs you that the enhanced __asm is a violation of ANSI C syntax, which the compiler is obliged to diagnose, and is not a compatible extension.

"asm" valid only for function definition

Type: Warning   *Options:* all

The asm storage class may only be used for function definitions. It is ignored here.

```
asm int f(void);
```

"file", line 1: warning: "asm" valid only for function
              definition

"#assert identifier (..." expected

Type: Error   *Options:* all

In a #assert directive, the token following the predicate was not the (that was expected.

```
#assert system unix
```

"file", line 1: "#assert identifier (..." expected

"#assert identifier" expected

Type: Error   *Options:* all

In a #assert directive, the token following the directive was not the name of the predicate.

```
#assert 5
```

"file", line 1: "#assert identifier" expected

"#assert" missing ")"

Type: Error   *Options:* all

In a #assert directive, the parenthesized form of the assertion lacked a
closing).

```
#assert system(unix
```

"file", line 1: "#assert" missing ")"

assignment type mismatch

Type: Warning, Error   *Options:* all

The operand types for an assignment operation are incompatible. The
message is a warning when the types are pointer types that do not
match. Otherwise the message is an error.

```
struct s { int x; } st;
f(void) {
    int i;
    char *cp;
    const char *ccp;
    i = st;
    cp = ccp;
}
```

"file", line 6: assignment type mismatch
"file", line 7: warning: assignment type mismatch

auto/register/asm inappropriate here

Type: Error   *Options:* all

A declaration outside any function has storage class auto or register
or a declaration within a function has storage class asm.

```
auto int i;
f(void){
      asm int j;
}
```

"*file*", line 1: auto/register/asm inappropriate here
"*file*", line 3: auto/register/asm inappropriate here

automatic redeclares external: *name*

> *Type:* Warning *Options:* all

You have declared an automatic variable *name* in the same block and
with the same name as another symbol that is extern. ANSI C prohibits such declarations, but previous versions of AT&T C allowed them.
For compatibility with previous versions, references to *name* in this
block will be to the automatic.

```
f(void){
      extern int i;
      int i;
}
```

"*file*", line 3: warning: automatic redeclares external: i

bad file specification

> *Type:* Error *Options:* all

The file specifier in a #include directive was neither a string literal nor
a well-formed header name.

```
#include stdio.h
```

"*file*", line 1: bad file specification

bad octal digit: *'digit'*

> *Type:* Warning   *Options:* −Xt

> An integer constant that began with 0 included the non-octal digit *digit*.
> An 8 is taken to have value 8, and a 9 is taken to have value 9, even
> though they are invalid.

> `int i = 08;`

> *"file"*, line 1: warning: bad octal digit: `'8'`

bad #pragma pack value: *n*

> *Type:* Warning   *Options:* all

> The value *n* that was specified in a #pragma pack directive was not one
> of the acceptable values: 1, 2, or 4. The erroneous value is ignored and
> the directive has no effect.

bad token in #error directive: *token*

> *Type:* Error   *Options:* all

> The tokens in a #error directive must be valid C tokens. The source
> program contained the invalid token *token*.

> `#error "this is an invalid token`

> *"file"*, line 1: bad token in #error directive: "
> *"file"*, line 1: #error: "this is an invalid token

bad use of "#" or "##" in macro #define

> *Type:* Warning   *Options:* all

> In a macro definition, a # or ## operator was followed by a # or ## operator.

> ```
> #define bug(s) # # s
> #define bug2(s) # ## s
> ```

> *"file"*, line 1: warning: bad use of "#" or "##" in macro #define
> *"file"*, line 2: warning: bad use of "#" or "##" in macro #define

base type is really "*type tag*": *name*

> *Type:* Warning   *Options:* −Xt

> A type was declared with a struct, union, or enum type specifier and with tag *tag*, and then used with a different type specifier to declare *name*. *type* is the type specifier that you used for the original declaration.

> For compatibility with previous releases of AT&T C, the compiler treats the two types as being the same. In ANSI C (with the −Xa or −Xc options), the types are different.

> ```
> struct s { int x,y,z; };
> f(void){
>         union s foo;
> }
> ```

> *"file"*, line 3: warning: base type is really "struct s": foo
> *"file"*, line 3: warning: declaration introduces new type in
>   ANSI C: union s

bit-field size <= 0: *name*

    Type: Error   *Options:* all

    The declaration for bit-field *name* specifies a zero or negative number of bits.

    struct s { int x:−3; };

    "file", line 1: bit-field size <= 0: x

bit-field too big: *name*

    Type: Error   *Options:* all

    The declaration for bit-field *name* specifies more bits than will fit in an object of the declared type.

    struct s { char c:20; };

    "file", line 1: bit-field too big: c

"break" outside loop or switch

    Type: Error   *Options:* all

    A function contains a break statement in an inappropriate place, namely outside any loop or switch statement.

```
f (void) {
    break;
}
```

    "file", line 2: "break" outside loop or switch

```
cannot access member of non-struct/union object
```

Type: Error   *Options:* all

The structure or union member must be completely contained within the left operand of the . operator.

```
f(void){
    struct s { int x; };
    char c;
    c.x = 1;
}
```

```
"file", line 4: warning: left operand of "." must be struct/
    union object
"file", line 4: cannot access member of non-struct/union object
```

```
cannot begin macro replacement with "##"
```

Type: Warning   *Options:* all

The ## operator is a binary infix operator and may not be the first token in the macro replacement list of a macro definition.

```
#define mac(s) ## s
```

```
"file", line 1: warning: cannot begin macro replacement with
    "##"
```

```
cannot concatenate wide and regular string literals
```

Type: Warning, Error   *Options:* all

Regular string literals and string literals for wide characters may be concatenated only if they are both regular or both wide. The compiler issues a warning if a wide string literal is followed by a regular one (and both are treated as wide); it issues an error if a regular string literal is followed by a wide one.

```
#include <stddef.h>
wchar_t wa[] = L"abc" "def";
char a[] = "abc" L"def";
```

"file", line 2: warning: cannot concatenate wide and regular
        string literals
"file", line 3: cannot concatenate wide and regular string
        literals

cannot declare array of functions or void

Type: Error   *Options:* all

You have attempted to declare an array of functions or an array of
void.

```
int f[5] ();
```

"file", line 1: cannot declare array of functions or void

cannot define "defined"

Type: Warning   *Options:* all

The predefined preprocessing operator defined may not be defined as a
macro name.

```
#define defined xyz
```

"file", line 1: warning: cannot define "defined"

cannot dereference non-pointer type

Type: Error   *Options:* all

The operand of the * (pointer dereference) operator must have pointer
type. This diagnostic is also issued for an array reference to a non-
array.

```
f () {
    int i;
    *i = 4;
    i[4] = 5;
}
```

"*file*", line 3: cannot dereference non-pointer type
"*file*", line 4: cannot dereference non-pointer type

cannot do pointer arithmetic on operand of unknown size

Type: Error   *Options:* all

An expression involves pointer arithmetic for pointers to objects whose size is unknown.

```
f (void) {
    struct s *ps;
    g (ps+1);
}
```

"*file*", line 3: cannot do pointer arithmetic on operand
            of unknown size

cannot end macro replacement with "#" or "##"

Type: Warning   *Options:* all

A # or ## operator may not be the last token in the macro replacement list of a macro definition.

```
#define mac1(s) abc ## s ##
#define mac2(s) s #
```

"*file*", line 1: warning: cannot end macro replacement with "#"
            or "##"
"*file*", line 2: warning: cannot end macro replacement with "#"
            or "##"

cannot find include file: *filename*

    Type: Error   *Options:* all

    The file *filename* specified in a #include directive could not be located in any of the directories along the search path.

    #include "where_is_it.h"

    "*file*", line 1: cannot find include file: "where_is_it.h"

cannot have "..." in asm function

    Type: Warning   *Options:* all

    An enhanced asm definition may not be a function prototype definition with ellipsis notation.

cannot have void object: *name*

    Type: Error   *Options:* all

    You may not declare an object of type void.

    void v;

    "*file*", line 1: cannot have void object: v

cannot initialize "extern" declaration: *name*

    Type: Error   *Options:* all

    Within a function, the declaration of an object with extern storage class may not have an initializer.

```
f(void) {
    extern int i = 1;
}
```

"*file*", line 2: cannot initialize "extern" declaration: i

cannot initialize function: *name*

    Type: Error   *Options:* all

    A name declared as a function may not have an initializer.

```
int f(void) = 3;
```

"*file*", line 1: cannot initialize function: f

cannot initialize parameter: *name*

    Type: Error   *Options:* all

    Old-style function parameter *name* may not have an initializer.

```
int f(i)
int i = 4;
{
}
```

"*file*", line 2: cannot initialize parameter: i

cannot initialize typedef: *name*

    Type: Error   *Options:* all

    A typedef may not have an initializer.

```
typedef int INT = 1;
```

"*file*", line 1: cannot initialize typedef: INT

cannot open *file*: *explanation*

    Type: Fatal   *Options:* all

The compiler was unable to open an input or output file. Usually this means the file name argument passed to the cc command was incorrect. *explanation* describes why *file* could not be opened.

```
cc glorch.c -c x.c
```

```
command line: fatal: cannot open  glorch.c: No such file or
        directory
```

cannot open include file (too many open files): *filename*

    Type: Error   *Options:* all

The compiler could not open a new include file, *filename*, because too many other include files are already open. Such a situation could arise if you have *file1* that includes *file2* that includes *file3*, and so on. The compiler supports at least eight levels of "nesting," up to a maximum defined by the operating system. The most likely reason for the diagnostic is that at some point an include file includes a file that had already been included. For example, this could happen if *file1* includes *file2*, which includes *file1* again.

In this example, imagine that the file i1.h contains #include "i1.h".

```
#include "i1.h"
```

```
"./i1.h", line 1: cannot open include file (too many open
        files): "i1.h"
```

cannot recover from previous errors

Type: Error   *Options:* all

Earlier errors in the compilation have confused the compiler, and it cannot continue to process your program. Please correct those errors and try again.

cannot return incomplete type

Type: Error   *Options:* all

When a function is called that returns a structure or union, the complete declaration for the structure or union must have been seen already. Otherwise this message results.

```
f () {
    struct s g ();
    g ();
}
```

"file", line 3: cannot return incomplete type

cannot take address of bit-field: *name*

Type: Error   *Options:* all

You cannot take the address of a bit-field member of a structure or union.

```
f (void) {
    struct s { int x:3, y:4; } st;
    int *ip = &st.y;
}
```

"file", line 3: cannot take address of bit-field: y

cannot take address of register: *name*

> *Type:* Warning, Error   *Options:* all

> You attempted to take the address of *name*, which is an object that was declared with the register storage class. You are not permitted to do so, whether or not the compiler actually allocates the object to a register. The attempt to take an object's address may have been implicit, such as when an array is dereferenced. The diagnostic is an error if a register was allocated for the object and a warning otherwise.

> ```
> f (void) {
>     register int i;
>     register int ia[5];
>     int *ip = &i;
>     ia[2] = 1;
> }
> ```

> *"file"*, line 4: cannot take address of register: i
> *"file"*, line 5: warning: cannot take address of register: ia

cannot take sizeof bit-field: *name*

> *Type:* Warning   *Options:* all

> The sizeof operator may not be applied to bit-fields.

> ```
> struct s { int x:3; } st;
> int i = sizeof(st.x);
> ```

> *"file"*, line 2: warning: cannot take sizeof bit-field: x

cannot take sizeof function: *name*

> *Type:* Error   *Options:* all

> The sizeof operator may not be applied to functions.

```
int f(void);
int i = sizeof(f);
```

```
"file", line 2: cannot take sizeof function: f
```

cannot take sizeof void

> *Type:* Error   *Options:* all

> The sizeof operator may not be applied to type void.

> ```
> void v(void);
> int i = sizeof(v());
> ```

> ```
> "file", line 2: cannot take sizeof void
> ```

cannot undefine "defined"

> *Type:* Error   *Options:* all

> The predefined preprocessing operator defined may not be undefined.

> ```
> #undef defined
> ```

> ```
> "file", line 1: warning: cannot undefine "defined"
> ```

case label affected by conversion: *value*

> *Type:* Warning   *Options:* -v

> The *value* for the case label cannot be represented by the type of the controlling expression of a switch statement. If the type of the case expression and the type of the controlling expression have the same size, the actual bit representation of the case expression is unchanged, but its interpretation is different. For example, the controlling expression may have type int and the case expression may have type unsigned int. In the diagnostic, *value* is represented as a hexadecimal value if the case expression is unsigned, decimal if it is signed.

```
f(){
    int i;

    switch( i ){
    case 0xffffffffu:

      ;
    }
}
```

"file", line 5: warning: case label affected by conversion:
          0xffffffff

In this example 0xffffffffu is not representable as an int. When the
case expression is converted to the type of the controlling expression
(int), its effective value is −1. That is, the case will be reached if i has
the value −1, rather than 0xffffffff.

"case" outside switch

Type: Error   *Options:* all

A case statement occurred outside the scope of any switch statement.

```
f(void){
    case 4: ;
}
```

"file", line 2: "case" outside switch

character constant too long

Type: Warning   *Options:* all

The character constant contains too many characters to fit in an integer.
Only the first four characters of a regular character constant, and only
the first character of a wide character constant, are used. (Character
constants that are longer than one character are non-portable.)

```
int i = 'abcde';
```

"file", line 1: warning: character constant too long

`character escape does not fit in character`

Type: Warning   *Options:* all

A hexadecimal or octal escape sequence in a character constant or string literal produces a value that is too big to fit in an unsigned char. The value is truncated to fit.

```
char *p = "\x1ff\400";
```


"file", line 1: warning: \x is ANSI C hex escape
"file", line 1: warning: character escape does not fit in
        character
"file", line 1: warning: character escape does not fit in
        character

`character escape does not fit in wide character`

Type: Warning   *Options:* all

This message diagnoses a condition similar to the previous one, except the character constant or string literal is prefixed by L to designate a wide character constant or string literal. The character escape is too large to fit in an object of type wchar_t and is truncated to fit.

`comment does not concatenate tokens`

Type: Warning   *Options:* −Xa, −Xc

In previous releases of AT&T C, it was possible to "paste" two tokens together by juxtaposing them in a macro with a comment between them. This behavior was never defined or guaranteed. ANSI C provides a well-defined operator, ##, that serves the same purpose and should be

used. This diagnostic warns that the old behavior is not being provided.

```
#define PASTE(a,b) a/*GLUE*/b
int PASTE(prefix,suffix) = 1;    /* does not create */
                                 /* prefixsuffix */
```

```
"file", line 1: warning: comment does not concatenate tokens
"file", line 2: syntax error, probably missing ",", ";" or "="
"file", line 2: syntax error before or at: suffix
"file", line 2: warning: old-style declaration; add "int"
```

comment is replaced by "##"

Type: Warning   *Options:* −Xt

This message is closely related to comment does not concatenate
tokens. The diagnostic tells you that the compiler is treating an
apparent concatenation as if it were the ## operator. The source code
should be updated to use the new operator.

```
#define PASTE(a,b) a/*GLUE*/b
int PASTE(prefix,suffix) = 1;    /* creates prefixsuffix */
```

```
"file", line 1: warning: comment is replaced by "##"
```

const object should have initializer: *name*

Type: Warning   *Options:* −v

A const object cannot be modified. If you do not supply an initial
value, the object will have a value of zero, or for automatics its value
will be indeterminate.

```
const int i;
```

```
"file", line 1: warning: const object should have initializer:
    i
```

"continue" outside loop

    Type: Error   *Options:* all

    Your program contains a continue statement outside the scope of any loop.

```
f(void) {
    continue;
}
```

    "file", line 2: "continue" outside loop

controlling expressions must have scalar type

    Type: Error   *Options:* all

    The expression for an if, for, while, or do–while must be an integral, floating-point, or pointer type.

```
f(void) {
    struct s {int x;} st;
    while (st) {}
}
```

    "file", line 3: controlling expressions must have scalar type

conversion of double to float is out of range

    Type: Warning, Error   *Options:* all

    A double expression has too large a value to fit in a float. The diagnostic is a warning if the expression is in executable code and an error otherwise.

```
float f = 1e30 * 1e30;
```

    "file", line 1: conversion of double to float is out of range

conversion of double to integral is out of range

> *Type:* Warning, Error   *Options:* all

> A double constant has too large a value to fit in an integral type. The diagnostic is a warning if the expression is in executable code and an error otherwise.

> int i = 1e100;

> "*file*", line 1: conversion of double to integral is out of
>   range

conversion of floating-point constant to *type* out of range

> *Type:* Error   *Options:* all

> A floating-point constant has too large a value to fit in type *type* (float, double, long double).

> float f = 1e300f;

> "*file*", line 1: conversion of floating-point constant to float
>   out of range

declaration hides parameter: *name*

> *Type:* Warning   *Options:* all

> You have declared an identifier *name* with the same name as one of the parameters of the function. References to *name* in this block will be to the new declaration.

```
int f(int i,int INT){
    int i;
    typedef int INT;
}
```

"file", line 2: warning: declaration hides parameter: i
"file", line 3: warning: declaration hides parameter: INT

declaration introduces new type in ANSI C: *type tag*

Type: Warning   *Options:* −Xt

struct, union, or enum *tag* has been redeclared in an inner scope. In
previous releases of AT&T C, this tag was taken to refer to the previous
declaration of tag. In ANSI C, the declaration introduces a new *type*.
When the −Xt option is selected, AT&T C reproduces the earlier
behavior.

```
struct s1 { int x; };
f(void){
    struct s1;
    struct s2 { struct s1 *ps1; };   /* s1 refers to line 1 */
    struct s1 { struct s2 *ps2; };
}
```

"file", line 3: warning: declaration introduces new type in
        ANSI C: struct s1

"default" outside switch

Type: Error   *Options:* all

A default label appears outside the scope of a switch statement.

```
f(void){
default: ;
}
```

"file", line 2: "default" outside switch

#define requires macro name

Type: Error   *Options:* all

A #define directive must be followed by the name of the macro to be defined.

```
#define +3
```

"file", line 1: #define requires macro name

digit sequence expected after "#line"

Type: Error   *Options:* all

The compiler expected to find the digit sequence that comprises a line number after #line, but the token it found there is either an inappropriate token or a digit sequence whose value is zero.

```
#line 09a
```

"file", line 1: digit sequence expected after "#line"

directive is an upward-compatible ANSI C extension

Type: Warning   *Options:* -Xc

This diagnostic is issued when the AT&T C compiler sees a directive that it supports, but that is not part of the ANSI C standard, and -Xc has been selected.

```
#assert system( unix )
```

"file", line 1: warning: directive is an upward–compatible
      ANSI C extension

directive not honored in macro argument list

Type: Warning, Error   *Options:* all

A directive has appeared between the ( )'s that delimit the arguments of a function-like macro invocation. The following directives are disallowed in such a context: #ident, #include, #line, #undef. The diagnostic is a warning if it appears within a false group of an if-group, and an error otherwise.

```
#define flm(a) a+4
int i = flm(
#ifdef flm          /* allowed */
    #undef flm          /* disallowed:  error */
        4
#else           /* allowed */
    #undef flm          /* disallowed:  warn */
        6
#endif          /* allowed */
);
```

"file", line 4: directive not honored in macro argument list
"file", line 7: warning: directive not honored in macro
        argument list

division by 0

Type: Warning, Error   *Options:* all

An expression contains a division by zero that was detected at compile-time. If the division is part of a #if or #elif directive, the result is taken to be zero.

The diagnostic is a warning if the division is in executable code, an error otherwise.

```
f(void) {
     int i = 1/0;
}
```

```
"file", line 2: warning: division by 0
```

dubious *type* declaration; use tag only: *tag*

Type: Warning   *Options:* all

You declared a new struct, union, or enum *type* with tag *tag* within a function prototype declaration or the parameter declaration list of an old-style function definition, and the declaration includes a declarator list for *type*. Calls to the function would always produce a type mismatch, because the tag declaration goes out of scope at the end of the function prototype declaration or definition, according to ANSI C's scope rules. You could never declare an object of that type outside the function. You should declare the struct, union, or enum ahead of the function prototype or function definition and then refer to it just by its tag.

```
int f(struct s {int x;} st)
{}
```

```
"file", line 1: warning: dubious struct declaration; use tag
          only: s
```

Rewrite this as

```
struct s {int x;};
int f(struct s st)
{}
```

dubious escape: \c

    Type: Warning   *Options:* all

    Only certain characters may follow \ in string literals and character constants; *c* was not one of them. AT&T C ignores the \.

    int i = '\q';

    "*file*", line 1: warning: dubious escape: \q

dubious escape: \<*hex value*>

    Type: Warning   *Options:* all

    This message diagnoses the same condition as the preceding one, but the character that follows \ in the program is a non-printing character. The *hex value* between the brackets in the diagnostic is the character's code, printed as a hexadecimal number.

dubious reference to *type* typedef: *typedef*

    Type: Warning   *Options:* all

    This message is similar to dubious tag in function prototype: *type tag*. A function prototype declaration refers to a *type* struct, union, or enum typedef with name *typedef*. Because the struct, union, or enum has been declared within a function, it could not be in scope when you define the function whose prototype is being declared. The prototype declaration and function definition thus could never match.

```
f () {
     struct s { int x; };
     typedef struct s ST;
     extern int g(ST, struct s);
}
```

"file", line 4: warning: dubious reference to struct typedef:
        ST
"file", line 4: warning: dubious tag in function prototype:
        struct s

dubious static function at block level

> *Type:* Warning   *Options:* -Xc

You declared a function with storage class static at block scope. The ANSI C standard says that the behavior is undefined if you declare a function at block scope with an explicit storage class other than extern. Although AT&T C allows you to declare functions this way, other implementations might not, or they might attach a different meaning to such a declaration.

```
void
f (void) {
     static void g (void);
}
```

"file", line 3: warning: dubious static function at block
        level

dubious tag declaration: *type tag*

> *Type:* Warning   *Options:* all

You declared a new struct, union, or enum *type* with tag *tag* within a function prototype declaration or the parameter declaration list of an old-style function definition. Calls to the function would always produce a type mismatch, because the tag declaration goes out of scope at the end of the function declaration or definition, according to ANSI C's scope rules. You could never declare an object of that type outside the function.

```
int f(struct s *);
```

`"file"`, line 1: warning: dubious tag declaration: struct s

`dubious tag in function prototype:` *type tag*

Type: Warning   *Options:* all

This message is similar to the previous one. A function prototype declaration refers to a `struct`, `union`, or `enum` *type* with tag *tag*. The *tag* has been declared within a function. Therefore it could not be in scope when you define the function whose prototype is being declared. The prototype declaration and function definition thus could never match.

```
f(){
     struct s {int x;};
     int g(struct s *);
}
```

`"file"`, line 3: warning: dubious tag in function prototype:
          struct s

`duplicate case in switch:` *value*

Type: Error   *Options:* all

There are two case statements in the current `switch` statement that have the same constant value *value*.

```
f(void){
    int i = 5;
    switch(i) {
    case 4:
    case 4:
        break;
    }
}
```

"file", line 5: duplicate case in switch: 4

duplicate "default" in switch

Type: Error   *Options:* all

There are two default labels in the current switch statement.

```
f(void){
    int i = 5;
    switch(i) {
    default:
    default:
        break;
    }
}
```

"file", line 5: duplicate "default" in switch

duplicate formal parameter: *name*

Type: Warning   *Options:* all

In a function-like macro definition, *name* was used more than once as a formal parameter.

```
#define add3(a,a,c) a + b + c
```

"file", line 1: warning: duplicate formal parameter: a

duplicate member name: *member*

> *Type:* Error   *Options:* all

> A struct or union declaration uses the name *member* for more than one member.

>  ```
>  union u {
>      int i;
>      float i;
>  };
>  ```

> *"file"*, line 3: duplicate member name: i

duplicate name in % line specification: *name*

> *Type:* Error   *Options:* all

> Formal parameter *name* was mentioned more than once in the % line of an enhanced asm function.

#elif follows #else

> *Type:* Warning   *Options:* all

> A preprocessing if-section must be in the order #if, optional #elif's, followed by optional #else and #endif. The code contains a #elif after the #else directive.

```
#if defined(ONE)
        int i = 1;
#elif defined(TWO)
        int i = 2;
#else
        int i = 3;
#elif defined(FOUR)
        int i = 4;
#endif
```

"file", line 7: warning: #elif follows #else

#elif has no preceding #if

Type: Error   *Options:* all

An #elif directive must be part of a preprocessing if-section, which
begins with a #if directive. The code in question lacked the #if.

```
#elif defined(TWO)
        int i = 2;
#endif
```

"file", line 1: #elif has no preceding #if
"file", line 3: #if-less #endif

#elif must be followed by a constant expression

Type: Error   *Options:* all

There was no expression following the #elif directive.

```
#if defined(ONE)
        int i = 1;
#elif
        int i = 4;
#endif
```

"*file*", line 3: warning: #elif must be followed by a constant
        expression

#else has no preceding #if

Type: Error   *Options:* all

An #else directive was encountered that was not part of a preprocessing if-section.

```
#else
        int i =7;
#endif
```

"*file*", line 1: #else has no preceding #if
"*file*", line 3: #if-less #endif

embedded NUL not permitted in asm()

Type: Error   *Options:* all

The string literal that appears in an old-style asm() contains an embedded NUL character (character code 0).

```
asm("this is an old-style asm with embedded NUL:  \0");
```

"*file*", line 1: embedded NUL not permitted in asm()

empty #assert directive

>   *Type:* Error   *Options:* all

>   A #assert directive contained no predicate name to assert.
>
>   #assert
>
>   *"file"*, line 1: empty #assert directive

empty character constant

>   *Type:* Error   *Options:* all

>   The program has a character constant without any characters in it.
>
>   int i = '';
>
>   *"file"*, line 1: empty character constant

empty constant expression after macro expansion

>   *Type:* Error   *Options:* all

>   A #if or #elif directive contained an expression that, after macro
>   expansion, consisted of no tokens.
>
>   #define EMPTY
>   #if EMPTY
>   char *mesg = "EMPTY is non-empty";
>   #endif
>
>   *"file"*, line 2: empty constant expression after macro
>   expansion

empty #define directive line

    Type: Error   *Options:* all

    A #define directive lacked both the name of the macro to define and any other tokens.

    #define

    "file", line 1: empty #define directive line

empty file name

    Type: Error   *Options:* all

    The file name in a #include directive is null.

    #include <>

    "file", line 1: empty file name

empty header name

    Type: Error   *Options:* all

    This diagnostic is similar to the preceding one, but the null file name arises after macro substitution.

    #define NULLNAME <>
    #include NULLNAME

    "file", line 2: empty header name

empty predicate argument

    Type: Error   *Options:* all

The compiler expects to find tokens between the ( )'s that delimit a predicate's assertions in a #unassert directive. None were present.

```
#unassert machine()
```

"*file*", line 1: empty predicate argument

empty translation unit

Type: Warning   *Options:* all

The source file has no tokens in it after preprocessing is complete. The ANSI C standard requires the compiler to diagnose a file that has no tokens in it.

```
#ifdef COMPILE
        int token;
#endif
```

"*file*", line 5: warning: empty translation unit

empty #unassert directive

Type: Error   *Options:* all

A #unassert contained no predicate name to discard.

```
#unassert
```

"*file*", line 1: empty #unassert directive

empty #undef directive, identifier expected

Type: Error   *Options:* all

A #undef directive lacked the name of a macro to "undefine."

#undef

"file", line 1: empty #undef directive, identifier expected

{}—enclosed initializer required

Type: Warning   *Options:* all

When you initialize an aggregate, except when you initialize a character array with a string literal or an automatic structure with an expression, you must enclose the initializer in { }'s.

```
int ia[5] = 1;
f(void) {
    struct s { int x,y; } st = 1;
}
```

"file", line 1: warning: {}—enclosed initializer required
"file", line 3: warning: {}—enclosed initializer required
"file", line 3: struct/union-valued initializer required

end—of—loop code not reached

Type: Warning   *Options:* all

You have written a loop in such a way that the code at the end of the loop that the compiler generates to branch back to the beginning of the loop is not reachable and will never be executed.

```
f(void) {
    int i = 1;
    while (i) {
        return 4;
    }
}
```

"file", line 5: warning: end—of—loop code not reached

enum constants have different types: op "*operator*"

> *Type:* Warning   *Options:* −v

You have used relational operator *operator* to compare enumeration constants from two different enumeration types. This may indicate a programming error. Note also that the sense of the comparison is known
at compile time, because the constants' values are known.

```
enum e1 { ec11, ec12 } ev1;
enum e2 { ec21, ec22 } ev2;
void v(void){
    if (ec11 > ec22)
        ;
}
```

"*file*", line 4: warning: enum constants have different types:
       op ">"

enum type mismatch: arg #*n*

> *Type:* Warning   *Options:* −v

The program is passing an enumeration constant or object to a function
for which a prototype declaration is in scope. The passed argument is
of a different enumerated type from the one in the function prototype,
which may indicate a programming error.

```
enum e1 { ec11 } ev1;
enum e2 { ec21 } ev2;
void ef(enum e1);

void v(void){
    ef(ec21);
}
```

"*file*", line 6: warning: enum type mismatch: arg #1

enum type mismatch: op *"operator"*

Type: Warning   *Options:* −v

This message is like the previous one. One of the operands of *operator* is an enumeration object or constant, and the other is an enumeration object or constant from a different enumerated type.

```
enum e1 { ec11, ec12 } ev1;
enum e2 { ec21, ec22 } ev2;
void v(void){
    if (ev1 > ec22)
        ;
}
```

"file", line 4: warning: enum type mismatch: op ">"

enumeration constant hides parameter: *name*

Type: Warning   *Options:* all

A declaration of an enumerated type within a function includes an enumeration constant with the same name as parameter *name*. The enumeration constant hides the parameter.

```
int
f(int i){
    enum e { l, k, j, i };
}
```

"file", line 3: warning: enumeration constant hides parameter:
        i

enumerator used in its own initializer: *name*

Type: Warning   *Options:* all

When setting the value of enumerator *name* in an enumeration type declaration, you have used *name* in the expression. ANSI C's scope rules take *name* in the expression to be whatever symbol was in scope at the time.

```
int i;
f(void){
    enum e { i = i+1, j, k };    /* uses global i in i+1 */
}
```

"*file*", line 3: warning: enumerator used in its own
        initializer: i
"*file*", line 3: integral constant expression expected

enumerator value overflows INT_MAX (2147483647)

Type: Warning   *Options:* all

The value for an enumeration constant overflowed the maximum integer value.

```
enum e { e1=2147483647, e2 };    /* overflow for e2 */
```

"*file*", line 1: warning: enumerator value overflows INT_MAX
        (2147483647)

#error: *tokens*

Type: Error   *Options:* all

A #error directive was encountered in the source file. The other *tokens* in the directive are printed as part of the message.

```
#define ONE 2
#if ONE != 1
#error ONE != 1
#endif
```

"*file*", line 3: #error: ONE != 1

`%error encountered in asm function`

> *Type:* Error   *Options:* all

> A `%error` specification line was encountered while an enhanced asm was being expanded.

`error in asm; expect ";" or "\n", saw 'c'`

> *Type:* Error   *Options:* all

> In a `%` line of an enhanced asm function, the compiler expected to read a semi-colon or new-line and found character *c* instead.

`error writing output file`

> *Type:* Error   *Options:* all

> An output error occurred while the compiler attempted to write its output file or a temporary file. The most likely problem is that a file system is out of space.

`")" expected`

> *Type:* Error   *Options:* all

> In an `#unassert` directive, the assertion of a predicate to be dropped must be enclosed in ( ).

> `#unassert system(unix`

> *"file",* `line 1: ")" expected`

`"(" expected after "# identifier"`

> *Type:* Error   *Options:* all

> When the `#` operator is used in a `#if` or `#elif` directive to select a

predicate instead of a like-named macro, the predicate must be followed by a parenthesized list of tokens.

```
#assert system(unix)
#define system "unix"
#if #system
        char *systype = system;
#endif
```

"file", line 3: "(" expected after "# identifier"

"(" expected after first identifier

Type: Error   *Options:* all

In an #unassert directive, the assertion of a predicate to be dropped must be enclosed in ( ) .

```
#unassert system unix
```

"file", line 1: "(" expected after first identifier

extern and prior uses redeclared as static: *name*

Type: Warning   *Options:* -Xc, -v

You declared *name* at file scope as an extern, then later declared the same object or function as static. ANSI C rules require that the first declaration of an object or function give its actual storage class. AT&T C accepts the declaration and treats the object or function as if the first declaration had been static.

```
extern int i;
static int i;
```

"file", line 2: warning: extern and prior uses redeclared as static: i

`first operand must have scalar type: op "?:"`

Type: Error   *Options:* all

The conditional expression in a ? : expression must have scalar (integral, floating-point, or pointer) type.

```
struct s { int x; } st;
f(void) {
     int i = st ? 3 : 4;
}
```

`"file", line 3: first operand must have scalar type: op "?:"`

`floating-point constant calculation out of range: op "operator"`

Type: Warning, Error   *Options:* all

The compiler detected an overflow at compile time when it attempted the *operator* operation between two floating-point operands. The diagnostic is a warning if the expression is in executable code and an error otherwise.

```
double d1 = 1e300 * 1e300;
```

`"file", line 1: floating-point constant calculation out of`
`        range: op "*"`

`floating-point constant folding causes exception`

Type: Error   *Options:* all

This message is like the previous one, except that the operation caused a floating-point exception that causes the compiler to exit.

formal parameter lacks name: param #*n*

   Type: Error   *Options:* all

In a function prototype definition, you failed to provide a name for the *n*-th parameter.

```
int f(int){
}
```

"*file*", line 1: formal parameter lacks name: param #1

function actually returns double: *name*

   Type: Warning   *Options:* -v

A function that was declared to return type float actually returns double. This information may be useful to know if you try to write an assembly language version of the called routine, or if you write the routine in C++.

```
float f();
```

"*file*", line 1: warning: function actually returns double: f

function cannot return function or array

   Type: Error   *Options:* all

You declared a function whose return type would be a function or array, rather than, perhaps, a pointer to one of those.

```
int f(void)[];     /* function returning array of ints */
```

"*file*", line 1: function cannot return function or array

`function designator is not of function type`

    Type: Error   *Options:* all

    You used an expression in a function call as if it were the name of a function or a pointer to a function when it was not.

```
f (void) {
    char *p;
    p ();
}
```

    "file", line 3: function designator is not of function type

`function expects to return value:` *name*

    Type: Warning   *Options:* −v

    The current function was declared with a non-void type, but you used a return statement with no return value expression.

```
f (void) {
    return;
}
```

    "file", line 2: warning: function expects to return value: f

`function prototype parameters must have types`

    Type: Warning   *Options:* all

    A function prototype declaration cannot contain an identifier list; it must declare types. The identifier list is ignored.

```
int f (i);
```

    "file", line 1: warning: function prototype parameters must
            have types

identifier expected after "#"

    Type: Error   *Options:* all

    The compiler expected to find an identifier, a predicate name, after a #
in a conditional compilation directive, and none was there.

```
#if #system(unix) || #
        char *os = "sys";
#endif
```

    "file", line 1: identifier expected after "#"

identifier expected after #undef

    Type: Error   *Options:* all

    A #undef must be followed by the name of the macro to be undefined.
The token following the directive was not an identifier.

```
#undef 4
```

    "file", line 1: identifier expected after #undef

identifier or "-" expected after -A

    Type: Error   *Options:* all

    The cc command line argument -A must be followed by the name of a
predicate to assert, or by a -, to eliminate all predefined macros and
predicates. The token following -A was neither of these.

```
cc -A3b2 -c x.c
```

    command line: identifier or "-" expected after -A

`identifier or digit sequence expected after "#"`

> *Type:* Error   *Options:* all

> An invalid token or non-decimal number follows the # that introduces a
> preprocessor directive line.

> `# 0x12`

> `"file", line 1: identifier or digit sequence expected after "#"`

`identifier redeclared:` *name*

> *Type:* Warning, Error   *Options:* all

> You declared the identifier *name* in a way that is inconsistent with a pre-
> vious appearance of *name*, or you declared *name* twice in the same
> scope.

> Previous releases of AT&T C were forgiving of inconsistent redeclara-
> tions if the types were "nearly" the same (such as `int` and `long` on an
> AT&T 3B2 computer). ANSI C considers the types to be different. The
> –Xt option will allow you to retain the previous behavior, although the
> compiler will issue a warning. When the types are manifestly different,
> the diagnostic is always an error. The –Xa and –Xc options always pro-
> duce an error when the types are different.

> ```
> int x;
> long x;
> int y;
> double y;
> ```

> `"file", line 2: warning: identifier redeclared: x`
> `"file", line 4: identifier redeclared: y`

> Declarations of functions with and without argument information can
> often lead to confusing diagnostics. The following example illustrates.

```
int f(char);
int f();
```

"file", line 2: warning: identifier redeclared: f

According to ANSI C's type compatibility rules, a function declaration that lacks type information (i.e., one that is not a function prototype declaration) is compatible with a function prototype only when each parameter type is unchanged by the default argument promotion rules. In the example, char would be affected by the promotion rules (it would be promoted to int). Therefore the two declarations have incompatible types.

identifier redeclared; ANSI C requires "static": *name*

   Type: Warning   *Options:* all

You declared *name* twice at file scope. The first one used storage class static, but the second one specified no storage class. ANSI C's rules for storage classes require that all redeclarations of *name* after the first must specify static.

```
static int i;
int i;
```

"file", line 2: warning: identifier redeclared; ANSI C
          requires "static": i

identifier redefined: *name*

   Type: Error   *Options:* all

You have defined *name* more than once. That is, you have declared an object more than once with an initializer, or you have defined a function more than once.

```
int i = 1;
int i = 1;
```

"file", line 2: identifier redefined: i

#if must be followed by a constant expression

Type: Warning   *Options:* all

No expression appeared after a #if directive.

```
#if
        int i = 4;
#endif
```

"file", line 1: warning: #if must be followed by a constant
          expression

#if on line *n* has no #endif

Type: Error   *Options:* all

The compiler reached end of file without finding the #endif that would
end the preprocessing if-section that began with the *if* directive that was
on line *n*. The *if* directive is one of #if, #ifdef, or #ifndef.

```
#ifdef NOENDIF
        int i = 1;
```

"file", line 5: #ifdef on line 1 has no matching #endif
"file", line 5: warning: empty translation unit

#if-less #endif

Type: Error   *Options:* all

An #endif directive was encountered that was not part of a preprocessing if-section.

```
            int i = 1;
    #endif
```

"file", line 2: #if-less #endif

#ifdef must be followed by an identifier

Type: Warning   *Options:* all

A #ifdef preprocessing directive must be followed by the name of the macro to check for being defined. The source code omitted the identifier. The #ifdef is treated as if it were false.

```
#ifdef
        int i = 1;
#endif
```

"file", line 1: warning: #ifdef must be followed by an
        identifier

#ifndef must be followed by an identifier

Type: Warning   *Options:* all

The #ifndef directive must be followed by the identifier that is to be tested for having been defined.

```
#ifndef
        int i = 5;
#endif
```

"file", line 1: warning: #ifndef must be followed by an
        identifier

ignoring malformed #pragma int_to_unsigned symbol

> *Type:* Warning   *Options:* all

> The compiler encountered a #pragma int_to_unsigned directive that did not have the form shown. The erroneous directive is ignored.

> #pragma int_to_unsigned strlen();

> *"file"*, line 1: warning: ignoring malformed #pragma
>   int_to_unsigned symbol

ignoring malformed #pragma pack(n)

> *Type:* Warning   *Options:* all

> The compiler encountered a #pragma pack directive that did not have the form shown. The erroneous directive is ignored.

ignoring malformed #pragma weak symbol [=value]

> *Type:* Warning   *Options:* all

> The compiler encountered a #pragma weak directive that did not have the form shown. The erroneous directive is ignored.

> #pragma weak write,_write

> *"file"*, line 1: warning: ignoring malformed #pragma weak
>   symbol [=value]

implicitly declaring function to return int: *name*()

> *Type:* Warning   *Options:* −v

> The program calls function *name*, which has not been previously declared. The compiler warns you that it is assuming that function *name* returns int.

```
void v(void){
     g();
}
```

```
"file", line 2: warning: implicitly declaring function to
          return int: g()
```

improper cast of void expression

Type: Error   *Options:* all

You cannot cast a void expression to something other than void.

```
f(void){
     void v(void);
     int i = (int) v();
}
```

```
"file", line 3: improper cast of void expression
```

improper member use: *name*

Type: Warning, Error   *Options:* all

Your program contains an expression with a -> or . operator, and
name is not a member of the structure or union that the left side of the
operator refers to, but it is a member of some other structure or union.

This diagnostic is an error if the member is not "unique." A unique
member is part of one or more structures or unions but has the same
type and offset in all of them.

```
struct s1 { int x,y; };
struct s2 { int q,r; };
f(void){
    struct s1 *ps1;
    ps1->r = 3;
}
```

"*file*", line 5: warning: improper member use: r

improper pointer subtraction

Type: Warning, Error   *Options:* all

The operands of a subtraction are both pointers, but they point at different types. You may only subtract pointers of the same type that point to the same array.

The diagnostic is a warning if the pointers point to objects of the same size, and an error otherwise.

```
f(void){
    int *ip;
    char *cp;
    int i = ip - cp;
}
```

"*file*", line 4: improper pointer subtraction

improper pointer/integer combination: arg #*n*

Type: Warning   *Options:* all

At a function call for which there is a function prototype declaration in scope, the code is passing an integer where a pointer is expected, or vice versa.

```
int f(char *);
g(void) {
    f(5);
}
```

```
"file", line 3: warning: improper pointer/integer combination:
          arg #1
```

improper pointer/integer combination: op "*operator*"

Type: Warning   *Options:* all

One of the operands of *operator* is a pointer and the other is an integer, but this combination is invalid.

```
f(void) {
    int i = "abc";
    int j = i ? 4 : "def";
}
```

```
"file", line 2: warning: improper pointer/integer combination:
          op "="
"file", line 3: warning: improper pointer/integer combination:
          op ":"
"file", line 3: warning: improper pointer/integer combination:
          op "="
```

inappropriate qualifiers with "void"

Type: Warning   *Options:* all

You may not qualify void (with const or volatile) when it stands by itself.

```
int f(const void);
```

```
"file", line 1: warning: inappropriate qualifiers with "void"
```

#include <... missing '>'

    Type: Warning   *Options:* all

    In a #include directive for which the header name began with <, the closing > character was omitted.

    #include <stdio.h

    "*file*", line 1: warning: #include <... missing '>'

#include directive missing file name

    Type: Error   *Options:* all

    A #include directive did not specify a file to include.

    #include

    "*file*", line 1: #include directive missing file name

#include of /usr/include/... may be non-portable

    Type: Warning   *Options:* all

    The source file included a file with the explicit prefix /usr/include. Such an inclusion is implementation-dependent and non-portable. On some systems the list of default places to look for a header might not include the /usr/include directory. In such a case the wrong file might be included.

    #include </usr/include/stdio.h>

    "*file*", line 1: warning: #include of /usr/include/... may be
        non-portable

`incomplete #define macro parameter list`

Type: Error   *Options:* all

In the definition of a function-like parameter, the compiler did not find a) character on the same (logical) line as the `#define` directive.

`#define mac(a`

`"`*file*`", line 1: incomplete #define macro parameter list`

`incomplete struct/union/enum` *tag*: *name*

Type: Error   *Options:* all

You declared an object *name*, with struct, union, or enum type and tag *tag*, but the type is incomplete.

`struct s st;`

`"`*file*`", line 1: incomplete struct/union/enum s: st`

`inconsistent redeclaration of extern:` *name*

Type: Warning   *Options:* all

You have redeclared function or object *name* with storage class extern for which there was a previous declaration that has since gone out of scope. The second declaration has a type that conflicts with the first.

```
f (void) {
    int *p = (int *) malloc(5*sizeof(int));
}
g (void) {
    void *malloc();
}
```

"*file*", line 5: warning: inconsistent redeclaration of extern:
        malloc

inconsistent redeclaration of static: *name*

Type: Warning   *Options:* all

You have redeclared an object or function that was originally declared
with storage class static. The second declaration has a type that
conflicts with the first.

The two most frequent conditions under which this diagnostic may be
issued are:

1. A function was originally declared at other than file scope and
   with storage class static. The subsequent declaration of the
   function has a type that conflicts with the first.

2. A function or object was originally declared at file scope and
   with storage class static. A subsequent declaration of the
   same object or function at other than file scope used storage
   class extern (or possibly no storage class, if a function), and
   there was an intervening, unrelated, declaration of the same
   name.

```
f(void){
      static int myfunc(void);
}
g(void){
      static char *myfunc(void);
}
```

"file", line 5: warning: inconsistent redeclaration of static:
        myfunc

```
static int x;
f(void){
      int x;                    /* unrelated */
      {
            extern float x;    /* related to first declaration */
      }
}
```
"file", line 5: warning: inconsistent redeclaration of static:
        x

inconsistent storage class for function: *name*

   Type: Warning   *Options:* all

   ANSI C requires that the first declaration of a function or object at file
   scope establish its storage class. You have redeclared function *name* in
   an inconsistent way according to these rules.

```
g(void){
      int f(void);
      static int f(void);
}
```

"file", line 3: warning: inconsistent storage class for
        function: f

initialization type mismatch

> *Type:* Warning   *Options:* all

> The type of an initializer value is incompatible with the type of the object being initialized. This specific message usually applies to pointers.

> ```
> int a;
> unsigned int *pa = &a;
> ```

> "*file*", line 2: warning: initialization type mismatch

initializer does not fit: *value*

> *Type:* Warning   *Options:* all

> The value *value* does not fit in the space provided for it. That is, if it were fetched from that space, it would not reproduce the same value as was put in. In the message, *value* is represented as a hexadecimal value if the initializer is unsigned, decimal if it is signed.

> ```
> struct s {signed int m1:3; unsigned int m2:3;} st = {4, 5};
> unsigned char uc = 300u;
> ```

> "*file*", line 1: warning: initializer does not fit: 4
> "*file*", line 2: warning: initializer does not fit: 0x12c

integer overflow detected: op "*operator*"

> *Type:* Warning   *Options:* all

> The compiler attempted to compute the result of an *operator* expression at compile-time, and determined that the result would overflow. The low-order 32 bits of the result are retained, and the compiler issues this diagnostic.

```
int i = 1000000 * 1000000;
```

`"file", line 1: warning: integer overflow detected: op "*"`

integral constant expression expected

> *Type:* Error   *Options:* all

The compiler expected (required) an integral constant or an expression that can be evaluated at compile time to yield an integral value. The expression you wrote contained either a non-integral value, a reference to an object, or an operator that cannot be evaluated at compile time.

```
int ia[5.0];
```

`"file", line 1: integral constant expression expected`

integral constant too large

> *Type:* Warning   *Options:* all

An integral constant is too large to fit in an unsigned long.

```
int i = 1234567890123;
```

`"file", line 1: warning: integral constant too large`

internal compiler error: *message*

> *Type:* Error   *Options:* all

This message does not diagnose a user programming error (usually), but rather a problem with the compiler itself. One of the compiler's internal consistency checks has failed. The problem diagnosed by *message* is important to AT&T's support staff but is probably meaningless to you.

You can help AT&T to identify the problem by performing the following and then calling an AT&T support center.

Run the cc command again with the same options as when it failed, plus the –P option. You will not get the internal compiler error message again. However, assuming you compiled *file*.c, the cc command will create a *file*.i file in your current directory. This file will help AT&T to identify the compiler problem.

`interpreted as a #line directive`

> *Type:* Warning   *Options:* –Xc

A source line was encountered that had a number where the directive name usually goes. Such a line is reserved for the compiler's internal use, but it must be diagnosed in the –Xc (strictly conforming) mode.

```
# 9
```

```
"file", line 1: warning: interpreted as a #line directive
"file", line 1: warning: directive is an upward-compatible
        ANSI C extension
```

`invalid cast expression`

> *Type:* Error   *Options:* all

You cannot apply the cast to the expression because the types are unsuitable for casting. Both the type of the expression being cast and the type of the cast must be scalar types. A pointer may only be cast to or from an integral type.

```
f(void) {
    struct s {int x;} st;
    int i = (int) st;
}
```

```
"file", line 3: invalid cast expression
```

invalid class in asm % line: *class*

Type: Error   *Options:* all

The storage class *class* that the compiler encountered in an enhanced asm
% line is not one of the acceptable classes.

invalid compiler control line in ".i" file

Type: Error   *Options:* all

A .i file, the result of a cc -P command, is assumed to be a reserved
communication channel between the preprocessing phase and the compilation phase of the compiler. The .i file lets you examine that intermediate form to detect errors that may otherwise be hard to detect.
However, the compiler expects to find only a few directives that are
used for internal communication. The source file that was compiled (a
.i file) contained a preprocessing directive other than one of the special
directives.

invalid directive

Type: Error   *Options:* all

The identifier that follows a # in a preprocessing directive line was one
that the compiler did not recognize.

unknown

"file", line 1: invalid directive

invalid initializer

Type: Error   *Options:* all

Your program contains an initializer for an extern or static that
attempts to store a pointer in a smaller than pointer-sized object. Such
initializations are not supported by AT&T C.

```
int j;
char c = (char) &j;
```

"*file*", line 2: invalid initializer

invalid multibyte character

Type: Error   *Options:* all

A multibyte character in a string literal or character constant could not be converted to a single wide character in the host environment.

invalid source character: '*c*'

Type: Error   *Options:* all

The compiler encountered a character (*c*) in the source program that is not a valid ANSI C token.

```
int i = 1$;
```

"*file*", line 1: invalid source character: '$'

invalid source character: <*hex value*>

Type: Error   *Options:* all

This message diagnoses the same condition as the previous one, but the invalid character is not printable. The *hex value* between the brackets in the diagnostic is the hexadecimal value of the character code.

invalid switch expression type

Type: Error   *Options:* all

The controlling expression of a switch statement could not be converted to int. This message always follows switch expression must have integral type.

```
f() {
    struct s {int x;} sx;
    switch(sx) {
    case 4: ;
    }
}
```

```
"file", line 3: switch expression must have integral type
"file", line 3: invalid switch expression type
```

invalid token: *non-token*

Type: Error   *Options:* all

The compiler encountered a sequence of characters that does not comprise a valid token. An invalid token may result from the preprocessing ## operator. The offending *non-token* is shown in the diagnostic. If the *non-token* is longer than 20 characters, the first 20 are printed, followed by "...". The offending invalid token is ignored.

```
#define PASTE(l,r) l ## r
double d1 = 1e;
double d2 = PASTE(1,e);
int i = 1veryverylongnontoken;
```

```
"file", line 2: invalid token: 1e
"file", line 2: syntax error before or at: ;
"file", line 2: warning: syntax error:  empty declaration
"file", line 3: invalid token: 1e
"file", line 3: syntax error before or at: ;
"file", line 3: warning: syntax error:  empty declaration
"file", line 4: invalid token: 1veryverylongnontoke...
"file", line 4: syntax error before or at: ;
"file", line 4: warning: syntax error:  empty declaration
```

invalid token in #define macro parameters: *token*

> *Type:* Error   *Options:* all

> The compiler encountered an inappropriate token while processing the
> argument list of a function-like macro definition. *token* is the erroneous
> token.

> #define mac(a,4) a b c

> "*file*", line 1: invalid token in #define macro parameters: 4

invalid token in directive

> *Type:* Error   *Options:* all

> The compiler found an invalid token at the end of what would other-
> wise be a correctly formed directive.

> #line 7 "file.c

> "*file*", line 1: warning: string literal expected after
>   #line <number>
> "*file*", line 1: invalid token in directive: "
> "*file*", line 1: warning: tokens ignored at end of directive
>   line

invalid type combination

> *Type:* Error   *Options:* all

> You used an inappropriate combination of type specifiers in a declara-
> tion.

> short float f;

> "*file*", line 1: invalid type combination

invalid type for bit-field: *name*

> *Type:* Error   *Options:* all

> The type you chose for bit-field *name* is not permitted for bit-fields. Bit-fields may only be declared with integral types.

> struct s { float f:3; };

> "*file*", line 1: invalid type for bit-field: f

invalid use of "defined" operator

> *Type:* Error   *Options:* all

> A defined operator in a #if or #elif directive must be followed by an identifier or ( )'s that enclose an identifier. The source code did not use it that way.

> #if defined
>   int i = 1;
> #endif

> "*file*", line 1: invalid use of "defined" operator

invalid white space character in directive

> *Type:* Warning   *Options:* all

> The only white space characters that are permitted in preprocessing directives are space and horizontal tab. The source code included some other white space character, such as form feed or vertical tab. The compiler treats this character like a space.

`label redefined:` *name*

    Type: Error   *Options:* all

The same label *name* has appeared more than once in the current function. (A label's scope is an entire function.)

```
f(void){
     int i;
     i = 1;
     if (i) {
L:
          while (i)
               g();
          goto L;
     }
L: ;
}
```

"*file*", line 10: label redefined: L

`left operand must be modifiable lvalue: op "`*operator*`"`

    Type: Error   *Options:* all

The operand on the left side of *operator* must be a modifiable lvalue, but it wasn't.

```
f(void){
     int i = 1;
     +i -= 1;
}
```

"*file*", line 3: left operand must be modifiable lvalue:
        op "-="

left operand of "->" must be pointer to struct/union

Type: Warning, Error   *Options:* all

The operand on the left side of a -> operator must be a pointer to a
structure or union, but it wasn't. The diagnostic is a warning if the
operand is a pointer, an error otherwise.

```
struct s { int x; };
f(void) {
    long *lp;
    lp->x = 1;
}
```

"file", line 4: warning: left operand of "->" must be pointer
        to struct/union

left operand of "." must be lvalue in this context

Type: Warning   *Options:* all

The operand on the left side of a . operator is an expression that does
not yield an lvalue. Usually this results from trying to change the
return value of a function that returns a structure.

```
struct s { int ia[10]; };
struct s sf(void);
f(void) {
    sf().ia[0] = 3;
}
```

"file", line 4: warning: left operand of "." must be lvalue in
        this context

left operand of "." must be struct/union object

Type: Warning, Error   *Options:* all

The . operator is only supposed to be applied to structure or union objects. The diagnostic is an error if the operand to the left of . is an array, pointer, function call, enumeration constant or variable, or a register value that got allocated to a register; it is a warning otherwise.

```
f (void) {
    struct s { short s; };
    int i;
    i.s = 4;
}
```

"*file*", line 4: warning: left operand of "." must be struct/
         union object

()-less function definition

    Type: Error   *Options:* all

The declarator portion of a function definition must include parentheses. You cannot define a function by writing a typedef name for a function type, followed by an identifier and the braces ({ }) that define a function.

```
typedef int F();
F f{ }
```

"*file*", line 2: ()-less function definition

"long double" not yet supported

    Type: Error   *Options:* -Xt, -Xa

AT&T C does not yet support long double as it will in the future. You are discouraged from using long double at this time.

"long double" not yet supported; using "double"

> *Type:* Warning   *Options:* -Xc

The AT&T implementation of ANSI C supports long double under the
-Xc flag by treating it the same as double. In future releases long
double will be fully supported, and you will have to recompile this
code.

loop not entered at top

> *Type:* Warning   *Options:* all

The controlling expression at the beginning of a for or while loop cannot be reached by sequential flow of control from the statement before
it.

```
f(void) {
     int i;
     goto lab;
     for (i = 1; i > 0; --i) {
lab:;
          i=5;
     }
}
```

"*file*", line 4: warning: loop not entered at top

macro recursion

> *Type:* Fatal   *Options:* -Xt

The source code calls a macro that calls itself, either directly or
indirectly. ANSI C's semantics prevent further attempts to rescan the
macro. Older C compilers would try to rescan the macro, which eventually leads to a fatal error.

Because the rescanning rules are different for ANSI C and its predecessor, the AT&T C compiler provides the old behavior in –Xt mode, which includes producing this diagnostic when macro recursion is detected.

```
#define a(x)  b(x)
#define b(x)  a(x)
a(3)
```

"*file*", line 3: fatal: macro recursion

macro redefined: *name*

> *Type:* Warning   *Options:* all

The source code redefined a macro. Previous releases of AT&T C allowed such redefinitions silently if both definitions were identical except for the order and spelling of formal parameters. ANSI C requires that, when a macro is redefined correctly, the definitions must be identical including the order and spelling of formal parameters. This diagnostic is produced under all options if the new macro definition disagrees with the old one. For strict conformance, it is also produced under the –Xc option when the macro definitions disagree only in the spelling of the formal parameters.

```
#define TIMES(a,b)  a * b
#define TIMES(a,b)  a - b
```

"*file*", line 2: warning: macro redefined: TIMES

macro replacement within a character constant

> *Type:* Warning   *Options:* –Xt

Previous releases of AT&T C allowed the value of a formal parameter to be substituted in a character constant that is part of a macro definition. ANSI C does not permit such a use.

```
#define      CTRL(x) ('x'&037)   /* form control character */

int ctrl_c = CTRL(c);
```

"*file*", line 1: warning: macro replacement within a character
          constant

The proper way to express this construct in ANSI C is the following:

```
#define      CTRL(x) (x&037)     /* form control character */

int ctrl_c = CTRL('c');
```

```
macro replacement within a string literal
```

    Type: Warning   *Options:* –Xt

This message diagnoses a similar condition to the preceding one, except
the substitution is being made into a string literal.

```
#define HELLO(name) "hello, name"

char *hello_dave = HELLO(Dave);
```

"*file*", line 1: warning: macro replacement within a string
          literal

ANSI C provides a way to accomplish the same thing. The # "string-
ize" operator turns the tokens of a macro argument into a string literal,
and adjacent string literals are concatenated. The correct form is:

```
#define HELLO(name) "hello, " #name

char *hello_dave = HELLO(Dave);
```

member cannot be function: *name*

> *Type:* Error   *Options:* all

> A function may not be a member of a structure or union, although a pointer to a function may. You declared member *name* as a function.

> ```
> struct s { int f(void); };
> ```

> *"file"*, line 1: member cannot be function: f

mismatched "?" and ":"

> *Type:* Error   *Options:* all

> An expression in a #if or #elif directive contained a malformed ? : expression.

> ```
> #if defined(foo) ? 5
>         int i;
> #endif
> ```

> *"file"*, line 1: mismatched "?" and ":"

mismatched parentheses

> *Type:* Error   *Options:* all

> Parentheses were mismatched in a preprocessing conditional compilation directive.

> ```
> #if ((1)
>         int i = 1;
> #endif
> ```

> *"file"*, line 1: mismatched parentheses

missing ")"

>Type: Error   Options: all

In a test of a predicate that follows a **#** operator in a **#if** or **#elif** directive, the) that follows the assertion was missing.

```
#if # system(unix
        char *system = "unix";
#endif
```

"*file*", line 1: missing ")"

missing formal name in % line

>Type: Error   Options: all

In an enhanced asm function, a % line specified a storage class, but not
the formal parameter than has that storage class.

missing operand

>Type: Error   Options: all

The constant expression of a preprocessing conditional compilation
directive is malformed. An expected operand for some operator was
missing.

```
#define EMPTY
#if EMPTY / 4
        int i = 1;
#endif
```

"*file*", line 2: missing operand

`missing operator`

Type: Error   *Options:* all

The constant expression of a preprocessing conditional compilation directive is malformed. An operator was expected but was not encountered.

```
#if 1 4
        int i = 1;
#endif
```

"file", `line 1: missing operator`

`missing tokens between parentheses`

Type: Error   *Options:* all

In a #assert directive, there are no assertions within the parentheses of the predicate.

```
#assert system()
```

"file", `line 1: missing tokens between parentheses`

`modifying typedef with "`*modifier*`"; only qualifiers allowed`

Type: Warning   *Options:* —Xt

You are applying a type *modifier* to a `typedef` name, which ANSI C prohibits. ANSI C only permits you to modify a `typedef` with a type qualifier (const, volatile). However, for compatibility, AT&T C accepts the declaration and treats it as did previous AT&T C compilers. Future releases will reject this declaration.

```
typedef int INT;
unsigned INT i;
```

"file", line 2: warning: modifying typedef with "unsigned";
        only qualifiers allowed

modulus by zero

> *Type:* Warning, Error   *Options:* all

The second operand of a % operator is zero. If the modulus operation is part of a #if or #elif directive, the result is taken to be zero.

The diagnostic is a warning if the modulus is in executable code, an error otherwise.

```
#if 42 % 0
        int i = 1;
#endif
```

"file", line 1: warning: modulus by zero

more than one character honored in character constant: *constant*

> *Type:* Warning   *Options:* all

A character constant has an integral value that derives from the character codes of the characters. If a character constant comprises more than one character, the encoding of the additional characters depends on the implementation. This warning alerts you that the encoding that the preprocessing phase uses for the character constant *constant* is different in this release of the AT&T C compiler from the one in previous releases, which only honored the first character. (The encoding for character constants you use in executable code is unchanged.)

```
#if 'ab' != ('b' * 256 + 'a')
#error unknown encoding
#endif
```

"*file*", line 1: warning: more than one character honored in
            character constant: 'ab'

"#" must be followed by formal identifier in #define

    Type: Error   *Options:* all

    The "string-ize" operator # must be followed by the name of a formal
    parameter in a function-like macro.

```
#define mac(a) # + a
```

"*file*", line 1: "#" must be followed by formal identifier in
            #define

must have type "function−returning−unsigned": *name*

    Type: Warning   *Options:* all

    The *name* that is a part of a #pragma int_to_unsigned directive must
    be an identifier whose type is function-returning-unsigned.

```
extern int f(int);
#pragma int_to_unsigned f
```

"*file*", line 2: warning: must have type
            "function−returning−unsigned": f

name in asm % line is not a formal: *name*

    Type: Error   *Options:* all

    The identifier *name* that followed a storage class specifier in the % line of an enhanced asm function was not one of the formal parameters of the function.

`nested asm calls not now supported`

> *Type:* Error   *Options:* all

The compiler does not now support calls to enhanced asm functions as part of the argument expression for another enhanced asm function.

`newline in character constant`

> *Type:* Error   *Options:* all

You wrote a character constant that had no closing ' on the same line as the beginning '.

```
int i = 'a
;
```

`"file", line 1: newline in character constant`

`newline in string literal`

> *Type:* Warning, Error   *Options:* all

You wrote a string literal that had no closing " on the same line as the beginning ". The diagnostic is a warning if the string literal is part of a preprocessing directive (and the compiler provides the missing ") and an error otherwise.

```
char *p = "abc
;
```

`"file", line 1: newline in string literal`

`newline not last character in file`

Type: Warning   *Options:* all

Every non-empty source file and header must consist of complete lines. This diagnostic warns that the last line of a file did not end with a newline.

`no actual for asm formal:` *name*

Type: Error   *Options:* all

An enhanced asm function was called with fewer arguments than there were parameters in the definition. Thus there was no actual argument for parameter *name*.

`no closing ">" in "#include <..."`

Type: Error   *Options:* all

A #include directive that used the < > form of header omitted the closing >.

`#include <stdio.h`

"file", `line 1: warning: #include <... missing '>'`

`no file name after expansion`

Type: Error   *Options:* all

You used the form of #include directive that permits macro expansion of its argument, but the resulting expansion left no tokens to be taken as a file name.

```
#define EMPTY
#include EMPTY
```

```
"file", line 2: no file name after expansion
```

no hex digits follow \x

Type: Warning   *Options:* −Xa, −Xc

The \x escape in character constants and string literals introduces a hex-adecimal character escape. The \x must be followed by at least one hex-adecimal digit.

```
char *cp = "\xz";
```

```
"file", line 1: warning: no hex digits follow \x
```

no macro replacement within a character constant

Type: Warning   *Options:* −Xa, −Xc

This message is the inverse of macro replacement within a charac-ter constant. It informs you that the macro replacement that was done for −Xt mode is not being done in −Xa or −Xt mode.

no macro replacement within a string literal

Type: Warning   *Options:* −Xa, −Xc

This message is the inverse of macro replacement within a string literal. It informs you that the macro replacement that was done for −Xt mode is not being done in −Xa or −Xt mode.

no tokens after expansion

>   *Type:* Error   *Options:* all

>   After macro expansion was applied to the expression in a #line direc-
>   tive, there were no tokens left to be interpreted as a line number.

>   #define EMPTY
>   #line EMPTY

>   *"file"*, line 2: no tokens after expansion

no tokens follow "#pragma"

>   *Type:* Warning   *Options:* -v

>   The compiler encountered a #pragma directive that contained no other
>   tokens.

>   #pragma

>   *"file"*, line 1: warning: no tokens follow "#pragma"

no tokens following "#assert name ("

>   *Type:* Error   *Options:* all

>   A use of the #assert directive is malformed. The assertions and the)
>   that should follow are missing.

>   #assert system(

>   *"file"*, line 1: no tokens following "#assert name ("

no tokens in #line directive

> *Type:* Error   *Options:* all

> The rest of a #line directive was empty; the line number and optional file name were missing.

> #line

> *"file"*, line 1: no tokens in #line directive

non-constant initializer: op *"operator"*

> *Type:* Error   *Options:* all

> The initializer for an extern, static, or array object must be a compile-time constant. The initializers for an automatic structure or union object, if enclosed in { }, must also be compile-time constants. *operator* is the operator whose operands could not be combined at compile time.

> int j;
> int k = j+1;

> *"file"*, line 2: non-constant initializer: op "+"

non-formal identifier follows "#" in #define

> *Type:* Warning   *Options:* all

> The identifier that follows a # operator in a macro definition must be a formal parameter of a function-like macro.

> #define mac(a) "abc" # b

> *"file"*, line 1: non-formal identifier follows "#" in #define

non-integral case expression

> *Type:* Error   *Options:* all

> The operand of a case statement must be an integral constant.

```
f (void) {
    int i = 1;
    switch (i) {
    case 5.0: ;
    }
}
```

> "*file*", line 4: non-integral case expression

non-unique member requires struct/union: *name*

> *Type:* Error   *Options:* all

> The operand on the left side of a . operator was not a structure, union, or a pointer to one, and member *name* was not unique among all structure and union members that you have declared. You should only use . with structures or unions, and the member should belong to the structure or union corresponding to the left operand.

```
struct s1 { int x,y; };
struct s2 { int y,z; };
f (void) {
    long *lp;
    lp.y = 1;
}
```

> "*file*", line 5: non-unique member requires struct/union object:
>   y
> "*file*", line 5: left operand of "." must be struct/union object

non-unique member requires struct/union pointer: *name*

> *Type:* Error   *Options:* all

> This message diagnoses the same condition as the preceding one, but for the -> operator.

null character in input

> *Type:* Error   *Options:* all

> The compiler encountered a null character (a character with a character code of zero).

null dimension: *name*

> *Type:* Warning, Error   *Options:* all

> A dimension of an array is null in a context where that is prohibited. The diagnostic is a warning if the offending dimension is outermost and an error otherwise.

> ```
> int ia[4][];
> struct s { int x, y[]; };
> int i = sizeof(int []);
> ```

> "*file*", line 1: null dimension: ia
> "*file*", line 2: warning: null dimension: y
> "*file*", line 3: warning: null dimension: sizeof()

number expected

> *Type:* Error   *Options:* all

> The compiler did not find a number where it expected to find one in a #if or #elif directive.

```
#if 1 +
        int i = 1;
#endif
```

"file", line 1: number expected

old-style declaration hides prototype declaration: *name*

Type: Warning   *Options:* −v

You redeclared function *name* in an inner scope. The outer declaration was a function prototype declaration, but the inner one lacks parameter information. By ANSI C's scoping rules, the parameter information is hidden and the automatic conversions of types that the prototype would have provided are suppressed.

```
extern double sin(double);
f(void) {
    extern double sin();
    double d;
    d = sin(1);     /* Note:  no conversion to double! */
}
```

"file", line 3: warning: old-style declaration hides prototype
          declaration: sin
"file", line 5: warning: argument does not match remembered
          type: arg #1

old-style declaration; add "int"

Type: Warning   *Options:* all

Objects and functions that are declared at file scope must have a storage class or type specifier. You will get this warning if you omit both.

```
i;
f(void);
```

```
"file", line 1: warning: old-style declaration; add "int"
"file", line 2: warning: old-style declaration; add "int"
```

only one storage class allowed

Type: Error   *Options:* all

You specified more than one storage class in a declaration.

```
f(void){
    register auto i;
}
```

```
"file", line 2: only one storage class allowed
```

only qualifiers allowed after *

Type: Error   *Options:* all

You may only specify the const or volatile type qualifiers after a * in a declaration.

```
int * const p;
int * unsigned q;
```

```
"file", line 2: only qualifiers allowed after *
```

only "register" valid as formal parameter storage class

Type: Error   *Options:* all

You may specify a storage class specifier in a function prototype declaration, but only register is permitted.

```
int f(
    register int x,
    auto int y
);
```

"file", line 3: only "register" valid as formal parameter
             storage class

operand cannot have void type: op *"operator"*

Type: Error   *Options:* all

One of the operands of *operator* has void type.

```
f(void){
    void v(void);
    int i = v();
}
```

"file", line 3: operand cannot have void type: op "="
"file", line 3: assignment type mismatch

operand must be modifiable lvalue: op *"operator"*

Type: Error   *Options:* all

The operand of *operator* must be a modifiable lvalue, but it wasn't.

```
f(void){
    int i = --3;
}
```

"file", line 2: operand must be modifiable lvalue: op "--"

operand treated as unsigned: *constant*

> *Type:* Warning   *Options:* -Xt

> An operand you used in a #if or #elif directive has a value greater than LONG_MAX (2147483647) but has no unsigned modifier suffix (u or U). Previous releases of AT&T C treated such *constant*s as signed quantities which, because of their values, actually became negative. ANSI C treats such constants as unsigned long integers, which may affect their behavior in expressions. This diagnostic is a transition aid that informs you that the value is being treated differently from before.

> ```
> #if 2147483648 > 0
>         char *mesg = "ANSI C-style";
> #endif
> ```

> "*file*", line 1: warning: operand treated as unsigned:
>   2147483648

operands have incompatible pointer types: op "*operator*"

> *Type:* Warning   *Options:* all

> You have applied *operator* to pointers to different types.

> ```
> f (void) {
>     char *cp;
>     int *ip;
>     if (ip < cp)
>         ;
> }
> ```

> "*file*", line 4: warning: operands have incompatible pointer
>   types: op "<"

operands have incompatible types: op *"operator"*

    Type: Error   *Options:* all

    The types of the operands for *operand* are unsuitable for that kind of operator.

```
f (void) {
    char *cp;
    int *ip;
    void *vp = ip + cp;
}
```

    "file", line 4: operands have incompatible types: op "+"

operands must have *category* type: op *"operator"*

    Type: Error   *Options:* all

    The operands for *operator* do not fall into the appropriate category for that operator. *category* may be arithmetic, integral, or scalar.

```
f (void) {
    int ia[5];
    int *ip = ia/4;
}
```

    "file", line 3: operands must have arithmetic type: op "/"

out of scope extern and prior uses redeclared as static: *name*

    Type: Warning   *Options:* -Xc, -v

    You declared *name* as extern in a block that has gone out of scope. Then you declared *name* again, this time as static. The AT&T C compiler treats the object or function as if it were static, and all references, including ones earlier in the source file, apply to the static version.

```
f(void) {
    extern int i;
}
static int i;
```

"file", line 4: warning: out of scope extern and prior uses
        redeclared as static: i

overflow in hex escape

Type: Warning   *Options:* all

In a hexadecimal escape (\x) in a character constant or string literal, the
accumulated value for the escape grew too large. Only the low-order 32
bits of value are retained.

```
int i = '\xabcdefedc';
```

"file", line 1: warning: \x is ANSI C hex escape
"file", line 1: warning: overflow in hex escape
"file", line 1: warning: character escape does not fit in
        character

parameter mismatch: *ndecl* declared, *ndef* defined

Type: Warning   *Options:* all

A function prototype declaration and an old-style definition of the function disagree in the number of parameters. The declaration had *ndecl*
parameters, while the definition had *ndef*.

```
int f(int);
int f(i,j)
int i,j;
{}
```

"file", line 4: warning: parameter mismatch: 1 declared,
        2 defined

`parameter not in identifier list:` *name*

> *Type:* Error   *Options:* all

> Variable *name* appears in an old-style function definition's parameter
> declarations, but it does not appear in the parameter identifier list.

> ```
> f(a,b)
> int i;
> {}
> ```

> `"`*file*`", line 2: parameter not in identifier list: i`

`parameter redeclared:` *name*

> *Type:* Error   *Options:* all

> You have used *name* more than once as the name for a parameter in a
> function definition.

> ```
> int f(int i, int i) { }
> int g(i,j)
> int i;
> int i;
> { }
> ```

> `"`*file*`", line 1: parameter redeclared: i`
> `"`*file*`", line 4: parameter redeclared: i`

`preprocessing a .i file`

> *Type:* Warning   *Options:* all

> The source file is a `.i` file, a file that has already been preprocessed, and
> the −E cc option was selected. The compiler will simply copy the input
> file to the standard output without further processing.

prototype mismatch: *n1* arg*[s]* passed, *n2* expected

   Type: Error   *Options:* all

   You called a function for which there is a function prototype declaration in scope, and the number of arguments in the call, *n2*, did not match the number of parameters in the declaration, *n1*.

```
int f(int);
g(void) {
    f(1,2);
}
```

   "file", line 3: prototype mismatch: 2 args passed, 1 expected

return value type mismatch

   Type: Error   *Options:* all

   You are attempting to return a value from a function that cannot be converted to the return-type of the function.

```
f(void) {
    struct s { int x; } st;
    return( st );
}
```

   "file", line 3: return value type mismatch

semantics of *"operator"* change in ANSI C; use explicit cast

   Type: Warning   *Options:* all

   The type promotion rules for ANSI C are slightly different from those of previous versions of AT&T C. In the current release the default behavior is to duplicate the previous rules. In future releases the default will be to use ANSI C rules. You may obtain the ANSI C interpretation by using the –Xa option for the cc command.

Previous AT&T C type promotion rules were "unsigned-preserving." If one of the operands of an expression was of unsigned type, the operands were promoted to a common unsigned type before the operation was performed.

ANSI C uses "value-preserving" type promotion rules. An unsigned type is promoted to a signed type if all its values may be represented in the signed type.

The different type promotion rules may lead to different program behavior for the operators that are affected by the unsigned-ness of their operands:

- The division operators: /, /=, %, %=.

- The right shift operators: >>, >>=.

- The relational operators: <, <=, >, >=.

The warning message tells you that your program contains an expression in which the behavior of *operator* will change in the future. You can guarantee the behavior you want by inserting an explicit cast in the expression.

```
f (void) {
    unsigned char uc;
    int i;
    /* was unsigned divide in AT&T C, signed in ANSI C */
    i /= uc;
}
```

"*file*", line 5: warning: semantics of "/=" change in ANSI C;
        use explicit cast

You can get the same behavior as in previous versions of AT&T C by adding an explicit cast:

```
f(void){
    unsigned char uc;
    int i;
    /* was unsigned divide in AT&T C, signed in ANSI C */
    i /= (unsigned int) uc;
}
```

shift count negative or too big: *op n*

Type: Warning   *Options:* all

The compiler determined that the shift count (the right operand) for
shift operator *op* is either negative or bigger than the size of the operand
being shifted.

```
f(){
    short s;
    s <<= 25;
}
```

"*file*", line 3: warning: shift count negative or too big:
        <<= 25

statement not reached

Type: Warning   *Options:* all

This statement in your program cannot be reached because of goto,
break, continue, or return statements preceding it.

```
f(void){
    int i;
    return i;
    i = 4;
}
```

"*file*", line 4: warning: statement not reached

`static function called but not defined:` *name* `()`

> *Type:* Warning   *Options:* all

The program calls function *name*, which has been declared `static`, but no definition of *name* appears in the translation unit. (The line number that is displayed in the message is one more than the number of lines in the file, because this condition can be diagnosed only after the entire translation unit has been seen.)

```
static int statfunc(int);
void
f() {
    int i = statfunc(4);
}
```

`"`*file*`", line 7: warning: static function called but not`
`        defined: statfunc()`

`static redeclares external:` *name*

> *Type:* Warning   *Options:* all

You reused *name* as the name of a `static` object or function after having used it in the same block as the name of an *extern* object or function. The version of *name* that remains visible is the `static` version.

```
f(void) {
    extern int i;
    static int i;
}
```

`"`*file*`", line 3: warning: static redeclares external: i`

```
storage class after type is obsolescent
```

> *Type:* Warning   *Options:* -v

According to the ANSI C standard, writing declarations in which the storage class specifier is not first is "obsolescent."

```
int static i;
```

```
"file", line 1: warning: storage class after type is
        obsolescent
```

```
storage class for function must be static or extern
```

> *Type:* Warning   *Options:* all

You used an inappropriate storage class specifier for a function declaration or definition. Only extern and static may be used, or the storage class may be omitted. The specifier is ignored.

```
f(void) {
    auto g(void);
}
```

```
"file", line 2: warning: storage class for function must be
        static or extern
```

```
string literal expected after # <number>
```

> *Type:* Warning   *Options:* all

The # line information directive takes an optional second token, a file name. If present, it must be in the form of a string literal.

```
# 1 x.c
```

```
"file", line 1: warning: string literal expected after
        # <number>
"file", line 1: warning: tokens ignored at end of directive
        line
```

string literal expected after #file

Type: Error   *Options:* all

The #file directive (which is reserved for the compilation system) is
used for internal communication between preprocessing and compilation phases. A string literal operand is expected as the operand.

string literal expected after #ident

Type: Error   *Options:* all

A #ident directive must be followed by a normal (not wide character)
string literal.

```
#ident no-string
```

```
"file", line 1: string literal expected after #ident
```

string literal expected after #line <number>

Type: Warning   *Options:* all

This diagnostic is similar to string literal expected after #
<number>, except that it applies to the standard #line directive.

string literal must be sole array initializer

> *Type:* Warning   *Options:* all

> You may not initialize a character array with both a string literal and other values in the same initialization.

> char ca[] = { "abc", 'd' };

> "*file*", line 1: warning: string literal must be sole array
>   initializer

struct/union has no named members

> *Type:* Warning   *Options:* all

> You have declared a structure or union in which none of the members is named.

> struct s { int :4; char :0; };

> "*file*", line 1: warning: struct/union has no named members

struct/union-valued initializer required

> *Type:* Error   *Options:* all

> ANSI C allows you to initialize an automatic structure or union, but the initializer must have the same type as the object being initialized.

> f (void) {
>   int i;
>   struct s { int x; } st = i;
> }

> "*file*", line 3: warning: {}-enclosed initializer required
> "*file*", line 3: struct/union-valued initializer required

`switch` expression must have integral type

> *Type:* Warning, Error   *Options:* all

> You wrote a `switch` statement in which the controlling expression did not have integral type. The message is a warning if the invalid type is a floating-point type and an error otherwise. A floating-point `switch` expression is converted to `int`.

```
f(void) {
    float x;
    switch (x) {
    case 4: ;
    }
}
```

> *"file"*, line 3: warning: switch expression must have integral
>   type

syntax error before or at: *token*

> *Type:* Error   *Options:* all

> This is an all-purpose diagnostic that means you have juxtaposed two (or more) language tokens inappropriately. The compiler shows you the *token* at which the error was detected.

```
f(void) {
    int i = 3+;
}
```

> *"file"*, line 2: syntax error before or at: ;

syntax error in macro parameters

> *Type:* Error   *Options:* all

> The macro parameter list part of a function-like macro definition is mal-formed. The list must be a comma-separated list of identifiers and was not.

```
#define mac(a,b,) a b
```

"file", line 1: syntax error in macro parameters

syntax error, probably missing ",", ";" or "="

> *Type:* Error   *Options:* all

> You wrote a declaration that looked like a function definition, except that the type of the symbol declared was not "function returning." You probably left out a ; or =.

```
int i
int j;
```

"file", line 2: syntax error, probably missing ",", ";" or "="
"file", line 2: parameter not in identifier list: j
"file", line 4: syntax error before or at: <EOF>

syntax error: empty declaration

> *Type:* Warning   *Options:* all

> You wrote a null statement at file scope. This looks like an empty declaration statement. AT&T C permitted this previously, but ANSI C does not.

```
int i;;
```

"file", line 1: warning: syntax error: empty declaration

syntax error: "&..." invalid

> *Type:* Warning   *Options:* -Xc

> You wrote &... in a program that was compiled with the -Xc option. &... is invalid ANSI C syntax. You should not use this notation explicitly.

syntax requires ";" after last struct/union member

    Type: Warning   *Options:* all

    You omitted the ; that C syntax requires after the last structure or union member in a structure or union declaration.

```
struct s { int x };
```

    "file", line 1: warning: syntax requires ";" after last
            struct/union member

(type) tag redeclared: *name*

    Type: Error   *Options:* all

    You have redeclared tag *name* that was originally a *type* (struct, union, or enum) tag.

```
struct q { int m1, m2; };
enum q { e1, e2 };
```

    "file", line 2: (struct) tag redeclared: q

token not allowed in directive: *token*

    Type: Error   *Options:* all

    You used a *token* in a #if or #elif directive that is neither a valid operator for constant expressions, nor a valid integer constant.

```
#if 1 > "1"
        int i = 1;
#endif
```

    "file", line 1: token not allowed in directive: "1"

token-less macro argument

> *Type:* Warning   *Options:* -Xc

> The actual argument to a preprocessor macro consisted of no tokens.
> The ANSI C standard regards this condition as undefined. The AT&T C
> compiler treats the empty list of tokens as an empty argument, and,
> under the -Xc mode, it also issues this warning.

> ```
> #define      m(x)  x+3
> int i = m();
> ```

> *"file"*, line 2: warning: token-less macro argument

tokens after -A- are ignored

> *Type:* Warning   *Options:* all

> In the -A- option to the cc command, there were additional tokens
> adjacent to the option. They are ignored.

> ```
> cc -A-extra -c x.c
> ```

> command line: warning: tokens after -A- are ignored

tokens expected after "# identifier ("

> *Type:* Error   *Options:* all

> When the # operator is used in a #if or #elif directive to select a
> predicate instead of a like-named macro, the predicate must be followed
> by a parenthesized list of tokens.

> ```
> #if #system(
>         char *system = "unix";
> #endif
> ```

> *"file"*, line 1: tokens expected after "# identifier ("

`tokens expected after "("`

Type: Error   *Options:* all

In a #unassert directive, the assertion(s) and closing) after the predicate were missing.

`#unassert system(`

`"file", line 1: tokens expected after "("`

`tokens expected between parentheses`

Type: Error   *Options:* all

The name of an assertion of a predicate to test was omitted in an #if or
#elif directive.

```
#if #system()
        char *sysname = "??";
#endif
```

`"file", line 1: tokens expected between parentheses`

`tokens ignored after "-U{identifier}"`

Type: Warning   *Options:* all

In the command line -U option, there were tokens following the name of
the macro to be undefined.

`cc -Uunix, u3b2 -c x.c`

`command line: warning: tokens ignored after "-U{identifier}"`

tokens ignored at end of directive line

> *Type:* Warning   *Options:* all

> A directive line contains extra tokens that are not expected as part of the directive.

> `#undef a b          /* can only undefine one */`

> *"file"*, line 1: warning: tokens ignored at end of directive line

too many array initializers

> *Type:* Error   *Options:* all

> You provided more initializers for an array than the array can hold.

> `int ia[3] = { 1, 2, 3, 4 };`

> *"file"*, line 1: too many array initializers

too many #else's

> *Type:* Warning   *Options:* all

> The code contained more that one #else directive in a preprocessing if-section. All #else directives after the first are taken to be false.

> ```
> #ifdef ONE
>         int i = 1;
> #else
>         int i = 2;
> #else
>         int i = 3;
> #endif
> ```

> *"file"*, line 5: warning: too many #else's

too many errors

> *Type:* Fatal   *Options:* all

> The compiler encountered too many errors to make further processing sensible. Rather than produce further diagnostics, the compiler exits.

too many initializers for scalar

> *Type:* Error   *Options:* all

> A { }-bracketed initialization for a scalar contains more than one value.
> int i = { 1, 2 };

> *"file"*, line 1: too many initializers for scalar

too many struct/union initializers

> *Type:* Error   *Options:* all

> You have provided too many initializers for a structure or union.
> struct s { int x,y; } st = { 1,2,3 };

> *"file"*, line 1: too many struct/union initializers

trailing "," prohibited in enum declaration

> *Type:* Warning   *Options:* -Xc, -v

> You supplied an extra comma at the end of an enumeration type declaration. The extra comma is prohibited by the syntax.
> enum e { e1, e2, };

> *"file"*, line 1: warning: trailing "," prohibited in enum
>   declaration

`trigraph sequence replaced`

>*Type:* Warning　　　　　　　*Options:* −Xt

ANSI C introduces the notion of trigraphs, three-character sequences that stand for a single character. All such sequences begin with ??. Because sequences that are interpreted as trigraphs may appear in existing code, the AT&T C compiler produces a transitional diagnostic when such sequences are encountered.

```
char *surprise = "this is a trigraph??!";
```

`"file"`, line 1: warning: trigraph sequence replaced

`type does not match prototype:` *name*

>*Type:* Warning　　　　　　　*Options:* all

You provided a function prototype declaration for a function, but used an old-style definition. The type for parameter *name* in that definition is incompatible with the type you used in the prototype declaration.

```
int f(char *);
int f(p)
int *p;
{}
```

`"file"`, line 4: warning: type does not match prototype: p

The following example shows an especially confusing instance of this diagnostic.

```
int f(char);
int f(c)
char c;
{}
```

`"file"`, line 3: warning: identifier redeclared: f
`"file"`, line 4: warning: type does not match prototype: c

f has an old-style definition. For compatibility reasons, f's arguments must therefore be promoted according to the default argument promotions, which is how they were promoted before the existence of function prototypes. Therefore the value that must actually be passed to f is an int, although the function will only use the char part of the value. The diagnostic, then, identifies the conflict between the int that the function expects and the char that the function prototype would (conceptually) cause to be passed.

There are two ways to fix the conflict:

1. Change the function prototype to read int f(int);

2. Define f with a function prototype definition:

```
int f(char);
int f(char c)
{}
```

typedef already qualified with "*qualifier*"

Type: Warning   *Options:* all

A type specifier includes a typedef and an explicit type qualifier, *qualifier*. The typedef already included *qualifier* when it was declared.

```
typedef volatile int VOL;
volatile VOL v;
```

"*file*", line 2: warning: typedef already qualified with "volatile"

typedef declares no type name

Type: Warning   *Options:* all

In a declaration with storage class typedef, no type name was actually declared. This is probably a programming error.

```
typedef struct s { int x; };
```

"file", line 1: warning: typedef declares no type name

typedef redeclared: *name*

    Type: Warning   *Options:* all

You have declared typedef *name* more than once. The later declaration has an identical type to the first.

```
typedef int i;
typedef int i;
```

"file", line 2: warning: typedef redeclared: i

typedef redeclares external: *name*

    Type: Warning   *Options:* all

You declared typedef *name*, but there is an extern of the same name in the same block. The typedef hides the external.

```
f(void) {
    extern int INT;
    typedef int INT;
}
```

"file", line 3: warning: typedef redeclares external: INT

"typedef" valid only for function declaration

    Type: Warning   *Options:* all

A function definition may not have the typedef storage class. It is ignored here.

```
typedef int f(void){}
```

```
"file", line 1: warning: "typedef" valid only for function
         declaration
```

unacceptable operand for unary &

Type: Error   *Options:* all

You attempted to take the address of something whose address cannot be taken.

```
f(void){
    int *ip = &g();
}
```

```
"file", line 2: unacceptable operand for unary &
```

#unassert requires an identifier token

Type: Error   *Options:* all

The #unassert directive must name a predicate to "un-assert."

```
#unassert 5
```

```
"file", line 1: #unassert requires an identifier token
```

undefined label: *label*

Type: Error   *Options:* all

You wrote a goto in the current function, but you never defined the target *label* anywhere within the function.

```
f (void) {
    goto L;
}
```

"file", line 3: undefined label: L

---

undefined struct/union member: *name*

Type: Error   *Options:* all

Your program made reference to a structure or union member, *name*, that has not been declared as part of any structure.

```
struct s { int x; };
f (void) {
    struct s q;
    q.y = 1;
}
```

"file", line 4: undefined struct/union member: y

---

undefined symbol: *name*

Type: Error   *Options:* all

You referred to symbol *name* for which there is no declaration in scope.

```
f (void) {
    g (i);
}
```

"file", line 2: undefined symbol: i

---

undefining __STDC__

Type: Warning   *Options:* −Xt

ANSI C prohibits undefining the predefined symbol __STDC__.

However, this release of AT&T C permits you to do so in transition mode (only). You may want to use this feature to test C code that you have written to work in both an ANSI C and non-ANSI C environment.

For example, suppose you have C code that checks __STDC__, declaring function prototype declarations if it is defined, and old-style function declarations (or definitions) if not. Because the AT&T C compiler predefines __STDC__, you would ordinarily be unable to check the old-style code, and you would have to run the code through another (non-ANSI C) compiler. By undefining __STDC__ (usually on the command line), you can use the AT&T C compiler to do the checking. This diagnostic tells you, as required, that you are violating ANSI C constraints.

```
#undef __STDC__        /* usually -U__STDC__ on cc line */

#ifdef __STDC__
int
myfunc(const char *arg1, int arg2)
#else                  /* non-ANSI C case */
int
myfunc(arg1,arg2)
char *arg1,            /* oops */
int arg2;
#endif
{
}


"file", line 1: warning: undefining __STDC__
"file", line 10: syntax error before or at: int
"file", line 12: syntax error before or at: {
```

unexpected "("

Type: Error   *Options:* all

A misplaced (was encountered in a #if or #elif directive.

```
#if 1 (
        int i = 1;
#endif
```

"file", line 1: unexpected "("

unexpected ")"

Type: Error   *Options:* all

A misplaced) was encountered in a #if or #elif directive.

```
#if ) 1
        int i = 1;
#endif
```

"file", line 1: unexpected ")"

unexpected character in asm % line: 'c'

Type: Error   *Options:* all

In the % specification line of an enhanced asm function, the compiler expected to see an alphabetic character that begins a storage class specifier. Instead it encountered the character *c*.

unknown operand size: op *"operator"*

Type: Error   *Options:* all

You applied *operator* ++, --, or = to an operand whose size is unknown. The operand is usually a pointer to a structure or union whose members have not been declared.

```
f (void) {
    struct s *sp;
    sp++;
}
```

"*file*", line 3: unknown operand size: op "++"

unnamed *type* member

Type: Warning   *Options:* all

In your *type* declaration, you failed to give a member a name.

```
union s { int; char c; };
```

"*file*", line 1: warning: unnamed union member

unreachable case label: *value*

Type: Warning   *Options:* all

The expression you specified in a case statement has a value outside
the range of the type of the controlling expression of the enclosing
switch statement. Therefore the case label can never be reached. In the
message, *value* is represented as a hexadecimal value if the case expression is unsigned, decimal if it is signed.

```
f () {
    unsigned char uc;

    switch( uc ) {
    case 256:
        ;
    }
}
```

"*file*", line 5: warning: unreachable case label: 256

unrecognized #pragma ignored: *pragma*

    Type: Warning   *Options:* −v

    Because #pragma directives are implementation-specific, when the −v compilation flag is set, the AT&T C compiler warns about any such directives that it is ignoring. The AT&T C compiler does not recognize #pragma *pragma*.

    #pragma list

    "*file*", line 1: warning: unrecognized #pragma ignored: list

use "double" instead of "long float"

    Type: Warning   *Options:* all

    You declared an object or function to be long float, which was a synonym for double. ANSI C does not permit long float, although AT&T C accepts it as a transition aid.

    long float f = 1.0;

    "*file*", line 1: warning: use "double" instead of "long float"

useless declaration

    Type: Warning   *Options:* all

    ANSI C requires that every declaration actually declare something, such as

        ■ a declarator,

        ■ a structure or union tag,

        ■ structure or union members, or

■ enumeration constants.

You wrote a declaration that provided no information to the compiler.

```
int;                    /* no identifier */
enum e { e1, e2 };      /* introduces enum e */
enum e;                 /* no new information */
```

```
"file", line 1: warning: useless declaration
"file", line 3: warning: useless declaration
```

using out of scope declaration: *name*

Type: Warning   *Options:* all

You previously declared *name* in a scope that is no longer active. In some ANSI C implementations, referring to such an object would yield an error; calling such a function would be interpreted as calling a function returning int. AT&T C remembers the previous declaration and uses it. This warning informs you what the compiler has done.

```
f (void) {
    extern int i;
    double sin (double);
}
g (void) {
    double d = sin(1.5);
    i = 1;
}
```

```
"file", line 6: warning: using out of scope declaration: sin
"file", line 7: warning: using out of scope declaration: i
```

void expressions may not be arguments: arg #*n*

Type: Error   *Options:* all

A function call contains an argument for which the expression type is void.

```
f(void){
    void v(void);
    g(v());
}
```

"file", line 3: void expressions may not be arguments: arg #1

void function cannot return value

Type: Warning   *Options:* all

You wrote a return statement with an expression, but the declared type of the function is void.

```
void v(void){
    return 3;
}
```

"file", line 2: void function cannot return value

"void" must be sole parameter

Type: Error   *Options:* all

Only the first parameter in a function prototype declaration may have void type, and it must be the only parameter.

```
int f(int,void);
```

"file", line 1: "void" must be sole parameter

void parameter cannot have name: *name*

Type: Error   *Options:* all

You have declared a parameter *name* in a function prototype declaration that has void type.

```
int f(void v);
```

```
"file", line 1: void parameter cannot have name: v
```

\x is ANSI C hex escape

Type: Warning   *Options:* −Xt

In earlier AT&T C products, '\x' was equivalent to 'x'. However, in ANSI C, '\x' introduces a hexadecimal character escape. This diagnostic warns of the new meaning.

If valid hexadecimal characters follow '\x', they are interpreted as part of the new escape sequence. Otherwise '\x' is treated as it was in previous AT&T C compilers.

```
int i = '\x';
```

```
"file", line 1: warning: \x is ANSI C hex escape
```

zero or negative subscript

Type: Warning, Error   *Options:* all

The size in an array declaration is zero or negative. The diagnostic is a warning if the size is zero and an error otherwise.

```
int ia[−5];
int ib[0];
```

```
"file", line 1: zero or negative subscript
"file", line 2: warning: zero or negative subscript
```

zero-sized struct/union

> *Type:* Error   *Options:* all
>
> You declared a structure or union with size of zero.
>
> struct s { int ia[0]; };
>
> *"file"*, line 1: warning: zero or negative subscript
> *"file"*, line 1: zero-sized struct/union

Operator Names

This section lists internal operator names that the compiler may use in error messages with definitions of these names.

,OP	The C "comma operator" (as distinct from the , that is used to separate function arguments).
ARG	A function argument. That is, a value passed to a function.
AUTO	An automatic variable that has not been allocated to a register.
CALL	A function call with arguments.
CBRANCH	A conditional branch. (This may be part of an if or loop statement.)
CONV	A conversion. It may have been explicit, in the form of a cast, or implicit, in the semantics of a C statement.
FCON	A floating-point constant.
ICON	An integer or address constant.
NAME	An object or function with extern or static storage class.
PARAM	A function parameter. That is, a value that is received by a function.
REG	An object that has been allocated to a register.
RETURN	The operation that corresponds to a return statement.
STAR	The indirection operator *, as in *p.
STRING	A string literal.
U&	The "take address of" operator (as distinct from the bit-wise AND operation).
U–	The arithmetic negation operator (as distinct from subtraction).
UCALL	A function call with no arguments.
UGE	An unsigned >= comparison.
UGT	An unsigned > comparison.

ULE   An unsigned <= comparison.

ULT   An unsigned < comparison.

UPLUS   The ANSI C "unary +" operator.

Other Error Messages

The following messages may appear at compile time, but they are not generated by the compiler. Messages beginning with `Assembler:` are produced by as. Messages beginning with `ld:` are generated by `ld`, the link editor. Note that the format of the messages varies, and some of the messages are displayed over several lines.

```
Assembler: file.c
        aline n (cline n) : trouble writing; probably out of
          temp-file space
```

The file system may be low on space, or the temporary file or output file exceeded the current ulimit.

```
Assembler: file.c aline n (cline n)
        Cannot open Output File filename
```

The directory containing the source file is unwritable, or
the file system containing source file is mounted read-only.

```
ld: Symbol name in file2.o is multiply defined. First defined in file1.o
```

A symbol name was defined more than once.

```
undefined                          first referenced
  symbol                              in file

  sym1                                 file1.o
```

`ld fatal: Symbol referencing errors. No output written to a.out`

A referenced symbol was not found. Compilation terminates.

5 lint

Introduction

`lint` checks for code constructs that may cause your C program not to compile, or to execute with unexpected results. `lint` issues every error and warning message produced by the C compiler. It also issues "`lint`-specific" warnings about potential bugs and portability problems.

In particular, `lint` compensates for separate and independent compilation in C by flagging inconsistencies in definition and use across files, including any libraries you have used. In a large project environment especially, where the same function may be used by different programmers in hundreds of separate modules of code, `lint` can help discover bugs that otherwise might be difficult to find. A function called with one less argument than expected, for example, looks at the stack for a value the call has never pushed, with results correct in one condition, incorrect in another, depending on whatever happens to be in memory at that stack location. By identifying dependencies like this one, and dependencies on machine architecture as well, `lint` can improve the reliability of code run on your machine or someone else's.

Options and Directives

`lint` is a static analyzer, which means that it cannot evaluate the run-time consequences of the dependencies it detects. Certain programs, for instance, may contain hundreds of unreachable `break` statements, of little importance, about which you typically can do nothing, and which `lint` will faithfully flag nevertheless. That's where `lint`'s command line options and directives — special comments embedded in the source text — come in. For the example we've cited here,

- you can invoke `lint` with the –b option to suppress all complaints about unreachable `break` statements;

- for a finer-grained control, you can precede any unreachable statement with the comment /* NOTREACHED */ to suppress the diagnostic for that statement.

The "Usage" section below discusses options and directives in greater detail and introduces the `lint` filter technique, which lets you tailor `lint`'s behavior even more finely to your project's needs. It also shows you how to use `lint` libraries to check your program for compatibility with the library functions you have called in it.

lint and the Compiler

Of the nearly five hundred diagnostics issued by lint, this chapter describes only the much smaller subset of lint-specific warnings: those not also issued by the compiler. The one exception to this rule applies to diagnostics issued both by lint and the compiler that are capable of being suppressed only by lint options. For the text and examples of all messages issued exclusively by lint or subject exclusively to its options, refer to the "lint-specific Messages" section at the end of this chapter. For the messages also issued by the compiler, consult the "C Compiler Diagnostics" chapter of the *Guide*.

Message Formats

Most of lint's messages are simple, one-line statements printed for each occurrence of the problem they diagnose. Errors detected in included files are reported multiply by the compiler but only once by lint, no matter how many times the file is included in other source files. Compound messages are issued for inconsistencies across files and, in a few cases, for problems within them as well. A single message describes every occurrence of the problem in the file or files being checked. When use of a lint filter (see the "Usage" section below) requires that a message be printed for each occurrence, compound diagnostics can be converted to the simple type by invoking lint with the −s option.

What lint Does

`lint`-specific diagnostics are issued for three broad categories of conditions: inconsistent use, nonportable code, and suspicious constructs. In this section, we'll review examples of `lint`'s behavior in each of these areas, and suggest possible responses to the issues they raise.

Consistency Checks

Inconsistent use of variables, arguments, and functions is checked within files as well as across them. Generally speaking, the same checks are performed for prototype uses, declarations, and parameters as for old-style functions. (If your program does not use function prototypes, `lint` will check the number and types of parameters in each call to a function more strictly than the compiler.) `lint` also identifies mismatches of conversion specifications and arguments in `[fs]printf()` and `[fs]scanf()` control strings. Examples:

- Within files, `lint` flags nonvoid functions that "fall off the bottom" without returning a value to the invoking function. In the past, programmers often indicated that a function was not meant to return a value by omitting the return type: `fun() {}`. That convention means nothing to the compiler, which regards `fun()` as having the return type `int`. Declare the function with the return type `void` to eliminate the problem.

- Across files, `lint` detects cases where a nonvoid function does not return a value, yet is used for its value in an expression, and the opposite problem, a function returning a value that is sometimes or always ignored in subsequent calls. When the value is always ignored, it may indicate an inefficiency in the function definition. When it is sometimes ignored, it's probably bad style (typically, not testing for error conditions). If you do not need to check the return values of string functions like `strcat()`, `strcpy()`, and `sprintf()`, or output functions like `printf()` and `putchar()`, cast the offending call(s) to `void`.

- `lint` identifies variables or functions that are declared but not used or defined; used but not defined; or defined but not used. That means that when `lint` is applied to some, but not all files of a collection to be loaded together, it will complain about functions and variables declared in those files but defined or used elsewhere; used there but defined elsewhere; or defined there and used elsewhere. Invoke the −x option to suppress the former complaint, −u to suppress the latter two.

Portability Checks

Some nonportable code is flagged by lint in its default behavior, and a few more cases are diagnosed when lint is invoked with –p and/or –Xc. The latter tells lint to check for constructs that do not conform to the ANSI C standard. For the messages issued under –p and –Xc, check the "Usage" section below. Examples:

■ In some C language implementations, character variables that are not explicitly declared signed or unsigned are treated as signed quantities with a range typically from -128 to 127. In other implementations, they are treated as nonnegative quantities with a range typically from 0 to 255. So the test

```
char c;

c = getchar();
if (c == EOF) ...
```

where EOF has the value -1, will always fail on machines where character variables take on nonnegative values. One of lint's –p checks will flag any comparison that implies a "plain" char may have a negative value. Note, however, that declaring c a signed char in the above example eliminates the diagnostic, not the problem. That's because getchar() must return all possible characters and a distinct EOF value, so a char cannot store its value. We cite this example, perhaps the most common one arising from implementation-defined sign-extension, to show how a thoughtful application of lint's portability option can help you discover bugs not related to portability. In any case, declare c as an int.

■ A similar issue arises with bit-fields. When constant values are assigned to bit-fields, the field may be too small to hold the value. On a machine that treats bit-fields of type int as unsigned quantities, the values allowed for int x:3 range from 0 to 7, whereas on machines that treat them as signed quantities they range from -4 to 3. However unintuitive it may seem, a three-bit field declared type int cannot hold the value 4 on the latter machines. lint invoked with –p flags all bit-field types other than unsigned int or signed int. Note that these are the only *portable* bit-field types. AT&T C supports int, char, short, and long bit-field types that may be unsigned, signed, or "plain." It also supports the enum bit-field type.

■ Bugs can arise when a larger-sized type is assigned to a smaller-sized type. If significant bits are truncated, accuracy is lost:

```
short s;
long l;
s = l;
```

lint flags all such assignments by default; the diagnostic can be suppressed by invoking the −a option. Bear in mind that you may be suppressing other diagnostics when you invoke lint with this or any other option. Check the list in the "Usage" section below for the options that suppress more than one diagnostic.

■ A cast of a pointer to one object type to a pointer to an object type with stricter alignment requirements may not be portable. lint flags

```
int *fun(y)
        char *y;
{
        return(int *)y;
}
```

because, on most machines, an int cannot start on an arbitrary byte boundary, whereas a char can. You can suppress the diagnostic by invoking lint with −h, although, again, you may be disabling other messages. Better still, eliminate the problem by using the generic pointer void *.

■ ANSI C leaves the order of evaluation of complicated expressions undefined. What this means is that when function calls, nested assignment statements, or the increment and decrement operators cause side effects — when a variable is changed as a byproduct of the evaluation of an expression — the order in which the side effects take place is highly machine dependent. By default, lint flags any variable changed by a side effect and used elsewhere in the same expression:

```
int a[10];
main()
{
    int i = 1;
    a[i++] = i;
}
```

Note that in this example the value of a[1] may be 1 if one compiler is used, 2 if another. The bitwise logical operator & can give rise to this diagnostic when it is mistakenly used in place of the logical operator &&:

```
if ((c = getchar()) != EOF & c != '0')
```

Suspicious Constructs

lint flags a miscellany of legal constructs that may not represent what the programmer intended. Examples:

- An unsigned variable always has a nonnegative value. So the test

```
unsigned x;
if (x < 0) ...
```

will always fail. Whereas the test

```
unsigned x;
if (x > 0) ...
```

is equivalent to

```
if (x != 0) ...
```

which may not be the intended action. lint flags suspicious comparisons of unsigned variables with negative constants or 0. To compare an unsigned variable to the bit pattern of a negative number, cast it to unsigned:

```
if (u == (unsigned) -1) ...
```

Or use the U suffix:

```
if (u == -1U) ...
```

- lint flags expressions without side effects that are used in a context where side effects are expected, that is, where the expression may not represent what the programmer intended. It issues an additional warning whenever the equality operator is found where the assignment operator was expected, in other words, where a side effect was expected:

```
int fun()
{
        int a, b, x, y;
        (a = x) && (b == y);
}
```

■ lint cautions you to parenthesize expressions that mix both the logical
and bitwise operators (specifically, &, | , ^, <<, >>), where misunder-
standing of operator precedence may lead to incorrect results. Because
the precedence of bitwise &, for example, falls below logical ==, the
expression

```
if (x & a == 0) ...
```

will be evaluated as

```
if (x & (a == 0)) ...
```

which is most likely not what you intended. Invoking lint with −h dis-
ables the diagnostic.

Usage

You invoke `lint` with a command of the form

```
$ lint file.c file.c
```

`lint` examines code in two passes. In the first, it checks for error conditions local to C source files, in the second for inconsistencies across them. This process is invisible to the user unless `lint` is invoked with `−c`:

```
$ lint −c file1.c file2.c
```

That command directs `lint` to execute the first pass only and collect information relevant to the second — about inconsistencies in definition and use across `file1.c` and `file2.c` — in intermediate files named `file1.ln` and `file2.ln`:

```
$ ls −1
file1.c
file1.ln
file2.c
file2.ln
```

In this way, the `−c` option to `lint` is analogous to the `−c` option to `cc`, which suppresses the link editing phase of compilation. Generally speaking, `lint`'s command line syntax closely follows `cc`'s.

When the `.ln` files are `lint`ed

```
$ lint file1.ln file2.ln
```

the second pass is executed. `lint` processes any number of `.c` or `.ln` files in their command line order. So

```
$ lint file1.ln file2.ln file3.c
```

directs `lint` to check `file3.c` for errors internal to it and all three files for consistency.

`lint` searches directories for included header files in the same order as `cc` (see "Searching for a Header File" in Chapter 2). You can use the `−I` option to `lint` as you would the `−I` option to `cc`. Namely, if you want `lint` to check an included header file that is stored in a directory other than your current directory or the standard place, specify the path of the directory with `−I` as follows:

```
$ lint −Idir file1.c file2.c
```

You can specify `−I` more than once on the `lint` command line. Directories are searched in the order they appear on the command line. Of course, you can specify multiple options to `lint` on the same command line. Options may be concatenated unless one of the options takes an argument:

```
$ lint -cp -Idir -Idir file1.c file2.c
```

That command directs `lint` to

- execute the first pass only;

- perform additional portability checks;

- search the specified directories for included header files.

lint Libraries

You can use `lint` libraries to check your program for compatibility with the library functions you have called in it: the declaration of the function return type, the number and types of arguments the function expects, and so on. The standard `lint` libraries correspond to libraries supplied by the C compilation system, and generally are stored in the standard place on your system, the directory /usr/ccs/lib. By convention, `lint` libraries have names of the form `llib-lx.ln`.

The `lint` standard C library, `llib-lc.ln`, is appended to the `lint` command line by default; checks for compatibility with it can be suppressed by invoking the -n option. Other `lint` libraries are accessed as arguments to -l. That is,

```
$ lint -lx file1.c file2.c
```

directs `lint` to check the usage of functions and variables in `file1.c` and `file2.c` for compatibility with the `lint` library `llib-lx.ln`. The library file, which consists only of definitions, is processed exactly as are ordinary source files and ordinary `.ln` files, except that functions and variables used inconsistently in the library file, or defined in the library file but not used in the source files, elicit no complaints.

To create your own `lint` library, insert the directive /* LINTLIBRARY */ at the head of a C source file, then invoke `lint` for that file with the -o option and the library name that will be given to -l:

```
$ lint -ox files headed by /* LINTLIBRARY */
```

causes only definitions in the source files headed by /* LINTLIBRARY */ to be
written to the file llib-l*x*.ln. (Note the analogy of lint -o to cc -o.) A
library can be created from a file of function prototype declarations in the same
way, except that both /* LINTLIBRARY */ and /* PROTOLIB*n* */ must be
inserted at the head of the declarations file. If *n* is 1, prototype declarations will
be written to a library .ln file just as are old-style definitions. If *n* is 0, the
default, the process is cancelled. Invoking lint with -y is another way of
creating a lint library:

        $ lint -y -o*x* file1.c file2.c

causes each source file named on the command line to be treated as if
it began with /* LINTLIBRARY */ and only its definitions to be written to
llib-l*x*.ln.

By default, lint searches for lint libraries in the standard place. To direct
lint to search for a lint library in a directory other than the standard place,
specify the path of the directory with the -L option:

        $ lint -L*dir* -l*x* file1.c file2.c

The specified directory is searched before the standard place.

lint Filters

A lint filter is a project-specific post-processor that typically uses an awk script
or similar program to read the output of lint and discard messages that your
project has decided do not identify real problems — string functions, for
instance, returning values that are sometimes or always ignored. It enables you
to generate customized diagnostic reports when lint options and directives do
not provide sufficient control over output.

Two options to lint are particularly useful in developing a filter. Invoking
lint with -s causes compound diagnostics to be converted into simple, one-
line messages issued for each occurrence of the problem diagnosed. The easily
parsed message format is suitable for analysis by an awk script.

Invoking lint with -k causes certain comments you have written in the source
file to be printed in output, and can be useful both in documenting project decisions and specifying the post-processor's behavior. In the latter instance, if the
comment identified an expected lint message, and the reported message was
the same, the message might be filtered out. To use -k, insert on the line

preceding the code you wish to comment the /* LINTED [*msg*] */ directive, where *msg* refers to the comment to be printed when lint is invoked with −k. (Refer to the list of directives below for what lint does when −k is *not* invoked for a file containing /* LINTED [*msg*] */.)

Options and Directives Listed

These options suppress specific messages:

−a   Suppress:

- assignment causes implicit narrowing conversion

- conversion to larger integral type may sign−extend incorrectly

−b   For unreachable break and empty statements, suppress:

- statement not reached

−h   Suppress:

- assignment operator "=" found where equality opera−tor "==" was expected

- constant operand to op: "!"

- fallthrough on case statement

- pointer cast may result in improper alignment

- precedence confusion possible; parenthesize

- statement has no consequent: if

- statement has no consequent: else

−m   Suppress:

- declared global, could be static

-u   Suppress:

   ■ name defined but never used

   ■ name used but not defined

-v   Suppress:

   ■ argument unused in function

-x   Suppress:

   ■ name declared but never used or defined

These options enable specific messages:

-p   Enable:

   ■ conversion to larger integral type may sign-extend incorrectly

   ■ may be indistinguishable due to truncation or case

   ■ pointer casts may be troublesome

   ■ nonportable bit-field type

   ■ suspicious comparison of char with *value*: op "*op*"

-Xc   Enable:

   ■ bitwise operation on signed value nonportable

   ■ function must return int: main()

   ■ may be indistinguishable due to truncation or case

   ■ only 0 or 2 parameters allowed: main()

   ■ nonportable character constant

Other options:

-c   Create a .ln file consisting of information relevant to lint's second pass for every .c file named on the command line. The second pass is not executed.

-F   When referring to the .c files named on the command line, print their path names as supplied on the command line rather than only their base names.

-I*dir*   Search the directory *dir* for included header files.

-k   When used with the directive /* LINTED [*msg*] */, print info: *msg*.

-l*x*   Access the lint library llib-l*x*.ln.

-L*dir*   When used with -l, search for a lint library in the directory *dir*.

-n   Suppress checks for compatibility with the default lint standard C library.

-o*x*   Create the file llib-l*x*.ln, consisting of information relevant to lint's second pass, from the .c files named on the command line. Generally used with -y or /* LINTLIBRARY */ to create lint libraries.

-s   Convert compound messages into simple ones.

-y   Treat every .c file named on the command line as if it began with the directive /* LINTLIBRARY */.

-V   Write the product name and release to standard error.

Directives:

/* ARGSUSED*n* */	Suppress:

 ■ argument unused in function

for every argument but the first *n* in the function definition it precedes. Default is 0.

/* CONSTCOND */	Suppress:

 ■ constant in conditional context

 ■ constant operand to op: "!"

 ■ logical expression always false: op "&&"

 ■ logical expression always true: op "||"

for the constructs it precedes. Also
/* CONSTANTCONDITION */.

/* EMPTY */	Suppress:

 ■ statement has no consequent: else

when inserted between the else and semicolon;

 ■ statement has no consequent: if

when inserted between the controlling expression of the if and semicolon.

/* FALLTHRU */	Suppress:

 ■ fallthrough on case statement

for the case statement it precedes. Also
/* FALLTHROUGH */.

/* LINTED [*msg*] */	When −k is not invoked, suppress every warning pertaining to an intrafile problem except:

- argument unused in function
- declaration unused in block
- set but not used in function
- static unused
- variable unused in function

for the line of code it precedes. *msg* is ignored.

/* LINTLIBRARY */   When −o is invoked, write to a library .ln file only definitions in the .c file it heads.

/* NOTREACHED */   Suppress:

- statement not reached

for the unreached statements it precedes;

- fallthrough on case statement

for the case it precedes that cannot be reached from the preceding case;

- function falls off bottom without returning value

for the closing curly brace it precedes at the end of the function.

/* PRINTFLIKE*n* */   Treat the *n*th argument of the function definition it precedes as a [fs]printf() format string and issue:

- malformed format string

for invalid conversion specifications in that argument, and

- function argument type inconsistent with format

- too few arguments for format

- too many arguments for format

for mismatches between the remaining arguments and the conversion specifications. lint issues these warnings by default for errors in calls to [fs]printf() functions provided by the standard C library.

/* PROTOLIB*n* */   When *n* is 1 and /* LINTLIBRARY */ is used, write to a library .ln file only function prototype declarations in the .c file it heads. Default is 0, cancelling the process.

/* SCANFLIKE*n* */   Same as /* PRINTFLIKE*n* */ except that the *n*th argument of the function definition is treated as a [fs]scanf() format string. By default, lint issues warnings for errors in calls to [fs]scanf() functions provided by the standard C library.

/* VARARGS*n* */   For the function whose definition it precedes, suppress:

- function called with variable number of arguments

for calls to the function with *n* or more arguments.

     ANSI C and Programming Support Tools

lint-specific Messages

This section lists alphabetically the warning messages issued exclusively by lint or subject exclusively to its options. The code examples illustrate conditions in which the messages are elicited. Note that some of the examples would elicit messages in addition to the one stated. For the remaining lint messages, consult the "C Compiler Diagnostics" chapter of the *Guide*.

argument unused in function

Format: Compound

A function argument was not used. Preceding the function definition with /* ARGSUSED*n* */ suppresses the message for all but the first *n* arguments; invoking lint with −v suppresses it for every argument.

```
1    int fun(int x, int y)
2    {
3         return x;
4    }
5    /* ARGSUSED1 */
6    int fun2(int x, int y)
7    {
8         return x;
9    }
```

argument unused in function
    (1) y in fun

array subscript cannot be > *value*: *value*

Format: Simple

The value of an array element's subscript exceeded the upper array bound.

```
1    int fun ()
2    {
3         int a[10];
4         int *p = a;
5         while (p != &a[10])   /* using address is ok */
6              p++;
7         return a[5 + 6];
8    }
```

(7) warning: array subscript cannot be > 9: 11

array subscript cannot be negative: *value*

Format: Simple

The constant expression that represents the subscript of a true array (as opposed to a pointer) had a negative value.

```
1    int f ()
2    {
3         int a[10];
4         return a[5 * 2 / 10 - 2];
5    }
```

(4) warning: array subscript cannot be negative: -1

assignment causes implicit narrowing conversion

Format: Compound

An object was assigned to one of a smaller type. Invoking lint with −a
suppresses the message. So does an explicit cast to the smaller type.

```
1    void fun()
2    {
3        short s;
4        long l = 0;
5        s = l;
6    }
```

assignment causes implicit narrowing conversion
      (5)

assignment of negative constant to unsigned type

Format: Simple

A negative constant was assigned to a variable of unsigned type. Use a cast or
the U suffix.

```
1    void fun()
2    {
3        unsigned i;
4        i = -1;
5        i = -1U;
6        i = (unsigned) (-4 + 3);
7    }
```

(4) warning: assignment of negative constant to unsigned type

```
assignment operator "=" found where "==" was expected
```

Format: Simple

An assignment operator was found where a conditional expression was
expected. The message is not issued when an assignment is made to a variable
using the value of a function call or in the case of string copying (see the example below). The warning is suppressed when lint is invoked with −h.

```
1    void fun ()
2    {
3        char *p, *q;
4        int a = 0, b = 0, c = 0, d = 0, i;
5        i = (a = b) && (c == d);
6        i = (c == d) && (a = b);
7        if (a = b)
8            i = 1;
9        while (*p++ = *q++);
10       while (a = b);
11       while ((a = getchar()) == b);
12       if (a = foo()) return;
13   }
```

```
(5)  warning: assignment operator "=" found where "=="
         was expected
(7)  warning: assignment operator "=" found where "=="
         was expected
(10) warning: assignment operator "=" found where "=="
         was expected
```

```
bitwise operation on signed value nonportable
```

Format: Compound

The operand of a bitwise operator was a variable of signed integral type, as
defined by ANSI C. Because these operators return values that depend on the
internal representations of integers, their behavior is implementation-defined for
operands of that type. The message is issued only when lint is invoked with
−Xc.

ANSI C and Programming Support Tools

```
1    fun ()
2    {
3         int i;
4         signed int j;
5         unsigned int k;
6         i = i & 055;
7         j = j | 022;
8         k = k >> 4;
9    }
```

```
warning: bitwise operation on signed value nonportable
     (6)            (7)
```

constant in conditional context

Format: Simple

The controlling expression of an if, while, or for statement was a constant. Preceding the statement with /* CONSTCOND */ suppresses the message.

```
1    void fun ()
2    {
3         if (! 1) return;
4         while (1) foo ();
5         for (;1;);
6         for (;;);
7         /* CONSTCOND */
8         while (1);
9    }
```

```
(3) warning: constant in conditional context
(4) warning: constant in conditional context
(5) warning: constant in conditional context
```

constant operand to op: "!"

Format: Simple

The operand of the NOT operator was a constant. Preceding the statement with
/* CONSTCOND */ suppresses the message for that statement; invoking lint
with −h suppresses it for every statement.

```
1    void fun ()
2    {
3         if   (! 0) return;
4         /* CONSTCOND */
5         if   (! 0) return;
6    }
```

(3) warning: constant operand to op: "!"

constant truncated by assignment

Format: Simple

An integral constant expression was assigned or returned to an object of an
integral type that cannot hold the value without truncation.

```
1    unsigned char f ()
2    {
3         unsigned char i;
4         i = 255;
5         i = 256;
6         return 256;
7    }
```

(5) warning: constant truncated by assignment
(6) warning: constant truncated by assignment

conversion of pointer loses bits

Format: Simple

A pointer was assigned to an object of an integral type that is smaller than the pointer.

```
1    void fun ()
2    {
3         char c;
4         int *i;
5         c = i;
6    }
```

(5) warning: conversion of pointer loses bits

conversion to larger integral type may sign-extend incorrectly

Format: Compound

A variable of type "plain" char was assigned to a variable of a larger integral type. Whether a "plain" char is treated as signed or unsigned is implementation-defined. The message is issued only when lint is invoked with −p, and is suppressed when it is invoked with −a.

```
1    void fun ()
2    {
3         char c = 0;
4         short s = 0;
5         long l;
6         l = c;
7         l = s;
8    }
```

conversion to larger integral type may sign-extend incorrectly
        (6)

declaration unused in block

Format: Compound

An external variable or function was declared but not used in an inner block.

```
1    int fun()
2    {
3          int foo();
4          int bar();
5          return foo();
6    }
```
==========

declaration unused in block
      (4) bar

declared global, could be static

Format: Compound

An external variable or function was declared global, that is, not declared static, but was referenced only in the file in which it was defined. The message is suppressed when lint is invoked with −m.

```
file f1.c
1    int i;
2    int foo() {return i;}
3    int fun() {return i;}
4    static int stfun() {return fun();}
file f2.c
1    main()
2    {
3      int a;
4      a = foo();
5    }
```
==========

declared global, could be static
      fun   f1.c(3)
      i   f1.c(1)

equality operator "==" found where "=" was expected

Format: Simple

An equality operator was found where a side effect was expected.

```
1    void fun(a, b)
2    int a, b;
3    {
4        a == b;
5        for (a == b; a < 10; a++);
6    }
```

(4) warning: equality operator "==" found where "="
     was expected
(5) warning: equality operator "==" found where "="
     was expected

evaluation order undefined: *name*

Format: Simple

A variable was changed by a side effect and used elsewhere in the same expression.

```
1    int a[10];
2    main()
3    {
4        int i = 1;
5        a[i++] = i;
6    }
```

(5) warning: evaluation order undefined: i

`fallthrough on case statement`

Format: Simple

Execution fell through one case to another without a break or return. Preceding a case statement with /* FALLTHRU */, or /* NOTREACHED */ when the case cannot be reached from the preceding case (see below), suppresses the message for that statement; invoking `lint` with −h suppresses it for every statement.

```
 1    void fun(i)
 2    {
 3        switch (i) {
 4        case 10:
 5            i = 0;
 6        case 12:
 7            return;
 8        case 14:
 9            break;
10        case 15:
11        case 16:
12            break;
13        case 18:
14            i = 0;
15            /* FALLTHRU */
16        case 20:
17            error("bad number");
18            /* NOTREACHED */
19        case 22:
20            return;
21        }
22    }
```

(6) warning: fallthrough on case statement

```
function argument ( number ) declared inconsistently
```

Format: Compound

The parameter types in a function prototype declaration or definition differed from their types in another declaration or definition. The message described after this one is issued for uses (not declarations or definitions) of a prototype with the wrong parameter types.

```
file i3a.c
1    int fun1(int);
2    int fun2(int);
3    int fun3(int);
file i3b.c
1    int fun1(int *i);
2    int fun2(int *i) {}
3    void foo()
4    {
5         int *i;
6         fun3(i);
7    }
```

```
function argument ( number ) declared inconsistently
       fun2 (arg 1)            i3b.c(2) int * :: i3a.c(2) int
       fun1 (arg 1)            i3a.c(1) int :: i3b.c(1) int *
function argument ( number ) used inconsistently
       fun3 (arg 1)            i3a.c(3) int :: i3b.c(6) int *
```

```
function argument ( number ) used inconsistently
```

Format: Compound

The argument types in a function call did not match the types of the formal parameters in the function definition. (And see the discussion of the preceding message.)

file f1.c
```
1    int fun(int x, int y)
2    {
3         return x + y;
4    }
```
file f2.c
```
1    int main()
2    {
3         int *x;
4         extern int fun();
5         return fun(1, x);
6    }
```

```
function argument ( number ) used inconsistently
      fun( arg 2 )          f1.c(2) int :: f2.c(5) int *
```

function argument type inconsistent with format

Format: Compound

An argument was inconsistent with the corresponding conversion specification in the control string of a `[fs]printf()` or `[fs]scanf()` function call. (See also `/* PRINTFLIKEn */` and `/* SCANFLIKEn */` in the list of directives in the "Usage" section above.)

```
1    #include <stdio.h>
2    main()
3    {
4         int i;
5         printf("%s", i);
6    }
```

```
function argument type inconsistent with format
      printf(arg 2) int :: (format) char *   test.c(5)
```

function called with variable number of arguments

Format: Compound

A function was called with the wrong number of arguments. Preceding a function definition with /* VARARGS*n* */ suppresses the message for calls with *n* or more arguments; defining and declaring a function with the ANSI C notation "..." suppresses it for every argument. (And see the discussion of the message following this one.)

```
file f1.c
1    int fun(int x, int y, int z)
2    {
3         return x + y + z;
4    }
5    int fun2(int x, ...)
6    {
7         return x;
8    }
10   /* VARARGS1 */
11   int fun3(int x, int y, int z)
12   {
13        return x;
14   }
file f2.c
1    int main()
2    {
3         extern int fun(), fun3(), fun2(int x, ...);
4         return fun(1, 2);
5         return fun2(1, 2, 3, 4);
6         return fun3(1, 2, 3, 4, 5);
7    }
```

```
function called with variable number of arguments
     fun          f1.c(2) :: f2.c(4)
```

function declared with variable number of arguments

Format: Compound

The number of parameters in a function prototype declaration or definition differed from their number in another declaration or definition. Declaring and
defining the prototype with the ANSI C notation "..." suppresses the warning
if all declarations have the same number of arguments. The message immediately preceding this one is issued for uses (not declarations or definitions) of a
prototype with the wrong number of arguments.

```
file i3a.c
1    int fun1(int);
2    int fun2(int);
3    int fun3(int);
file i3b.c
1    int fun1(int, int);
2    int fun2(int a, int b)  {}
3    void foo()
4    {
5         int i, j, k;
6         i = fun3(j, k);
7    }
```
```
function declared with variable number of arguments
      fun2              i3a.c(2) :: i3b.c(2)
      fun1              i3a.c(1) :: i3b.c(1)
function called with variable number of arguments
      fun3              i3a.c(3) :: i3b.c(6)
```

function falls off bottom without returning value

Format: Compound

A nonvoid function did not return a value to the invoking function. If the closing curly brace is truly not reached, preceding it with /* NOTREACHED */
suppresses the message.

```
1    fun ()
2    { }
3    void fun2 ()
4    { }
5    foo ()
6    {
7        exit (1);
8    /* NOTREACHED */
9    }
```

function falls off bottom without returning value
    (2) fun

function must return int: main ()

Format: Simple

You used a main () that did not return int, in violation of ANSI C restrictions. The message is issued only when lint is invoked with −Xc.

```
1    void main ()
2    { }
```

    (2) warning: function must return int: main ()

function returns pointer to [automatic/parameter]

Format: Simple

A function returned a pointer to an automatic variable or a parameter. Since an object with automatic storage duration is no longer guaranteed to be reserved after the end of the block, the value of the pointer to that object will be indeterminate after the end of the block.

```
1    int *fun(int x)
2    {
3         int a[10];
4         int b;
5         if (x == 1)
6             return a;
7         else if (x == 2)
8             return &b;
9         else return &x;
10   }
```

```
(6)  warning: function returns pointer to automatic
(8)  warning: function returns pointer to automatic
(9)  warning: function returns pointer to parameter
```

function returns value that is always ignored

Format: Compound

A function contained a return statement and every call to the function ignored its return value.

file f1.c
```
1    int fun()
2    {
3         return 1;
4    }
```
file f2.c
```
1    extern int fun();
2    int main()
3    {
4         fun();
5         return 1;
6    }
```

```
function returns value that is always ignored
        fun
```

ANSI C and Programming Support Tools

function returns value that is sometimes ignored

Format: Compound

A function contained a return statement and some, but not all, calls to the
function ignored its return value.

```
file f1.c
1    int fun()
2    {
3         return 1;
4    }
file f2.c
1    extern int fun();
2    int main()
3    {
4         if(1) {
5              return fun();
6         }
          else {
7              fun();
8              return 1;
9         }
10   }
```

function returns value that is sometimes ignored
        fun

function value is used, but none returned

Format: Compound

A nonvoid function did not contain a return statement, yet was used for its
value in an expression.

file f1.c
```
1    extern int fun();
2    main()
3    {
4         return fun();
5    }
```
file f2.c
```
1    int fun()
2    {}
```

```
function value is used, but none returned
      fun
```

```
logical expression always false: op "&&"
```

Format: Simple

A logical AND expression checked for equality of the same variable to two different constants, or had the constant 0 as an operand. In the latter case, preceding the expression with /* CONSTCOND */ suppresses the message.

```
1    void fun(a)
2    int a;
3    {
4         a = (a == 1) && (a == 2);
5         a = (a == 1) && (a == 1);
6         a = (1 == a) && (a == 2);
7         a = (a == 1) && 0;
8         /* CONSTCOND */
9         a = (0 && (a == 1));
10   }
```

```
(4) warning: logical expression always false: op "&&"
(6) warning: logical expression always false: op "&&"
(7) warning: logical expression always false: op "&&"
```

logical expression always true: op "||"

Format: Simple

A logical OR expression checked for inequality of the same variable to two different constants, or had a nonzero integral constant as an operand. In the latter case, preceding the expression with /* CONSTCOND */ suppresses the message.

```
1    void fun(a)
2    int a;
3    {
4        a = (a != 1) || (a != 2);
5        a = (a != 1) || (a != 1);
6        a = (1 != a) || (a != 2);
7        a = (a == 10) || 1;
8        /* CONSTCOND */
9        a = (1 || (a == 10));
10   }
```

```
(4) warning: logical expression always true: op "||"
(6) warning: logical expression always true: op "||"
(7) warning: logical expression always true: op "||"
```

malformed format string

Format: Compound

A [fs]printf() or [fs]scanf() control string was formed incorrectly. (See also /* PRINTFLIKE*n* */ and /* SCANFLIKE*n* */ in the list of directives in the "Usage" section above.)

```
1    #include <stdio.h>
2    main()
3    {
4        printf("%y");
5    }
```

```
malformed format string
       printf        test.c(4)
```

may be indistinguishable due to truncation or case

Format: Compound

External names in your program may be indistinguishable when it is ported to
another machine due to implementation-defined restrictions as to length or case.
The message is issued only when lint is invoked with −Xc or −p. Under −Xc,
external names are truncated to the first 6 characters with one case, in accordance with the ANSI C lower bound; under −p, to the first 8 characters with one
case.

```
file f1.c
1    int foobar1;
2    int FooBar12;
file f2.c
1    int foobar2;
2    int FOOBAR12;
```

```
under −p
may be indistinguishable due to truncation or case
     FooBar12   f1.c(2)   ::   FOOBAR12   f2.c(2)
```

```
under −Xc
may be indistinguishable due to truncation or case
     foobar1    f1.c(1)   ::   FooBar12   f1.c(2)
     foobar1    f1.c(1)   ::   foobar2    f2.c(1)
     foobar1    f1.c(1)   ::   FOOBAR12   f2.c(2)
```

name declared but never used or defined

Format: Compound

A nonstatic external variable or function was declared but not used or defined
in any file. The message is suppressed when lint is invoked with −x.

```
file f.c
1    extern int fun();
2    static int foo();
```

```
name declared but never used or defined
     fun              f.c(1)
```

name defined but never used

Format: Compound

A variable or function was defined but not used in any file. The message is suppressed when lint is invoked with −u.

```
file f.c
1    int i, j, k = 1;
2    main()
3    {
4         j = k;
5    }
```

```
name defined but never used
     i               f.c(1)
```

name multiply defined

Format: Compound

A variable was defined in more than one source file.

```
file f1.c
1    char i = 'a';
file f2.c
1    long i = 1;
```

```
name multiply defined
     i               f1.c(1) :: f2.c(1)
```

name used but not defined

Format: Compound

A nonstatic external variable or function was declared but not defined in any file. The message is suppressed when lint is invoked with −u.

```
file f.c
1    extern int fun();
2    int main()
3    {
4        return fun();
5    }
```

name used but not defined
        fun   f.c(4)

nonportable bit-field type

Format: Simple

You used a bit-field type other than signed int or unsigned int. The message is issued only when lint is invoked with −p. Note that these are the only *portable* bit-field types. AT&T C supports int, char, short, and long bit-field types that may be unsigned, signed, or "plain." It also supports the enum bit-field type.

```
1    struct u {
2        unsigned v:1;
3        int      w:1;
4        char     x:8;
5        long     y:8;
6        short    z:8;
7    };
```

(3) warning: nonportable bit-field type
(4) warning: nonportable bit-field type
(5) warning: nonportable bit-field type
(6) warning: nonportable bit-field type

nonportable character constant

Format: Simple

A multi-character character constant in your program may not be portable. The message is issued only when lint is invoked with −Xc.

```
1    int c = 'abc';
```

(1) warning: nonportable character constant

only 0 or 2 parameters allowed: main()

Format: Simple

The function main() in your program was defined with only one parameter or more than two parameters, in violation of the ANSI C requirement. The message is issued only when lint is invoked with −Xc.

```
1    main(int argc, char **argv, char **envp)
2    {}
```

(2) warning: only 0 or 2 parameters allowed: main()

pointer cast may result in improper alignment

Format: Compound

You cast a pointer to one object type to a pointer to an object type with stricter alignment requirements. Doing so may result in a value that is invalid for the second pointer type. The warning is suppressed when lint is invoked with −h.

```
1    void fun ()
2    {
3         short *s;
4         int *i;
5         i = (int *) s;
6    }
=========
```

```
pointer cast may result in improper alignment
    (5)
```

pointer casts may be troublesome

Format: Compound

You cast a pointer to one object type to a pointer to a different object type. The message is issued only when lint is invoked with −p, and is not issued for the generic pointer void *.

```
1    void fun ()
2    {
3         int *i;
4         char *c;
5         void *v;
6         i = (int *) c;
7         i = (int *) v;
8    }
=========
```

```
warning: pointer casts may be troublesome
    (6)
```

precedence confusion possible; parenthesize

Format: Simple

You did not parenthesize an expression that mixes a logical and a bitwise operator. The message is suppressed when lint is invoked with −h.

```
1    void fun()
2    {
3         int x = 0, m = 0, MASK = 0, i;
4         i = (x + m == 0);
5         i = (x & MASK == 0);    /* eval'd (x & (MASK == 0)) */
6         i = (MASK == 1 & x);    /* eval'd ((MASK == 1) & x) */
7    }
```

(5) warning: precedence confusion possible; parenthesize
(6) warning: precedence confusion possible; parenthesize

precision lost in bit-field assignment

Format: Simple

A constant was assigned to a bit-field too small to hold the value without truncation. Note that in the following example the bit-field z may have values that
range from 0 to 7 or −4 to 3, depending on the machine.

```
1    void fun()
2    {
3         struct {
4              signed x:3;      /* max value allowed is 3 */
5              unsigned y:3;    /* max value allowed is 7 */
6              int z:3;         /* max value allowed is 7 */
7         } s;
8         s.x = 3;
9         s.x = 4;
10        s.y = 7;
11        s.y = 8;
12        s.z = 7;
13        s.z = 8;
14   }
```

(9) warning: precision lost in bit-field assignment: 4
(11) warning: precision lost in bit-field assignment: 0x8
(13) warning: precision lost in bit-field assignment: 8

set but not used in function

Format: Compound

An automatic variable or a function parameter was declared and set but not used in a function.

```
1    void fun(y)
2    int y;
3    {
4         int x;
5         x = 1;
6         y = 1;
7    }
```

```
set but not used in function
     (4) x in fun
     (1) y in fun
```

statement has no consequent: else

Format: Simple

An if statement had a null else part. Inserting /* EMPTY */ between the else and semicolon suppresses the message for that statement; invoking lint with −h suppresses it for every statement.

```
1    void f(a)
2    int a;
3    {
4         if (a)
5              return;
6         else;
7    }
```

```
(6) warning: statement has no consequent: else
```

statement has no consequent: if

Format: Simple

An if statement had a null if part. Inserting /* EMPTY */ between the controlling expression of the if and semicolon suppresses the message for that statement; invoking lint with −h suppresses it for every statement.

```
1    void f(a)
2    int a;
3    {
4        if (a);
5        if (a == 10)
6            /* EMPTY */;
7        else return;
8    }
```

(4) warning: statement has no consequent: if

statement has null effect

Format: Compound

An expression did not generate a side effect where a side effect was expected. Note that the message is issued for every subsequent sequence point that is reached at which a side effect is not generated.

```
1    void fun ()
2    {
3         int a, b, c, x;
4         a;
5         a == 5;
6         ;
7         while (x++ != 10);
8         (a == b) && (c = a);
9         (a = b) && (c == a);
10        (a, b);
11   }
```

statement has null effect
        (4)   (5)   (9)   (10)

statement not reached

Format: Compound

A function contained a statement that cannot be reached. Preceding an
unreached statement with /* NOTREACHED */ suppresses the message for that
statement; invoking lint with −b suppresses it for every unreached break and
empty statement. Note that this message is also issued by the compiler but cannot be suppressed.

```
1    void fun(a)
2    {
3         switch (a) {
4              case 1:
5                   return;
6                   break;
7              case 2:
8                   return;
9                   /* NOTREACHED */
10                  break;
11        }
12   }
```

statement not reached
    (6)

static unused

Format: Compound

A variable or function was defined or declared static in a file but not used in
that file. Doing so is probably a programming error because the object cannot
be used outside the file.

```
1    static int x;
2    static int main() {}
3    static int foo();
4    static int y = 1;
```

static unused
    (4) y   (3) foo   (2) main   (1) x

suspicious comparison of char with *value*: op "*op*"

Format: Simple

A comparison was performed on a variable of type "plain" char that implied it
may have a negative value (< 0, <= 0, >= 0, > 0). Whether a "plain" char is

treated as signed or nonnegative is implementation-defined. The message is issued only when lint is invoked with −p.

```
1    void fun(c, d)
2    char c;
3    signed char d;
4    {
5        int i;
6        i = (c == −5);
7        i = (c < 0);
8        i = (d < 0);
9    }
```

(6) warning: suspicious comparison of char with negative
    constant: op "=="
(7) warning: suspicious comparison of char with 0: op "<"

suspicious comparison of unsigned with *value*: op "*op*"

Format: Simple

A comparison was performed on a variable of unsigned type that implied it may have a negative value (< 0, <= 0, >= 0, > 0).

```
 1    void fun(x)
 2    unsigned x;
 3    {
 4        int i;
 5        i = (x > -2);
 6        i = (x < 0);
 7        i = (x <= 0);
 8        i = (x >= 0);
 9        i = (x > 0);
10        i = (-2 < x);
11        i = (x == -1);
12        i = (x == -1U);
13    }
```

(5) warning: suspicious comparison of unsigned with negative
      constant: op ">"
(6) warning: suspicious comparison of unsigned with 0: op "<"
(7) warning: suspicious comparison of unsigned with 0: op "<="
(8) warning: suspicious comparison of unsigned with 0: op ">="
(9) warning: suspicious comparison of unsigned with 0: op ">"
(10) warning: suspicious comparison of unsigned with negative
      constant: op "<"
(11) warning: suspicious comparison of unsigned with negative
      constant: op "=="

too few arguments for format

Format: Compound

A control string of a [fs]printf() or [fs]scanf() function call had more
conversion specifications than there were arguments remaining in the call. (See
also /* PRINTFLIKE*n* */ and /* SCANFLIKE*n* */ in the list of directives in the
"Usage" section above.)

```
1    #include <stdio.h>
2    main ()
3    {
4         int i;
5         printf("%d%d", i);
6    }
```

```
too few arguments for format
     printf        test.c(5)
```

too many arguments for format

Format: Compound

A control string of a [fs]printf() or [fs]scanf() function call had fewer conversion specifications than there were arguments remaining in the call. (See also /* PRINTFLIKE*n* */ and /* SCANFLIKE*n* */ in the list of directives in the "Usage" section above.)

```
1    #include <stdio.h>
2    main ()
3    {
4         int i, j;
5         printf("%d", i, j);
6    }
```

```
too many arguments for format
     printf        test.c(5)
```

value type declared inconsistently

Format: Compound

The return type in a function declaration or definition did not match the return type in another declaration or definition of the function. The message is also issued for inconsistent declarations of variable types.

ANSI C and Programming Support Tools

file f1.c
```
1    void fun() {}
2    void foo();
3    extern int a;
```
file f2.c
```
1    extern int fun();
2    extern int foo();
3    extern char a;
```
══════════

```
value type declared inconsistently
       fun          f1.c(1) void() :: f2.c(1) int()
       foo          f1.c(2) void() :: f2.c(2) int()
       a            f1.c(3) int :: f2.c(3) char
```

`value type used inconsistently`

Format: Compound

The return type in a function call did not match the return type in the function definition.

file f1.c
```
1    int *fun(p)
2    int *p;
3    {
4        return p;
5    }
```
file f2.c
```
1    main()
2    {
3        int i, *p;
4        i = fun(p);
5    }
```
══════════

```
value type used inconsistently
       fun          f1.c(3) int *() :: f2.c(4) int()
```

variable may be used before set: *name*

Format: Simple

The first reference to an automatic, non-array variable occurred at a line number earlier than the first assignment to the variable. Note that taking the address of a variable implies both a set and a use, and that the first assignment to any member of a struct or union implies an assignment to the entire struct or union.

```
1    void fun()
2    {
3          int i, j, k;
4          static int x;
5          k = j;
6          i = i + 1;
7          x = x + 1;
8    }
```

```
(5)  warning: variable may be used before set: j
(6)  warning: variable may be used before set: i
```

variable unused in function

Format: Compound

A variable was declared but never used in a function.

```
1    void fun()
2    {
3          int x, y;
4          static z;
5    }
```

```
variable unused in function
     (4)  z in fun
     (3)  y in fun
     (3)  x in fun
```

6 sdb

Introduction

The symbolic debugger sdb is a source-level debugging program that lets you interactively reference variables and the program statements in which they occur by their symbolic names and line numbers in your C source code. You can also use sdb to debug C and assembly language programs at the machine level.

You typically want to debug a program in two situations. sdb was designed to work in both of them.

- *Postmortem debugging.* When the UNIX system aborts an executing program, it creates in your current directory a file called core that contains the current memory image of the process at the time of the failure. You receive a message such as

      Memory Fault - core dumped

  which means that the program tried to reference an area of memory that it was not allowed to — a pointer pointed somewhere wild, for instance — or

      Bus Error - core dumped

  typically caused by scanning a non-terminated string. core dumped means that the system saved the core image of the process in the file core. You then use sdb to examine the image, usually by printing a stack trace: the function that was executing when the process died, the function that called it, and so forth. That way you can check each function for variables with unexpected values.

- *Debugging a live process.* Sometimes you need to do more than examine a core image file to locate a problem in a process that has aborted. And, of course, programs can also fail by running to completion with unexpected results. In these cases, you can use sdb to examine and change the values of variables as each statement in your program executes or as sections of the program execute up to preset breakpoints. You can trace back variables from these breakpoints and, in general, stop and restart your program as you see fit. In the case of a program that has aborted, sdb lets you examine the core image file, then start a live process in the same session, so you can see what your program was doing up to the point at which it failed.

We'll show you how to do these things below. First we'll look at sdb's command line syntax, then at the interactive commands you can use to examine a core image file or monitor and control a live process. We'll close with an extended example.

Command Line Syntax

To use sdb to full advantage you must compile your program with the –g
option:

```
$ cc -g -o prog prog.c
```

–g tells the compiler and link editor to store in your executable information
about the names of variables and functions in your program, and their line
numbers in your source code. (When you have finished debugging your program, you can remove the debugging information with the strip command,
described in Section 1 of the *Programmer's Reference Manual*. strip removes
other information as well, so you may want simply to recompile the program
without –g.) Because optimization will occasionally confuse sdb, it's best, as a
general rule, not to compile your program with both –g and –O. All the same,
there may be times when an unoptimized program that appears to have executed correctly will fail after it has been optimized. (An optimized program
with an uninitialized variable, for example, will probably misbehave, even
though its unoptimized version produced an apparently correct result earlier.)
In situations like this, it's usually better to recompile the program with both –g
and –O. Although you will have to make some adjustments for optimization —
you may not be able to set breakpoints in all the places you set them before, for
example — you will be able to debug the program at the source rather than the
assembly language level. Note that you can link object files that were compiled
with –g with object files that were compiled without it.

Now we'll execute the program we compiled in the previous example:

```
$ prog
Memory Fault - core dumped
```

To examine the executable program and its core image, you use the following
command:

```
$ sdb prog
```

sdb accepts three command line arguments. The first is the name of the executable file to be debugged, or whose core image is to be debugged; it defaults to
a.out when not specified. The second is the name of the core file to be
debugged, defaulting to core. The third is a list of colon-separated directories
containing the source files of the executable; the default is the current directory.
In the example, the second and third arguments defaulted to the correct values,
so only the first was specified.

You can also use sdb to "grab" an executing process, that is, stop it temporarily so that you can examine it under sdb control. Suppose, for instance, you are running the program myprog in the background. You notice that a portion of it is executing more slowly than you think it should. You want to look at that portion with sdb without killing the process. You enter the command

> $ sdb /proc/12345

where /proc is the UNIX system directory that contains information about each process currently active on your system, and 12345 is the process ID of the program myprog. (You can use the ps command, described in Section 1 of the *User's Reference Manual*, to determine the process ID of any process currently active on your system.) The process stops at the first system call it executes or signal it receives after the sdb command is invoked. You then use sdb to examine the values of variables, set breakpoints, resume execution, stop at breakpoints, and so on. When you quit sdb, control returns to the program. That is, the process continues execution where it left off.

Occasionally, the core file of another program may be in the directory of an executable you want to run under control of sdb. When you specify a hyphen as the second argument

> $ sdb myprog −

you tell sdb to ignore the core image file.

Ordinarily, sdb will stop a live process when the process receives a signal. When you specify a signal number with the −s option

> $ sdb −s 14 myprog

you tell sdb not to stop the process for that signal. The signal is passed to the process. You should use −s if your program will receive and handle numerous signals.

When you use the −w option

> $ sdb −w myprog

sdb lets you edit the executable or core file to be debugged.

Interactive Commands

When you use sdb to examine an executable file, it prompts you with an asterisk (*), which shows that it is waiting for a command. When you use it to examine a core image file, such as the one in the previous section, its output will look something like this:

```
sub:30:         z[i] = 0;
    *
```

sdb reports that the program quit at line 30 in the function sub () and displays the source text of the offending line. It then prompts you to continue. Line numbers are always counted relative to the beginning of the file and include comments and blank lines. sdb has a notion of current file and current function, and when the file was compiled with –g, of current line. If you are debugging an executable file, sdb sets the current function and line to main () and the first line of main (), respectively. If you are debugging a core image file, it sets the current line and function to the last line and function that were executed — in the example, 30 and sub (), respectively. In the latter case, if the function was not compiled with –g, sdb prints a warning to that effect and displays the function name and the address at which the error occurred.

Once you have received the * prompt, you can proceed as you like. You can examine the core image file, for instance, or set a breakpoint and start a live process. In the next three sections, we'll look at tasks common to debugging core files and live processes: printing a stack trace, examining the values of variables, and displaying source files. Since these are pretty much the only things you can do in debugging core, we'll concentrate after that on how you debug a live process.

Printing a Stack Trace

To trace function calls in a stopped process or a core image file, you use the t command. In the following example, assume we are debugging core:

```
*t
sub(x=2,y=3)         [prog.c:25]
inter(i=16012)       [prog.c:96]
main(argc=1,argv=0x7fffff54,envp=0x7fffff5c)  [prog.c:15]
    _start()
```

sdb's output shows that the function sub () at line 25 in the file prog.c was called with the integer arguments x and y from inter () at line 96. inter ()

was called from main() at line 15. main() is always called by a startup routine named _start(), and accepts three arguments, conventionally referred to as argc, argv, and envp (see "How C Programs Communicate with the Shell" in Chapter 1 for a discussion). argv and envp are pointers, so their values are printed in hexadecimal. Argument values are printed in hexadecimal regardless of type if the source file was not compiled with −g.

Examining Variables

You can display the value of a variable by entering its name followed by the / command:

```
*errflag/
```

Unless otherwise specified, variables are assumed to be either local to or accessible from the current function. To specify a different function, enter the name of the function and a colon before the name of the variable:

```
*inter:i/
```

sdb will display the value of the variable i in the function inter(). We'll show you how to change the current function in the next section.

To display the address of the variable i in inter(), you can specify

```
*inter:i=
```

An easier way to do it is to enter

```
*.=
```

The period tells sdb to look for the last variable entered, in this case, i in inter(). So

```
*./
```

tells sdb to redisplay the value of i in inter().

sdb supports a limited form of pattern matching for variable and function names. The symbol * is used to match any sequence of characters of a variable name, the symbol ? to match any single character. Consider the following commands:

```
*x*/
*inter:y?/
**/
```

The first prints the values of all variables local to or accessible from the current function that begin with x. The second prints the values of all two-letter variables local to or accessible from the function inter() that begin with y. The last prints the values of all variables local to or accessible from the current function.

If you have multiple calls to a function, you can display the value of a variable in a given call by using a comma as follows:

```
*inter:*,2/
```

That command displays the values of all variables in the second call to inter() from the top of the stack. The command

```
**:*/
```

displays the values of variables in each function on the call stack. Note that you cannot use the metacharacters * and ? in any command that specifies a line number, or in the commands to call a function, change the current function, or set a watchpoint. Nor can you use them to match a file name.

sdb normally displays the value of a variable in a format determined by its type as declared in the source program. To request a different format, you place a specifier after the /. The specifier consists of an optional length specifier followed by a format specifier. The length specifiers are:

b   One byte

h   Two bytes (half word)

1   Four bytes (long word)

The format specifiers are:

c   Character

d   Decimal

u   Decimal unsigned

o   Octal

x   Hexadecimal

f   32-bit single-precision floating point

g   64-bit double-precision floating point

s   Assume variable is a string pointer and print characters starting at the address pointed to by the variable until a null is reached.

a   Print characters starting at the variable's address until a null is reached.

p   Pointer to function.

i   Interpret as a machine-language instruction.

So, to display the value of i in hexadecimal, you enter

        `*inter:i/x`

or, more simply,

        `*./x`

provided i in inter() was the last variable entered.

The length specifiers are effective only with the format specifiers d, o, x, and u. If no length is specified, sdb uses the length for the type of the object being examined. A number can be entered with the s or a format specifiers to control the number of characters printed. The s and a specifiers normally print characters until either a null is reached or 128 characters have been printed. The number specifies exactly how many characters should be printed. So

        `*str/10s`

tells sdb to print ten characters starting at the address pointed to by the variable str.

sdb also knows about C structures, arrays, and pointers, so that all of the following commands work:

        `*array[2][3]/`
        `*sym.id/`
        `*psym->usage/`
        `*xsym[20].p->usage/`

The only restriction is that array subscripts must be a number, *, or a range. (A range is two numbers separated by a semicolon.) Note that as a special case

    `*psym[0]`

displays the structure pointed to by psym.

You can display the contents of core locations by specifying their absolute addresses. The command

    `*1024/`

displays the contents of location 1024 in decimal. As in C, numbers can also be specified in octal or hexadecimal so the above command is equivalent to both

    `*02000/`

and

    `*0x400/`

You can mix numbers and variables, so that

    `*1000.x/`

refers to an element of a structure starting at address 1000, and

    `*1000->x/`

refers to an element of a structure whose address is at 1000. For commands of the type *1000.x/ and *1000->x/, sdb uses the structure template of the last structure referenced.

You can print the value of a specified register, say r3, with the command

    `*%r3/`

The x command prints the current instruction and the values of all registers.

If you are debugging a live process, you can set the value of a variable or a register with the ! command. To set the value of the variable i to 10, for example, you enter

    `*inter:i!10`

To set the value of the register r3 to 10, you enter

    `*%r3!10`

The value can be a number, a character constant — specified by *character* — or another variable. (You can set a character to any of the C language escape sequences described in the section "Source Files and Tokenization" of Chapter 3.) The value must be well-defined; expressions that produce more than one value are not allowed, except when assigning a structure to a variable of the same type. Numbers are treated as integers unless a decimal point or exponent is used, in which case they are treated as having the type double. Register values, except those for floating-point registers, are treated as integers. If the address of a variable is given, it is regarded as the address of a variable of type int. C language conventions govern any type conversions necessary to perform the indicated assignment.

File Display and Manipulation

sdb has been designed to make it easy to debug a program without constant reference to a current source listing. You can use it to display, and perform context searches in, the source files of the executable you are debugging or whose core image you are debugging. The commands are similar to those of the UNIX system text editor ed. Like the editor, sdb has a notion of current file and current line. sdb also knows how the lines of a file are partitioned into functions, so it also has a notion of current function.

Five commands exist for displaying lines in a file:

l	Print the line corresponding to the current instruction.
p	Print the current line.
w	Print a window of ten lines around the current line.
z	Print ten lines starting at the current line.
control-d	Print the next ten lines.

When a line from a file is printed, it is preceded by its line number. You can use line numbers as input to some sdb commands.

z and control-d advance the current line by nine and ten, respectively. You can also use the + and − commands to move the current line forward or backward, respectively, a specified number of lines. If the last command displayed source, a carriage return advances the current line by one. Entering a line number by itself causes that line to become the current line. You can combine these commands with the display commands, so that

```
*+15z
```

advances the current line by 15, prints ten lines starting with the current line, then advances the current line by nine. Note that the current line determines the current function.

To change the current source file, you use the e command:

```
*e file.c
```

causes the named file to become current. The current line is set to the first line of the named file. If the first line of the file is a function, that function becomes current. Otherwise, there is no current function. If the directory of the file is not in the search path, you use e to add its path name to the search path. The path name must be followed by a /:

```
*e /home/tm/
*e file.c
```

You can also change the current file with the command

```
*e function
```

which causes the named function to become the current function, and the file containing it to become the current file. The current line becomes the first line of the function. If the directory of the file containing the function is not in the search path, you must add its name to the search path as described above. Note that you can use this form of the e command to change the current function in a core file. Note, finally, that an e command with no arguments causes the names of the current function and file to be printed.

You can use two commands to search for instances of a regular expression in a file:

```
*/regular expression/
*?regular expression?
```

The first searches forward through the file for a line containing a string that matches the regular expression; the second searches backward. In either case, the search wraps around. The current line becomes the line containing the matched string. The trailing / and ? can be omitted, provided they are not embedded in a command associated with a breakpoint. Regular expression matching is identical to that of ed.

Debugging a Live Process

As we noted earlier, you can use sdb to examine and change the values of variables as each statement in your program executes, or as sections of the program execute up to preset breakpoints. To do either of these things, you must set at least one breakpoint before you start the program — otherwise you will not be able to stop it. If, for example, you are stepping through your program on a statement-by-statement basis, you might set a breakpoint at the first executable line of main(). The command

    *main:b

does exactly that. If the first executable line of main() is line 3 of your current file, the command

    *3b

does the same thing. So does

    *b

if the line is the current line, and

    *main:3b

if line 3 of the current file occurs in main(). You can set a breakpoint at any executable statement of a function compiled with −g, and at any function whether or not it was compiled with −g. Of course, you can set as many breakpoints as you like before you execute your program, and as many as you like while your live process is stopped. We'll show you how to delete breakpoints below.

Now you are ready to run the program:

    *r *args*

That command runs the program with the given arguments as if they had been entered on the shell command line. If no arguments are specified, the arguments from sdb's last execution of the program are used. In other words, you can start your program again in the same sdb session, creating a new live process, by specifying r without arguments. To run a program with no arguments, you use the R command.

Once the program starts, execution continues until a breakpoint is encountered, a watchpoint condition occurs (we'll explain watchpoints in a moment), a signal such as INTERRUPT or QUIT is received, or the process terminates. In all cases, after an appropriate message is printed, control returns to you.

Now that our program has stopped at the first executable line of main(), we can execute that line — step through it — with the s command:

```
*s
```

The S command works the same way except that it does not stop in called functions. You use it when you are sure that the called function works correctly, and want to test the calling routine. Both s and S take as an argument a count of the number of statements to be executed. So, at the first executable statement of main(), the command

```
*s 2
```

will cause that and the next executable statement to be executed. Note that if you are single-stepping with s or S, and sdb reaches a function that was not compiled with −g, it will continue execution until a function is reached that was compiled with −g.

In these situations, you can use the i command to run your program one machine-level instruction at a time. sdb will ignore any signal that stopped the program. The I command does the same thing except that it passes the signal that stopped the program back to the program. We'll talk a bit more about signal handling in a moment. We'll look at machine-level debugging later in the chapter.

Now suppose we are done stepping through our program and are ready to run it to another breakpoint. Once a live process has stopped, you can resume its execution with the c (for "continue") command:

```
*c
```

When you enter a line number before c

```
*9c
```

sdb places a breakpoint at the named line in your current file, and resumes execution. When execution stops at that line, the breakpoint is deleted. In contrast, when you specify

```
*c 9
```

sdb continues execution until the ninth breakpoint is encountered. In either case, it will ignore any signal that stopped the program.

The C command does the same thing except that it passes the signal that stopped the program back to the program. That can be useful in testing user-written signal handlers. As we have noted, the −s option can be used on the sdb command line to specify the number of a signal that will automatically be sent to a live process without stopping it. Again, you should use it if your program will receive and handle numerous signals.

You can tell sdb to continue execution at a given line with the g command:

```
*3g
```

That command causes execution to resume at line 3 of the current file. sdb will resume execution at that line and skip two breakpoints with the command

```
*3g 2
```

You should be sure not to resume execution in a function different from that in which the process was stopped, or at a line that bypasses needed initializations. Generally speaking, you should try to avoid using g unless you are sure that the section of code you are skipping is bad.

Except for the breakpoint counts, the syntax of c, C, and g is identical to that of b. So

```
*main:6c
```

tells sdb to continue execution until it reaches the breakpoint it set at line 6 in main().

The syntax is also the same to delete breakpoints with the d command:

```
*main:d
```

for example, tells sdb to delete the breakpoint at the first executable line of main(). If the d command is given by itself, breakpoints are deleted interactively; as the location of each breakpoint is printed, you enter y or d to remove it. The D command deletes all breakpoints; the B command lists them.

sdb will set a breakpoint, and when it reaches it, automatically perform a sequence of commands when you specify the b command with a so-called "associated command":

```
*12b t;x/;c
```

That directs sdb, first, to set a breakpoint at line 12 of the current file, then to print a stack trace and display the value of the variable x each time it reaches the breakpoint. You can use the a (for "announce") command to do something similar:

        *function:a

tells sdb to print the name of the specified function and its arguments each time it is called. The command

        *function:12a

tells sdb to print line 12 in the specified function each time the line is about to be executed.

You can call a function in either of two ways:

        *proc(arg1, arg2, . . .)
        *proc(arg1, arg2, . . .)/m

The first simply executes the function, the second executes the function and displays the value it returns. The value is printed in decimal unless some other format is specified by *m*. Arguments to functions may be register names, integers, floating point, character, or string constants, or variables local to or accessible from the current function. You can use this feature to test the same function with different arguments or to call a user-supplied function that prints structured data.

Finally, you can use watchpoints to monitor changes in the value of a variable or the contents of an address. In the former case, you set the watchpoint with the command

        *x$m

where x is the variable to be monitored; in the latter, with the command

        *1024:m

where 1024 is the address to be monitored. sdb will begin single-stepping as with the s command, and stop when the value of the variable or the contents of the address have changed. If they have, or if the process stops for any other reason, including a breakpoint, the watchpoint is deleted automatically. The variable must be local to or accessible from the current function.

The following is a summary of sdb commands discussed in this section:

r   Run the program.

R   Run the program with no arguments.

s   Step through one or more program statements.

S   Same as s except step over function calls.

i   Step through one or more machine-level instructions.

I   Same as i except pass the signal that stopped the program back to the program.

c   Continue execution.

C   Same as c except pass the signal that stopped the program back to the program.

g   Continue execution at a given line.

b   Set a breakpoint.

a   Announce a line or a function and its arguments.

B   List all breakpoints.

D   Delete all breakpoints.

d   Delete a breakpoint.

m   Set a watchpoint.

Machine Language Debugging

As we noted in the previous section, you can use the i or I commands to step through your program one machine-level instruction at a time. These and the commands described below effectively disassemble your program for machine-level debugging. That is, you can use sdb to display the machine language statements associated with a line in your source program and to place breakpoints at arbitrary addresses. You can also use it to display or modify the contents of machine registers, as described in "Examining Variables" above.

To display the machine language statements associated with line 25 in main(), for example, you use the command

    *main:25?

The ? command is identical to the / command except that it displays from text space. The default format for printing text space is given by the i specifier, described in "Examining Variables" above. You can use control-d to print the next ten instructions.

Absolute addresses can be specified instead of line numbers by appending a colon to them, so that

    *0x1024:?

displays the instruction at address 0x1024 in text space. Note that the command

    *0x1024?

displays the first instruction corresponding to line 0x1024 in the current file.

You can set or delete a breakpoint by specifying its absolute address:

    *0x1024:b

for example, sets a breakpoint at address 0x1024.

As noted, the x command prints the current instruction and the values of all registers; X prints the current instruction.

Exiting

To quit sdb, use the q command:

    *q

The ! command, when used immediately after the * prompt, is identical to that in ed and is used to execute a shell command. Other commands are described on the sdb page in Section 1 of the *Programmer's Reference Manual*.

Example

Figure 6-2 shows how you can use sdb to debug an aborted program. The source code for the program is shown in Figure 6-1. The program consists of a main() routine and a recursively called function foo(). The number of calls to foo() is determined by the argument passed in argv[1]. That is, an argument of 50 causes 50 calls to foo(), an argument of 150 causes 150 calls, and so on. We have inserted line numbers in the source code and comments in the sdb output to help you follow the session. Note that the example is for the 3B2. Register names and other processor-specific information would be different on the 6386.

Figure 6-1: Source Program c_recurse.c

```
1    #define        DEFAULT_MAX        150
2    int call_max;
3    int ab_val = 0;
4
5    void foo(int);
6
7    main(argc, argv)
8    int argc;
9    char *argv[];
10   {
11       int start_stack=1;
12
13       if (argc < 2)
14               call_max = DEFAULT_MAX;
15       else
16               call_max = atoi(argv[1]);
17
18       foo (start_stack);
19
20   }
21
22   void foo(keepcalling)
23   int keepcalling;
24   {
25
26       if (keepcalling <= call_max) {
27               if (keepcalling == 8)
28                       /* forces a core dump, for example */
29                       ab_val = keepcalling/ab_val;
30               else {
31                       keepcalling++;
32                       foo(keepcalling);
33               }
34       }
35       return;
36   }
```

Example _____

_____

Figure 6-2: sdb Usage Example

```
$ cc -g c_recurse.c
$ a.out
Arithmetic Exception - core dumped
$ sdb
29:                   ab_val = keepcalling/ab_val;
*t                          # print stack trace
foo(keepcalling=8)    [c_recurse.c:29]
foo(keepcalling=8)    [c_recurse.c:32]
foo(keepcalling=7)    [c_recurse.c:32]
foo(keepcalling=6)    [c_recurse.c:32]
foo(keepcalling=5)    [c_recurse.c:32]
foo(keepcalling=4)    [c_recurse.c:32]
foo(keepcalling=3)    [c_recurse.c:32]
foo(keepcalling=2)    [c_recurse.c:32]
main(argc=1,argv=0xc00201c0,0xc00201c8) [c_recurse.c:18]
_start()
*x                          # print register set and current instruction
%r0         0x1        %r1         0x180       %r2         0x25
%r3         0x7d3  %r4            0        %r5     0x8001ef8a
%r6     0x8001ef0f      %r7     0x8001ef8a      %r8     0x8001ed14
%fp     0xc00203c8      %ap     0xc00203a0      %psw     0x1f03
%sp     0xc00203c8      %pcbp   0xc000007c      %isp        0
%pc     0x8000044e      %asr    0x80000000
%dr     0x00020000_02000000_00000000 - 0
%x0     0x00000000_00000000_00000000 - 0
%x1     0x00000000_00000000_00000000 - 0
%x2     0x00000000_00000000_00000000 - 0
%x3     0x00000000_00000000_00000000 - 0
0x8000044e (foo:29)    DIVW3   $0x8000247c,(%ap),%r0   [0x8000247c,(%ap),%r0]
*1                          # print line corresponding to current instruction
29:                   ab_val = keepcalling/ab_val;
*X                          # print current instruction
0x8000044e (foo:29)    DIVW3   $0x8000247c,(%ap),%r0   [0x8000247c,(%ap),%r0]
*p                          # print current line
29:                   ab_val = keepcalling/ab_val;
*keepcalling/               # print value of keepcalling, all foos
foo:keepcalling/8
foo:keepcalling/8
foo:keepcalling/7
foo:keepcalling/6
foo:keepcalling/5
foo:keepcalling/4
foo:keepcalling/3
foo:keepcalling/2
```

(continued on next page)

ANSI C and Programming Support Tools

Figure 6-2: sdb Usage Example (continued)

```
*foo:*,1                      # print values of all variables, top foo
foo:keepcalling/8
foo:ab_val/0
Assuming foo:main is int
foo:main/0x10499c4f
Assuming foo:foo is int
foo:foo/0x10499c4f
foo:call_max/150
:ab_val/0
Assuming :main is int
:main/0x10499c4f
Assuming :foo is int
:foo/0x10499c4f
:call_max/150
*foo:keepcalling,3            # print value of keepcalling, third foo
foo:keepcalling/7
*foo:ab_val,1/x              # print ab_val in hex format, top foo
foo:ab_val/0
:ab_val/0
*foo:b                        # set a breakpoint
0x80000437   c_recurse.c:24    foo
*r 10                         # run with an argument of 10 calls to foo
BREAKPOINT process 12465 function foo() in c_recurse.c
24:     {
*c 7                          # continue to 7th breakpoint
BREAKPOINT process 12465 function foo() in c_recurse.c
24:     {
*s                            # single step to see error
STEPPED process 12465 function foo() in c_recurse.c
26:           if (keepcalling <= call_max) {
*foo:keepcalling,1           # check keepcalling -- is value 8?
foo:keepcalling/8
*w                            # see the code -- confirm offending lines 27 & 29
21:
22:     void foo (keepcalling)
23:     int keepcalling;
24:     {
25:
26:           if (keepcalling <= call_max) {
27:                 if (keepcalling == 8)
28:                     /* forces a core dump, for example */
29:                   ab_val = keepcalling/ab_val;
30:               else {
*keepcalling!9                # set to 9 instead of 8, avoid dump at line 29
```

(continued on next page)

Figure 6-2: sdb Usage Example (continued)

```
foo:keepcalling/9
foo:keepcalling/8
foo:keepcalling/7
foo:keepcalling/6
foo:keepcalling/5
foo:keepcalling/4
foo:keepcalling/3
foo:keepcalling/2
*c;c;c                          # should terminate normally, could quit here
BREAKPOINT process 12465 function foo() in c_recurse.c
24:     {
BREAKPOINT process 12465 function foo() in c_recurse.c
24:     {
Process 12465 has terminated.
*q                              # know the problem, quit sdb
```

7 lprof

Overview of C Profiling Utilities

Profilers are tools that analyze the dynamic behavior of your program: how fast and how often the parts of its code are executed when the program is run. First, the profilers interpret data that have been collected about that behavior at run time; then they display the interpreted data in a format you choose from a number of options.

Two complementary utilities are available for profiling C source programs:

- prof is a time profiler. It reports the amount of time and the percentage of time that was spent executing the parts of a program. It also reports the number of calls to each function and the average execution time of the calls. For an example of prof output, see Figure 7-4 below.

- lprof is a line-by-line frequency profiler. It reports whether and how many times each line of source code was executed. In other words, it lets you identify the unexecuted and most frequently executed parts of your code. For an example of lprof output, see Figure 7-1 below.

The profilers are complementary in this sense. You can use prof to identify the most time-consuming parts of a program. You can then use lprof to obtain line-specific information only about those parts. In that way, you can avoid generating uninformative output while targeting the lines of code whose performance needs to be improved. You may then be able to rewrite those lines to execute more efficiently.

We'll see an example of this approach in the section "Improving Program Performance" below. For now it's enough to note that this complementary use of the profilers takes the guesswork out of determining the small part of code that usually accounts for a high percentage of run time.

We'll also look at ways of improving test coverage with lprof. By default, lprof displays source code line by line with a count of the number of times each line was executed, 0 if a line was never executed. You can obtain a summary of coverage by invoking lprof with the −s option. The summary reports the percentage of lines of code that were exercised for each function, by a test suite or otherwise. You may then want to highlight the unexecuted lines in functions with less than 100% coverage. The −x option to lprof causes it to generate a source listing in which only unexecuted lines are marked. See the sections "Invoking lprof" and "Improving Test Coverage" below for details.

One last feature of lprof ought to be mentioned here. You can obtain a more representative sample of a program's dynamic behavior by running it more than once, then invoking lprof with its merging options to obtain sums of the execution counts for the multiple runs. You can do the same thing by setting the environment variable PROFOPTS to its merging option before you run the program. See the sections "Running the Profiled Program," "Invoking lprof," and "Profiling Archive or Shared Object Library Code" below for details.

How to Use the Profilers

To use either of these profilers, you must follow a three-step procedure:

Step 1:   Compile and link the program with a profiling option:

        for prof: $ cc −qp (or −p)
        for lprof: $ cc −ql

    The rules stated in the next section for compiling and linking a program with −ql (lprof) are identical for −qp (prof).

Step 2:   Run the profiled program. At the end of execution, run-time data are written to a file known as a data file. A data file consists of a header section, a section for each function, and an end of data marker. The coverage datum (execution count) for each function is recorded beside the name of the function. Data files have the following default names:

        for prof: mon.out
        for lprof: *prog*.cnt

    where *prog* is the name of the profiled program. For prof, the PROFDIR environment variable and, for lprof, the PROFOPTS environment variable enable you to specify names other than mon.out and *prog*.cnt, respectively. They also allow you to write data files to a directory other than the current directory and, when they are set to the null string, to turn off profiling.

Step 3:   Execute the prof or lprof commands. By default, both profilers expect a.out as the input. Both permit specification of a differently named program on the command line (for lprof, as an argument to the −o option), and both accept data files as input (for prof, as an argument to the −m option; for lprof, as an argument to the −c option).

In the next four sections, we'll take a closer look at the steps you must follow to profile a program with lprof. For further details of prof usage, check the manual page in Section 1 of the *Programmer's Reference Manual.*

Compiling the Program

Suppose you have a program that consists of the source files `travel.c` and `misc.c`. As we have seen, you must compile your source files with the −ql option to profile a program with `lprof`:

```
$ cc −ql −o travel travel.c misc.c
```

When you specify −ql, you arrange for data about your program's run-time behavior to be written to a data file at the end of execution.

If you compile and link your program in separate steps, you must specify −ql when you link as well as when you compile:

```
$ cc −ql −c travel.c
$ cc −ql −c misc.c
$ cc −ql −o travel travel.o misc.o
```

See the section "Invoking `lprof`" below for the options you must specify to use the profiler on a program with a name other than `a.out`.

These command lines illustrate what you must do to profile an entire program. You may be interested in profiling only a piece of a large program. Suppose, for instance, you have run `prof` on both source files and found out that 70% of the total execution time can be accounted for by one function in `travel.c`. Now you want to examine that function with `lprof` to determine how you can improve its performance. To produce profiling data only for `travel.c`, you enter the commands

```
$ cc −ql −c travel.c
$ cc −c misc.c
$ cc −ql −o travel travel.o misc.o
```

Note, finally, that the −ql option overrides the −O option. That is, the command

```
$ cc −ql −O −o travel travel.c misc.c
```

will not invoke the optimizer. Of course, you can optimize your program after you have profiled it by recompiling your source files with −O and without −ql.

Running the Profiled Program

When you execute the profiled program

```
$ travel
```

run-time data are written to the data file `travel.cnt` in your current directory. The following message is printed to `stderr`:

```
dumping profiling data from process 'travel' . . .
        CNTFILE 'travel.cnt' created
```

The PROFOPTS Environment Variable

The environment variable `PROFOPTS` provides run-time control over profiling. When the profiled program is about to terminate execution, it examines the value of `PROFOPTS` to determine how the profiling data are to be handled.

The `PROFOPTS` environment variable is a comma-separated list of options interpreted by the program being profiled. If `PROFOPTS` is not defined in the environment, then the default action is taken: the profiling data are saved in *prog*.cnt in the current directory. If `PROFOPTS` is set to the null string, no profiling data are produced.

The following options can be specified in `PROFOPTS`. They are explained in more detail in the section "Examples of Using `PROFOPTS`" below.

msg=y|n	If `msg=y` is specified, print a message to `stderr` stating that profiling data are being created. If `msg=n` is specified, print only profiling error messages. The default is `msg=y`.
merge=y|n	If `merge=n` is specified, do not merge data files after successive runs; the data file will be overwritten after each execution. If `merge=y` is specified, the data will be merged. The merge will fail if the program has been recompiled between runs; the data file associated with the second run will be stored in `TMPDIR`. The default is `merge=n`.

pid=y|n	If pid=y is specified, the name of the data file will include the process ID of the profiled program. This allows the creation of different data files for programs calling fork(2). If pid=n is specified, the default name is used. The default is pid=n.
dir=*dir*	Store the data file in the directory *dir*. Otherwise the data file is created in the directory that is current at the end of execution.
file=*file*	Use *file* as the name of the data file. Otherwise the default name is used. (See "Profiling within a Shell Script" for an example.)

Examples of Using PROFOPTS

The following sections provide examples of how PROFOPTS might be used to tailor the environment to specific tasks.

Turning Off Profiling

If you do not want to profile a particular run, you can set PROFOPTS to the null string when you execute the profiled program:

```
$ PROFOPTS="" travel
```

Because you did not export PROFOPTS, this value will remain in effect for only one execution of the program. If you want to turn off profiling for more than one program and/or run, export the value of PROFOPTS:

```
$ PROFOPTS="" export PROFOPTS
$ travel
```

Exporting the variable eliminates the need to specify it every time you execute travel. It also makes the value of PROFOPTS applicable to all runs of any profiled program, not just travel. Once you have exported PROFOPTS, it keeps the value you have given it until you unset or redefine the variable.

Merging Data Files

Suppose you are not interested in the data from a single run; you want the information collected from all runs. A data file that contains information from multiple executions is called a merged data file. When data files are merged, the line execution counts for all runs are added together arithmetically.

The following screen shows how you must specify the environment if you want your data files from successive runs to be merged:

```
$ PROFOPTS="merge=y" export PROFOPTS
$ travel

        dumping profiling data from process 'travel' . . .
            CNTFILE 'travel.cnt' created

$ travel

        dumping profiling data from process 'travel' . . .
            CNTFILE 'travel.cnt' updated
```

As noted, the merge will fail if the program has been recompiled between runs; the data file associated with the second run will be stored in TMPDIR, and its path name will be printed to stderr. See the section "Invoking lprof" below for command line options to lprof that enable you to merge existing data files of a recompiled program.

Keeping Data Files in a Separate Directory

To avoid clutter in your current directory, you may want to create a directory specifically for data files. When you assign that directory to the PROFOPTS environment variable, your data files will be created in that directory:

```
$ PROFOPTS="dir=cntfiles" travel
```

In this case, travel.cnt will be created in the directory cntfiles.

Profiling within a Shell Script

You may want to write a shell script that runs a profiled program automatically. That could be useful for tasks you perform frequently, such as determining test coverage. In that case,

- you might not want to receive notification that profiling data are being created;

- you might want to have data from successive runs merged automatically;

- you might want to give the data file a name you can associate with a given test case.

You can specify these conditions in PROFOPTS as follows:

```
$ PROFOPTS="msg=n,merge=y,file=test1.cnt" prog < test1
```

In this example, the profiling data will be written to a merged data file with the name test1.cnt rather than the default name myprog.cnt.

Profiling Programs That Fork

If a profiled program uses the system call fork(), the data files of both the parent and child processes will have the same name by default. You can avoid that by using the PROFOPTS option pid. By setting pid to y, you insure that the data file name will include the process ID of the program being profiled. As a result, multiple data files will be created, each with a unique name.

What happens when you run a program that forks without using the pid option? If you have set merge=y, the data will be merged; data from separate processes will be indistinguishable. If you have set merge=n, the last process to dump data will overwrite the data file.

The following screen shows how the pid option works, where forkprog is a program that uses fork():

ANSI C and Programming Support Tools

```
$ PROFOPTS="pid=y" forkprog

        dumping profiling data from process 'forkprog' . . .
                CNTFILE '922.forkprog.cnt' created

        dumping profiling data from process 'forkprog' . . .
                CNTFILE '923.forkprog.cnt' created
```

Invoking lprof

lprof correlates the data file with the profiled program to produce its report. By default, lprof expects the profiled program to be called a.out and the data file a.out.cnt. If the default names are used, and both the profiled program and the data file are in your current directory, you invoke lprof without arguments:

    $ lprof

If the program and data file are in a different directory, you specify their paths relative to the current directory with the −o and −c options, respectively:

    $ lprof −o *dir*/a.out −c *dir*/a.out.cnt

To invoke lprof for a program with a name other than a.out, you specify its name after the −o option:

    $ lprof −o travel

lprof will assume the data file is called travel.cnt.

You can also invoke lprof for the data file. You specify the name of the data file after the −c option:

    $ lprof −c travel.cnt

The name of the profiled program is stored in the data file exactly as it appeared on the command line when the program was run. When the −c option is invoked, lprof consults the data file for the name of the profiled program. That is, even if run-time data have been written to a data file other than the default *prog*.cnt — say, to a data file whose name you have specified in the PROFOPTS environment variable — lprof will be able to determine the name of the profiled program with which the data file is to be correlated. Because the name of the data file is not stored in the profiled program, however, the reverse is not true: you cannot specify the name of the program and expect lprof to determine the name of the data file if it is other than *prog*.cnt.

The simplest way to invoke lprof, then, is to specify the name of the data file and let lprof determine the name of the profiled program. Note, however, that because the name of the program is stored in the data file exactly as it appeared on the command line when it was run, lprof will not be able to access the profiled program if you

- use a relative path name on the command line when you run the profiled program;

- invoke `lprof` in a different directory, specifying only the path name of the data file, that is, without also specifying the profiled program's full path name or its path name relative to your current directory.

Suppose, for instance, you are working in the directory `/home/cur.dir`. You enter the commands

```
$ cc -ql -o newprog newprog.c
$ newprog
```

A data file called `newprog.cnt` is created in `cur.dir`. The data file contains the name of the profiled program exactly as it appeared on the command line when the program was run, `newprog`. Now you change directories to `/home` and enter the command

```
$ lprof -c cur.dir/newprog.cnt
```

`lprof` looks for `newprog` in the current directory and fails to find it:

```
***cannot access object file 'newprog'***
```

To make sure that `lprof` can access both the data file and the profiled program, you should specify their paths relative to `/home` with the `-c` and `-o` options, respectively:

```
$ lprof -c cur.dir/newprog.cnt -o cur.dir/newprog
```

Searching for Source Files

To produce the source listing output described in the next section, `lprof` must be able to access the source and header files that comprise the profiled program (or the profiled part of it). By default, `lprof` searches

- the current directory for the source files to be displayed in the listing;

- the current directory and the standard place for header files — usually `/usr/include` — for the header files to be displayed.

If your source or header files are in directories different from these, you must specify their paths with the −I option. (That is, unlike cc −I, you use lprof −I to specify directories to be searched for source files as well as header files.) So if some of the source and header files for the profiled program sample are stored in the directory /usr/src/cmd, and the rest in your current directory and the standard place for header files, you use the command

```
$ lprof -c sample.cnt -I/usr/src/cmd
```

to produce a source listing for all your profiled files. You can specify −I more than once on the lprof command line. Directories are searched in the order they appear on the command line.

If you want a source listing for selected source files, you specify the files with the −r option:

```
$ lprof -c sample.cnt -r sample1.c -r sample2.c
```

That command will produce source listing output only for sample1.c and sample2.c of the profiled program sample, provided, of course, that the source files are in your current directory.

Source Listing Output

By default, lprof displays profiled source code line by line with a count of the number of times each line was executed, 0 if an executable line was never executed. Line numbers of executable lines are enclosed in brackets, with the number of times each line was executed printed to the left of the line number, as shown in Figure 7-1. Note that lines that are not executable — declarations, comments, and blank lines, for example — are marked neither with a line number or an execution count.

Figure 7-1: Example of Iprof Default Output

```
SOURCE FILE:  sample1.c

              #include <stdio.h>

              main()
    1 [4]     {
                  /* declarations are not executable lines
                     and therefore have no line number or execution
                     status associated with them */
                  int i;

    1 [10]        for (i = 0; i < 10; i++)
   10 [11]           sub1();

    1 [13]     }

              sub1()
   10 [16]    {
                  /* this initialization is an executable statement */
   10 [18]        int i = 0;

   10 [20]        if (i > 0) {
    0 [21]           sub2();
                  }
    0 [23]        else {
   10 [24]           sub3();
                  }
   10 [26]    }

              sub2()
    0 [29]    {
                  /* do nothing */
    0 [31]    }

              sub3()
   10 [34]    {
                  /* do nothing */
   10 [36]    }
```

Highlighting Unexecuted Lines

If you specify the −x option to lprof, the source listing output will highlight lines that have not been executed. Lines that have been executed will be marked only by line numbers. Executable lines that have not been executed will be marked with a line number preceded by a [U]. Figure 7-2 shows an example of output produced with the −x option.

Figure 7-2: Example of Iprof –x Output

```
SOURCE FILE:  sample1.c

              #include <stdio.h>

              main()
      [4]     {
                   /* declarations are not executable lines
                   and therefore have no line number or execution
                   status associated with them */
                   int i;

     [10]          for (i = 0; i < 10; i++)
     [11]              sub1();

     [13]     }

              sub1()
     [16]     {
                   /* this initialization is an executable statement */
     [18]          int i = 0;

     [20]          if (i > 0) {
 [U] [21]              sub2();
                   }
 [U] [23]          else {
     [24]              sub3();
                   }
     [26]     }

              sub2()
 [U] [29]     {
                   /* do nothing */
 [U] [31]     }

              sub3()
     [34]     {
                   /* do nothing */
     [36]     }
```

Summary Report

You can obtain a summary of profiling data by invoking lprof with the −s option:

```
$ lprof −s −c sample.cnt
```

Because a source listing is not produced by lprof −s, the −I option need not be specified. The summary reports the percentage of lines of code that were executed for each function in the profiled program, as shown in Figure 7-3.

Figure 7-3: Example of lprof −s Output

```
Coverage Data Source: sample.cnt
Date of Coverage Data Source: Mon Apr  7 17:19:43 1988
Object: sample

percent    lines    total      function
covered    covered  lines      name

100.0        4         4        main
 71.4        5         7        sub1
  0.0        0         2        sub2
100.0        2         2        sub3

 78.6       11        14        TOTAL
```

To obtain both a source listing report and a summary report, you can invoke lprof with the −s and −p options. As an exercise, you might want to consider what the following command does:

```
$ lprof −p −s −c sample.cnt −r sample3.c −I/usr/src/cmd
```

Merged Data

You can merge existing data files with the `lprof` command as follows:

```
$ lprof -d destfile -m run1.cnt run2.cnt run3.cnt
```

where the data file `run1.cnt` was specified in the PROFOPTS environment variable the first time the program was executed, the data file `run2.cnt` the second time the program was executed, and so on. The command line requires both `-d` and `-m`. The `-m` option takes the names of two or more data files to be merged. The `-d` option specifies the destination file that will contain the merged data. The command will fail if the data files were not created by the same program or if the program was recompiled between runs.

You can, however, use the `-T` option to merge existing data files of a recompiled program. Suppose, for example, you have run the profiled program `travel`, specifying the data file `run1.cnt` in the PROFOPTS environment variable. Now you recompile `travel` with `-ql` and run it again, this time specifying the data file `run2.cnt`. The profiled programs have the same name, `travel`, but different time stamps. Because the time stamps do not match, the data files cannot be merged unless you override the time stamp check by specifying the `-T` option to `lprof`:

```
$ lprof -d merged.cnt -m run1.cnt run2.cnt -T
```

NOTE Use the `-T` option with care. If the control flow of the recompiled program has changed, the merged data file is very likely to be erroneous; `lprof` will produce an incorrect report.

Profiling Archive or Shared Object Library Code

You can use lprof to profile archive library code as long as you specify -ql when you compile the library source files, and again when you link the library with your program:

```
$ cc -ql -c function1.c function2.c
$ ar -r libfoo.a function1.o function2.o
$ cc -c test1.c
$ cc -dn -ql -o test1 -L. test1.o -lfoo
$ test1
```

Profiling data for the library functions are written to the data file test1.cnt. The command

```
$ lprof -c test1.cnt
```

generates the default lprof output for the profiled archive library.

To profile test1 as well as the library code, you specify -ql when you compile test1.c. Profiling data for both the library code and the test program are written to test1.cnt.

You can profile shared object library code with lprof by specifying -ql when you compile and link the library functions, and again when you link the library with your program. Note that if you are not profiling the test program, you must specify -g when you compile the source:

```
$ cc -K PIC -ql -c function1.c function2.c
$ cc -ql -G -o libfoo.so function1.o function2.o
$ cc -g -c test1.c
$ cc -ql -o test1 -L. test1.o -lfoo
$ LD_LIBRARY_PATH=. export LD_LIBRARY_PATH
$ test1
```

Profiling data for the library functions are written to the data file libfoo.so.cnt. That is, whereas profiling data for archive library functions are stored in a data file that takes its name from the program, profiling data for shared library functions are stored in a data file that takes its name from the library. And whereas profiling data for archive library functions are stored in the same data file as profiling data for the program, profiling data for shared library functions are stored in a different data file. Had we specified -ql when we compiled test1.c, two data files would have been created: test1.cnt and `libfoo.so.cnt`. Whether or not you profile the test program, you specify

```
$ lprof -c libfoo.so.cnt
```

to generate `lprof` default output for the profiled shared library.

Note that because profiling data for shared library functions are stored in a data file that takes its name from the library, you can obtain merged ouput for multiple test runs of a shared library even though the library was linked with a different executable each time. Consider the following commands:

```
$ mv libfoo.so.cnt libfoo.cnt
$ cc -g -c test2.c
$ cc -ql -o test2 -L. test2.o -lfoo
$ test2
$ lprof -d merged.cnt -m libfoo.cnt libfoo.so.cnt
```

That is, the data files `libfoo.cnt` and `libfoo.so.cnt` can be merged because both were created by executing a program that used `libfoo.so`.

For a discussion of how libraries are created and linked with your program, see the "Link Editing" section of Chapter 2.

Notes

This section describes certain problems that may arise when you use `lprof` and how to avoid them.

Trouble at Run Time

You may get no data after running a profiled program. The program terminates normally, and you receive neither a message about data being saved or an error message. This may be caused by one of three problems:

- You may not have specified -ql at both compile time and link time. If you forget to specify -ql when you link, the program will run but a data file will not be created.

- Because profiling data are saved at termination by the system call exit(2), no profiling data are saved if exit () is never called. The profiled program may include a call to _exit () that is causing the program to quit without calling exit (). Replace calls to _exit () with calls to exit () in order to save profiling data.

- The PROFOPTS environment variable may be set to the null string.

Finally, you may see the following error message at the end of execution:

```
Dumping profiling data from process 'a.out' . . .
fatal error: Cannot find symbol table section in ./a.out.
```

Usually this is caused by running a stripped version of a profiled program. Never strip files to be profiled. If necessary, change makefiles so that they do not produce stripped files.

Data File Cannot Be Found

Occasionally, you may not be able to find the data file, despite the fact that the profiled program has terminated normally and you have received a message saying that the data file has been created.

The profiled program creates the data file in the directory in which the program is located when it terminates. If the program changes directories during execution, the data file may be created in a directory different from both the directory in which you executed the program and the directory in which the shell is located when the program terminates.

Use the `dir` option of PROFOPTS to specify exactly where the data file is to be created so you will be able to find it.

Improving Program Performance

This section presents an extended example of how you might use `prof` and `lprof` together to improve program performance.

prof and lprof on lprof

During the development of `lprof` it was observed that the process of merging profiling data was slow. The profiling data being merged came from two runs of the C compiler, a medium-sized program with, at the time, 284 functions. It took forty cpu seconds (two minutes of real time) to merge the two coverage files. We wanted to improve on that.

The first step was to produce a time profile of `lprof` to see which functions were taking the most time. Here is part of the output from `prof`:

Figure 7-4: prof Output

%Time	Seconds	Cumsecs	#Calls	msec/call	Name
34.8	13.52	13.52	226638	0.0597	fread
12.1	4.72	18.24	228254	0.0207	memcpy
9.5	3.69	21.93	40286	0.0918	CAjump
9.2	3.60	5.52			_mcount
7.7	2.99	28.51	284	10.53	CAfind
7.6	2.94	31.45	42472	0.0692	malloc
6.3	2.45	33.90	1154	2.123	read
3.0	1.17	35.07	40475	0.0289	strcmp
2.8	1.09	36.16	42471	0.0257	free
2.5	0.96	37.13	2	482.	creat
1.4	0.55	37.68	1	550.	fputc
0.8	0.33	38.01	1431	0.231	lseek
0.4	0.16	38.17	1518	0.105	fwrite
0.3	0.11	38.28	569	0.19	CAread

The two most time-consuming user functions were `CAjump()` and `CAfind()`. We wondered why `CAjump()` was called 40,286 times and why the average time per call for `CAfind()` was so high, 10.53 milliseconds. The next step was to invoke `lprof` only for the source files containing the functions `CAjump()` and `CAfind()`. Here are the results for `CAfind()`:

Figure 7-5: Iprof Output for the Function CAfind()

```
                short
                CAfind(filedata, searchfunc)
                struct caFILEDATA *filedata;
                char *searchfunc;
   284 [61]     {
                    short ret_code,findflag;
                    unsigned char fname_size;
                    char *name;

   284 [66]         CArewind(filedata);  /* rewind file pointers */
   284 [67]         findflag = 1;

 40754 [69]         while (findflag)
 40470 [70]             if ((fread((char *) &fname_size, sizeof(unsigned char),
                            1, filedata->cov_data_ptr)) > 0) {
 40470 [72]                 name = (char *) malloc(fname_size+1);
 40470 [73]                 fread(name, (int)fname_size, 1, filedata->cov_data_ptr);
                            /* make null-terminated */
 40470 [75]                 name[fname_size] = '\0';
 40470 [76]                 if (strcmp(name,searchfunc) == 0)
                            {   /* this is the function, move
                                        ptr back to beginning of
                                        function name        */
   284 [80]                     fseek(filedata->cov_data_ptr,
                                    -(long)(fname_size+sizeof(unsigned char)),1);
   284 [82]                     ret_code = OK;
   284 [83]                     findflag = 0;
                            }
                            else        /* this is not it, move to next function */
                            {
 40186 [87]                     if (fname_size != EOD)
 40186 [88]                         if (CAjump(filedata->cov_data_ptr) == EOF_FAIL)
                                    {   /* error - end of file found */
     0 [90]                             ret_code = FUNC_FAIL;
     0 [91]                             findflag = 0;
                                    }
                            }
 40470 [94]                 free(name);
                        }
                        else
                        {       /* end of file before function found */
     0 [98]                 ret_code = FUNC_FAIL;
     0 [99]                 findflag = 0;
                        }
```

(continued on next page)

Figure 7-5: lprof Output for the Function CAfind() (continued)

```
284 [101]        return(ret_code);
  0 [102]    }
```

> **NOTE** The data shown in the previous screen were reported by an earlier release of lprof. The current release would treat the else statements in lines 85 and 96 as executable. Similarly, the case statements shown in Figure 7-9 below would be treated by the current release as executable.

CAfind() searches the data file for data pertaining to a particular function. Recall that a data file consists of a header section, a section for each function, and an end of data marker. The coverage datum (execution count) for each function is recorded beside the function's name.

Notice that the while loop (shown between lines 70 and 94) was executed 40,470 times; for 284 successful searches, there were 40,186 unsuccessful searches. We were getting a low rate of return for computing resources spent. A look at the while loop also shows why fread() was executed so many times: the loop contains two calls to fread() (lines 70 and 73). Finally, the prof output reports that CAjump() was called 40,186 times, once for each unsuccessful search.

Our goals were to minimize the number of unsuccessful searches and, if possible, decrease the number of calls to fread(), because these are relatively expensive.

The lprof algorithm for merging files consists of two steps: traversing the functions in one of the files sequentially, and calling CAfind() to locate the data for a given function in the other coverage file.

The first thing that happens in CAfind() is the resetting of the file pointers so they point to the first function in the file (line 66). Then, because the given function (which was passed to CAfind() as an argument) has not been found, the next function in the file is examined to see if it is the correct function. If it is, we are finished. If not, we can skip over the data and try the next function. If we have reached the end of the file, there will be no data for that function in the coverage file and we will return with a failure. By itself, CAfind() looked fine. There didn't seem to be much we could do to improve its performance.

Looking over the entire program, however, we were able to observe that in almost all situations the order of the coverage data in the two files to be merged was identical. This meant that on subsequent calls to CAfind(), the next function being sought was immediately after the one found on the last call to CAfind(). The original implementation did not take advantage of the fact that the search was usually sequential. The file pointers were always reset to the beginning of the file before the search began. Because the functions were in sequential order, this meant that each successive search took progressively longer.

We changed the search strategy so that instead of starting at the beginning of the file on each call to CAfind(), we started at the place in the file where the previous search had ended. This could have been anywhere in the file. Because files being merged are usually identical, the function being sought is almost always the function following the last one found.

The new search strategy required a slightly more complicated algorithm. Whereas the original strategy demanded only that we check for the end of the file, the new strategy required that we both check for the end of the file and keep track of our current location. The need to do both arose from the sequence of events involved in this type of searching.

The new strategy dictated that each iteration of searching begin where the last search ended. CAfind() was to search until the function being sought was found. If CAfind() reached the end of the file before finding that function, it had to continue the search between the first line of the file and the place where it had started the search. Thus CAfind() had to keep track of when the end of the file was reached. Because the goal of the new strategy was to start each search iteration at the place where the last search had ended, it was obviously necessary to keep track of our current location in the file.

The following screen shows the lprof output for CAfind() after we changed it to accommodate our new strategy:

Figure 7-6: lprof Output for New Version of CAfind()

```
                short
                CAfind(filedata, searchfunc)
                struct caFILEDATA *filedata;
                char *searchfunc;
  284 [61]      {
                    short ret_code;
                    unsigned char fname_size;
                    char *name;
                    long init_loc;

  284 [67]          init_loc = -1;
  284 [68]          while (1) {
  284 [69]              if (init_loc == -1) {
                            /* first time through */
  284 [71]                  init_loc = ftell(filedata->cov_data_ptr);
                        }
                        else {
                            /* have we wrapped completely around? */
    0 [75]                  if (ftell(filedata->cov_data_ptr) == init_loc) {
                                /* searched all functions */
    0 [77]                      ret_code = FUNC_FAIL;
    0 [78]                      break;
                            }
                        }
  284 [81]              if ((fread((char *) &fname_size, sizeof(unsigned char),
                                1, filedata->cov_data_ptr)) > 0) {
  284 [83]                  if (fname_size == EOD) {
                                /* wrap around to beginning */
    0 [85]                      CArewind(filedata);
                                /* go back to top of loop */
                                continue;
                            }
  284 [89]                  name = (char *) malloc(fname_size+1);
  284 [90]                  fread(name, (int)fname_size, 1, filedata->cov_data_ptr);
                            /* make null-terminated */
  284 [92]                  name[fname_size] = '\0';
  284 [93]                  if (strcmp(name, searchfunc) == 0)
                            {   /* this is the function, move
                                     ptr back to beginning of
                                     function name        */
  284 [97]                      fseek(filedata->cov_data_ptr,
                                    -(long)(fname_size+sizeof(unsigned char)),1);
  284 [99]                      ret_code = OK;
                                break;
```

(continued on next page)

Figure 7-6: lprof Output for New Version of CAfind() (continued)

```
                             }
                             else          /* this is not it, move to next function */
                             {
    0 [104]                      if (CAjump(filedata->cov_data_ptr) == EOF_FAIL)
                                 {   /* error - end of file found */
    0 [106]                          ret_code = FUNC_FAIL;
                                     break;
                                 }
                             }
    0 [110]                  free(name);
                         }
                         else
                         {   /* end of file before function found */
    0 [114]                  ret_code = FUNC_FAIL;
                             break;
                         }
                     }

  284 [119]          return(ret_code);
    0 [120]     }
```

Note that not only did we greatly reduce the number of calls to fread(), but in typical situations we eliminated calls to CAjump() entirely! Remember, CAjump() originally took 3.69 seconds (9.5% of the total execution time), which was more than any other user function.

The prof output for the new version is shown in the following screen:

Figure 7-7: prof Output for New Version of lprof

%Time	Seconds	Cumsecs	#Calls	msec/call	Name
25.4	0.54	0.54	298	1.81	read
11.7	0.25	0.79	2002	0.125	malloc
10.6	0.22	1.01	2848	0.079	fread
8.9	0.19	1.20	579	0.33	lseek
7.0	0.15	1.35	1518	0.099	fwrite
6.1	0.13	1.48			_mcount
4.2	0.09	1.57	569	0.16	CAread
3.8	0.08	1.65	4369	0.018	memcpy
2.8	0.06	1.71	284	0.21	CAor
2.8	0.06	1.77	2	30.	creat
2.8	0.06	1.83	1	60.	CAcov_join
1.9	0.04	1.87	284	0.14	CAfind
1.9	0.04	1.91	284	0.14	CAdata_entry
1.9	0.04	1.95	1717	0.023	free
1.4	0.03	1.98	7	4.	open

The execution time for CAfind() decreased from 2.99 seconds to 0.04 seconds, and for CAjump() from 3.69 seconds to 0 seconds. The overall performance of the entire program decreased from forty cpu seconds (two minutes of real time) to two cpu seconds (six seconds of real time).

Improving Test Coverage

It is difficult to write test suites that fully cover programs if you have no way of determining how much of the code is exercised. lprof removes the guesswork by showing, on a line-by-line basis, which lines of code are executed. That allows the tester to know exactly what has been tested. It also makes it easier to refine and improve tests.

Suppose we want to measure how well a given test suite tests a program. First we compile and link the program with −ql so that profiling information will be saved. Then we run the program with the tests to get the profiling data. By looking at the summary output, we can see how much of the code is exercised.

Figure 7-8: lprof Summary Output for a Test Suite

```
Coverage Data Source: test.cnt
Date of Coverage Data Source: Wed Mar  5 11:11:58 1985
Object: myprog

percent   lines    total function
covered   covered  lines name

  91.5      97       106  compile
 100.0      18        18  step
 100.0      73        73  advance
 100.0       4         4  getrnge
  42.9      12        28  main
 100.0      29        29  execute
 100.0      19        19  succeed
  42.9       3         7  putdata
   0.0       0        19  regerr
 100.0      21        21  fgetl

  85.2     276       324  TOTAL
```

Now we can examine individual functions that do not have 100% coverage to find ways of improving the tests.

The rest of this section consists of three examples that show why certain functions may not have 100% coverage. The first example demonstrates how to uncover an option that is usually missed because it is not documented. The second example shows how to uncover a function that is never called. The third example examines code that is never executed because of an error condition that is difficult to produce. Each section also explains how to resolve the problem of lack of coverage.

Searching for Undocumented Options

First, examine the function `main()` to see what parts of the code are not exe-cuted. Use the −x option to `lprof` to highlight the unexecuted lines:

Figure 7-9: Fragment of Output from lprof −x

```
                              while((c=getopt(argc, argv, "blcnsvi")) != EOF)
        [32]                      switch(c) {
                                  case 'v':
   [U] [34]                           vflag++;
                                      break;
                                  case 'c':
        [37]                          cflag++;
                                      break;
                                  case 'n':
        [40]                          nflag++;
                                      break;
                                  case 'b':
        [43]                          bflag++;
                                      break;
                                  case 's':
        [46]                          sflag++;
                                      break;
                                  case 'l':
        [49]                          lflag++;
                                      break;
                                  case 'i':
        [52]                          iflag++;
                                      break;
                                  case '?':
   [U] [55]                           errflg++;
        [56]                      }
```

The output shows that the −v option was not tested. By checking the docu-mentation you can confirm that −v is an undocumented option. To correct this, create a test that exercises the −v option and add the −v option to the manual page.

Functions That Are Never Called

None of the lines in the function `regerr()` are executed. To find out why, invoke `cscope` (Chapter 8) and request a list of the functions that call `regerr()`. `cscope` reports that no function calls `regerr()`. Because `regerr()` will never be exercised, it ought to be — but, for arcane reasons, cannot be — deleted from the code. You can, though, discount the 19 lines of `regerr()` in calculating the percentage of code that is covered by the test suite.

Hard to Produce Error Conditions

Now take a look at the function `putdata()`.

Figure 7-10: Output from lprof −x for putdata()

```
                    void
                    putdata(output, data)
                    char    *data;
                    FILE    *output;
        [9]         {
                        /* check for file system out of space */
        [11]            if (fprintf(output, "%s", data) < 0) {
   [U] [12]                 fprintf(stderr, "write error with file '%s'", filename);
   [U] [13]                 fclose(output);
   [U] [14]                 unlink(newreffile);
   [U] [15]                 exit(1);

                        }
        [17]        }
```

Because this error is hard to produce, the error recovery part of the function usually does not get tested. You can simulate the error, however, by writing your own `fprintf()` function that returns a value less than 0. That will cause the error recovery part of the function to be exercised, allowing you to see the following error message:

        write error with file '@%#&HP'

Further inspection reveals that the variable `filename` was never initialized. That oversight caused the error message to be garbled.

8 cscope

Introduction

The cscope browser is an interactive program that locates specified elements of code in C, lex, or yacc source files. It lets you search and, if you want, edit your source files more efficiently than you could with a typical editor. That's because cscope knows about function calls — when a function is being called, when it is doing the calling — and C language identifiers and keywords. This chapter is a tutorial on the cscope browser.

How cscope Works

When you invoke cscope for a set of C, lex, or yacc source files, it builds a symbol cross-reference table for the functions, function calls, macros, variables, and preprocessor symbols in those files. It then lets you query that table about the locations of symbols you specify. First, it presents a menu and asks you to choose the type of search you would like to have performed. You may, for instance, want cscope to find all functions that call a specified function.

When cscope has completed this search, it prints a list. Each list entry contains the name of the file, the number of the line, and the text of the line in which cscope has found the specified code. In our case, the list will also include the names of the functions that call the specified function. You now have the option of requesting another search or examining one of the listed lines with the editor. If you choose the latter, cscope invokes the editor for the file in which the line appears, with the cursor on that line. You may now view the code in context and, if you wish, edit the file as you would any other file. You can then return to the menu from the editor to request a new search.

Because the procedure you follow will depend on the task at hand, there is no single set of instructions for using cscope. For an extended example of its use, review the cscope session described in the next section. It shows how you can locate a bug in a program without learning all the code.

How to Use cscope

Suppose you are given responsibility for maintaining the program prog. You are told that an error message, out of storage, sometimes appears just as the program starts up. Now you want to use cscope to locate the parts of the code that are generating the message. Here is how you do it.

Step 1: Set Up the Environment

cscope is a screen-oriented tool that can only be used on terminals listed in the Terminal Information Utilities (terminfo) database. Be sure you have set the TERM environment variable to your terminal type so that cscope can verify that it is listed in the terminfo database. If you have not done so, assign a value to TERM and export it to the shell as follows:

$ TERM=*term_name* export TERM

You may now want to assign a value to the EDITOR environment variable. By default, cscope invokes the vi editor. (The examples in this chapter illustrate vi usage.) If you prefer not to use vi, set the EDITOR environment variable to the editor of your choice and export EDITOR:

$ EDITOR=emacs export EDITOR

Note that you may have to write an interface between cscope and your editor. For details, see the section "Command Line Syntax for Editors" below.

If you want to use cscope only for browsing (without editing), you can set the VIEWER environment variable to pg and export VIEWER. cscope will then invoke pg instead of vi.

An environment variable called VPATH can be set to specify directories to be searched for source files. See the section "Using Viewpaths" below.

Step 2: Invoke cscope

By default, cscope builds a symbol cross-reference table for all the C, lex, and yacc source files in the current directory, and for any included header files in the current directory or the standard place. So if all the source files for the program to be browsed are in the current directory, and if its header files are there or in the standard place, invoke cscope without arguments:

        $ cscope

To browse through selected source files, invoke cscope with the names of those files as arguments:

        $ cscope file1.c file2.c file3.h

For other ways to invoke cscope, see the section "Command Line Options" below.

cscope builds the symbol cross-reference table the first time it is used on the source files for the program to be browsed. By default, the table is stored in the file cscope.out in the current directory. On a subsequent invocation, cscope rebuilds the cross-reference only if a source file has been modified or the list of source files is different. When the cross-reference is rebuilt, the data for the unchanged files are copied from the old cross-reference, which makes rebuilding faster than the initial build and startup time less for subsequent invocations.

Step 3: Locate the Code

Now let's return to the task we undertook at the beginning of this section: to identify the problem that is causing the error message out of storage to be printed. You have invoked cscope, the cross-reference table has been built. The cscope menu of tasks appears on the screen:

Figure 8-1: The cscope Menu of Tasks

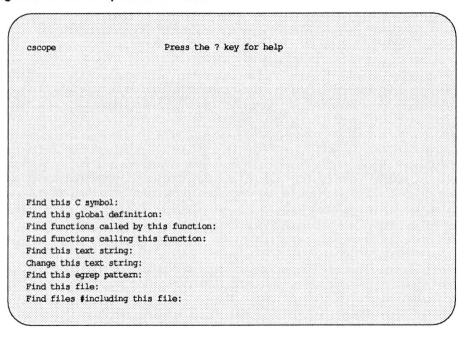

```
cscope                          Press the ? key for help




















Find this C symbol:
Find this global definition:
Find functions called by this function:
Find functions calling this function:
Find this text string:
Change this text string:
Find this egrep pattern:
Find this file:
Find files #including this file:
```

Press the RETURN key to move the cursor down the screen (with wraparound at the bottom of the display), and ^p (control-p) to move the cursor up; or use the up (↑) and down (↓) arrow keys if your keyboard has them. You can manipulate the menu, and perform other tasks, with the following single-key commands:

Figure 8-2: Menu Manipulation Commands

TAB	move to next input field
RETURN	move to next input field
^n	move to next input field
^p	move to previous input field
^y	search with the last text typed
^b	move to previous input field and search pattern
^f	move to next input field and search pattern
^c	toggle ignore/use letter case when searching (a search for FILE will match, for example, File and file when ignoring letter case)
^r	rebuild the cross-reference
!	start an interactive shell (type ^d to return to cscope)
^l	redraw the screen
?	display list of commands
^d	exit cscope

If the first character of the text for which you are searching matches one of these commands, you can escape the command by entering a backslash (\) before the character.

Now move the cursor to the fifth menu item, Find this text string, enter the text out of storage, and press the RETURN key:

Figure 8-3: Requesting a Search for a Text String

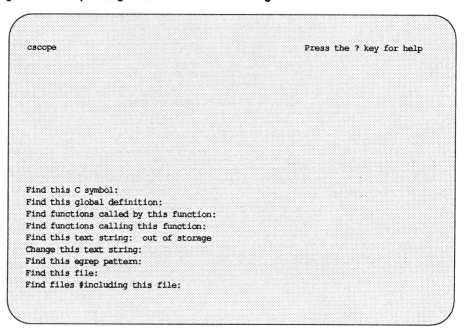

```
cscope                                              Press the ? key for help




Find this C symbol:
Find this global definition:
Find functions called by this function:
Find functions calling this function:
Find this text string:  out of storage
Change this text string:
Find this egrep pattern:
Find this file:
Find files #including this file:
```

> **NOTE** Follow the same procedure to perform any other task listed in the menu except the sixth, Change this text string. Because this task is slightly more complex than the others, there is a different procedure for performing it. For a description of how to change a text string, see the "Examples" section below.

cscope searches for the specified text, finds one line that contains it, and reports its finding as follows:

Figure 8-4: cscope Lists Lines Containing the Text String

```
Text string: out of storage

  File    Line
  1 alloc.c 63 (void) fprintf(stderr, "\n%s: out of storage\n", argv0);




  Find this C symbol:
  Find this global definition:
  Find functions called by this function:
  Find functions calling this function:
  Find this text string:
  Change this text string:
  Find this egrep pattern:
  Find this file:
  Find files #including this file:
```

After cscope shows you the results of a successful search, you have several options. You may want to change one of the lines or examine the code surrounding it in the editor. Or, if cscope has found so many lines that a list of them will not fit on the screen at once, you may want to look at the next part of the list. The following table shows the commands available after cscope has found the specified text:

Figure 8-5: Commands for Use after Initial Search

1-9	edit the file referenced by this line (the number you type corresponds to an item in the list of lines printed by cscope)
space	display next set of matching lines
+	display next set of matching lines
^v	display next set of matching lines
-	display previous set of matching lines
^e	edit displayed files in order
>	append the list of lines being displayed to a file
|	pipe all lines to a shell command

Again, if the first character of the text for which you are searching matches one of these commands, you can escape the command by entering a backslash before the character.

Now examine the code around the newly found line. Enter 1 (the number of the line in the list). The editor will be invoked with the file alloc.c; the cursor will be at the beginning of line 63 of alloc.c:

ANSI C and Programming Support Tools

Figure 8-6: Examining a Line of Code Found by cscope

```
{
        return(alloctest(realloc(p, (unsigned) size)));
}

/* check for memory allocation failure */

static  char *
alloctest(p)
char    *p;
{
        if (p == NULL) {
                (void) fprintf(stderr, "\n%s: out of storage\n", argv0);
                exit(1);
        }
        return(p);
}
~
~
~
~
~
~
"alloc.c" 67 lines, 1283 characters
```

You can see that the error message is generated when the variable p is NULL.
To determine how an argument passed to alloctest() could have been
NULL, you must first identify the functions that call alloctest().

Exit the editor by using normal quit conventions. You are returned to the menu
of tasks. Now type alloctest after the fourth item, Find functions calling this function:

Figure 8-7: Requesting a List of Functions That Call alloctest()

```
Text string: out of storage

  File    Line
1 alloc.c 63 (void) fprintf(stderr, "\n%s: out of storage\n", argv0);




Find this C symbol:
Find this global definition:
Find functions called by this function:
Find functions calling this function:  alloctest
Find this text string:
Change this text string:
Find this egrep pattern:
Find this file:
Find files #including this file:
```

cscope finds and lists three such functions:

Figure 8-8: cscope Lists Functions That Call alloctest()

```
Functions calling this function: alloctest

   File    Function  Line
1 alloc.c mymalloc  33 return(alloctest(malloc((unsigned) size)));
2 alloc.c mycalloc  43 return(alloctest(calloc((unsigned) nelem, (unsigned)
                       size)));
3 alloc.c myrealloc 53 return(alloctest(realloc(p, (unsigned) size)));




Find this C symbol:
Find this global definition:
Find functions called by this function:
Find functions calling this function:
Find this text string:
Change this text string:
Find this egrep pattern:
Find this file:
Find files #including this file:
```

Now you want to know which functions call mymalloc(). cscope finds ten
such functions. It lists nine of them on the screen and instructs you to press the
space bar to see the rest of the list:

Figure 8-9: cscope Lists Functions That Call mymalloc()

```
Functions calling this function: mymalloc

    File       Function     Line
1 alloc.c      stralloc      24 return(strcpy(mymalloc(strlen(s) + 1), s));
2 crossref.c   crossref      47 symbol = (struct symbol *) mymalloc(msymbols *
                                 sizeof(struct symbol));
3 dir.c        makevpsrcdirs 63 srcdirs = (char **) mymalloc(nsrcdirs * sizeof(char
                                 *));
4 dir.c        addincdir    167 incdirs = (char **) mymalloc(sizeof(char *));
5 dir.c        addincdir    168 incnames = (char **) mymalloc(sizeof(char *));
6 dir.c        addsrcfile   439 p = (struct listitem *) mymalloc(sizeof(struct
                                 listitem));
7 display.c    dispinit      87 displine = (int *) mymalloc(mdisprefs * sizeof(int ));
8 history.c    addcmd        19 h = (struct cmd *) mymalloc(sizeof(struct cmd));
9 main.c       main         212 s = mymalloc((unsigned ) (strlen(reffile) +
                                 strlen(home) + 2));

* 9 more lines - press the space bar to display more *
Find this C symbol:
Find this global definition:
Find functions called by this function:
Find functions calling this function:
Find this text string:
Change this text string:
Find this egrep pattern:
Find this file:
Find files #including this file:
```

Because you know that the error message out of storage is generated at the beginning of the program, you can guess that the problem may have occurred in the function dispinit () (display initialization). To view dispinit (), the seventh function on the list, type 7:

ANSI C and Programming Support Tools

Figure 8-10: Viewing dispinit() in the Editor

```
void
dispinit()
{
        /* calculate the maximum displayed reference lines */
        lastdispline = FLDLINE - 4;
        mdisprefs = lastdispline - REFLINE + 1;
        if (mdisprefs > 9) {
                mdisprefs = 9;
        }
        /* allocate the displayed line array */
        displine = (int *) mymalloc(mdisprefs * sizeof(int));
}
^L/* display a page of the references */

void
display()
{
        char    file[PATHLEN + 1];      /* file name */
        char    function[PATLEN + 1];   /* function name */
        char    linenum[NUMLEN + 1];    /* line number */
        int     screenline;             /* screen line number */
        int     width;                  /* source line display width */
        register int    i, j;
"display.c" 622 lines, 14326 characters
```

mymalloc() failed because it was called either with a very large number or a negative number. By examining the possible values of FLDLINE and REFLINE, you can see that there are situations in which the value of mdisprefs is nega-tive, that is, in which you are trying to call mymalloc() with a negative number.

Step 4: Edit the Code

On a windowing terminal you may have multiple windows of arbitrary size. The error message out of storage might have appeared as a result of running prog in a window with too few lines. In other words, that may have been one of the situations in which mymalloc () was called with a negative number. Now you want to be sure that when the program aborts in this situation in the future, it does so after printing the more meaningful error message screen too small. Edit the function dispinit () as follows:

Figure 8-11: Using cscope to Fix the Problem

```
/* initialize display parameters */

void
dispinit ()
{
        /* calculate the maximum displayed reference lines */
        lastdispline = FLDLINE - 4;
        mdisprefs = lastdispline - REFLINE + 1;
        if (mdisprefs <= 0) {
                (void) fprintf (stderr, "\n%s: screen too small\n", argv0);
                exit (1);
        }
        if (mdisprefs > 9) {
                mdisprefs = 9;
        }
        /* allocate the displayed line array */
        displine = (int *) mymalloc (mdisprefs * sizeof (int));
}
^L/* display a page of the references */

void
display ()
```

You have fixed the problem we began investigating at the beginning of this section. Now if prog is run in a window with too few lines, it will not simply fail with the unedifying error message out of storage. Instead, it will check the window size and generate a more meaningful error message before exiting.

Command Line Options

As noted, cscope builds a symbol cross-reference table for the C, lex, and yacc source files in the current directory by default. That is,

        $ cscope

is equivalent to

        $ cscope *.[chly]

We have also seen that you can browse through selected source files by invoking cscope with the names of those files as arguments:

        $ cscope file1.c file2.c file3.h

cscope provides command line options that allow you greater flexibility in specifying source files to be included in the cross-reference. When you invoke cscope with the −s option and any number of directory names (separated by commas)

        $ cscope −s *dir,dir,dir*

cscope will build a cross-reference for all the source files in the specified directories as well as the current directory. To browse through all of the source files whose names are listed in *file* (file names separated by spaces, tabs, or newlines), invoke cscope with the −i option and the name of the file containing the list:

        $ cscope −i *file*

If your source files are in a directory tree, the following commands will allow you to browse through all of them easily:

        $ find . −name '*.[chly]' −print | sort > *file*
        $ cscope −i *file*

Note that if this option is selected, cscope ignores any other files appearing on the command line.

The −I option to cscope is similar to the −I option to cc. By default, cscope searches for included header files in the current directory, then the standard place. If you want cscope to search for an included header file in a different directory, specify the path of the directory with −I:

```
$ cscope -I dir
```

In this case, cscope will search the directory *dir* for #include files called into the source files in the current directory. Directories are searched for #include files in the following order:

1. the current directory;

2. the directories specified with -I;

3. the standard place for header files, usually usr/include.

You can invoke the -I option more than once on a command line. cscope will search the specified directories in the order they appear on the command line.

You can specify a cross-reference file other than the default cscope.out by invoking the -f option. This is useful for keeping separate symbol cross-reference files in the same directory. You may want to do this if two programs are in the same directory, but do not share all the same files:

```
$ cscope -f admin.ref admin.c common.c aux.c libs.c
$ cscope -f delta.ref delta.c common.c aux.c libs.c
```

In this example, the source files for two programs, admin and delta, are in the same directory, but the programs consist of different groups of files. By specifying different symbol cross-reference files when you invoke cscope for each set of source files, the cross-reference information for the two programs is kept separate.

You can use the -p*n* option to specify that cscope display the path name, or part of the path name, of a file when it lists the results of a search. The number you give to -p stands for the last *n* elements of the path name you want to be displayed. The default is 1, the name of the file itself. So if your current directory is home/common, the command

```
$ cscope -p2
```

will cause cscope to display common/file1.c, common/file2.c, and so forth when it lists the results of a search.

If the program you want to browse contains a large number of source files, you can use the -b option to tell cscope to stop after it has built a cross-reference; cscope will not display a menu of tasks. When you use cscope -b in a pipeline with the batch command, described in Section 1 of the *User's Reference Manual*, cscope will build the cross-reference in the background:

```
$ echo 'cscope -b' | batch
```

Once the cross-reference is built (and as long as you have not changed a source file or the list of source files in the meantime), you need only specify

```
$ cscope
```

for the cross-reference to be copied and the menu of tasks to be displayed in the normal way. In other words, you can use this sequence of commands when you want to continue working without having to wait for cscope to finish its initial processing.

The −d option instructs cscope not to update the symbol cross-reference. You can use it to save time — cscope will not check the source files for changes — if you are sure that no such changes have been made.

 NOTE Use the −d option with care. If you specify −d under the erroneous impression that your source files have not been changed, cscope will refer to an outdated symbol cross-reference in responding to your queries.

Check the cscope page in Section 1 of the *Programmer's Reference Manual* for other command line options.

Using Viewpaths

As we have seen, cscope searches for source files in the current directory by default. When the environment variable VPATH is set, cscope searches for source files in directories that comprise your viewpath. A viewpath is an ordered list of directories, each of which has the same directory structure below it.

For example, suppose you are part of a software project. There is an "official" set of source files in directories below /fs1/ofc. Each user has a home directory (/usr/you). If you make changes to the software system, you may have copies of just those files you are changing in /usr/you/src/cmd/prog1. The official versions of the entire program can be found in in the directory /fs1/ofc/src/cmd/prog1.

Suppose you use cscope to browse through the three files that comprise progl, namely, f1.c, f2.c, and f3.c. You would set VPATH to /usr/you and /fs1/ofc and export it, as in

        $ VPATH=/usr/you:/fs1/ofc export VPATH

You would then make your current directory /usr/you/src/cmd/progl, and invoke cscope:

        $ cscope

The program will locate all files in the viewpath. In case duplicates are found, cscope uses the file whose parent directory appears earlier in VPATH. Thus if f2.c is in your directory (and all three files are in the official directory), cscope will examine f2.c from your directory and f1.c and f3.c from the official directory.

The first directory in VPATH must be a prefix (usually $HOME) of the directory you will be working in. Each colon-separated directory in VPATH must be absolute: it should begin at /.

Stacking cscope and Editor Calls

cscope and editor calls can be stacked. That means that when cscope puts you in the editor to view a reference to a symbol and there is another reference of interest, you can invoke cscope again from within the editor to view the second reference without exiting the current invocation of either cscope or the editor. You can then back up by exiting the most recent invocation with the appropriate cscope and editor commands.

Examples

This section presents examples of how cscope can be used to perform three tasks: changing a constant to a preprocessor symbol, adding an argument to a function, and changing the value of a variable. The first example demonstrates the procedure for changing a text string, which differs slightly from the other tasks on the cscope menu. That is, once you have entered the text string to be changed, cscope prompts you for the new text, displays the lines containing the old text, and waits for you to specify which of these lines you want it to change.

Changing a Constant to a Preprocessor Symbol

Suppose you want to change a constant, 100, to a preprocessor symbol,
MAXSIZE. Select the sixth menu item, Change this text string, and
enter \100. The 1 must be escaped with a backslash because it has a special
meaning (item 1 on the menu) to cscope. Now press RETURN. cscope will
prompt you for the new text string. Type MAXSIZE:

Figure 8-12: Changing a Text String

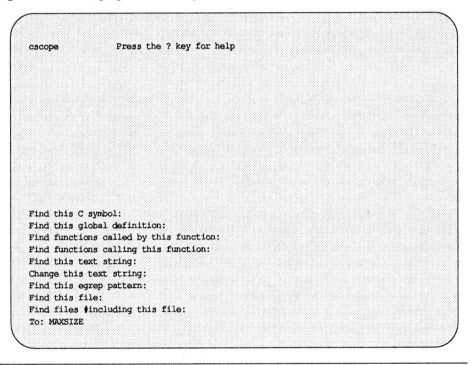

```
cscope                    Press the ? key for help
















Find this C symbol:
Find this global definition:
Find functions called by this function:
Find functions calling this function:
Find this text string:
Change this text string:
Find this egrep pattern:
Find this file:
Find files #including this file:
To: MAXSIZE
```

cscope displays the lines containing the specified text string, and waits for you
to select those in which you want the text to be changed:

Figure 8-13: cscope Prompts for Lines to Be Changed

```
Change "100" to "MAXSIZE"

  File  Line
1 init.c   4 char s[100];
2 init.c  26 for (i = 0; i < 100; i++)
3 find.c   8 if (c < 100) {
4 read.c  12 f = (bb & 0100);
5 err.c   19 p = total/100.0; /* get percentage */




Find this C symbol:
Find this global definition:
Find functions called by this function:
Find functions calling this function:
Find this text string:
Change this text string:
Find this egrep pattern:
Find this file:
Find files #including this file:
Select lines to change (press the ? key for help):
```

You know that the constant 100 in lines 1, 2, and 3 of the list (lines 4, 26, and 8 of the listed source files) should be changed to MAXSIZE. You also know that 0100 in read.c and 100.0 in err.c (lines 4 and 5 of the list) should not be changed. You select the lines you want changed with the following single-key commands:

Figure 8-14: Commands for Selecting Lines to Be Changed

1–9	mark or unmark the line to be changed
*	mark or unmark all displayed lines to be changed
space	display next set of lines
+	display next set of lines
–	display previous set of lines
a	mark all lines to be changed
^d	change the marked lines and exit
ESC	exit without changing the marked lines

In this case, enter 1, 2, and 3. Note that the numbers you type are not printed on the screen. Instead, cscope marks each list item you want to be changed by printing a > (greater than) symbol after its line number in the list:

Figure 8-15: Marking Lines to Be Changed

```
Change "100" to "MAXSIZE"

  File  Line
1>init.c   4 char s[100];
2>init.c 26 for (i = 0; i < 100; i++)
3>find.c   8 if (c < 100) {
4 read.c 12 f = (bb & 0100);
5 err.c  19 p = total/100.0; /* get percentage */







Find this C symbol:
Find this global definition:
Find functions called by this function:
Find functions calling this function:
Find this text string:
Change this text string:
Find this egrep pattern:
Find this file:
Find files #including this file:
Select lines to change (press the ? key for help):
```

Now type ^d to change the selected lines. cscope displays the lines that have been changed and prompts you to continue:

Figure 8-16: cscope Displays Changed Lines of Text

```
Changed lines:

     char s[MAXSIZE];
     for (i = 0; i < MAXSIZE; i++)
         if (c < MAXSIZE) {

Press the RETURN key to continue:
```

When you press RETURN in response to this prompt, cscope redraws the screen, restoring it to its state before you selected the lines to be changed, as shown in Figure 8-17.

The next step is to add the #define for the new symbol MAXSIZE. Because the header file in which the #define is to appear is not among the files whose lines are displayed, you must escape to the shell by typing !. The shell prompt will appear at the bottom of the screen. Then enter the editor and add the #define:

Figure 8-17: Escaping from cscope to the Shell

```
Text string: 100

   File  Line
1 init.c   4 char s[100];
2 init.c  26 for (i = 0; i < 100; i++)
3 find.c   8 if (c < 100) {
4 read.c  12 f = (bb & 0100);
5 err.c   19 p = total/100.0; /* get percentage */




Find this C symbol:
Find this global definition:
Find functions called by this function:
Find functions calling this function:
Find this text string:
Change this text string:
Find this egrep pattern:
Find this file:
Find files #including this file:
$ vi defs.h
```

To resume the cscope session, quit the editor and type ^d to exit the shell.

ANSI C and Programming Support Tools

Adding an Argument to a Function

Adding an argument to a function involves two steps: editing the function itself and adding the new argument to every place in the code where the function is called. cscope makes that easy.

First, edit the function by using the second menu item, Find this global definition. Next, find out where the function is called. Use the fourth menu item, Find functions calling this function, to get a list of all the functions that call it. With this list, you can either invoke the editor for each line found by entering the list number of the line individually, or invoke the editor for all the lines automatically by typing ^e. Using cscope to make this kind of change assures that none of the functions you need to edit will be over-looked.

Changing the Value of a Variable

The value of cscope as a browser becomes apparent when you want to see how a proposed change will affect your code. Suppose you want to change the value of a variable or preprocessor symbol. Before doing so, use the first menu item, Find this C symbol, to obtain a list of references that will be affected. Then use the editor to examine each one. This will help you predict the overall effects of your proposed change. Later, you can use cscope in the same way to verify that your changes have been made.

Notes

This section describes certain problems that may arise when you use `cscope` and how to avoid them.

Unknown Terminal Type

You may see the error message

```
Sorry, I don't know how to deal with your "term"
    terminal
```

If this message appears, your terminal may not be listed in the Terminal Information Utilities (`terminfo`) database that is currently loaded. Make sure you have assigned the correct value to TERM. If the message reappears, try reloading the Terminal Information Utilities.

You may also see

```
Sorry, I need to know a more specific terminal type
    than "unknown"
```

If this message appears, set and export the TERM variable as described in the section "Step 1: Set Up the Environment" above.

Command Line Syntax for Editors

As noted, `cscope` invokes the `vi` editor by default. You may override the default setting by assigning your preferred editor to the EDITOR environment variable and exporting EDITOR, as described in the section "Step 1: Set Up the Environment" above. Note, however, that `cscope` expects the editor it uses to have a command line syntax of the form

$ *editor +linenum filename*

as does `vi`. If the editor you want to use does not have this command line syntax, you must write an interface between `cscope` and the editor.

Suppose you want to use ed, for example. Because ed does not allow specification of a line number on the command line, you will not be able to use it to view or edit files with `cscope` unless you write a shell script (called `myedit` here) that contains the following line:

```
/usr/bin/ed $2
```

Now set the value of EDITOR to your shell script and export EDITOR:

```
$ EDITOR=myedit export EDITOR
```

When cscope invokes the editor for the list item you have specified, say, line 17 in main.c, it will invoke your shell script with the command line

```
$ myedit +17 main.c
```

myedit will discard the line number ($1) and call ed correctly with the file name ($2). Of course, you will then have to execute the appropriate ed commands to display and edit the line. That is, you will not be moved automatically to line 17 of the file.

9 make

Introduction

The trend toward increased modularity of programs means that a project may have to cope with a large assortment of individual files. There may also be a wide range of generation procedures needed to turn the assortment of individual files into the final executable product.

make provides a method for maintaining up-to-date versions of programs that consist of a number of files that may be generated in a variety of ways.

An individual programmer can easily forget

- file-to-file dependencies

- files that were modified and the impact that has on other files

- the exact sequence of operations needed to generate a new version of the program

In a description file, make keeps track of the commands that create files and the relationship between files. Whenever a change is made in any of the files that make up a program, the make command creates the finished program by recompiling only those portions directly or indirectly affected by the change.

The basic operation of make is to

- find the target in the description file

- ensure that all the files on which the target depends, the files needed to generate the target, exist and are up to date

- (re)create the target file if any of the generators have been modified more recently than the target

The description file that holds the information on interfile dependencies and command sequences is conventionally called makefile, Makefile, s.makefile, or s.Makefile. If this naming convention is followed, the simple command make is usually sufficient to regenerate the target regardless of the number of files edited since the last make. In most cases, the description file is not difficult to write and changes infrequently. Even if only a single file has been edited, rather than entering all the commands to regenerate the target, entering the make command ensures that the regeneration is done in the prescribed way.

Basic Features

The basic operation of make is to update a target file by ensuring that all of the files on which the target file depends exist and are up to date. The target file is regenerated if it has not been modified since the dependents were modified. The make program searches the graph of dependencies. The operation of make depends on its ability to find the date and time that a file was last modified.

The make program operates using three sources of information:

- a user-supplied description file
- file names and last-modified times from the file system
- built-in rules to bridge some of the gaps

To illustrate, consider a simple example in which a program named prog is made by compiling and loading three C language files x.c, y.c, and z.c with the math library, libm. By convention, the output of the C language compilations will be found in files named x.o, y.o, and z.o. Assume that the files x.c and y.c share some declarations in a file named defs.h, but that z.c does not. That is, x.c and y.c have the line

```
#include "defs.h"
```

The following specification describes the relationships and operations:

```
prog :   x.o  y.o  z.o
         cc  x.o  y.o  z.o  -lm  -o  prog

x.o  y.o :   defs.h
```

If this information were stored in a file named makefile, the command

```
$ make
```

would perform the operations needed to regenerate prog after any changes had been made to any of the four source files x.c, y.c, z.c, or defs.h. In the example above, the first line states that prog depends on three .o files. Once these object files are current, the second line describes how to load them to create prog. The third line states that x.o and y.o depend on the file defs.h. From the file system, make discovers that there are three .c files corresponding to the needed .o files and uses built-in rules on how to generate an object from a C source file (that is, issue a cc -c command).

If make did not have the ability to determine automatically what needs to be done, the following longer description file would be necessary:

```
prog :   x.o  y.o  z.o
         cc  x.o  y.o  z.o  -lm  -o prog
x.o :   x.c  defs.h
         cc  -c  x.c
y.o :   y.c  defs.h
         cc  -c  y.c
z.o :   z.c
         cc  -c  z.c
```

If none of the source or object files have changed since the last time prog was made, and all of the files are current, the command make announces this fact and stops. If, however, the defs.h file has been edited, x.c and y.c (but not z.c) are recompiled; and then prog is created from the new x.o and y.o files, and the existing z.o file. If only the file y.c had changed, only it is recompiled; but it is still necessary to reload prog. If no target name is given on the make command line, the first target mentioned in the description is created; otherwise, the specified targets are made. The command

```
$ make x.o
```

would regenerate x.o if x.c or defs.h had changed.

A method often useful to programmers is to include rules with mnemonic names and commands that do not actually produce a file with that name. These entries can take advantage of make's ability to generate files and substitute macros (for information about macros, see "Description Files and Substitutions" below.) Thus, an entry save might be included to copy a certain set of files, or an entry clean might be used to throw away unneeded intermediate files.

If a file exists after such commands are executed, the file's time of last modification is used in further decisions. If the file does not exist after the commands are executed, the current time is used in making further decisions.

You can maintain a zero-length file purely to keep track of the time at which certain actions were performed. This technique is useful for maintaining remote archives and listings.

A simple macro mechanism for substitution in dependency lines and command strings is used by make. Macros can either be defined by command-line arguments or included in the description file. In either case, a macro consists of a name followed by the symbol = followed by what the macro stands for. A macro is invoked by preceding the name by the symbol $. Macro names longer than one character must be parenthesized. The following are valid macro invocations:

```
$ (CFLAGS)
$2
$ (xy)
$Z
$ (Z)
```

The last two are equivalent.

$*, $@, $?, and $< are four special macros that change values during the execution of the command. (These four macros are described later in this chapter under "Description Files and Substitutions.") The following fragment shows assignment and use of some macros:

```
OBJECTS = x.o  y.o  z.o
LIBES = -lm
prog: $ (OBJECTS)
        cc $ (OBJECTS)  $ (LIBES)  -o prog
     . . .
```

The command

```
$ make  LIBES="-ll -lm"
```

loads the three objects with both the lex (-ll) and the math (-lm) libraries, because macro definitions on the command line override definitions in the description file. (In UNIX system commands, arguments with embedded blanks must somehow be quoted.)

As an example of the use of make, a description file that might be used to maintain the make command itself is given. The code for make is spread over a number of C language source files and has a yacc grammar. The description file contains the following:

```
# Description file for the make command
FILES = Makefile defs.h main.c doname.c misc.c \
        files.c dosys.c gram.y
OBJECTS = main.o doname.o misc.o files.o \
          dosys.o gram.o
LIBES =
LINT = lint -p
CFLAGS = -O
LP = lp

make:   $(OBJECTS)
        $(CC) $(CFLAGS) -o make $(OBJECTS) $(LIBES)
        @size make

$(OBJECTS): defs.h

cleanup:
        -rm *.o gram.c
        -du

install:
        make
        @size make /usr/bin/make
        cp make /usr/bin/make && rm make

lint:   dosys.c doname.c files.c main.c misc.c gram.c
        $(LINT) dosys.c doname.c files.c main.c misc.c \
        gram.c

                  # print files that are out-of-date
                  # with respect to "print" file.

print:  $(FILES)
        pr $? | $(LP)
        touch print
```

The make program prints out each command before issuing it.

The following output results from entering the command make in a directory containing only the source and description files:

```
cc  -O -c main.c
cc  -O -c doname.c
cc  -O -c misc.c
cc  -O -c files.c
cc  -O -c dosys.c
yacc  gram.y
mv y.tab.c gram.c
cc  -O -c gram.c
cc  -o make  main.o doname.o misc.o files.o dosys.o gram.o
13188 + 3348 + 3044 = 19580
```

The last line results from the size make command. The printing of the command line itself was suppressed by the symbol @ in the description file.

Description Files and Substitutions

The following section will explain the customary elements of the description file.

Comments

The comment convention is that the symbol # and all characters on the same line after it are ignored. Blank lines and lines beginning with # are totally ignored.

Continuation Lines

If a noncomment line is too long, the line can be continued by using the symbol \, which must be the last character on the line. If the last character of a line is \, then it, the new-line, and all following blanks and tabs are replaced by a single blank. Comments can be continued on to the next line as well.

Macro Definitions

A macro definition is an identifier followed by the symbol =. The identifier must not be preceded by a colon (:) or a tab. The name (string of letters and digits) to the left of the = (trailing blanks and tabs are stripped) is assigned the string of characters following the = (leading blanks and tabs are stripped). The following are valid macro definitions:

```
2 = xyz
abc = -ll -ly -lm
LIBES =
```

The last definition assigns LIBES the null string. A macro that is never explicitly defined has the null string as its value. Remember, however, that some macros are explicitly defined in make's own rules. (See Figure 9-2 at the end of the chapter.)

General Form

The general form of an entry in a description file is

> *target1* [*target2* ...] : [:] [*dependent1* ...] [; *commands*] [# ...]
> [\t *commands*] [# ...]
> . . .

Items inside brackets may be omitted and targets and dependents are strings of letters, digits, periods, and slashes. Shell metacharacters such as * and ? are expanded when the commands are evaluated. Commands may appear either after a semicolon on a dependency line or on lines beginning with a tab (denoted above as \t) immediately following a dependency line. A command is any string of characters not including #, except when # is in quotes.

Dependency Information

A dependency line may have either a single or a double colon. A target name may appear on more than one dependency line, but all of those lines must be of the same (single or double colon) type. For the more common single colon case, a command sequence may be associated with at most one dependency line. If the target is out of date with any of the dependents on any of the lines and a command sequence is specified (even a null one following a semicolon or tab), it is executed; otherwise, a default rule may be invoked. In the double colon case, a command sequence may be associated with more than one dependency line. If the target is out of date with any of the files on a particular line, the associated commands are executed. A built-in rule may also be executed. The double colon form is particularly useful in updating archive-type files, where the target is the archive library itself. (An example is included in the "Archive Libraries" section later in this chapter.)

Executable Commands

If a target must be created, the sequence of commands is executed. Normally, each command line is printed and then passed to a separate invocation of the shell after substituting for macros. The printing is suppressed in the silent mode (−s option of the make command) or if the command line in the description file begins with an @ sign. make normally stops if any command signals an error by returning a nonzero error code. Errors are ignored if the −i flag has been specified on the make command line, if the fake target name .IGNORE appears in the description file, or if the command string in the description file begins with a hyphen (−). If a program is known to return a meaningless status, a hyphen in front of the command that invokes it is appropriate. Because each command line is passed to a separate invocation of the shell, care must be taken with certain commands (cd and shell control commands, for instance) that have meaning only within a single shell process. These results are forgotten before the next line is executed.

Before issuing any command, certain internally maintained macros are set. The $@ macro is set to the full target name of the current target. The $@ macro is evaluated only for explicitly named dependencies. The $? macro is set to the string of names that were found to be younger than the target. The $? macro is evaluated when explicit rules from the makefile are evaluated. If the command was generated by an implicit rule, the $< macro is the name of the related file that caused the action; and the $* macro is the prefix shared by the current and the dependent file names. If a file must be made but there are no explicit commands or relevant built-in rules, the commands associated with the name .DEFAULT are used. If there is no such name, make prints a message and stops.

In addition, a description file may also use the following related macros: $(@D), $(@F), $(*D), $(*F), $(<D), and $(<F) (see below).

Extensions of $*, $@, and $<

The internally generated macros $*, $@, and $< are useful generic terms for current targets and out-of-date relatives. To this list is added the following related macros: $(@D), $(@F), $(*D), $(*F), $(<D), and $(<F). The D refers to the directory part of the single character macro. The F refers to the file name part of the single character macro. These additions are useful when building hierarchical makefiles. They allow access to directory names for purposes of using the cd command of the shell. Thus, a command can be

        cd $(<D); $(MAKE) $(<F)

Output Translations

The values of macros are replaced when evaluated. The general form, where brackets indicate that the enclosed sequence is optional, is as follows:

        $ (macro [: string1= [string2]])

The parentheses are optional if there is no substitution specification and the macro name is a single character. If a substitution sequence is present, the value of the macro is considered to be a sequence of "words" separated by sequences of blanks, tabs, and new-line characters. Then, for each such word that ends with string1, string1 is replaced with string2 (or no characters if string2 is not present).

This particular substitution capability was chosen because make usually concerns itself with suffixes. The usefulness of this type of translation occurs when maintaining archive libraries. Now, all that is necessary is to accumulate the out-of-date members and write a shell script that can handle all the C language programs (that is, files ending in .c). Thus, the following fragment optimizes the executions of make for maintaining an archive library:

        $(LIB) : $(LIB) (a.o) $(LIB) (b.o) $(LIB) (c.o)
                $(CC) -c $(CFLAGS) $(?:.o=.c)
                $(AR) $(ARFLAGS) $(LIB) $?
                rm $?

A dependency of the preceding form is necessary for each of the different types of source files (suffixes) that define the archive library. These translations are added in an effort to make more general use of the wealth of information that make generates.

Recursive Makefiles

Another feature of make concerns the environment and recursive invocations. If the sequence $ (MAKE) appears anywhere in a shell command line, the line is executed even if the −n flag is set. Since the −n flag is exported across invocations of make (through the MAKEFLAGS variable), the only thing that is executed is the make command itself. This feature is useful when a hierarchy of makefiles describes a set of software subsystems. For testing purposes, make −n can be executed and everything that would have been done will be printed including output from lower-level invocations of make.

Suffixes and Transformation Rules

make uses an internal table of rules to learn how to transform a file with one suffix into a file with another suffix. If the −r flag is used on the make command line, the internal table is not used.

The list of suffixes is actually the dependency list for the name . SUFFIXES. make searches for a file with any of the suffixes on the list. If it finds one, make transforms it into a file with another suffix. Transformation rule names are the concatenation of the before and after suffixes. The name of the rule to transform a . r file to a . o file is thus . r . o. If the rule is present and no explicit command sequence has been given in the user's description files, the command sequence for the rule . r . o is used. If a command is generated by using one of these suffixing rules, the macro $* is given the value of the stem (everything but the suffix) of the name of the file to be made; and the macro $< is the full name of the dependent that caused the action.

The order of the suffix list is significant since the list is scanned from left to right. The first name formed that has both a file and a rule associated with it is used. If new names are to be appended, the user can add an entry for . SUFFIXES in the description file. The dependents are added to the usual list.

make   **9-11**

A .SUFFIXES line without any dependents deletes the current list. It is necessary to clear the current list if the order of names is to be changed.

Implicit Rules

make uses a table of suffixes and a set of transformation rules to supply default
dependency information and implied commands. The default suffix list (in
order) is as follows:

.o	Object file
.c	C source file
.c~	SCCS C source file
.y	yacc C source grammar
.y~	SCCS yacc C source grammar
.l	lex C source grammar
.l~	SCCS lex C source grammar
.s	Assembler source file
.s~	SCCS assembler source file
.sh	Shell file
.sh~	SCCS shell file
.h	Header file
.h~	SCCS header file
.f	FORTRAN source file
.f~	SCCS FORTRAN source file
.C	C++ source file
.C~	SCCS C++ source file
.Y	yacc C++ source grammar

.Y~   SCCS yacc C++ source grammar

.L   lex C++ source grammar

.L~   SCCS lex C++ source grammar

Figure 9-1 summarizes the default transformation paths. If there are two paths connecting a pair of suffixes, the longer one is used only if the intermediate file exists or is named in the description.

Figure 9-1: Summary of Default Transformation Path

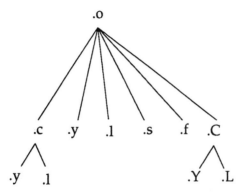

If the file x.o is needed and an x.c is found in the description or directory, the x.o file would be compiled. If there is also an x.l, that source file would be run through lex before compiling the result. However, if there is no x.c but there is an x.l, make would discard the intermediate C language file and use the direct link as shown in Figure 9-1.

It is possible to change the names of some of the compilers used in the default or the flag arguments with which they are invoked by knowing the macro names used. The compiler names are the macros AS, CC, C++C, F77, YACC, and LEX. The command

```
$ make CC=newcc
```

will cause the newcc command to be used instead of the usual C language compiler. The macros CFLAGS, YFLAGS, LFLAGS, ASFLAGS, FFLAGS, and

C++FLAGS may be set to cause these commands to be issued with optional flags. Thus

        $ make CFLAGS=-g

causes the cc command to include debugging information.

Archive Libraries

The make program has an interface to archive libraries. A user may name a member of a library in the following manner:

        projlib(object.o)

or

        projlib((entry_pt))

where the second method actually refers to an entry point of an object file within the library. (make looks through the library, locates the entry point, and translates it to the correct object file name.)

To use this procedure to maintain an archive library, the following type of makefile is required:

```
projlib::   projlib(pfile1.o)
            $(CC) -c $(CFLAGS) pfile1.c
            $(AR) $(ARFLAGS) projlib pfile1.o
            rm pfile1.o
projlib::   projlib(pfile2.o)
            $(CC) -c $(CFLAGS) pfile2.c
            $(AR) $(ARFLAGS) projlib pfile2.o
            rm pfile2.o
```

and so on for each object. This is tedious and error prone. Obviously, the command sequences for adding a C language file to a library are the same for each invocation; the file name being the only difference each time. (This is true in most cases.)

The make command also gives the user access to a rule for building libraries. The handle for the rule is the .a suffix. Thus, a .c.a rule is the rule for compiling a C language source file, adding it to the library, and removing the .o file. Similarly, the .y.a, the .s.a, and the .l.a rules rebuild yacc, assembler, and lex files, respectively. The archive rules defined internally are .c.a, .c~.a, .f.a, .f~.a, and .s~.a. (The tilde (~) syntax will be described shortly.) The user may define other needed rules in the description file.

The above two-member library is then maintained with the following shorter makefile:

```
projlib:          projlib(pfile1.o) projlib(pfile2.o)
          @echo projlib up-to-date.
```

The internal rules are already defined to complete the preceding library maintenance. The actual .c.a rule is as follows:

```
.c.a:
          $(CC) -c $(CFLAGS) $<
          $(AR) $(ARFLAGS) $@ $*.o
          rm -f $*.o
```

Thus, the $@ macro is the .a target (projlib); the $< and $* macros are set to the out-of-date C language file, and the file name minus the suffix, respectively (pfile1.c and pfile1). The $< macro (in the preceding rule) could have been changed to $*.c.

It is useful to go into some detail about exactly what make does when it sees the construction

```
projlib:     projlib(pfile1.o)
          @echo projlib up-to-date
```

Assume the object in the library is out of date with respect to pfile1.c. Also, there is no pfile1.o file.

1.   make projlib.

2.   Before makeing projlib, check each dependent of projlib.

3.   projlib(pfile1.o) is a dependent of projlib and needs to be generated.

4.   Before generating projlib(pfile1.o), check each dependent of projlib(pfile1.o). (There are none.)

5.   Use internal rules to try to create projlib(pfile1.o). (There is no explicit rule.) Note that projlib(pfile1.o) has a parenthesis in the name to identify the target suffix as .a. This is the key. There is no explicit .a at the end of the projlib library name. The

parenthesis implies the .a suffix. In this sense, the .a is hard-wired
into make.

6. Break the name `projlib(pfile1.o)` up into `projlib` and
    `pfile1.o`. Define two macros, `$@` (`projlib`) and
    `$*` (`pfile1`).

7. Look for a rule `.X.a` and a file `$*.X`. The first `.X` (in the
    `.SUFFIXES` list) which fulfills these conditions is `.c` so the rule is
    `.c.a`, and the file is `pfile1.c`. Set `$<` to be `pfile1.c` and execute
    the rule. In fact, make must then compile `pfile1.c`.

8. The library has been updated. Execute the command associated with
    the `projlib`: dependency, namely

    ```
    @echo projlib up-to-date
    ```

It should be noted that to let `pfile1.o` have dependencies, the following syntax is required:

```
projlib(pfile1.o) :          $(INCDIR)/stdio.h   pfile1.c
```

There is also a macro for referencing the archive member name when this form
is used. The `$%` macro is evaluated each time `$@` is evaluated. If there is no
current archive member, `$%` is null. If an archive member exists, then `$%` evaluates to the expression between the parenthesis.

Source Code Control System File Names

The syntax of make does not directly permit referencing of prefixes. For most
types of files on UNIX operating system machines, this is acceptable since nearly
everyone uses a suffix to distinguish different types of files. SCCS files are the
exception. Here, `s.` precedes the file name part of the complete path name.

To allow make easy access to the prefix `s.` the symbol `~` is used as an identifier
of SCCS files. Hence, `.c~.o` refers to the rule which transforms an SCCS C
language source file into an object file. Specifically, the internal rule is

```
.c~.o:
        $(GET)  $(GFLAGS)  $<
        $(CC)  $(CFLAGS)  -c  $*.c
        rm  -f  $*.c
```

Thus, ~ appended to any suffix transforms the file search into an SCCS file name search with the actual suffix named by the dot and all characters up to (but not including) ~.

The following SCCS suffixes are internally defined:

.c~	.sh~	.C~
.y~	.h~	.Y~
.l~	.f~	.L~
.s~		

The following rules involving SCCS transformations are internally defined:

.c~:	.s~.s:	.C~:
.c~.c:	.s~.a:	.C~.C:
.c~.a:	.s~.o:	.C~.a:
.c~.o:	.sh~:	.C~.o:
.y~.c:	.sh~.sh:	.Y~.C:
.y~.o:	.h~.h:	.Y~.o:
.y~.y:	.f~:	.Y~.Y:
.l~.c:	.f~.f:	.L~.C:
.l~.o:	.f~.a:	.L~.o:
.l~.l:	.f~.o:	.L~.L:
.s~:		

Obviously, the user can define other rules and suffixes that may prove useful. The ~ provides a handle on the SCCS file name format so that this is possible.

The Null Suffix

There are many programs that consist of a single source file. make handles this case by the null suffix rule. Thus, to maintain the UNIX system program cat, a rule in the makefile of the following form is needed:

```
.c:
        $(CC) -o $@ $(CFLAGS) $(LDFLAGS) $<
```

In fact, this .c: rule is internally defined so no makefile is necessary at all. The user only needs to enter

```
$ make cat dd echo date
```

(these are all UNIX system single-file programs) and all four C language source files are passed through the above shell command line associated with the .c: rule. The internally defined single suffix rules are

.c:	.sh:	.f~:
.c~:	.sh~:	.C:
.s:	.f:	.C~:
.s~:		

Others may be added in the makefile by the user.

Included Files

The make program has a capability similar to the #include directive of the C preprocessor. If the string include appears as the first seven letters of a line in a makefile and is followed by a blank or a tab, the rest of the line is assumed to be a file name, which the current invocation of make will read. Macros may be used in file names. The file descriptors are stacked for reading include files so that no more than 16 levels of nested includes are supported.

SCCS Makefiles

Makefiles under SCCS control are accessible to make. That is, if make is typed and only a file named s.makefile or s.Makefile exists, make will do a get on the file, then read and remove the file.

Dynamic Dependency Parameters

A dynamic dependency parameter has meaning only on the dependency line in a makefile. The $$@ refers to the current "thing" to the left of the : symbol (which is $@). Also the form $$(@F) exists, which allows access to the file part of $@. Thus, in the following:

    cat: $$@.c

the dependency is translated at execution time to the string cat.c. This is useful for building a large number of executable files, each of which has only one source file. For instance, the UNIX system software command directory could have a `makefile` like:

```
CMDS = cat dd echo date cmp comm chown

$(CMDS):           $$@.c
           $(CC) $(CFLAGS) $? -o $@
```

Obviously, this is a subset of all the single file programs. For multiple file programs, a directory is usually allocated and a separate `makefile` is made. For any particular file that has a peculiar compilation procedure, a specific entry must be made in the `makefile`.

The second useful form of the dependency parameter is $$(@F). It represents the file name part of $$@. Again, it is evaluated at execution time. Its usefulness becomes evident when trying to maintain the /usr/include directory from `makefile` in the /usr/src/head directory. Thus, the /usr/src/head/makefile would look like

```
INCDIR = /usr/include

INCLUDES = \
           $(INCDIR)/stdio.h \
           $(INCDIR)/pwd.h \
           $(INCDIR)/dir.h \
           $(INCDIR)/a.out.h

$(INCLUDES): $$(@F)
           cp $? $@
           chmod 0444 $@
```

This would completely maintain the /usr/include directory whenever one of the above files in /usr/src/head was updated.

Command Usage

The make command description is found under make in Section 1 of the *Programmer's Reference Manual*.

The make Command

The make command takes macro definitions, options, description file names, and target file names as arguments in the form:

$ make [*options*] [*macro definitions and targets*]

The following summary of command operations explains how these arguments are interpreted.

First, all macro definition arguments (arguments with embedded = symbols) are analyzed and the assignments made. Command line macros override corresponding definitions found in the description files. Next, the option arguments are examined. The permissible options are as follows:

-i   Ignore error codes returned by invoked commands. This mode is entered if the fake target name .IGNORE appears in the description file.

-s   Silent mode. Do not print command lines before executing. This mode is also entered if the fake target name .SILENT appears in the description file.

-r   Do not use the built-in rules.

-n   No execute mode. Print commands, but do not execute them. Even lines beginning with an @ sign are printed.

-t   Touch the target files (causing them to be up to date) rather than issue the usual commands.

-q   Question. The make command returns a zero or nonzero status code depending on whether the target file is or is not up to date.

-p   Print out the complete set of macro definitions and target descriptions.

-k   Abandon work on the current entry if something goes wrong, but
continue on other branches that do not depend on the current entry.

-e   Environment variables override assignments within makefiles.

-f   Description file name. The next argument is assumed to be the name
of a description file. A file name of – denotes the standard input. If
there are no −f arguments, the file named makefile, Makefile,
s.makefile, or s.Makefile in the current directory is read. The
contents of the description files override the built-in rules if they are
present.

The following two fake target names are evaluated in the same manner as flags:

.DEFAULT   If a file must be made but there are no explicit commands or relevant built-in rules, the commands associated with the name .DEFAULT are used if it exists.

.PRECIOUS   Dependents on this target are not removed when quit
or interrupt is pressed.

Finally, the remaining arguments are assumed to be the names of targets to be
made and the arguments are done in left-to-right order. If there are no such
arguments, the first name in the description file that does not begin with the
symbol . is made.

Environment Variables

Environment variables are read and added to the macro definitions each time
make executes. Precedence is a prime consideration in doing this properly. The
following describes make's interaction with the environment. A macro,
MAKEFLAGS, is maintained by make. The macro is defined as the collection of
all input flag arguments into a string (without minus signs). The macro is
exported and thus accessible to recursive invocations of make. Command line
flags and assignments in the makefile update MAKEFLAGS. Thus, to describe
how the environment interacts with make, the MAKEFLAGS macro (environment
variable) must be considered.

When executed, make assigns macro definitions in the following order:

1. Read the MAKEFLAGS environment variable. If it is not present or
    null, the internal make variable MAKEFLAGS is set to the null string.
    Otherwise, each letter in MAKEFLAGS is assumed to be an input flag
    argument and is processed as such. (The only exceptions are the −f,
    −p, and −r flags.)

2. Read the internal list of macro definitions.

3. Read the environment. The environment variables are treated as
    macro definitions and marked as exported (in the shell sense).

4. Read the makefile(s). The assignments in the makefile(s) over-
    ride the environment. This order is chosen so that when a
    makefile is read and executed, you know what to expect. That is,
    you get what is seen unless the −e flag is used. The −e is the input
    flag argument, which tells make to have the environment override
    the makefile assignments. Thus, if make −e is entered, the vari-
    ables in the environment override the definitions in the makefile.
    Also MAKEFLAGS overrides the environment if assigned. This is use-
    ful for further invocations of make from the current makefile.

It may be clearer to list the precedence of assignments. Thus, in order from
least binding to most binding, the precedence of assignments is as follows:

1. internal definitions

2. environment

3. makefile(s)

4. command line

The −e flag has the effect of rearranging the order to:

1. internal definitions

2. makefile(s)

3. environment

4. command line

This order is general enough to allow a programmer to define a makefile or
set of makefiles whose parameters are dynamically definable.

Suggestions and Warnings

The most common difficulties arise from make's specific meaning of dependency. If file x.c has a

        #include "defs.h"

line, then the object file x.o depends on defs.h; the source file x.c does not. If defs.h is changed, nothing is done to the file x.c while file x.o must be recreated.

To discover what make would do, the −n option is very useful. The command

        $ make −n

orders make to print out the commands that make would issue without actually taking the time to execute them. If a change to a file is absolutely certain to be mild in character (adding a comment to an include file, for example), the −t (touch) option can save a lot of time. Instead of issuing a large number of superfluous recompilations, make updates the modification times on the affected file. Thus, the command

        $ make −ts

(touch silently) causes the relevant files to appear up to date. Obvious care is necessary because this mode of operation subverts the intention of make and destroys all memory of the previous relationships.

Internal Rules

The standard set of internal rules used by make are reproduced below.

Figure 9-2: make Internal Rules

```
#
#          SUFFIXES RECOGNIZED BY MAKE
#
.SUFFIXES: .o .c .c~ .y .y~ .l .l~ .s .s~ .sh .sh~ .h .h~ .f .f~ .C .C~ \
           .Y .Y~ .L .L~

#
#          PREDEFINED MACROS
#
AR=ar
ARFLAGS=-rv
AS=as
ASFLAGS=
BUILD=build
CC=cc
CFLAGS=-O
C++C=CC
C++FLAGS=-O
F77=f77
FFLAGS=-O
GET=get
GFLAGS=
LEX=lex
LFLAGS=
LD=ld
LDFLAGS=
MAKE=make
MAKEFLAGS=
YACC=yacc
YFLAGS=
$=$
#
#          SPECIAL RULES
#
markfile.o : markfile
        A=@; echo "static char _sccsid[]=\042'grep $$A'(#)' markfile'\042;" \
        > markfile.c
        $(CC) -c markfile.c
        rm -f markfile.c
```

(continued on next page)

ANSI C and Programming Support Tools

Figure 9-2: make Internal Rules (continued)

```
#
#          SINGLE SUFFIX RULES
#
.c:
          $(CC) $(CFLAGS) $(LDFLAGS) -o $@ $<

.c~:
          $(GET) $(GFLAGS) $<
          $(CC) $(CFLAGS) $(LDFLAGS) -o $* $*.c
          rm -f $*.c

.s:
          $(AS) $(AFLAGS) -o $@ $<

.s~:
          $(GET) $(GFLAGS) $<
          $(AS) $(AFLAGS) -o $@ $*.s
          rm -f $*.s

.sh:
          cp $< $@; chmod 0777 $@

.sh~:
          $(GET) $(GFLAGS) $<
          cp $*.sh $*; chmod 0777 $@
          rm -f $*.sh

.f:
          $(F77) $(FFLAGS) $(LDFLAGS) -o $@ $<

.f~:
          $(GET) $(GFLAGS) $<
          $(F77) $(FFLAGS) -o $@ $(LDFLAGS) $*.f
          rm -f $*.f

.C~:
          $(GET) $(GFLAGS) $<
          $(C++C) $(C++FLAGS) -o $@ $(LDFLAGS) $*.C
          rm -f $*.C

.C:
          $(C++C) $(C++FLAGS) -o $@ $(LDFLAGS) $<
```

(continued on next page)

Figure 9-2: make Internal Rules (continued)

```
#
#            DOUBLE SUFFIX RULES
#
.c~.c .y~.y .l~.l .s~.s .sh~.sh .h~.h: .f~.f .C~.C .Y~.Y .L~.L:
            $(GET) $(GFLAGS) $<

.c.a:
            $(CC) -c $(CFLAGS) $<
            $(AR) $(ARFLAGS) $@ $*.o
            rm -f $*.o

.c~.a:
            $(GET) $(GFLAGS) $<
            $(CC) -c $(CFLAGS) $*.c
            $(AR) $(ARFLAGS) $@ $*.o
            rm -f $*.[co]

.c.o:
            $(CC) $(CFLAGS) -c $<

.c~.o:
            $(GET) $(GFLAGS) $<
            $(CC) $(CFLAGS) -c $*.c
            rm -f $*.c

.y.c:
            $(YACC) $(YFLAGS) $<
            mv y.tab.c $@

.y~.c:
            $(GET) $(GFLAGS) $<
            $(YACC) $(YFLAGS) $*.y
            mv y.tab.c $*.c
            rm -f $*.y

.y.o:
            $(YACC) $(YFLAGS) $<
            $(CC) $(CFLAGS) -c y.tab.c
            rm -f y.tab.c
            mv y.tab.o $@

.y~.o:
            $(GET) $(GFLAGS) $<
            $(YACC) $(YFLAGS) $*.y
            $(CC) $(CFLAGS) -c y.tab.c
            rm -f y.tab.c $*.y
            mv y.tab.o $*.o
```

(continued on next page)

ANSI C and Programming Support Tools

Figure 9-2: make Internal Rules (continued)

```
.l.c:
        $(LEX) $(LFLAGS) $<
        mv lex.yy.c $@
.l~.c:
        $(GET) $(GFLAGS) $<
        $(LEX) $(LFLAGS) $*.l
        mv lex.yy.c $@
        rm -f $*.l
.l.o:
        $(LEX) $(LFLAGS) $<
        $(CC) $(CFLAGS) -c lex.yy.c
        rm -f lex.yy.c
        mv lex.yy.o $@
.l~.o:
        $(GET) $(GFLAGS) $<
        $(LEX) $(LFLAGS) $*.l
        $(CC) $(CFLAGS) -c lex.yy.c
        rm -f lex.yy.c $*.l
        mv lex.yy.o $@
.s.a:
        $(AS) $(ASFLAGS) -o $*.o $*.s
        $(AR) $(ARFLAGS) $@ $*.o
.s~.a:
        $(GET) $(GFLAGS) $<
        $(AS) $(ASFLAGS) -o $*.o $*.s
        $(AR) $(ARFLAGS) $@ $*.o
        rm -f $*.[so]
.s.o:
        $(AS) $(ASFLAGS) -o $@ $<
.s~.o:
        $(GET) $(GFLAGS) $<
        $(AS) $(ASFLAGS) -o $*.o $*.s
        rm -f $*.s
.f.a:
        $(F77) $(FFLAGS) -c $*.f
        $(AR) $(ARFLAGS) $@ $*.o
        rm -f $*.o
```

(continued on next page)

make

Figure 9-2: make Internal Rules (continued)

```
.f~.a:
          $(GET) $(GFLAGS) $<
          $(F77) $(FFLAGS) -c $*.f
          $(AR) $(ARFLAGS) $@ $*.o
          rm -f $*.[fo]

.f.o:
          $(F77) $(FFLAGS) -c $*.f

.f~.o:
          $(GET) $(GFLAGS) $<
          $(F77) $(FFLAGS) -c $*.f
          rm -f $*.f

.C.a:
          $(C++C) $(C++FLAGS) -c $<
          $(AR) $(ARFLAGS) $@ $*.o
          rm -f $*.o

.C~.a:
          $(GET) $(GFLAGS) $<
          $(C++C) $(C++FLAGS) -c $*.C
          $(AR) $(ARFLAGS) $@ $*.o
          rm -f $*.[Co]

.C.o:
          $(C++C) $(C++FLAGS) -c $<

.C~.o:
          $(GET) $(GFLAGS) $<
          $(C++C) $(C++FLAGS) -c $*.C
          rm -f $*.C

.Y.C:
          $(YACC) $(YFLAGS) $<
          mv y.tab.c $@

.Y~.C:
          $(GET) $(GFLAGS) $<
          $(YACC) $(YFLAGS) $*.Y
          mv y.tab.c $*.C
          rm -f $*.Y

.Y.o:
          $(YACC) $(YFLAGS) $<
          $(C++C) $(C++FLAGS) -c y.tab.c
          rm -f y.tab.c
          mv y.tab.o $@
```

(continued on next page)

Figure 9-2: make Internal Rules (continued)

```
.Y~.o:
        $(GET) $(GFLAGS) $<
        $(YACC) $(YFLAGS) $*.Y
        $(C++C) $(C++FLAGS) -c y.tab.c
        rm -f y.tab.c $*.Y
        mv y.tab.o $*.o

.L.C:
        $(LEX) $(LFLAGS) $<
        mv lex.yy.c $@

.L~.C:
        $(GET) $(GFLAGS) $<
        $(LEX) $(LFLAGS) $*.L
        mv lex.yy.c $@
        rm -f $*.L

.L.o:
        $(LEX) $(LFLAGS) $<
        $(C++C) $(C++FLAGS) -c lex.yy.c
        rm -f lex.yy.c
        mv lex.yy.o $@

.L~.o:
        $(GET) $(GFLAGS) $<
        $(LEX) $(LFLAGS) $*.L
        $(C++C) $(C++FLAGS) -c lex.yy.c
        rm -f lex.yy.c $*.L
        mv lex.yy.o $@
```

make

10 SCCS

SCCS Files

Introduction

The Source Code Control System, SCCS, is a a set of programs that you can use to track evolving versions of files, ordinary text files as well as source files. SCCS takes custody of a file and, when changes are made, identifies and stores them in the file with the original source code and/or documentation. As other changes are made, they too are identified and retained in the file.

Retrieval of the original or any set of changes is possible. Any version of the file as it develops can be reconstructed for inspection or additional modification. History information can be stored with each version: why the changes were made, who made them, and when they were made.

This chapter covers the following topics:

- the basics of creating, retrieving, and updating an SCCS file;

- delta numbering: how versions of an SCCS file are named;

- SCCS command conventions: what rules apply to SCCS commands;

- SCCS commands: the 14 SCCS commands and their more useful arguments;

- SCCS files: protection, format, and auditing of SCCS files.

Basic Usage

Several terminal session fragments are presented in this section. Try them all. The best way to learn SCCS is to use it.

Terminology

A delta is a set of changes made to a file under SCCS custody. To identify and keep track of a delta, it is assigned an SID (SCCS IDentification) number. The SID for any original file turned over to SCCS is composed of release number 1 and level number 1, stated as 1.1. The SID for the first set of changes made to that file, that is, its first delta, is release 1 version 2, or 1.2. The next delta would be 1.3, the next 1.4, and so on. More on delta numbering later. At this point, it is enough to know that by default SCCS assigns SIDs automatically.

Creating an SCCS File with admin

Suppose you have a file called lang that is simply a list of five programming language names:

```
C
PL/I
FORTRAN
COBOL
ALGOL
```

Custody of your lang file can be given to SCCS using the admin (for administer) command. The following creates an SCCS file from the lang file:

```
$ admin -ilang s.lang
```

All SCCS files must have names that begin with s., hence s.lang. The -i keyletter, together with its value lang, means admin is to create an SCCS file and initialize it with the contents of the file lang.

The admin command replies

```
No id keywords (cm7)
```

This is a warning message that may also be issued by other SCCS commands. Ignore it for now. Its significance is described later under the get command in the section "SCCS Commands." In the following examples, this warning message is not shown although it may be issued.

Remove the lang file. It is no longer needed because it exists now under SCCS as s.lang.

```
$ rm lang
```

Retrieving a File with get

The command

```
$ get s.lang
```

retrieves the latest version of s.lang and prints

```
1.1
5 lines
```

This tells you that get retrieved version 1.1 of the file, which is made up of five lines of text.

The retrieved text is placed in a new file called lang. That is, if you list the contents of your directory, you will see both lang and s.lang.

The get s.lang command creates lang as read-only and keeps no information regarding its creation. Because you are going to make changes to it, get must be informed of your intention to do so. This is done as follows:

```
$ get -e s.lang
```

get -e causes SCCS to create lang for both reading and writing (editing). It also places certain information about lang in another new file, called p.lang, which is needed later by the delta command. Now if you list the contents of your directory, you will see s.lang, lang, and p.lang.

get -e prints the same messages as get, except that the SID for the first delta you will create also is issued:

```
1.1
new delta 1.2
5 lines
```

Change lang by adding two more programming languages:

```
SNOBOL
ADA
```

Recording Changes with delta

Next, use the delta command as follows:

```
$ delta s.lang
```

delta then prompts with

```
comments?
```

Your response should be an explanation of why the changes were made. For example,

```
added more languages
```

delta now reads the file p.lang and determines what changes you made to lang. It does this by doing its own get to retrieve the original version and applying the diff command (described in Section 1 of the *User's Reference Manual*), to the original version and the edited version. Next, delta stores the changes in s.lang and destroys the no longer needed p.lang and lang files.

When this process is complete, delta outputs

```
1.2
2 inserted
0 deleted
5 unchanged
```

The number 1.2 is the SID of the delta you just created, and the next three lines summarize what was done to s.lang.

More on get

The command

```
$ get s.lang
```

retrieves the latest version of the file s.lang, now 1.2. SCCS does this by starting with the original version of the file and applying the delta you made. If
you use the get command now, any of the following will retrieve version 1.2:

```
$ get s.lang
$ get -r1 s.lang
$ get -r1.2 s.lang
```

The numbers following -r are SIDs. When you omit the level number of the
SID (as in get -r1 s.lang), the default is the highest level number that exists
within the specified release. Thus, the second command requests the retrieval of
the latest version in release 1, namely 1.2. The third command requests the
retrieval of a particular version, in this case also 1.2.

Whenever a major change is made to a file, you may want to signify it by
changing the release number, the first number of the SID. This, too, is done
with the get command:

```
$ get -e -r2 s.lang
```

Because release 2 does not exist, get retrieves the latest version before release 2.
get also interprets this as a request to change the release number of the new
delta to 2, thereby naming it 2.1 rather than 1.3. The output is

```
1.2
new delta 2.1
7 lines
```

which means version 1.2 has been retrieved, and 2.1 is the version the delta
command will create. If the file is now edited — for example, by deleting
COBOL from the list of languages — and delta is executed

```
$ delta s.lang
comments? deleted cobol from list of languages
```

you will see by delta's output that version 2.1 is indeed created:

```
2.1
0 inserted
1 deleted
6 unchanged
```

Deltas can now be created in release 2 (deltas 2.2, 2.3, etc.), or another new release can be created in a similar manner.

The help Command

If the command

```
$ get lang
```

is now executed, the following message will be output:

```
ERROR [lang]: not an SCCS file (co1)
```

The code co1 can be used with help to print a fuller explanation of the message:

```
$ help co1
```

This gives the following explanation of why get lang produced an error message:

```
co1:
"not an SCCS file"
A file that you think is an SCCS file
does not begin with the characters "s.".
```

help is useful whenever there is doubt about the meaning of almost any SCCS message.

Delta Numbering

Think of deltas as the nodes of a tree in which the root node is the original version of the file. The root node is normally named 1.1 and deltas (nodes) are named 1.2, 1.3, etc. The components of these SIDs are called release and level numbers, respectively. Thus, normal naming of new deltas proceeds by incrementing the level number. This is done automatically by SCCS whenever a delta is made.

Because the user may change the release number to indicate a major change, the release number then applies to all new deltas unless specifically changed again. Thus, the evolution of a particular file could be represented by Figure 10-1.

Figure 10-1: Evolution of an SCCS File

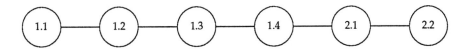

This is the normal sequential development of an SCCS file, with each delta dependent on the preceding deltas. Such a structure is called the trunk of an SCCS tree.

There are situations that require branching an SCCS tree. That is, changes are planned to a given delta that will not be dependent on all previous deltas. For example, consider a program in production use at version 1.3 and for which development work on release 2 is already in progress. Release 2 may already have a delta in progress as shown in Figure 10-1. Assume that a production user reports a problem in version 1.3 that cannot wait to be repaired in release 2. The changes necessary to repair the trouble will be applied as a delta to version 1.3 (the version in production use). This creates a new version that will then be released to the user but will not affect the changes being applied for release 2 (i.e., deltas 1.4, 2.1, 2.2, etc.). This new delta is the first node of a new branch of the tree.

Branch delta names always have four SID components: the same release number and level number as the trunk delta, plus a branch number and sequence number. The format is as follows:

release . level . branch . sequence

The branch number of the first delta branching off any trunk delta is always 1, and its sequence number is also 1. For example, the full SID for a delta branching off trunk delta 1.3 will be 1.3.1.1. As other deltas on that same branch are created, only the sequence number changes: 1.3.1.2, 1.3.1.3, etc. This is shown in Figure 10-2.

Figure 10-2: Tree Structure with Branch Deltas

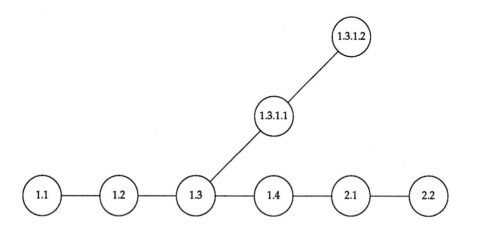

The branch number is incremented only when a delta is created that starts a new branch off an existing branch, as shown in Figure 10-3. As this secondary branch develops, the sequence numbers of its deltas are incremented (1.3.2.1, 1.3.2.2, etc.), but the secondary branch number remains the same.

Figure 10-3: Extended Branching Concept

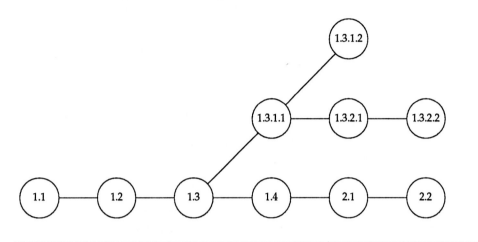

The concept of branching may be extended to any delta in the tree, and the numbering of the resulting deltas proceeds as shown above. SCCS allows the generation of complex tree structures. Although this capability has been pro-vided for certain specialized uses, the SCCS tree should be kept as simple as possible. Comprehension of its structure becomes difficult as the tree becomes complex.

SCCS Command Conventions

SCCS commands accept two types of arguments, keyletters and file names. Keyletters are options that begin with a hyphen (–) followed by a lowercase letter and, in some cases, a value.

File and/or directory names specify the file(s) the command is to process. Naming a directory is equivalent to naming all the SCCS files within the directory. Non-SCCS files and unreadable files in the named directories are silently ignored.

In general, file name arguments may not begin with a hyphen. If a lone hyphen is specified, the command will read the standard input (usually your terminal) for lines and take each line as the name of an SCCS file to be processed. The standard input is read until end-of-file. This feature is often used in pipelines.

Keyletters are processed before file names, so the placement of keyletters is arbitrary — they may be interspersed with file names. File names, however, are processed left to right. Somewhat different conventions apply to help, what, sccsdiff, and val, detailed later under "SCCS Commands."

Certain actions of various SCCS commands are controlled by flags appearing in SCCS files. Some of these flags will be discussed, but for a complete description see the admin page in Section 1 of the *Programmer's Reference Manual*.

The distinction between real user (see passwd in Section 1 of the *User's Reference Manual*) and effective user will be of concern in discussing various actions of SCCS commands. For now, assume that the real and effective users are the same — the person logged into the UNIX system.

x.files and z.files

All SCCS commands that modify an SCCS file do so by first writing and modifying a copy called x.*file*. This is done to ensure that the SCCS file is not damaged if processing terminates abnormally. x.*file* is created in the same directory as the SCCS file, given the same mode (see chmod, described in Section 1 of the *User's Reference Manual*), and is owned by the effective user. It exists only for the duration of the execution of the command that creates it. When processing is complete, the contents of s.*file* are replaced by the contents of x.*file*, whereupon x.*file* is destroyed.

To prevent simultaneous updates to an SCCS file, the same modifying commands also create a lock-file called z.*file*. z.*file* contains the process number of the command that creates it, and its existence prevents other commands from processing the SCCS file. z.*file* is created with access permission mode 444 (read-only for owner, group, and other) in the same directory as the SCCS file and is owned by the effective user. It exists only for the duration of the execution of the command that creates it.

In general, you can ignore these files. They are useful only in the event of system crashes or similar situations.

Error Messages

SCCS commands produce error messages on the diagnostic output in this format:

ERROR [*file*] : *message text* (*code*)

The code in parentheses can be used as an argument to the help command to obtain a further explanation of the message. Detection of a fatal error during the processing of a file causes the SCCS command to stop processing that file and proceed with the next file specified.

SCCS Commands

This section describes the major features of the fourteen SCCS commands and their most common arguments. Full descriptions with details of all arguments are in the *Programmer's Reference Manual*.

Here is a quick-reference overview of the commands:

get
: retrieves versions of SCCS files.

unget
: undoes the effect of a get −e prior to the file being deltaed.

delta
: applies deltas (changes) to SCCS files and creates new versions.

admin
: initializes SCCS files, manipulates their descriptive text, and controls delta creation rights.

prs
: prints portions of an SCCS file in user-specified format.

sact
: prints information about files that are currently out for editing.

help
: gives explanations of error messages.

rmdel
: removes a delta from an SCCS file — allows removal of deltas created by mistake.

cdc
: changes the commentary associated with a delta.

what
: searches any UNIX system file(s) for all occurrences of a special pattern and prints out what follows it — useful in finding identifying information inserted by the get command.

sccsdiff
: shows differences between any two versions of an SCCS file.

comb
: combines consecutive deltas into one to reduce the size of an SCCS file.

val
: validates an SCCS file.

vc
: a filter that may be used for version control.

The get Command

The get command creates a file that contains a specified version of an SCCS file. The version is retrieved by beginning with the initial version and then applying deltas, in order, until the desired version is obtained. The resulting file, called a *g-file* (for gotten), is created in the current directory and is owned by the real user. The mode assigned to the *g-file* depends on how the get command is used.

The most common use of get is

```
$ get s.abc
```

which normally retrieves the latest version of s.abc from the SCCS file tree trunk and produces (for example) on the standard output

```
1.3
67 lines
No id keywords (cm7)
```

meaning version 1.3 of s.abc was retrieved (assuming 1.3 is the latest trunk delta), it has 67 lines of text, and no ID keywords were substituted in the file.

The *g-file*, namely, file abc, is given access permission mode 444 (read-only for owner, group, and other). This particular way of using get is intended to produce *g-files* only for inspection, compilation, or copying, for example. It is not intended for editing (making deltas).

When several files are specified, the same information is output for each one. For example,

```
$ get s.abc s.xyz
```

produces

```
s.abc:
1.3
67 lines
No id keywords (cm7)

s.xyz:
1.7
85 lines
No id keywords (cm7)
```

ID Keywords

In generating a *g-file* for compilation, it is useful to record the date and time of creation, the version retrieved, the module's name, and so on in the *g-file* itself. This information appears in a load module when one is eventually created. SCCS provides a convenient mechanism for doing this automatically. Identification (ID) keywords appearing anywhere in the *g-file* are replaced by appropriate values according to the definitions of those ID keywords. The format of an ID keyword is an uppercase letter enclosed by percent signs (%). For example,

        %I%

is the ID keyword replaced by the SID of the retrieved version of a file. Similarly, %H% and %M% are the date and name of the *g-file*, respectively. Thus, executing get on an SCCS file that contains the PL/I declaration

        DCL ID CHAR(100) VAR INIT('%M% %I% %H%');

gives (for example) the following:

        DCL ID CHAR(100) VAR INIT('MODNAME 2.3 07/18/85');

When no ID keywords are substituted by get, the following message is issued:

        No id keywords (cm7)

This message is normally treated as a warning by get although the presence of the i flag in the SCCS file causes it to be treated as an error. For a complete list of the keywords provided, see the get page in Section 1 of the *Programmer's Reference Manual*.

Retrieval of Different Versions

The version of an SCCS file that get retrieves by default is the most recently created delta of the highest numbered trunk release. However, any other version can be retrieved with get −r by specifying the version's SID. Thus,

        $ get −r1.3 s.abc

retrieves version 1.3 of s.abc and produces (for example) on the standard output

        1.3
        64 lines

A branch delta may be retrieved similarly,

```
$ get -r1.5.2.3 s.abc
```

which produces (for example) on the standard output

```
1.5.2.3
234 lines
```

When a SID is specified and the particular version does not exist in the SCCS file, an error message results.

Omitting the level number, as in

```
$ get -r3 s.abc
```

causes retrieval of the trunk delta with the highest level number within the given release. Thus, the above command might output

```
3.7
213 lines
```

If the given release does not exist, get retrieves the trunk delta with the highest level number within the highest-numbered existing release that is lower than the given release. For example, assume release 9 does not exist in file s.abc and release 7 is the highest-numbered release below 9. Executing

```
$ get -r9 s.abc
```

might produce

```
7.6
420 lines
```

which indicates that trunk delta 7.6 is the latest version of file s.abc below release 9. Similarly, omitting the sequence number, as in

```
$ get -r4.3.2 s.abc
```

results in the retrieval of the branch delta with the highest sequence number on the given branch. (If the given branch does not exist, an error message results.) This might result in the following output:

```
4.3.2.8
89 lines
```

get −t will retrieve the latest (top) version of a particular release when no −r is used or when its value is simply a release number. The latest version is the delta produced most recently, independent of its location on the SCCS file tree. Thus, if the most recent delta in release 3 is 3.5,

```
$ get −r3 −t s.abc
```

might produce

```
3.5
59 lines
```

However, if branch delta 3.2.1.5 were the latest delta (created after delta 3.5), the same command might produce

```
3.2.1.5
46 lines
```

Retrieval With Intent to Make a Delta

get −e indicates an intent to make a delta. First, get checks the following:

- The user list to determine if the login name or group ID of the person executing get is present. The login name or group ID must be present for the user to be allowed to make deltas. (See "The admin Command" for a discussion of making user lists.)

- The release number (R) of the version being retrieved to determine if the release being accessed is a protected release. That is, the release number must satisfy the relation

    floor is less than or equal to R,
    which is less than or equal to *ceiling*

    Floor and *ceiling* are flags in the SCCS file representing start and end of the range of valid releases.

- R is not locked against editing. The lock is a flag in the SCCS file.

- Whether multiple concurrent edits are allowed for the SCCS file by the j flag in the SCCS file.

A failure of any of the first three conditions causes the processing of the corresponding SCCS file to terminate.

If the above checks succeed, get −e causes the creation of a *g-file* in the current directory with mode 644 (readable by everyone, writable only by the owner) that is owned by the real user. If a writable *g-file* already exists, get terminates with an error. This is to prevent inadvertent destruction of a *g-file* being edited for the purpose of making a delta.

Any ID keywords appearing in the *g-file* are not replaced by get −e because the generated *g-file* is subsequently used to create another delta. Replacement of ID keywords causes them to be permanently changed in the SCCS file. Because of this, get does not need to check for their presence in the *g-file*. Thus, the message

        No id keywords (cm7)

is never output when get −e is used.

In addition, get −e causes the creation (or updating) of the p.*file* that is used to pass information to the delta command.

The following

        $ get −e s.abc

produces (for example) on the standard output

        1.3
        new delta 1.4
        67 lines

Undoing a get −e

There may be times when a file is retrieved accidentally for editing; there is really no editing that needs to be done at this time. In such cases, the unget command can be used to cancel the delta reservation that was set up.

Additional get Options

If get −r and/or −t are used together with −e, the version retrieved for editing is the one specified with −r and/or −t.

get −i and −x are used to specify a list of deltas to be included and excluded, respectively (see the get page in the *Programmer's Reference Manual* for the syntax of such a list). Including a delta means forcing its changes to be included in the retrieved version. This is useful in applying the same changes to more than one version of the SCCS file. Excluding a delta means forcing it not to be applied. This may be used to undo the effects of a previous delta in the version to be created.

Whenever deltas are included or excluded, get checks for possible interference with other deltas. Two deltas can interfere, for example, when each one changes the same line of the retrieved *g-file*. A warning shows the range of lines within the retrieved *g-file* where the problem may exist. The user should examine the *g-file* to determine what the problem is and take appropriate corrective steps (edit the file if necessary).

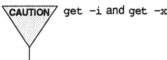 get −i and get −x should be used with extreme care.

get −k is used either to regenerate a *g-file* that may have been accidentally removed or ruined after get −e, or simply to generate a *g-file* in which the replacement of ID keywords has been suppressed. A *g-file* generated by get −k is identical to one produced by get −e, but no processing related to p.*file* takes place.

Concurrent Edits of Different SID

The ability to retrieve different versions of an SCCS file allows several deltas to be in progress at any given time. This means that several get −e commands may be executed on the same file as long as no two executions retrieve the same version (unless multiple concurrent edits are allowed).

The p.*file* created by get −e is created in the same directory as the SCCS file, given mode 644 (readable by everyone, writable only by the owner), and owned by the effective user. It contains the following information for each delta that is still in progress:

- the SID of the retrieved version

- the SID given to the new delta when it is created

- the login name of the real user executing get

The first execution of get −e causes the creation of p.*file* for the corresponding SCCS file. Subsequent executions only update p.*file* with a line containing the above information. Before updating, however, get checks to assure that no entry already in p.*file* specifies that the SID of the version to be retrieved is already retrieved (unless multiple concurrent edits are allowed). If the check succeeds, the user is informed that other deltas are in progress and processing continues. If the check fails, an error message results.

It should be noted that concurrent executions of get must be carried out from different directories. Subsequent executions from the same directory will attempt to overwrite the *g-file*, which is an SCCS error condition. In practice, this problem does not arise since each user normally has a different working directory. See "Protection" in the section "SCCS Files" for a discussion of how different users are permitted to use SCCS commands on the same files.

Figure 10-4 shows the possible SID components a user can specify with get (left-most column), the version that will then be retrieved by get, and the resulting SID for the delta, which delta will create (right-most column). In the table

- R, L, B, and S mean release, level, branch, and sequence numbers in the SID, and m means maximum. Thus, for example, R.mL means the maximum level number within release R. R.L.(mB+1).1 means the first sequence number on the new branch (i.e., maximum branch number plus 1) of level L within release R. Note that if the SID specified is R.L, R.L.B, or R.L.B.S, each of these specified SID numbers must exist.

- The −b keyletter is effective only if the b flag (see admin in Section 1 of the *Programmer's Reference Manual*) is present in the file. An entry of − means irrelevant.

- The first two entries in the left-most column apply only if the d (default SID) flag is not present. If the d flag is present in the file, the SID is interpreted as if specified on the command line. Thus, one of the other cases in this figure applies.

- R.1 (the third entry in the right-most column) is used to force the creation of the first delta in a new release.

- hR (the seventh entry in the fourth column) is the highest existing release that is lower than the specified, nonexistent release R.

Figure 10-4: Determination of New SID

SID Specified in get	−b Key-Letter Used	Other Conditions	SID Retrieved by get	SID of Delta To be Created by delta
none	no	R defaults to mR	mR.mL	mR.(mL+1)
none	yes	R defaults to mR	mR.mL	mR.mL.(mB+1).1
R	no	R > mR	mR.mL	R.1
R	no	R = mR	mR.mL	mR.(mL+1)
R	yes	R > mR	mR.mL	mR.mL.(mB+1).1
R	yes	R = mR	mR.mL	mR.mL.(mB+1).1
R	−	R< mR and R does not exist	hR.mL	hR.mL.(mB+1).1
R	−	Trunk successor number in release > R and R exists	R.mL	R.mL.(mB+1).1
R.L	no	No trunk successor	R.L	R.(L+1)
R.L	yes	No trunk successor	R.L	R.L.(mB+1).1
R.L	−	Trunk successor in release ≥ R	R.L	R.L.(mB+1).1
R.L.B	no	No branch successor	R.L.B.mS	R.L.B.(mS+1)

Figure 10-4: Determination of New SID (continued)

SID Specified in get	-b Key-Letter Used	Other Conditions	SID Retrieved by get	SID of Delta To be Created by delta
R.L.B	yes	No branch successor	R.L.B.mS	R.L.(mB+1).1
R.L.B.S	no	No branch successor	R.L.B.S	R.L.B.(S+1)
R.L.B.S	yes	No branch successor	R.L.B.S	R.L.(mB+1).1
R.L.B.S	−	Branch successor	R.L.B.S	R.L.(mB+1).1

Concurrent Edits of Same SID

Under normal conditions, more than one get −e for the same SID is not permitted. That is, delta must be executed before a subsequent get −e is executed on the same SID.

Multiple concurrent edits are allowed if the j flag is set in the SCCS file. Thus:

```
$ get -e s.abc
1.1
new delta 1.2
5 lines
```

may be immediately followed by

```
$ get -e s.abc
1.1
new delta 1.1.1.1
5 lines
```

without an intervening delta. In this case, a delta after the first get will produce delta 1.2 (assuming 1.1 is the most recent trunk delta), and a delta after the second get will produce delta 1.1.1.1.

Keyletters that Affect Output

get –p causes the retrieved text to be written to the standard output rather than to a *g-file*. In addition, all output normally directed to the standard output (such as the SID of the version retrieved and the number of lines retrieved) is directed instead to the standard error. get –p is used, for example, to create a *g-file* with an arbitrary name, as in

    $ get –p s.abc > *arbitrary file name*

get –s suppresses output normally directed to the standard output, such as the SID of the retrieved version and the number of lines retrieved, but it does not affect messages normally directed to the standard error. get –s is used to prevent nondiagnostic messages from appearing on the user's terminal and is often used with –p to pipe the output, as in

    $ get –p –s s.abc | pg

get –g suppresses the retrieval of the text of an SCCS file. This is useful in several ways. For example, to verify a particular SID in an SCCS file

    $ get –g –r4.3 s.abc

outputs the SID 4.3 if it exists in the SCCS file s.abc or an error message if it does not. Another use of get –g is in regenerating a p.*file* that may have been accidentally destroyed, as in

    $ get –e –g s.abc

get –l causes SCCS to create l.*file* in the current directory with mode 444 (read-only for owner, group, and other) and owned by the real user. The l.*file* contains a table (whose format is described on the get page in the *Programmer's Reference Manual*) showing the deltas used in constructing a particular version of the SCCS file. For example

    $ get –r2.3 –l s.abc

generates an l.*file* showing the deltas applied to retrieve version 2.3 of s.abc. Specifying p with –l, as in

    $ get –lp –r2.3 s.abc

causes the output to be written to the standard output rather than to l.*file*. get –g can be used with –l to suppress the retrieval of the text.

get −m identifies the changes applied to an SCCS file. Each line of the *g-file* is preceded by the SID of the delta that caused the line to be inserted. The SID is separated from the text of the line by a tab character.

get −n causes each line of a *g-file* to be preceded by the value of the %M% ID keyword and a tab character. This is most often used in a pipeline with grep, described in Section 1 of the *User's Reference Manual*. For example, to find all lines that match a given pattern in the latest version of each SCCS file in a directory, the following may be executed:

$ get −p −n −s *directory* | grep *pattern*

If both −m and −n are specified, each line of the *g-file* is preceded by the value of the %M% ID keyword and a tab (this is the effect of −n) and is followed by the line in the format produced by −m.

Because use of −m and/or −n causes the contents of the *g-file* to be modified, such a *g-file* must not be used for creating a delta. Therefore, neither −m nor −n may be specified together with get −e. See the get page in the *Programmer's Reference Manual* for a description of other options.

The delta Command

The delta command is used to incorporate changes made to a *g-file* into the corresponding SCCS file — that is, to create a delta and, therefore, a new version of the file.

The delta command requires the existence of p. *file* (created by get −e). It examines p. *file* to verify the presence of an entry containing the user's login name. If none is found, an error message results.

The delta command performs the same permission checks that get −e performs. If all checks are successful, delta determines what has been changed in the *g-file* by comparing it with its own temporary copy of the *g-file* as it was before editing. This temporary copy is called d. *file* and is obtained by performing an internal get on the SID specified in the p. *file* entry.

The required p. *file* entry is the one containing the login name of the user executing delta, because the user who retrieved the *g-file* must be the one who creates the delta. However, if the login name of the user appears in more than one entry, the same user has executed get −e more than once on the same

SCCS file. Then, delta -r must be used to specify the SID that uniquely identifies the p.*file* entry. This entry is then the one used to obtain the SID of the delta to be created.

In practice, the most common use of delta is

    $ delta s.abc

which prompts

    comments?

to which the user replies with a description of why the delta is being made, ending the reply with a new-line character. The user's response may be up to 512 characters long with new-lines (not intended to terminate the response) escaped by backslashes (\).

If the SCCS file has a v flag, delta first prompts with

    MRs?

(Modification Requests) on the standard output. The standard input is then read for MR numbers, separated by blanks and/or tabs, ended with a new-line character. A Modification Request is a formal way of asking for a correction or enhancement to the file. In some controlled environments where changes to source files are tracked, deltas are permitted only when initiated by a trouble report, change request, trouble ticket, and so on, collectively called MRs. Recording MR numbers within deltas is a way of enforcing the rules of the change management process.

delta -y and/or -m can be used to enter comments and MR numbers on the command line rather than through the standard input, as in

    $ delta -y"*descriptive comment*" -m"*mrnum1 mrnum2*" s.abc

In this case, the prompts for comments and MRs are not printed, and the standard input is not read. These two keyletters are useful when delta is executed from within a shell procedure. Note that delta -m is allowed only if the SCCS file has a v flag.

No matter how comments and MR numbers are entered with delta, they are recorded as part of the entry for the delta being created. Also, they apply to all SCCS files specified with the delta.

If `delta` is used with more than one file argument and the first file named has a v flag, all files named must have this flag. Similarly, if the first file named does not have the flag, none of the files named may have it.

When `delta` processing is complete, the standard output displays the SID of the new delta (from p.*file*) and the number of lines inserted, deleted, and left unchanged. For example:

```
1.4
14 inserted
7 deleted
345 unchanged
```

If line counts do not agree with the user's perception of the changes made to a g-*file*, it may be because there are various ways to describe a set of changes, especially if lines are moved around in the g-*file*. However, the total number of lines of the new delta (the number inserted plus the number left unchanged) should always agree with the number of lines in the edited g-*file*.

If you are in the process of making a delta and the `delta` command finds no ID keywords in the edited g-*file*, the message

```
No id keywords (cm7)
```

is issued after the prompts for commentary but before any other output. This means that any ID keywords that may have existed in the SCCS file have been replaced by their values or deleted during the editing process. This could be caused by making a delta from a g-*file* that was created by a `get` without −e (ID keywords are replaced by `get` in such a case). It could also be caused by accidentally deleting or changing ID keywords while editing the g-*file*. Or, it is possible that the file had no ID keywords. In any case, the delta will be created unless there is an i flag in the SCCS file (meaning the error should be treated as fatal), in which case the delta will not be created.

After the processing of an SCCS file is complete, the corresponding p.*file* entry is removed from p.*file*. All updates to p.*file* are made to a temporary copy, q.*file*, whose use is similar to that of x.*file* described under "SCCS Command Conventions." If there is only one entry in p.*file*, then p.*file* itself is removed.

In addition, `delta` removes the edited g-*file* unless −n is specified. For example

```
$ delta −n s.abc
```

will keep the g-*file* after processing.

delta -s suppresses all output normally directed to the standard output, other than comments? and MRs?. Thus, use of -s with -y (and/or -m) causes delta neither to read from the standard input nor to write to the standard output.

The differences between the *g-file* and the d. *file* constitute the delta and may be printed on the standard output by using delta -p. The format of this output is similar to that produced by diff.

The admin Command

The admin command is used to administer SCCS files — that is, to create new SCCS files and change the parameters of existing ones. When an SCCS file is created, its parameters are initialized by use of keyletters with admin or are assigned default values if no keyletters are supplied. The same keyletters are used to change the parameters of existing SCCS files.

Two keyletters are used in detecting and correcting corrupted SCCS files (see "Auditing" in the section "SCCS Files").

Newly created SCCS files are given access permission mode 444 (read-only for owner, group and other) and are owned by the effective user. Only a user with write permission in the directory containing the SCCS file may use the admin command on that file.

Creation of SCCS Files

An SCCS file can be created by executing the command

```
$ admin -ifirst s.abc
```

in which the value first with -i is the name of a file from which the text of the initial delta of the SCCS file s.abc is to be taken. Omission of a value with -i means admin is to read the standard input for the text of the initial delta.

The command

```
$ admin -i s.abc < first
```

is equivalent to the previous example.

If the text of the initial delta does not contain ID keywords, the message

      `No id keywords (cm7)`

is issued by `admin` as a warning. However, if the command also sets the `i` flag (not to be confused with the −i keyletter), the message is treated as an error and the SCCS file is not created. Only one SCCS file may be created at a time using `admin −i`.

`admin −r` is used to specify a release number for the first delta. Thus:

      `admin −ifirst −r3 s.abc`

means the first delta should be named 3.1 rather than the normal 1.1. Because −r has meaning only when creating the first delta, its use is permitted only with −i.

Inserting Commentary for the Initial Delta

When an SCCS file is created, the user may want to record why this was done. Comments (`admin −y`) and/or MR numbers (−m) can be entered in exactly the same way as with `delta`.

If −y is omitted, a comment line of the form

      date and time created YY/MM/DD HH:MM:SS by logname

is automatically generated.

If it is desired to supply MR numbers (`admin −m`), the `v` flag must be set with −f. The `v` flag simply determines whether MR numbers must be supplied when using any SCCS command that modifies a delta commentary in the SCCS file (see `sccsfile` in Section 4 of the *Programmer's Reference Manual*). An example would be

      `$ admin −ifirst −mmrnum1 −fv s.abc`

Note that −y and −m are effective only if a new SCCS file is being created.

Initialization and Modification of SCCS File Parameters

Part of an SCCS file is reserved for descriptive text, usually a summary of the file's contents and purpose. It can be initialized or changed by using admin −t.

When an SCCS file is first being created and −t is used, it must be followed by the name of a file from which the descriptive text is to be taken. For example, the command

        $ admin −ifirst −tdesc s.abc

specifies that the descriptive text is to be taken from file desc.

When processing an existing SCCS file, −t specifies that the descriptive text (if any) currently in the file is to be replaced with the text in the named file. Thus:

        $ admin −tdesc s.abc

specifies that the descriptive text of the SCCS file is to be replaced by the contents of desc. Omission of the filename after the −t keyletter as in

        $ admin −t s.abc

causes the removal of the descriptive text from the SCCS file.

The flags of an SCCS file may be initialized or changed by admin −f, or deleted by admin −d.

SCCS file flags are used to direct certain actions of the various commands. (See the admin page in the *Programmer's Reference Manual* for a description of all the flags.) For example, the i flag specifies that a warning message (stating that there are no ID keywords contained in the SCCS file) should be treated as an error. The d (default SID) flag specifies the default version of the SCCS file to be retrieved by the get command.

admin −f is used to set flags and, if desired, their values. For example

        $ admin −ifirst −fi −fm*modname* s.abc

sets the i and m (module name) flags. The value *modname* specified for the m flag is the value that the get command will use to replace the %M% ID keyword. (In the absence of the m flag, the name of the *g-file* is used as the replacement for the %M% ID keyword.) Several −f keyletters may be supplied on a single admin, and they may be used whether the command is creating a new SCCS file or processing an existing one.

admin −d is used to delete a flag from an existing SCCS file. As an example, the command

```
$ admin −dm s.abc
```

removes the m flag from the SCCS file. Several −d keyletters may be used with one admin and may be intermixed with −f.

SCCS files contain a list of login names and/or group IDs of users who are allowed to create deltas. This list is empty by default, allowing anyone to create deltas. To create a user list (or add to an existing one), admin −a is used. For example,

```
$ admin −axyz −awql −a1234 s.abc
```

adds the login names xyz and wql and the group ID 1234 to the list. admin −a may be used whether creating a new SCCS file or processing an existing one.

admin −e (erase) is used to remove login names or group IDs from the list.

The prs Command

The prs command is used to print all or part of an SCCS file on the standard output. If prs −d is used, the output will be in a format called data specification. Data specification is a string of SCCS file data keywords (not to be confused with get ID keywords) interspersed with optional user text.

Data keywords are replaced by appropriate values according to their definitions. For example,

```
:I:
```

is defined as the data keyword replaced by the SID of a specified delta. Similarly, :F: is the data keyword for the SCCS filename currently being processed, and :C: is the comment line associated with a specified delta. All parts of an SCCS file have an associated data keyword. For a complete list, see the prs page in the *Programmer's Reference Manual*.

There is no limit to the number of times a data keyword may appear in a data specification. Thus, for example,

```
$ prs −d":I: this is the top delta for :F: :I:" s.abc
```

may produce on the standard output

```
2.1 this is the top delta for s.abc 2.1
```

Information may be obtained from a single delta by specifying its SID using prs
−r. For example,

```
$ prs −d":F:: :I: comment line is: :C:" −r1.4 s.abc
```

may produce the following output:

```
s.abc: 1.4 comment line is: THIS IS A COMMENT
```

If −r is not specified, the value of the SID defaults to the most recently created
delta.

In addition, information from a range of deltas may be obtained with −l or −e.
The use of prs −e substitutes data keywords for the SID designated with −r
and all deltas created earlier, while prs −l substitutes data keywords for the
SID designated with −r and all deltas created later. Thus, the command

```
$ prs −d:I: −r1.4 −e s.abc
```

may output

```
1.4
1.3
1.2.1.1
1.2
1.1
```

and the command

```
$ prs −d:I: −r1.4 −l s.abc
```

may produce

```
3.3
3.2
3.1
2.2.1.1
2.2
2.1
1.4
```

Substitution of data keywords for all deltas of the SCCS file may be obtained by specifying both −e and −l.

The sact Command

sact is a special form of the prs command that produces a report about files that are out for edit. The command takes only one type of argument: a list of file or directory names. The report shows the SID of any file in the list that is out for edit, the SID of the impending delta, the login of the user who executed the get −e command, and the date and time the get −e was executed. It is a useful command for an administrator.

The help Command

The help command prints information about messages that may appear on the user's terminal. Arguments to help are the code numbers that appear in parentheses at the end of SCCS messages. (If no argument is given, help prompts for one.) Explanatory information is printed on the standard output. If no information is found, an error message is printed. When more than one argument is used, each is processed independently, and an error resulting from one will not stop the processing of the others. For more information, see the help page in the *Programmer's Reference Manual*.

The rmdel Command

The rmdel command allows removal of a delta from an SCCS file. Its use should be reserved for deltas in which incorrect global changes were made. The delta to be removed must be a leaf delta. That is, it must be the most recently created delta on its branch or on the trunk of the SCCS file tree. In Figure 10-3, only deltas 1.3.1.2, 1.3.2.2, and 2.2 can be removed. Only after they are removed can deltas 1.3.2.1 and 2.1 be removed.

To be allowed to remove a delta, the effective user must have write permission in the directory containing the SCCS file. In addition, the real user must be either the one who created the delta being removed or the owner of the SCCS file and its directory.

The −r keyletter is mandatory with rmdel. It is used to specify the complete SID of the delta to be removed. Thus

        $ rmdel −r2.3 s.abc

specifies the removal of trunk delta 2.3.

Before removing the delta, rmdel checks that the release number (R) of the given SID satisfies the relation

> *floor* is less than or equal to R,
> which is less than or equal to *ceiling*

Floor and *ceiling* are flags in the SCCS file representing start and end of the range of valid releases.

The rmdel command also checks the SID to make sure it is not for a version on which a get for editing has been executed and whose associated delta has not yet been made. In addition, the login name or group ID of the user must appear in the file's user list (or the user list must be empty). Also, the release specified cannot be locked against editing. That is, if the l flag is set (see admin in the *Programmer's Reference Manual*), the release must not be contained in the list. If these conditions are not satisfied, processing is terminated, and the delta is not removed.

Once a specified delta has been removed, its type indicator in the delta table of the SCCS file is changed from D (delta) to R (removed).

The cdc Command

The cdc command is used to change the commentary made when the delta was created. It is similar to the rmdel command (e.g., −r and full SID are necessary), although the delta need not be a leaf delta. For example,

        $ cdc −r3.4 s.abc

specifies that the commentary of delta 3.4 is to be changed. New commentary is then prompted for as with delta.

The old commentary is kept, but it is preceded by a comment line indicating that it has been superseded, and the new commentary is entered ahead of the comment line. The inserted comment line records the login name of the user executing cdc and the time of its execution.

The cdc command also allows for the insertion of new and deletion of old MR numbers with the ! symbol. Thus

```
cdc -r1.4 s.abc
MRs? mrnum3 !mrnum1          (The MRs? prompt appears only
                            if the v flag has been set.)
comments? deleted wrong MR no. and inserted correct MR no.
```

inserts mrnum3 and deletes mrnum1 for delta 1.4.

The what Command

The what command is used to find identifying information in any UNIX system file whose name is given as an argument. No keyletters are accepted. The what command searches the given file(s) for all occurrences of the string @ (#), which is the replacement for the %Z% ID keyword (see the get page in the *Programmer's Reference Manual*). It prints on the standard output whatever follows the string until the first double quote ("), greater than symbol (>), backslash (\ ), new-line, null, or nonprinting character.

For example, if an SCCS file called s.prog.c (a C language source file) contains the following line

```
char id[]= "%W%";
```

and the command

```
$ get -r3.4 s.prog.c
```

is used, the resulting *g-file* is compiled to produce prog.o and a.out. Then, the command

```
$ what prog.c prog.o a.out
```

produces

```
prog.c:
   prog.c:   3.4
prog.o:
   prog.c:   3.4
a.out:
   prog.c:   3.4
```

The string searched for by what need not be inserted with an ID keyword of get; it may be inserted in any convenient manner.

The sccsdiff Command

The sccsdiff command determines (and prints on the standard output) the differences between any two versions of an SCCS file. The versions to be compared are specified with sccsdiff −r in the same way as with get −r. SID numbers must be specified as the first two arguments. The SCCS file or files to be processed are named last. Directory names and a lone hyphen are not acceptable to sccsdiff.

The following is an example of the format of sccsdiff:

```
$ sccsdiff −r3.4 −r5.6 s.abc
```

The differences are printed the same way as by diff.

The comb Command

The comb command lets the user reduce the size of an SCCS file. It generates a shell procedure on the standard output, which reconstructs the file by discarding unwanted deltas and combining other specified deltas. (It is not recommended that comb be used as a matter of routine.)

In the absence of any keyletters, comb preserves only leaf deltas and the minimum number of ancestor deltas necessary to preserve the shape of an SCCS tree. The effect of this is to eliminate middle deltas on the trunk and on all branches of the tree. Thus, in Figure 10-3, deltas 1.2, 1.3.2.1, 1.4, and 2.1 would be eliminated.

Some of the keyletters used with this command are:

comb −s	This option generates a shell procedure that produces a report of the percentage space (if any) the user will save. This is often useful as a preliminary check.
comb −p	This option is used to specify the oldest delta the user wants preserved.

ANSI C and Programming Support Tools

comb −c   This option is used to specify a list (see the get page in the
            Programmer's Reference Manual for its syntax) of deltas the
            user wants preserved. All other deltas will be discarded.

The shell procedure generated by comb is not guaranteed to save space. A
reconstructed file may even be larger than the original. Note, too, that the
shape of an SCCS file tree may be altered by the reconstruction process.

The val Command

The val command is used to determine whether a file is an SCCS file meeting
the characteristics specified by certain keyletters. It checks for the existence of a
particular delta when the SID for that delta is specified with −r.

The string following −y or −m is used to check the value set by the t or m flag,
respectively. See admin in the *Programmer's Reference Manual* for descriptions of
these flags.

The val command treats the special argument hyphen differently from other
SCCS commands. It allows val to read the argument list from the standard
input instead of from the command line, and the standard input is read until an
end-of-file (control−d) is entered. This permits one val command with different values for keyletters and file arguments. For example,

```
$ val −
−yc −mabc s.abc
−mxyz −ypll s.xyz
control_d
```

first checks if file s.abc has a value c for its type flag and value abc for the
module name flag. Once this is done, val processes the remaining file, in this
case s.xyz.

The val command returns an 8-bit code. Each bit set shows a specific error (see
val in the *Programmer's Reference Manual* for a description of errors and codes).
In addition, an appropriate diagnostic is printed unless suppressed by −s. A
return code of 0 means all files met the characteristics specified.

The vc Command

The vc command is an awk-like tool used for version control of sets of files. While it is distributed as part of the SCCS package, it does not require the files it operates on to be under SCCS control. A complete description of vc can be found in Section 1 of the *Programmer's Reference Manual*.

SCCS Files

This section covers protection mechanisms used by SCCS, the format of SCCS files, and the recommended procedures for auditing SCCS files.

Protection

SCCS relies on the capabilities of the UNIX system for most of the protection mechanisms required to prevent unauthorized changes to SCCS files — that is, changes by non-SCCS commands. Protection features provided directly by SCCS are the release lock flag, the release floor and ceiling flags, and the user list.

Files created by the admin command are given access permission mode 444 (read-only for owner, group, and other). This mode should remain unchanged because it (generally) prevents modification of SCCS files by non-SCCS commands. Directories containing SCCS files should be given mode 755, which allows only the owner of the directory to modify it.

SCCS files should be kept in directories that contain only SCCS files and any temporary files created by SCCS commands. This simplifies their protection and auditing. The contents of directories should be logical groupings — subsystems of the same large project, for example.

SCCS files should have only one link (name) because commands that modify them do so by creating and modifying a copy of the file. When processing is done, the contents of the old file are automatically replaced by the contents of the copy, whereupon the copy is destroyed. If the old file had additional links, this would break them. Then, rather than process such files, SCCS commands would produce an error message.

When only one person uses SCCS, the real and effective user IDs are the same; and the user ID owns the directories containing SCCS files. Therefore, SCCS may be used directly without any preliminary preparation.

When several users with unique user IDs are assigned SCCS responsibilities (on large development projects, for example), one user — that is, one user ID — must be chosen as the owner of the SCCS files. This person will administer the files (use the admin command) and will be SCCS administrator for the project. Because other users do not have the same privileges and permissions as the SCCS administrator, they are not able to execute directly those commands that require write permission in the directory containing the SCCS files. Therefore, a project-dependent program is required to provide an interface to the get, delta, and, if desired, rmdel and cdc commands.

The interface program must be owned by the SCCS administrator and must have the set-user-ID-on-execution bit on (see chmod in Section 1 of the *User's Reference Manual*). This assures that the effective user ID is the user ID of the SCCS administrator. With the privileges of the interface program during command execution, the owner of an SCCS file can modify it at will. Other users whose login names or group IDs are in the user list for that file (but are not the owner) are given the necessary permissions only for the duration of the execution of the interface program. Thus, they may modify SCCS only with delta and, possibly, rmdel and cdc.

Formatting

SCCS files are composed of lines of ASCII text arranged in six parts as follows:

Checksum	a line containing the logical sum of all the characters of the file (not including the checksum line itself)
Delta Table	information about each delta, such as type, SID, date and time of creation, and commentary
User Names	list of login names and/or group IDs of users who are allowed to modify the file by adding or removing deltas
Flags	indicators that control certain actions of SCCS commands
Descriptive Text	usually a summary of the contents and purpose of the file
Body	the text administered by SCCS, intermixed with internal SCCS control lines

Details on these file sections may be found on the sccsfile page in Section 4 of the *Programmer's Reference Manual*. The checksum line is discussed below under "Auditing."

Since SCCS files are ASCII files they can be processed by non-SCCS commands like ed, grep, and cat. This is convenient when an SCCS file must be modified manually (a delta's time and date were recorded incorrectly, for example, because the system clock was set incorrectly), or when a user wants simply to look at the file.

Extreme care should be exercised when modifying SCCS files with non-SCCS commands.

Auditing

When a system or hardware malfunction destroys an SCCS file, any command will issue an error message. Commands also use the checksum stored in an SCCS file to determine whether the file has been corrupted since it was last accessed (possibly by having lost one or more blocks or by having been modified with ed). No SCCS command will process a corrupted SCCS file except the admin −h or −z, as described below.

SCCS files should be audited for possible corruptions on a regular basis. The simplest and fastest way to do an audit is to use admin −h and specify all SCCS files:

        admin −h s.*file1* s.*file2* ...

or

        admin −h *directory1 directory2* ...

If the new checksum of any file is not equal to the checksum in the first line of that file, the message

        `corrupted file (co6)`

is produced for that file. The process continues until all specified files have been examined. When examining directories (as in the second example above), the checksum process will not detect missing files. A simple way to learn whether files are missing from a directory is to execute the ls command periodically, and compare the outputs. Any file whose name appeared in a previous output but not in the current one no longer exists.

When a file has been corrupted, the way to restore it depends on the extent of the corruption. If damage is extensive, the best solution is to contact the local UNIX system operations group and request that the file be restored from a backup copy. If the damage is minor, repair through editing may be possible. After such a repair, the admin command must be executed:

$ admin −z s.*file*

The purpose of this is to recompute the checksum and bring it into agreement with the contents of the file. After this command is executed, any corruption that existed in the file will no longer be detectable.

11 **lex**

Introduction

`lex` is a software tool that lets you solve a wide class of problems drawn from text processing, code enciphering, compiler writing, and other areas. In text processing, you might check the spelling of words for errors; in code enciphering, you might translate certain patterns of characters into others; and in compiler writing, you might determine what the tokens (smallest meaningful sequences of characters) are in the program to be compiled. The task common to all these problems is lexical analysis: recognizing different strings of characters that satisfy certain characteristics. Hence the name `lex`.

You don't have to use `lex` to handle problems of this kind. You could write programs in a standard language like C to handle them, too. In fact, what `lex` does is produce such C programs. (`lex` is therefore called a program generator.) What `lex` offers you, once you acquire a facility with it, is typically a faster, easier way to create programs that perform these tasks. Its weakness is that it often produces C programs that are longer than necessary for the task at hand and that execute more slowly than they otherwise might. In many applications this is a minor consideration, and the advantages of using `lex` considerably outweigh it.

`lex` can also be used to collect statistical data on features of an input text, such as character count, word length, number of occurrences of a word, and so forth. In the remaining sections of this chapter, we will see

- how to generate a lexical analyzer program

- how to write `lex` source

- how to translate `lex` source

- how to use `lex` with `yacc`

Generating a Lexical Analyzer Program

lex generates a C language scanner from a source specification that you write to solve the problem at hand. This specification consists of a list of rules indicating sequences of characters — expressions — to be searched for in an input text, and the actions to take when an expression is found. We'll show you how to write a lex specification in the next section.

The C source code for the lexical analyzer is generated when you enter

```
$ lex lex.l
```

where lex.l is the file containing your lex specification. (The name lex.l is conventionally the favorite, but you may use whatever name you want. Keep in mind, though, that the .l suffix is a convention recognized by other UNIX system tools, in particular, make.) The source code is written to an output file called lex.yy.c by default. That file contains the definition of a function called yylex() that returns 1 whenever an expression you have specified is found in the input text, 0 when end of file is encountered. Each call to yylex() parses one token (assuming a return); when yylex() is called again, it picks up where it left off.

Note that running lex on a specification that is spread across several files

```
$ lex lex1.l lex2.l lex3.l
```

produces one lex.yy.c. Invoking lex with the -t option causes it to write its output to stdout rather than lex.yy.c, so that it can be redirected:

```
$ lex -t lex.l > lex.c
```

Options to lex must appear between the command name and the file name argument.

The lexical analyzer code stored in lex.yy.c (or the .c file to which it was redirected) must be compiled to generate the executable object program, or scanner, that performs the lexical analysis of an input text. The lex library supplies a default main() that calls the function yylex(), so you need not supply your own main(). The library is accessed by invoking the -ll option to cc:

```
$ cc lex.yy.c -ll
```

Alternatively, you may want to write your own driver. The following is similar to the library version:

```
extern int yylex();

int yywrap()
{
        return(1);
}

main()
{
        while (yylex())
                ;
}
```

We'll take a closer look at the function yywrap() in the "lex Routines" section below. For now it's enough to note that when your driver file is compiled with lex.yy.c

```
$ cc lex.yy.c driver.c
```

its main() will call yylex() at run time exactly as if the lex library had been loaded. The resulting executable reads stdin and writes its output to stdout. Figure 11-1 shows how lex works.

Figure 11-1: Creation and Use of a Lexical Analyzer with lex

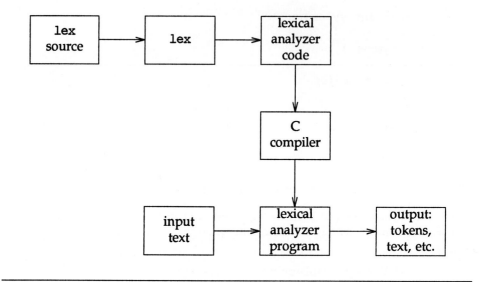

Writing lex Source

`lex` source consists of at most three sections: definitions, rules, and user-defined routines. The rules section is mandatory. Sections for definitions and user routines are optional, but if present, must appear in the indicated order:

> *definitions*
> %%
> *rules*
> %%
> *user routines*

The Fundamentals of lex Rules

The mandatory rules section opens with the delimiter %%. If a routines section follows, another %% delimiter ends the rules section. The %% delimiters must be entered at the beginning of a line, without leading blanks. If there is no second delimiter, the rules section is presumed to continue to the end of the program. Lines in the rules section that begin with white space and that appear before the first rule are copied to the beginning of the function `yylex()`, immediately after the first brace. You might use this feature to declare local variables for `yylex()`.

Each rule consists of a specification of the pattern sought and the action(s) to take on finding it. The specification of the pattern must be entered at the beginning of a line. The scanner writes input that does not match a pattern directly to the output file. So the simplest lexical analyzer program is just the beginning rules delimiter, %%. It writes out the entire input to the output with no changes at all. Typically, the rules are more elaborate than that.

Regular Expressions

You specify the patterns you are interested in with a notation called a regular expression. A regular expression is formed by stringing together characters with or without operators. The simplest regular expressions are strings of text characters with no operators at all:

```
apple
orange
pluto
```

These three regular expressions match any occurrences of those character strings in an input text. If you want to have the scanner remove every occurrence of orange from the input text, you could specify the rule

orange   ;

Because you specified a null action on the right with the semicolon, the scanner does nothing but print out the original input text with every occurrence of this regular expression removed, that is, without any occurrence of the string orange at all.

Operators

Unlike orange above, most of the expressions that we want to search for cannot be specified so easily. The expression itself might simply be too long. More commonly, the class of desired expressions is too large; it may, in fact, be infinite. Thanks to the use of operators — summarized in Figure 11-2 below — we can form regular expressions to signify any expression of a certain class. The + operator, for instance, means one or more occurrences of the preceding expression, the ? means 0 or 1 occurrence(s) of the preceding expression (which is equivalent, of course, to saying that the preceding expression is optional), and * means 0 or more occurrences of the preceding expression. (It may at first seem odd to speak of 0 occurrences of an expression and to need an operator to capture the idea, but it is often quite helpful. We will see an example in a moment.) So m+ is a regular expression that matches any string of ms:

mmm
m
mmmmm

and 7* is a regular expression that matches any string of zero or more 7s:

77
77777

777

The empty third line matches simply because it has no 7s in it at all.

The | operator indicates alternation, so that ab|cd matches either ab or cd. The operators {} specify repetition, so that a{1,5} looks for 1 to 5 occurrences of a. Brackets, [], indicate any one character from the string of characters specified between the brackets. Thus, [dgka] matches a single d, g, k, or a. Note that the characters between brackets must be adjacent, without spaces or punctuation. The ^ operator, when it appears as the first character after the left bracket, indicates all characters in the standard set except those specified between the brackets. (Note that |, {}, and ^ may serve other purposes as well; see below.) Ranges within a standard alphabetic or numeric order (A through Z, a through z, 0 through 9) are specified with a hyphen. [a-z], for instance, indicates any lowercase letter. Somewhat more interestingly,

        [A-Za-z0-9*&#]

is a regular expression that matches any letter (whether upper or lowercase), any digit, an asterisk, an ampersand, or a sharp character. Given the input text

        $$$$?? ????!!!*$$ $$$$$$&+====r~~# ((

the lexical analyzer with the previous specification in one of its rules will recognize *, &, r, and #, perform on each recognition whatever action the rule specifies (we have not indicated an action here), and print out the rest of the text as it stands. If you want to include the hyphen character in the class, it should appear as the first or last character in the brackets: [-A-Z] or [A-Z-].

The operators become especially powerful in combination. For example, the regular expression to recognize an identifier in many programming languages is

        [a-zA-Z][0-9a-zA-Z]*

An identifier in these languages is defined to be a letter followed by zero or more letters or digits, and that is just what the regular expression says. The first pair of brackets matches any letter. The second, if it were not followed by a *, would match any digit or letter. The two pairs of brackets with their enclosed characters would then match any letter followed by a digit or a letter. But with the *, the example matches any letter followed by any number of letters or digits. In particular, it would recognize the following as identifiers:

        e
        not
        idenTIFIER
        pH
        EngineNo99
        R2D2

Note that it would not recognize the following as identifiers:

        not_idenTIFIER
        5times
        $hello

because not_idenTIFIER has an embedded underscore; 5times starts with a digit, not a letter; and $hello starts with a special character.

A potential problem with operator characters is how we can specify them as characters to look for in a search pattern. The last example, for instance, will not recognize text with a * in it.   lex solves the problem in one of two ways: an operator character preceded by a backslash, or characters (except backslash) enclosed in double quotation marks, are taken literally, that is, as part of the text to be searched for. To use the backslash method to recognize, say, a * followed by any number of digits, we can use the pattern

    [1-9]

To recognize a \ itself, we need two backslashes: \\. Similarly, "x*x" matches x*x, and "y\"z" matches y"z. Other lex operators are noted as they arise in the discussion below.   lex recognizes all the C language escape sequences described in "Source Files and Tokenization" in Chapter 3.

Figure 11-2: lex Operators

Expression	Description
\x	x, if x is a lex operator
"xy"	xy, even if x or y are lex operators (except \)
[xy]	x or y
[x−z]	x, y, or z
[^x]	any character but x
.	any character but new-line
^x	x at the beginning of a line
<y>x	x when lex is in start condition y
x$	x at the end of a line
x?	optional x
x*	0, 1, 2, ... instances of x
x+	1, 2, 3, ... instances of x
x{m,n}	m through n occurrences of x
xx|yy	either xx or yy
x |	the action on x is the action for the next rule
(x)	x
x/y	x but only if followed by y
{xx}	the translation of xx from the definitions section

Actions

Once the scanner recognizes a string matching the regular expression at the start of a rule, it looks to the right of the rule for the action to be performed. You supply the actions. Kinds of actions include recording the token type found and its value, if any; replacing one token with another; and counting the number of instances of a token or token type. You write these actions as program fragments in C. An action may consist of as many statements as are needed for the job at hand. You may want to change the text in some way or simply print a message noting that the text has been found. So, to recognize the expression Amelia Earhart and to note such recognition, the rule

```
"Amelia Earhart"   printf("found Amelia");
```

would do. And to replace in a text lengthy medical terms with their equivalent acronyms, a rule such as

```
Electroencephalogram      printf("EEG");
```

would be called for. To count the lines in a text, we need to recognize the ends
of lines and increment a linecounter. As we have noted, lex uses the standard
C escape sequences, including \n for new-line. So, to count lines we might
have

```
\n    lineno++;
```

where lineno, like other C variables, is declared in the definitions section that
we discuss later.

Input is ignored when the C language null statement ; is specified. So the rule

```
[ \t\n]   ;
```

causes blanks, tabs, and new-lines to be ignored. Note that the alternation
operator | can also be used to indicate that the action for a rule is the action for
the next rule. The previous example could have been written:

```
" "    |
\t     |
\n     ;
```

with the same result.

The scanner stores text that matches an expression in a character array called
yytext[]. You can print or manipulate the contents of this array as you like.
In fact, lex provides a macro called ECHO that is equivalent to printf("%s",
yytext). We'll see an example of its use in the "Start Conditions" section
below.

Sometimes your action may consist of a long C statement, or two or more C
statements, and you must (or for style and clarity, you choose to) write it on
several lines. To inform lex that the action is for one rule only, simply enclose
the C code in braces. For example, to count the total number of all digit strings
in an input text, print the running total of the number of digit strings, and print
out each one as soon as it is found, your lex code might be

```
\+?[1-9]+                  { digstrngcount++;
                           printf("%d",digstrngcount);
                           printf("%s", yytext);   }
```

This specification matches digit strings whether they are preceded by a plus
sign or not, because the ? indicates that the preceding plus sign is optional. In
addition, it will catch negative digit strings because that portion following the

minus sign will match the specification. The next section explains how to distinguish negative from positive integers.

Advanced lex Usage

`lex` provides a suite of features that let you process input text riddled with quite complicated patterns. These include rules that decide what specification is relevant when more than one seems so at first; functions that transform one matching pattern into another; and the use of definitions and subroutines. Before considering these features, you may want to affirm your understanding thus far by examining an example that draws together several of the points already covered:

```
%%
-[0-9]+             printf("negative integer");
\+?[0-9]+           printf("positive integer");
-0.[0-9]+           printf("negative fraction, no whole number part");
rail[ \t]+road      printf("railroad is one word");
crook               printf("Here's a crook");
function            subprogcount++;
G[a-zA-Z]*          { printf("may have a G word here:%s", yytext);
                    Gstringcount++; }
```

The first three rules recognize negative integers, positive integers, and negative fractions between 0 and -1. The use of the terminating + in each specification ensures that one or more digits compose the number in question. Each of the next three rules recognizes a specific pattern. The specification for `railroad` matches cases where one or more blanks intervene between the two syllables of the word. In the cases of `railroad` and `crook`, we could have simply printed a synonym rather than the messages stated. The rule recognizing a `function` simply increments a counter. The last rule illustrates several points:

- The braces specify an action sequence that extends over several lines.

- Its action uses the `lex` array `yytext[]`, which stores the recognized character string.

■ Its specification uses the * to indicate that zero or more letters may follow the G.

Some Special Features

Besides storing the matched input text in yytext [], the scanner automatically counts the number of characters in a match and stores it in the variable yyleng. You may use this variable to refer to any specific character just placed in the array yytext []. Remember that C language array indices start with 0, so to print out the third digit (if there is one) in a just recognized integer, you might enter

```
[1-9]+              {if   (yyleng > 2)
                    printf("%c", yytext[2]); }
```

lex follows a number of high-level rules to resolve ambiguities that may arise from the set of rules that you write. In the following lexical analyzer example, the "reserved word" end could match the second rule as well as the eighth, the one for identifiers:

```
begin                    return (BEGIN);
end                      return (END);
while                    return (WHILE);
if                       return (IF);
package                  return (PACKAGE);
reverse                  return (REVERSE);
loop                     return (LOOP);
[a-zA-Z][a-zA-Z0-9]*     { tokval = put_in_tabl ();
                         return (IDENTIFIER); }
[0-9]+                   { tokval = put_in_tabl ();
                         return (INTEGER); }
\+                       { tokval = PLUS;
                         return (ARITHOP); }
\-                       { tokval = MINUS;
                         return (ARITHOP); }
>                        { tokval = GREATER;
                         return (RELOP); }
>=                       { tokval = GREATEREQL;
                         return (RELOP); }
```

lex follows the rule that, where there is a match with two or more rules in a specification, the first rule is the one whose action will be executed. By placing the rule for end and the other reserved words before the rule for identifiers, we ensure that our reserved words will be duly recognized.

Another potential problem arises from cases where one pattern you are searching for is the prefix of another. For instance, the last two rules in the lexical analyzer example above are designed to recognize > and >=. If the text has the string >= at one point, you might worry that the lexical analyzer would stop as soon as it recognized the > character and execute the rule for >, rather than read the next character and execute the rule for >=. lex follows the rule that it matches the longest character string possible and executes the rule for that. Here the scanner would recognize the >= and act accordingly. As a further example, the rule would enable you to distinguish + from ++ in a C program.

Still another potential problem exists when the analyzer must read characters beyond the string you are seeking because you cannot be sure that you've in fact found it until you've read the additional characters. These cases reveal the importance of trailing context. The classic example here is the DO statement in FORTRAN. In the statement

```
DO 50 k = 1 , 20, 1
```

we cannot be sure that the first 1 is the initial value of the index k until we read the first comma. Until then, we might have the assignment statement

```
DO50k = 1
```

(Remember that FORTRAN ignores all blanks.) The way to handle this is to use the slash, /, which signifies that what follows is trailing context, something not to be stored in yytext [], because it is not part of the pattern itself. So the rule to recognize the FORTRAN DO statement could be

```
DO/([ ]*[0-9]+[ ]*[a-zA-Z0-9]+=[a-zA-Z0-9]+,)    {
        printf("found DO");
        }
```

Different versions of FORTRAN have limits on the size of identifiers, here the index name. To simplify the example, the rule accepts an index name of any length. See the "Start Conditions" section below for a discussion of lex's similar handling of prior context.

lex uses the $ symbol as an operator to mark a special trailing context — the end of a line. An example would be a rule to ignore all blanks and tabs at the end of a line:

```
[  \t]+$      ;
```

which could also be written:

```
[  \t]+/\n    ;
```

On the other hand, if you want to match a pattern only when it starts a line or a file, you can use the ^ operator. Suppose a text-formatting program requires that you not start a line with a blank. You might want to check input to the program with some such rule as

```
^[ ]          printf("error: remove leading blank");
```

Note the difference in meaning when the ^ operator appears inside the left bracket, as described in the "Operators" section above.

lex Routines

Some of your action statements themselves may require your reading another character, putting one back to be read again a moment later, or writing a character on an output device. **lex** supplies three macros to handle these tasks — input (), unput (c), and output (c), respectively. One way to ignore all characters between two special characters, say between a pair of double quotation marks, would be to use input (), thus:

```
\"            while (input() != '"');
```

Upon finding the first double quotation mark, the scanner will simply continue reading all subsequent characters so long as none is a double quotation mark, and not look for a match again until it finds a second double quotation mark. (See the further examples of input () and unput (c) usage in the "User Routines" section below.)

By default, these routines are provided as macro definitions. To handle special I/O needs, such as writing to several files, you may use standard I/O routines in C to rewrite the functions. Note, however, that they must be modified consistently. In particular, the character set used must be consistent in all routines, and a value of 0 returned by input () must mean end of file. The relationship between input () and unput (c) must be maintained or the **lex** lookahead will not work.

If you do provide your own input(), output(c), or unput(c), you will have to write a #undef input and so on in your definitions section first:

```
#undef input
#undef output
         .
         .
         .
#define input()    ... etc.
more declarations
         .
         .
         .
```

Your new routines will replace the standard ones. See the "Definitions" section below for further details.

A lex library routine that you may sometimes want to redefine is yywrap(), which is called whenever the scanner reaches end of file. If yywrap() returns 1, the scanner continues with normal wrapup on end of input. Occasionally, however, you may want to arrange for more input to arrive from a new source. In that case, redefine yywrap() to return 0 whenever further processing is required. The default yywrap() always returns 1. Note that it is not possible to write a normal rule that recognizes end of file; the only access to that condition is through yywrap(). Unless a private version of input() is supplied, a file containing nulls cannot be handled because a value of 0 returned by input() is taken to be end of file.

There are a number of lex routines that let you handle sequences of characters to be processed in more than one way. These include yymore(), yyless(n), and REJECT. Recall that the text that matches a given specification is stored in the array yytext[]. In general, once the action is performed for the specification, the characters in yytext[] are overwritten with succeeding characters in the input stream to form the next match. The function yymore(), by contrast, ensures that the succeeding characters recognized are appended to those already in yytext[]. This lets you do one thing and then another, when one string of characters is significant and a longer one including the first is significant as well. Consider a language that defines a string as a set of characters between double quotation marks and specifies that to include a double quotation mark in a string it must be preceded by a backslash. The regular expression matching that is somewhat confusing, so it might be preferable to write:

```
\"[^"]*        {
               if (yytext[yyleng-1] == '\\')
                   yymore();
               else
               ... normal processing
               }
```

When faced with the string `"abc\"def"`, the scanner will first match the characters `"abc\`, whereupon the call to `yymore()` will cause the next part of the string `"def` to be tacked on the end. The double quotation mark terminating the string should be picked up in the code labeled "normal processing."

The function `yyless(n)` lets you specify the number of matched characters on which an action is to be performed: only the first n characters of the expression are retained in `yytext[]`. Subsequent processing resumes at the nth + 1 character. Suppose you are again in the code deciphering business and the idea is to work with only half the characters in a sequence that ends with a certain one, say upper or lowercase Z. The code you want might be

```
[a-yA-Y]+[Zz]    {  yyless(yyleng/2);
                 ... process first half of string ... }
```

Finally, the function `REJECT` lets you more easily process strings of characters even when they overlap or contain one another as parts. `REJECT` does this by immediately jumping to the next rule and its specification without changing the contents of `yytext[]`. If you want to count the number of occurrences both of the regular expression `snapdragon` and of its subexpression `dragon` in an input text, the following will do:

```
snapdragon        {countflowers++; REJECT;}
dragon            countmonsters++;
```

As an example of one pattern overlapping another, the following counts the number of occurrences of the expressions `comedian` and `diana`, even where the input text has sequences such as `comediana..`:

```
comedian          {comiccount++; REJECT;}
diana             princesscount++;
```

Note that the actions here may be considerably more complicated than simply incrementing a counter. In all cases, you declare the counters and other necessary variables in the definitions section commencing the `lex` specification.

Definitions

The `lex` definitions section may contain any of several classes of items. The most critical are external definitions, preprocessor statements like `#include`, and abbreviations. Recall that for legal `lex` source this section is optional, but in most cases some of these items are necessary. Preprocessor statements and C source code should appear between a line of the form `%{` and one of the form `%}`. All lines between these delimiters — including those that begin with white space — are copied to `lex.yy.c` immediately before the definition of `yylex()`. (Lines in the definition section that are not enclosed by the delimiters are copied to the same place *provided* they begin with white space.) The definitions section is where you would normally place C definitions of objects accessed by actions in the rules section or by routines with external linkage.

One example occurs in using `lex` with `yacc`, which generates parsers that call a lexical analyzer. In this context, you should include the file `y.tab.h`, which may contain `#defines` for token names:

```
%{
#include "y.tab.h"
extern int tokval;
int lineno;
%}
```

After the `%}` that ends your `#include`'s and declarations, you place your abbreviations for regular expressions to be used in the rules section. The abbreviation appears on the left of the line and, separated by one or more spaces, its definition or translation appears on the right. When you later use abbreviations in your rules, be sure to enclose them within braces. Abbreviations avoid needless repetition in writing your specifications and make them easier to read.

As an example, reconsider the `lex` source reviewed at the beginning of this section on advanced `lex` usage. The use of definitions simplifies our later reference to digits, letters, and blanks. This is especially true if the specifications appear several times:

```
D               [0-9]
L               [a-zA-Z]
B               [ \t]+
%%
-{D}+           printf("negative integer");
\+?{D}+         printf("positive integer");
-0.{D}+         printf("negative fraction");
G{L}*           printf("may have a G word here");
rail{B}road     printf("railroad is one word");
crook           printf("criminal");
   .               .
   .               .
```

Start Conditions

Some problems require for their solution a greater sensitivity to prior context than is afforded by the ^ operator alone. You may want different rules to be applied to an expression depending on a prior context that is more complex than the end of a line or the start of a file. In this situation you could set a flag to mark the change in context that is the condition for the application of a rule, then write code to test the flag. Alternatively, you could define for lex the different "start conditions" under which it is to apply each rule.

Consider this problem: copy the input to the output, except change the word magic to the word first on every line that begins with the letter a; change magic to second on every line that begins with b; change magic to third on every line that begins with c. Here is how the problem might be handled with a flag. Recall that ECHO is a lex macro equivalent to printf("%s", yytext):

```
int flag
%%
^a    {flag = 'a'; ECHO;}
^b    {flag = 'b'; ECHO;}
^c    {flag = 'c'; ECHO;}
\n    {flag = 0; ECHO;}
magic {
            switch (flag)
            {
                    case 'a': printf("first"); break;
                    case 'b': printf("second"); break;
                    case 'c': printf("third"); break;
                    default: ECHO; break;
            }
      }
```

To handle the same problem with start conditions, each start condition must be introduced to lex in the definitions section with a line reading

> %Start *name1 name2* ...

where the conditions may be named in any order. The word Start may be abbreviated to S or s. The conditions are referenced at the head of a rule with <> brackets. So

> *<name1>expression*

is a rule that is only recognized when the scanner is in start condition *name1*. To enter a start condition, execute the action statement

> BEGIN *name1*;

which changes the start condition to *name1*. To resume the normal state

> BEGIN 0;

resets the initial condition of the scanner. A rule may be active in several start conditions. That is,

> <*name1*, *name2*, *name3*>

is a legal prefix. Any rule not beginning with the <> prefix operators is always active.

The example can be written with start conditions as follows:

```
%Start AA BB CC
%%
^a          {ECHO; BEGIN AA;}
^b          {ECHO; BEGIN BB;}
^c          {ECHO; BEGIN CC;}
\n          {ECHO; BEGIN 0;}
<AA>magic       printf("first");
<BB>magic       printf("second");
<CC>magic       printf("third");
```

User Routines

You may want to use your own routines in `lex` for much the same reason that you do so in other programming languages. Action code that is to be used for several rules can be written once and called when needed. As with definitions, this can simplify the writing and reading of programs. The function `put_in_tabl()`, to be discussed in the next section on `lex` and `yacc`, is a good candidate for the user routines section of a `lex` specification.

Another reason to place a routine in this section is to highlight some code of interest or to simplify the rules section, even if the code is to be used for one rule only. As an example, consider the following routine to ignore comments in a language like C where comments occur between /* and */:

```
%{
static skipcmnts();
%}
%%
"/*"                      skipcmnts();
.
.                 /* rest of rules */
%%
static
skipcmnts()
{
      for(;;)
      {
          while (input() != '*')
                ;
          if (input() != '/')
                unput(yytext[yyleng-1])
          else return;
      }
}
```

There are three points of interest in this example. First, the unput(c) macro (putting back the last character read) is necessary to avoid missing the final / if the comment ends unusually with a **/. In this case, eventually having read a *, the scanner finds that the next character is not the terminal / and must read some more. Second, the expression yytext[yyleng-1] picks out that last character read. Third, this routine assumes that the comments are not nested. That is indeed the case with the C language.

Using lex with yacc

If you work on a compiler project or develop a program to check the validity of an input language, you may want to use the UNIX system tool yacc (Chapter 12). yacc generates parsers, programs that analyze input to insure that it is syntactically correct. lex often forms a fruitful union with yacc in the compiler development context. Whether or not you plan to use lex with yacc, be sure to read this section because it covers information of interest to all lex programmers.

As noted, a program uses the lex-generated scanner by repeatedly calling the function yylex(). This name is convenient because a yacc-generated parser calls its lexical analyzer with this very name. To use lex to create the lexical analyzer for a compiler, you want to end each lex action with the statement return *token*, where *token* is a defined term whose value is an integer. The integer value of the token returned indicates to the parser what the lexical analyzer has found. The parser, called yyparse() by yacc, then resumes control and makes another call to the lexical analyzer when it needs another token.

In a compiler, the different values of the token indicate what, if any, reserved word of the language has been found or whether an identifier, constant, arithmetic operator, or relational operator has been found. In the latter cases, the analyzer must also specify the exact value of the token: what the identifier is, whether the constant is, say, 9 or 888, whether the operator is + or *, and whether the relational operator is = or >. Consider the following portion of lex source (discussed in another context earlier) for a scanner that recognizes tokens in a "C-like" language:

```
begin                         return (BEGIN);
end                           return (END);
while                         return (WHILE);
if                            return (IF);
package                       return (PACKAGE);
reverse                       return (REVERSE);
loop                          return (LOOP);
[a-zA-Z][a-zA-Z0-9]*          { tokval = put_in_tabl();
                                return (IDENTIFIER); }
[0-9]+                        { tokval = put_in_tabl();
                                return (INTEGER); }
\+                            { tokval = PLUS;
                                return (ARITHOP); }
\-                            { tokval = MINUS;
                                return (ARITHOP); }
>                             { tokval = GREATER;
                                return (RELOP); }
>=                            { tokval = GREATEREQL;
                                return (RELOP); }
```

Despite appearances, the tokens returned, and the values assigned to tokval, are indeed integers. Good programming style dictates that we use informative terms such as BEGIN, END, WHILE, and so forth to signify the integers the parser understands, rather than use the integers themselves. You establish the association by using #define statements in your parser calling routine in C. For example,

```
#define BEGIN  1
#define END   2

  .

#define PLUS 7

  .
```

If the need arises to change the integer for some token type, you then change the #define statement in the parser rather than hunt through the entire program changing every occurrence of the particular integer. In using yacc to generate your parser, insert the statement

```
#include "y.tab.h"
```

in the definitions section of your lex source. The file y.tab.h, which is created when yacc is invoked with the -d option, provides #define

lex

statements that associate token names such as BEGIN, END, and so on with the integers of significance to the generated parser.

To indicate the reserved words in the example, the returned integer values suffice. For the other token types, the integer value of the token type is stored in the programmer-defined variable tokval. This variable, whose definition was an example in the definitions section, is globally defined so that the parser as well as the lexical analyzer can access it. yacc provides the variable yylval for the same purpose.

Note that the example shows two ways to assign a value to tokval. First, a function put_in_tabl() places the name and type of the identifier or constant in a symbol table so that the compiler can refer to it in this or a later stage of the compilation process. More to the present point, put_in_tabl() assigns a type value to tokval so that the parser can use the information immediately to determine the syntactic correctness of the input text. The function put_in_tabl() would be a routine that the compiler writer might place in the user routines section of the parser. Second, in the last few actions of the example, tokval is assigned a specific integer indicating which arithmetic or relational operator the scanner recognized. If the variable PLUS, for instance, is associated with the integer 7 by means of the #define statement above, then when a + is recognized, the action assigns to tokval the value 7, which indicates the +. The scanner indicates the general class of operator by the value it returns to the parser (that is, the integer signified by ARITHOP or RELOP).

In using lex with yacc, either may be run first. The command

```
$ yacc -d grammar.y
```

generates a parser in the file y.tab.c. As noted, the -d option creates the file y.tab.h, which contains the #define statements that associate the yacc-assigned integer token values with the user-defined token names. Now you can invoke lex with the command

```
$ lex lex.l
```

then compile and link the output files with the command

```
$ cc lex.yy.c y.tab.c -ly -ll
```

Note that the yacc library is loaded (with the -ly option) before the lex library (with the -ll option) to insure that the supplied main() will call the yacc parser.

Miscellaneous

Recognition of expressions in an input text is performed by a deterministic finite automaton generated by lex. The −v option prints out for you a small set of statistics describing the finite automaton. (For a detailed account of finite automata and their importance for lex, see the Aho, Sethi, and Ullman text, *Compilers: Principles, Techniques, and Tools*, Addison-Wesley, 1986.)

lex uses a table to represent its finite automaton. The maximum number of states that the finite automaton allows is set by default to 500. If your lex source has a large number of rules or the rules are very complex, this default value may be too small. You can enlarge the value by placing another entry in the definitions section of your lex source as follows:

```
%n 700
```

This entry tells lex to make the table large enough to handle as many as 700 states. (The −v option will indicate how large a number you should choose.) If you have need to increase the maximum number of state transitions beyond 2000, the designated parameter is a, thus:

```
%a 2800
```

Finally, check the *Programmer's Reference Manual* for a list of all the options available with the lex command.

Summary of Source Format

■ The general form of a `lex` source file is

> *definitions*
> %%
> *rules*
> %%
> *user routines*

■ The definitions section contains any combination of

□ definitions of abbreviations in the form

> *name space translation*

□ included code in the form

> %{
> *C code*
> %}

□ start conditions in the form

> Start *name1 name2* . . .

□ changes to internal array sizes in the form

> %*x nnn*

where *nnn* is a decimal integer representing an array size and *x* selects the parameter as follows:

p	positions
n	states
e	tree nodes
a	transitions
k	packed character classes
o	output array size

■ Lines in the rules section have the form

> *expression action*

where the action may be continued on succeeding lines by using braces to delimit it.

- The `lex` operator characters are

    " \ [] ^ - ? . * | () $ / {} <> +

- Important `lex` variables, functions, and macros are

yytext []	array of char
yyleng	int
yylex ()	function
yywrap ()	function
yymore ()	function
yyless (n)	function
REJECT	macro
ECHO	macro
input ()	macro
unput (c)	macro
output (c)	macro

12 yacc

Introduction

yacc provides a general tool for imposing structure on the input to a computer program. When you use yacc, you prepare a specification that includes

- a set of rules to describe the elements of the input;
- code to be invoked when a rule is recognized;
- either a definition or declaration of a low-level scanner to examine the input.

yacc then turns the specification into a C language function that examines the input stream. This function, called a parser, works by calling the low-level scanner. The scanner, called a lexical analyzer, picks up items from the input stream. The selected items are known as tokens. Tokens are compared to the input construct rules, called grammar rules. When one of the rules is recognized, the code you have supplied for the rule is invoked. This code is called an action. Actions are fragments of C language code. They can return values and make use of values returned by other actions.

The heart of the yacc specification is the collection of grammar rules. Each rule describes a construct and gives it a name. For example, one grammar rule might be

        date : month_name day ´,´ year ;

where date, month_name, day, and year represent constructs of interest; presumably, month_name, day, and year are defined in greater detail elsewhere. In the example, the comma is enclosed in single quotes. This means that the comma is to appear literally in the input. The colon and semicolon merely serve as punctuation in the rule and have no significance in evaluating the input. With proper definitions, the input

        July 4, 1776

might be matched by the rule.

The lexical analyzer is an important part of the parsing function. This user-supplied routine reads the input stream, recognizes the lower-level constructs, and communicates these as tokens to the parser. The lexical analyzer recognizes constructs of the input stream as terminal symbols; the parser recognizes constructs as nonterminal symbols. To avoid confusion, we will refer to terminal symbols as tokens.

There is considerable leeway in deciding whether to recognize constructs using the lexical analyzer or grammar rules. For example, the rules

```
month_name : 'J' 'a' 'n'  ;
month_name : 'F' 'e' 'b'  ;
             . . .
month_name : 'D' 'e' 'c'  ;
```

might be used in the above example. While the lexical analyzer only needs to recognize individual letters, such low-level rules tend to waste time and space, and may complicate the specification beyond the ability of yacc to deal with it. Usually, the lexical analyzer recognizes the month names and returns an indication that a month_name is seen. In this case, month_name is a token and the detailed rules are not needed.

Literal characters such as a comma must also be passed through the lexical analyzer and are also considered tokens.

Specification files are very flexible. It is relatively easy to add to the above example the rule

```
date   :   month '/' day '/' year    ;
```

allowing

```
7/4/1776
```

as a synonym for

```
July 4, 1776
```

on input. In most cases, this new rule could be slipped into a working system with minimal effort and little danger of disrupting existing input.

The input being read may not conform to the specifications. With a left-to-right scan, input errors are detected as early as is theoretically possible. Thus, not only is the chance of reading and computing with bad input data substantially reduced, but the bad data usually can be found quickly. Error handling, provided as part of the input specifications, permits the reentry of bad data or the continuation of the input process after skipping over the bad data.

In some cases, yacc fails to produce a parser when given a set of specifications. For example, the specifications may be self-contradictory, or they may require a more powerful recognition mechanism than that available to yacc. The former cases represent design errors; the latter cases often can be corrected by making the lexical analyzer more powerful or by rewriting some of the grammar rules.

While yacc cannot handle all possible specifications, its power compares favorably with similar systems. Moreover, the constructs that are difficult for yacc to handle are also frequently difficult for human beings to handle. Some users have reported that the discipline of formulating valid yacc specifications for their input revealed errors of conception or design early in program development.

The remainder of this chapter describes the following subjects:

- basic process of preparing a yacc specification
- parser operation
- handling ambiguities
- handling operator precedences in arithmetic expressions
- error detection and recovery
- the operating environment and special features of the parsers yacc produces
- suggestions to improve the style and efficiency of the specifications
- advanced topics

In addition, there are two examples and a summary of the yacc input syntax.

Basic Specifications

Names refer to either tokens or nonterminal symbols. yacc requires token names to be declared as such. While the lexical analyzer may be included as part of the specification file, it is perhaps more in keeping with modular design to keep it as a separate file. Like the lexical analyzer, other subroutines may be included as well. Thus, every specification file theoretically consists of three sections: the declarations, (grammar) rules, and subroutines. The sections are separated by double percent signs (%%; the percent sign is generally used in yacc specifications as an escape character).

A full specification file looks like

```
declarations
%%
rules
%%
subroutines
```

when all sections are used. The *declarations* and *subroutines* sections are optional. The smallest legal yacc specification might be

```
%%
S:;
```

Blanks, tabs, and new-lines are ignored, but they may not appear in names or multicharacter reserved symbols. Comments may appear wherever a name is legal. They are enclosed in /* and */, as in the C language.

The rules section is made up of one or more grammar rules. A grammar rule has the form

```
A  :  BODY ;
```

where *A* represents a nonterminal symbol, and *BODY* represents a sequence of zero or more names and literals. The colon and the semicolon are yacc punctuation.

Names may be of any length and may be made up of letters, periods, underscores, and digits although a digit may not be the first character of a name. Uppercase and lowercase letters are distinct. The names used in the body of a grammar rule may represent tokens or nonterminal symbols.

A literal consists of a character enclosed in single quotes. As in the C language, the backslash is an escape character within literals. yacc recognizes all the C language escape sequences described in the section "Source Files and Tokenization" of Chapter 3. For a number of technical reasons, the null character should never be used in grammar rules.

If there are several grammar rules with the same left-hand side, the vertical bar can be used to avoid rewriting the left-hand side. In addition, the semicolon at the end of a rule is dropped before a vertical bar. Thus the grammar rules

```
A   :   B   C   D   ;
A   :   E   F   ;
A   :   G   ;
```

can be given to yacc as

```
A   :   B   C   D
    |   E   F
    |   G
    ;
```

by using the vertical bar. It is not necessary that all grammar rules with the same left side appear together in the grammar rules section although it makes the input more readable and easier to change.

If a nonterminal symbol matches the empty string, this can be indicated by

```
epsilon :   ;
```

The blank space following the colon is understood by yacc to be a nonterminal symbol named epsilon.

Names representing tokens must be declared. This is most simply done by writing

```
%token   name1   name2   name3
```

and so on in the declarations section. Every name not defined in the declarations section is assumed to represent a nonterminal symbol. Every nonterminal symbol must appear on the left side of at least one rule.

Of all the nonterminal symbols, the start symbol has particular importance. By default, the symbol is taken to be the left-hand side of the first grammar rule in the rules section. It is possible and desirable to declare the start symbol explicitly in the declarations section using the %start keyword:

```
%start    symbol
```

The end of the input to the parser is signaled by a special token, called the end-marker. The end-marker is represented by either a zero or a negative number. If the tokens up to but not including the end-marker form a construct that matches the start symbol, the parser function returns to its caller after the end-marker is seen and accepts the input. If the end-marker is seen in any other context, it is an error.

It is the job of the user-supplied lexical analyzer to return the end-marker when appropriate. Usually the end-marker represents some reasonably obvious I/O status, such as end of file or end of record.

Actions

With each grammar rule, you can associate actions to be performed when the rule is recognized. Actions may return values and may obtain the values returned by previous actions. Moreover, the lexical analyzer can return values for tokens if desired.

An action is an arbitrary C language statement and as such can do input and output, call subroutines, and alter arrays and variables. An action is specified by one or more statements enclosed in { and }. For example,

```
A    :   '(' B ')'
     {
         hello( 1, "abc" );
     }
```

and

```
XXX    :  YYY  ZZZ
       {
           (void) printf("a message\n");
           flag = 25;
       }
```

are grammar rules with actions.

The $ symbol is used to facilitate communication between the actions and the parser, The pseudo-variable $$ represents the value returned by the complete action. For example, the action

```
{   $$ = 1;   }
```

returns the value of one; in fact, that's all it does.

To obtain the values returned by previous actions and the lexical analyzer, the action can use the pseudo-variables $1, $2, ... $n. These refer to the values returned by components 1 through n of the right side of a rule, with the components being numbered from left to right. If the rule is

```
A    :   B  C  D    ;
```

then $2 has the value returned by C, and $3 the value returned by D. The rule

```
expr    :    '('  expr  ')'    ;
```

provides a common example. One would expect the value returned by this rule to be the value of the expr within the parentheses. Since the first component of the action is the literal left parenthesis, the desired logical result can be indicated by

```
expr    :    '('  expr  ')'
            {
                $$ = $2 ;
            }
```

By default, the value of a rule is the value of the first element in it ($1). Thus, grammar rules of the form

```
A    :    B    ;
```

frequently need not have an explicit action. In previous examples, all the actions came at the end of rules. Sometimes, it is desirable to get control before a rule is fully parsed. yacc permits an action to be written in the middle of a rule as well as at the end. This action is assumed to return a value accessible through the usual $ mechanism by the actions to the right of it. In turn, it may access the values returned by the symbols to its left. Thus, in the rule below the effect is to set x to 1 and y to the value returned by C:

```
A   :   B
            {
                $$ = 1;
            }
            C
        {
            x = $2;
            y = $3;
        }
        ;
```

Actions that do not terminate a rule are handled by yacc by manufacturing a
new nonterminal symbol name and a new rule matching this name to the empty
string. The interior action is the action triggered by recognizing this added rule.
yacc treats the above example as if it had been written

```
$ACT    :   /* empty */
            {
                $$ = 1;
            }
            ;

A       :   B  $ACT  C
            {
                x = $2;
                y = $3;
            }
            ;
```

where $ACT is an empty action.

In many applications, output is not done directly by the actions. A data structure, such as a parse tree, is constructed in memory and transformations are
applied to it before output is generated. Parse trees are particularly easy to construct given routines to build and maintain the tree structure desired. For
example, suppose there is a C function node written so that the call

```
node ( L, n1, n2 )
```

creates a node with label L and descendants n1 and n2 and returns the index of the newly created node. Then a parse tree can be built by supplying actions such as

```
expr    :   expr  '+'  expr
        {
            $$ = node( '+', $1, $3 );
        }
```

in the specification.

You may define other variables to be used by the actions. Declarations and definitions can appear in the declarations section enclosed in %{ and %}. These declarations and definitions have global scope, so they are known to the action statements and can be made known to the lexical analyzer. For example:

```
%{   int variable = 0;    %}
```

could be placed in the declarations section making variable accessible to all of the actions. You should avoid names beginning with yy because the yacc parser uses only such names. Note, too, that in the examples shown thus far all the values are integers. A discussion of values of other types is found in the section "Advanced Topics" below. Finally, note that in the following case

```
%{
        int i;
        printf("%}");
%}
```

yacc will start copying after %{ and stop copying when it encounters the first %}, the one in printf(). In contrast, it would copy %{ in printf() if it encountered it there.

Lexical Analysis

You must supply a lexical analyzer to read the input stream and communicate tokens (with values, if desired) to the parser. The lexical analyzer is an integer-valued function called yylex(). The function returns an integer, the token number, representing the kind of token read. If there is a value associated with that token, it should be assigned to the external variable yylval.

The parser and the lexical analyzer must agree on these token numbers in order for communication between them to take place. The numbers may be chosen by yacc or the user. In either case, the #define mechanism of C language is used to allow the lexical analyzer to return these numbers symbolically. For example, suppose that the token name DIGIT has been defined in the declarations section of the yacc specification file. The relevant portion of the lexical analyzer might look like

```
int yylex()
{
        extern int yylval;
        int c;
        ...
        c = getchar();
        ...
        switch (c)
        {
            ...
            case '0':
            case '1':
            ...
            case '9':
            yylval = c - '0';
            return (DIGIT);
            ...
        }
        ...
}
```

to return the appropriate token.

The intent is to return a token number of DIGIT and a value equal to the numerical value of the digit. You put the lexical analyzer code in the subroutines section and the declaration for DIGIT in the declarations section. Alternatively, you can put the lexical analyzer code in a separately compiled file, provided

- you invoke yacc with the −d option, which generates a file called y.tab.h that contains #define statements for the tokens, and

- you #include y.tab.h in the separately compiled lexical analyzer.

This mechanism leads to clear, easily modified lexical analyzers. The only pitfall to avoid is using any token names in the grammar that are reserved or
significant in C language or the parser. For example, the use of token names
`if` or `while` will almost certainly cause severe difficulties when the lexical
analyzer is compiled. The token name `error` is reserved for error handling
and should not be used naively.

In the default situation, token numbers are chosen by `yacc`. The default token
number for a literal character is the numerical value of the character in the local
character set. Other names are assigned token numbers starting at 257.

If you prefer to assign the token numbers, the first appearance of the token
name or literal in the declarations section must be followed immediately by a
nonnegative integer. This integer is taken to be the token number of the name
or literal. Names and literals not defined this way are assigned default
definitions by `yacc`. The potential for duplication exists here. Care must be
taken to make sure that all token numbers are distinct.

For historical reasons, the end-marker must have token number 0 or negative.
You cannot redefine this token number. Thus, all lexical analyzers should be
prepared to return 0 or a negative number as a token upon reaching the end of
their input.

As noted in the previous chapter, lexical analyzers produced by `lex` are
designed to work in close harmony with `yacc` parsers. The specifications for
these lexical analyzers use regular expressions instead of grammar rules. `lex`
can be used to produce quite complicated lexical analyzers, but there remain
some languages that do not fit any theoretical framework and whose lexical
analyzers must be crafted by hand.

Parser Operation

yacc turns the specification file into a C language procedure, which parses the input according to the specification given. The algorithm used to go from the specification to the parser is complex and will not be discussed here. The parser itself, though, is relatively simple and understanding its usage will make treatment of error recovery and ambiguities easier.

The parser produced by yacc consists of a finite state machine with a stack. The parser is also capable of reading and remembering the next input token, called the lookahead token. The current state is always the one on the top of the stack. The states of the finite state machine are given small integer labels. Initially, the machine is in state 0 (the stack contains only state 0) and no lookahead token has been read.

The machine has only four actions available: shift, reduce, accept, and error. A step of the parser is done as follows:

1. Based on its current state, the parser decides if it needs a look-ahead token to choose the action to be taken. If it needs one and does not have one, it calls yylex() to obtain the next token.

2. Using the current state and the lookahead token if needed, the parser decides on its next action and carries it out. This may result in states being pushed onto the stack or popped off of the stack and in the lookahead token being processed or left alone.

The shift action is the most common action the parser takes. Whenever a shift action is taken, there is always a lookahead token. For example, in state 56 there may be an action

```
    IF    shift 34
```

which says, in state 56, if the lookahead token is IF, the current state (56) is pushed down on the stack, and state 34 becomes the current state (on the top of the stack). The lookahead token is cleared.

The reduce action keeps the stack from growing without bounds. reduce actions are appropriate when the parser has seen the right-hand side of a grammar rule and is prepared to announce that it has seen an instance of the rule replacing the right-hand side by the left-hand side. It may be necessary to consult the lookahead token to decide whether or not to reduce. In fact, the default action (represented by .) is often a reduce action.

reduce actions are associated with individual grammar rules. Grammar rules are also given small integer numbers, and this leads to some confusion. The action

.   `reduce 18`

refers to grammar rule 18, while the action

`IF    shift 34`

refers to state 34.

Suppose the rule

`A   :   x  y  z    ;`

is being reduced. The reduce action depends on the left-hand symbol (A in this case) and the number of symbols on the right-hand side (three in this case). To reduce, first pop off the top three states from the stack. (In general, the number of states popped equals the number of symbols on the right side of the rule.) In effect, these states were the ones put on the stack while recognizing x, y, and z and no longer serve any useful purpose. After popping these states, a state is uncovered, which was the state the parser was in before beginning to process the rule. Using this uncovered state and the symbol on the left side of the rule, perform what is in effect a shift of A. A new state is obtained, pushed onto the stack, and parsing continues. There are significant differences between the processing of the left-hand symbol and an ordinary shift of a token, however, so this action is called a goto action. In particular, the lookahead token is cleared by a shift but is not affected by a goto. In any case, the uncovered state contains an entry such as

`A    goto 20`

causing state 20 to be pushed onto the stack and become the current state.

In effect, the reduce action turns back the clock in the parse, popping the states off the stack to go back to the state where the right-hand side of the rule was first seen. The parser then behaves as if it had seen the left side at that time. If the right-hand side of the rule is empty, no states are popped off the stacks. The uncovered state is in fact the current state.

The reduce action is also important in the treatment of user-supplied actions and values. When a rule is reduced, the code supplied with the rule is executed before the stack is adjusted. In addition to the stack holding the states, another stack running in parallel with it holds the values returned from the lexical analyzer and the actions. When a shift takes place, the external variable yylval is copied onto the value stack. After the return from the user code, the reduction is carried out. When the goto action is done, the external variable yyval is copied onto the value stack. The pseudo-variables $1, $2, and so on refer to the value stack.

The other two parser actions are conceptually much simpler. The accept action indicates that the entire input has been seen and that it matches the specification. This action appears only when the lookahead token is the end-marker and indicates that the parser has successfully done its job. The error action, on the other hand, represents a place where the parser can no longer continue parsing according to the specification. The input tokens it has seen (together with the lookahead token) cannot be followed by anything that would result in a legal input. The parser reports an error and attempts to recover the situation and resume parsing. The error recovery (as opposed to the detection of error) will be discussed later.

Consider

```
%token  DING  DONG  DELL
%%
rhyme   :    sound  place
        ;
sound   :    DING  DONG
        ;
place   :    DELL
        ;
```

as a yacc specification. When yacc is invoked with the –v (verbose) option, a file called y.output is produced with a human-readable description of the parser. The y.output file corresponding to the above grammar (with some statistics stripped off the end) follows.

```
state 0
        $accept  :  _rhyme  $end

        DING  shift 3
        .  error

        rhyme  goto 1
        sound  goto 2
state 1
        $accept  :  rhyme_$end

        $end  accept
        .  error

state 2
        rhyme  :  sound_place

        DELL  shift 5
        .  error

        place   goto 4

state 3
        sound  :  DING_DONG

        DONG  shift 6
        .  error

state 4
        rhyme  :  sound  place_     (1)

        .   reduce  1

state 5
        place  :  DELL_     (3)

        .  reduce  3

state 6
        sound  :  DING  DONG_     (2)

        .  reduce  2
```

The actions for each state are specified and there is a description of the parsing rules being processed in each state. The _ character is used to indicate what has been seen and what is yet to come in each rule. The following input

        DING DONG DELL

can be used to track the operations of the parser. Initially, the current state is state 0. The parser needs to refer to the input in order to decide between the actions available in state 0, so the first token, DING, is read and becomes the lookahead token. The action in state 0 on DING is shift 3, state 3 is pushed onto the stack, and the lookahead token is cleared. State 3 becomes the current state. The next token, DONG, is read and becomes the lookahead token. The action in state 3 on the token DONG is shift 6, state 6 is pushed onto the stack, and the lookahead is cleared. The stack now contains 0, 3, and 6. In state 6, without even consulting the lookahead, the parser reduces by

        sound   :   DING DONG

which is rule 2. Two states, 6 and 3, are popped off the stack, uncovering state 0. Consulting the description of state 0 (looking for a goto on sound),

        sound   goto 2

is obtained. State 2 is pushed onto the stack and becomes the current state.

In state 2, the next token, DELL, must be read. The action is shift 5, so state 5 is pushed onto the stack, which now has 0, 2, and 5 on it, and the lookahead token is cleared. In state 5, the only action is to reduce by rule 3. This has one symbol on the right-hand side, so one state, 5, is popped off, and state 2 is uncovered. The goto in state 2 on place (the left side of rule 3) is state 4. Now, the stack contains 0, 2, and 4. In state 4, the only action is to reduce by rule 1. There are two symbols on the right, so the top two states are popped off, uncovering state 0 again. In state 0, there is a goto on rhyme causing the parser to enter state 1. In state 1, the input is read and the end-marker is obtained indicated by $end in the y.output file. The action in state 1 (when the end-marker is seen) successfully ends the parse.

You might want to consider how the parser works when confronted with such incorrect strings as DING DONG DONG, DING DONG, DING DONG DELL DELL, and so on. A few minutes spent with this and other simple examples is repaid when problems arise in more complicated contexts.

Ambiguity and Conflicts

A set of grammar rules is ambiguous if there is some input string that can be structured in two or more different ways. For example, the grammar rule

        expr   :   expr '-' expr

is a natural way of expressing the fact that one way of forming an arithmetic expression is to put two other expressions together with a minus sign between them. Unfortunately, this grammar rule does not completely specify the way that all complex inputs should be structured. For example, if the input is

        expr - expr - expr

the rule allows this input to be structured as either

        (expr - expr) - expr

or as

        expr - (expr - expr)

The first is called left association, the second right association.

yacc detects such ambiguities when it is attempting to build the parser. Given the input

        expr - expr - expr

consider the problem that confronts the parser. When the parser has read the second expr, the input seen

        expr - expr

matches the right side of the grammar rule above. The parser could reduce the input by applying this rule. After applying the rule, the input is reduced to expr (the left side of the rule). The parser would then read the final part of the input

         - expr

and again reduce. The effect of this is to take the left associative interpretation.

Alternatively, if the parser sees

        expr - expr

it could defer the immediate application of the rule and continue reading the input until

        expr - expr - expr

is seen. It could then apply the rule to the rightmost three symbols, reducing them to `expr`, which results in

        expr - expr

being left. Now the rule can be reduced once more. The effect is to take the right associative interpretation. Thus, having read

        expr - expr

the parser can do one of two legal things, shift or reduce. It has no way of deciding between them. This is called a `shift-reduce` conflict. It may also happen that the parser has a choice of two legal reductions. This is called a `reduce-reduce` conflict. Note that there are never any `shift-shift` conflicts.

When there are `shift-reduce` or `reduce-reduce` conflicts, yacc still produces a parser. It does this by selecting one of the valid steps wherever it has a choice. A rule describing the choice to make in a given situation is called a disambiguating rule.

yacc invokes two default disambiguating rules:

1. In a `shift-reduce` conflict, the default is to do the shift.

2. In a `reduce-reduce` conflict, the default is to reduce by the earlier grammar rule (in the yacc specification).

Rule 1 implies that reductions are deferred in favor of shifts when there is a choice. Rule 2 gives the user rather crude control over the behavior of the parser in this situation, but `reduce-reduce` conflicts should be avoided when possible.

Conflicts may arise because of mistakes in input or logic or because the grammar rules (while consistent) require a more complex parser than yacc can construct. The use of actions within rules can also cause conflicts if the action must be done before the parser can be sure which rule is being recognized. In these cases, the application of disambiguating rules is inappropriate and leads to an incorrect parser. For this reason, yacc always reports the number of `shift-reduce` and `reduce-reduce` conflicts resolved by rules 1 and 2 above.

In general, whenever it is possible to apply disambiguating rules to produce a correct parser, it is also possible to rewrite the grammar rules so that the same inputs are read but there are no conflicts. For this reason, most previous parser generators have considered conflicts to be fatal errors. Our experience has suggested that this rewriting is somewhat unnatural and produces slower parsers. Thus, yacc will produce parsers even in the presence of conflicts.

As an example of the power of disambiguating rules, consider

```
stat    :   IF  '('  cond  ')'  stat
        |   IF  '('  cond  ')'  stat  ELSE  stat
        ;
```

which is a fragment from a programming language involving an if-then-else statement. In these rules, IF and ELSE are tokens, cond is a nonterminal symbol describing conditional (logical) expressions, and stat is a nonterminal symbol describing statements. The first rule will be called the simple if rule and the second the if-else rule.

These two rules form an ambiguous construction because input of the form

```
IF    (  C1  )   IF   (  C2  )   S1   ELSE   S2
```

can be structured according to these rules in two ways

```
IF   ( C1 )
{
        IF   ( C2 )
                S1
}
ELSE
        S2
```

or

```
IF   ( C1 )
{
        IF   ( C2 )
                S1
        ELSE
                S2
}
```

where the second interpretation is the one given in most programming languages having this construct; each ELSE is associated with the last preceding un-ELSE'd IF. In this example, consider the situation where the parser has seen

```
IF   (  C1  )   IF   (  C2  )   S1
```

and is looking at the ELSE. It can immediately reduce by the simple if rule to get

        IF   (C1   )   stat

and then read the remaining input

        ELSE   S2

and reduce

        IF   (C1   )   stat   ELSE   S2

by the if-else rule. This leads to the first of the above groupings of the input.

On the other hand, the ELSE may be shifted, S2 read, and then the right-hand portion of

        IF   (C1   )   IF   (C2   )   S1   ELSE   S2

can be reduced by the if-else rule to get

        IF   (C1   )   stat

which can be reduced by the simple if rule. This leads to the second of the above groupings of the input, which is usually the one desired.

Once again, the parser can do two valid things — there is a shift-reduce conflict. The application of disambiguating rule 1 tells the parser to shift in this case, which leads to the desired grouping.

This shift-reduce conflict arises only when there is a particular current input symbol, ELSE, and particular inputs, such as

        IF   (C1   )   IF   (C2   )   S1

have already been seen. In general, there may be many conflicts, and each one will be associated with an input symbol and a set of previously read inputs. The previously read inputs are characterized by the state of the parser.

The conflict messages of yacc are best understood by examining the -v output. For example, the output corresponding to the above conflict state might be

```
23: shift-reduce conflict (shift 45, reduce 18) on ELSE

state 23

    stat  :  IF  (  cond  )  stat_            (18)
    stat  :  IF  (  cond  )  stat_ELSE  stat

    ELSE      shift 45
     .        reduce 18
```

where the first line describes the conflict — giving the state and the input symbol. The ordinary state description gives the grammar rules active in the state and the parser actions. Recall that the underscore marks the portion of the grammar rules that has been seen. Thus in the example, in state 23, the parser has seen input corresponding to

        IF   (cond   )   stat

and the two grammar rules shown are active at this time. The parser can do two possible things. If the input symbol is ELSE, it is possible to shift into state 45. State 45 will have, as part of its description, the line

        stat   :   IF   (cond   )   stat   ELSE_stat

because the ELSE will have been shifted in this state. In state 23, the alternative action (specified by .) is to be done if the input symbol is not mentioned explicitly in the actions. In this case, if the input symbol is not ELSE, the parser reduces to

        stat   :   IF   '('   cond   ')'   stat

by grammar rule 18.

Once again, notice that the numbers following shift commands refer to other states, while the numbers following reduce commands refer to grammar rule numbers. In the y.output file, rule numbers are printed in parentheses after those rules that can be reduced. In most states, there is a reduce action possible, and reduce is the default command. If you encounter unexpected shift-reduce conflicts, you will probably want to look at the -v output to decide whether the default actions are appropriate.

Precedence

There is one common situation where the rules given above for resolving conflicts are not sufficient. This is in the parsing of arithmetic expressions. Most of the commonly used constructions for arithmetic expressions can be naturally described by the notion of precedence levels for operators, together with information about left or right associativity. It turns out that ambiguous grammars with appropriate disambiguating rules can be used to create parsers that are faster and easier to write than parsers constructed from unambiguous grammars. The basic notion is to write grammar rules of the form

```
expr  :  expr  OP  expr
```

and

```
expr  :  UNARY  expr
```

for all binary and unary operators desired. This creates a very ambiguous grammar with many parsing conflicts. You specify as disambiguating rules the precedence or binding strength of all the operators and the associativity of the binary operators. This information is sufficient to allow yacc to resolve the parsing conflicts in accordance with these rules and construct a parser that realizes the desired precedences and associativities.

The precedences and associativities are attached to tokens in the declarations section. This is done by a series of lines beginning with the yacc keywords %left, %right, or %nonassoc, followed by a list of tokens. All of the tokens on the same line are assumed to have the same precedence level and associativity; the lines are listed in order of increasing precedence or binding strength. Thus

```
%left   '+'   '-'
%left   '*'   '/'
```

describes the precedence and associativity of the four arithmetic operators. + and − are left associative and have lower precedence than * and /, which are also left associative. The keyword %right is used to describe right associative operators. The keyword %nonassoc is used to describe operators, like the operator .LT. in FORTRAN, that may not associate with themselves. That is, because

```
A .LT. B .LT. C
```

is illegal in FORTRAN, .LT. would be described with the keyword %nonassoc in yacc.

As an example of the behavior of these declarations, the description

```
%right '='
%left '+' '-'
%left '*' '/'

%%

expr  :    expr '=' expr
      |    expr '+' expr
      |    expr '-' expr
      |    expr '*' expr
      |    expr '/' expr
      |    NAME
      ;
```

might be used to structure the input

```
a  =  b  =  c * d  -  e  -  f * g
```

as follows

```
a = ( b = ( ((c * d) - e) - (f * g) ) )
```

in order to achieve the correct precedence of operators. When this mechanism is used, unary operators must, in general, be given a precedence. Sometimes a unary operator and a binary operator have the same symbolic representation but different precedences. An example is unary and binary minus.

Unary minus may be given the same strength as multiplication, or even higher, while binary minus has a lower strength than multiplication. The keyword %prec changes the precedence level associated with a particular grammar rule. %prec appears immediately after the body of the grammar rule, before the action or closing semicolon, and is followed by a token name or literal. It causes the precedence of the grammar rule to become that of the following token name or literal. For example, the rules

```
%left  '+'  '-'
%left  '*'  '/'

%%

expr   :   expr  '+'  expr
       |   expr  '-'  expr
       |   expr  '*'  expr
       |   expr  '/'  expr
       |   '-'  expr       %prec  '*'
       |   NAME
       ;
```

might be used to give unary minus the same precedence as multiplication.

A token declared by %left, %right, and %nonassoc need not, but may, be declared by %token as well.

Precedences and associativities are used by yacc to resolve parsing conflicts. They give rise to the following disambiguating rules:

1. Precedences and associativities are recorded for those tokens and literals that have them.

2. A precedence and associativity is associated with each grammar rule. It is the precedence and associativity of the last token or literal in the body of the rule. If the %prec construction is used, it overrides this default. Some grammar rules may have no precedence and associativity associated with them.

3. When there is a reduce-reduce or shift-reduce conflict, and either the input symbol or the grammar rule has no precedence and associativity, then the two default disambiguating rules given in the preceding section are used, and the conflicts are reported.

4. If there is a shift-reduce conflict and both the grammar rule and the input character have precedence and associativity associated with them, then the conflict is resolved in favor of the action — shift or reduce — associated with the higher precedence. If precedences are equal, then associativity is used. Left associative implies reduce; right associative implies shift; nonassociating implies error.

Conflicts resolved by precedence are not counted in the number of shift-reduce and reduce-reduce conflicts reported by yacc. This means that mistakes in the specification of precedences may disguise errors in the input grammar. It is a good idea to be sparing with precedences and use them in a cookbook fashion until some experience has been gained. The y.output file is useful in deciding whether the parser is actually doing what was intended.

To illustrate further how you might use the precedence keywords to resolve a shift-reduce conflict, we'll look at an example similar to the one described in the previous section. Consider the following C statement:

```
if (flag) if (anotherflag) x = 1;
else x = 2;
```

The problem for the parser is whether the else goes with the first or the second if. C programmers will recognize that the else goes with the second if, contrary to to what the misleading indentation suggests. The following yacc grammar for an if-then-else construct abstracts the problem. That is, the input iises will model the C statement shown above.

```
%{
#include <stdio.h>
%}
%token SIMPLE IF ELSE
%%
S                       : stmnt '\n'
                        ;
stmnt                   : SIMPLE
                        | if_stmnt
                        ;
if_stmnt                : IF stmnt
                                { printf("simple if\n");}
                        | IF stmnt ELSE stmnt
                                { printf("if_then_else\n");}
                        ;
%%
int
yylex() {
        int c;
        c=getchar();
        if (c==EOF) return 0;
        else switch(c) {
                case 'i': return IF;
                case 's': return SIMPLE;
                case 'e': return ELSE;
                default: return c;
                }
}
```

When the specification is passed to yacc, however, we get the following message:

        conflicts: 1 shift/reduce

The problem is that when yacc has read iis in trying to match iises, it has two choices: recognize is as a statement (reduce), or read some more input (shift) and eventually recognize ises as a statement.

One way to resolve the problem is to invent a new token REDUCE whose sole purpose is to give the correct precedence for the rules:

```
%{
#include <stdio.h>
%}
%token SIMPLE IF
%nonassoc REDUCE
%nonassoc ELSE
%%
s                       : stmnt '\n'
                        ;
stmnt                   : SIMPLE
                        | if_stmnt
                        ;
if_stmnt                : IF stmnt %prec REDUCE
                                { printf("simple if");}
                        | IF stmnt ELSE stmnt
                                { printf("if_then_else");}
                        ;
%%
```

Since the precedence associated with the second form of `if_stmnt` is higher now, `yacc` will try to match that rule first, and no conflict will be reported.

Actually, in this simple case, the new token is not needed:

```
%nonassoc IF
%nonassoc ELSE
```

would also work. Moreover, it is not really necessary to resolve the conflict in this way, because, as we have seen, `yacc` will shift by default in a `shift-reduce` conflict. Resolving conflicts is a good idea, though, in the sense that you should not see diagnostic messages for correct specifications.

Error Handling

Error handling is an extremely difficult area, and many of the problems are semantic ones. When an error is found, for example, it may be necessary to reclaim parse tree storage, delete or alter symbol table entries, and/or, typically, set switches to avoid generating any further output.

It is seldom acceptable to stop all processing when an error is found. It is more useful to continue scanning the input to find further syntax errors. This leads to the problem of getting the parser restarted after an error. A general class of algorithms to do this involves discarding a number of tokens from the input string and attempting to adjust the parser so that input can continue.

To allow the user some control over this process, yacc provides the token name error. This name can be used in grammar rules. In effect, it suggests where errors are expected and recovery might take place. The parser pops its stack until it enters a state where the token error is legal. It then behaves as if the token error were the current lookahead token and performs the action encountered. The lookahead token is then reset to the token that caused the error. If no special error rules have been specified, the processing halts when an error is detected.

In order to prevent a cascade of error messages, the parser, after detecting an error, remains in error state until three tokens have been successfully read and shifted. If an error is detected when the parser is already in error state, no message is given, and the input token is quietly deleted.

As an example, a rule of the form

```
stat    :    error
```

means that on a syntax error the parser attempts to skip over the statement in which the error is seen. More precisely, the parser scans ahead, looking for three tokens that might legally follow a statement, and starts processing at the first of these. If the beginnings of statements are not sufficiently distinctive, it may make a false start in the middle of a statement and end up reporting a second error where there is in fact no error.

Actions may be used with these special error rules. These actions might attempt to reinitialize tables, reclaim symbol table space, and so forth.

Error rules such as the above are very general but difficult to control. Rules such as

```
stat    :    error ';'
```

are somewhat easier. Here, when there is an error, the parser attempts to skip over the statement but does so by skipping to the next semicolon. All tokens after the error and before the next semicolon cannot be shifted and are discarded. When the semicolon is seen, this rule will be reduced and any cleanup action associated with it performed.

Another form of `error` rule arises in interactive applications where it may be desirable to permit a line to be reentered after an error. The following example

```
input : error   '\n'
                {
                        (void) printf("Reenter last line: " );
                }
                input
        {
          $$ = $4;
        }
        ;
```

is one way to do this. There is one potential difficulty with this approach. The parser must correctly process three input tokens before it admits that it has correctly resynchronized after the error. If the reentered line contains an error in the first two tokens, the parser deletes the offending tokens and gives no message. This is clearly unacceptable. For this reason, there is a mechanism that can force the parser to believe that error recovery has been accomplished. The statement

```
yyerrok ;
```

in an action resets the parser to its normal mode. The last example can be rewritten as

```
input : error   '\n'
                {
                        yyerrok;
                        (void) printf("Reenter last line: " );
                }
                input
        {
          $$ = $4;
        }
        ;
```

As previously mentioned, the token seen immediately after the error symbol
is the input token at which the error was discovered. Sometimes this is inappropriate; for example, an error recovery action might take upon itself the job of
finding the correct place to resume input. In this case, the previous lookahead
token must be cleared. The statement

```
yyclearin ;
```

in an action will have this effect. For example, suppose the action after error
were to call some sophisticated resynchronization routine (supplied by the user)
that attempted to advance the input to the beginning of the next valid statement. After this routine is called, the next token returned by yylex() is
presumably the first token in a legal statement. The old illegal token must be
discarded and the error state reset. A rule similar to

```
stat    :    error
        {
            resynch();
            yyerrok  ;
            yyclearin;
        }
        ;
```

could perform this.

These mechanisms are admittedly crude but do allow for a simple, fairly effective recovery of the parser from many errors. Moreover, the user can get control to deal with the error actions required by other portions of the program.

The yacc Environment

You create a yacc parser with the command

```
$ yacc grammar.y
```

where grammar.y is the file containing your yacc specification. (The .y suffix is a convention recognized by other UNIX system commands. It is not strictly necessary.) The output is a file of C language subroutines called y.tab.c. The function produced by yacc is called yyparse(), and is integer-valued. When it is called, it in turn repeatedly calls yylex(), the lexical analyzer supplied by the user (see "Lexical Analysis" above), to obtain input tokens. Eventually, an error is detected, yyparse() returns the value 1, and no error recovery is possible, or the lexical analyzer returns the end-marker token and the parser accepts. In this case, yyparse() returns the value 0.

You must provide a certain amount of environment for this parser in order to obtain a working program. For example, as with every C language program, a routine called main() must be defined that eventually calls yyparse(). In addition, a routine called yyerror() is needed to print a message when a syntax error is detected.

These two routines must be supplied in one form or another by the user. To ease the initial effort of using yacc, a library has been provided with default versions of main() and yyerror(). The library is accessed by a −ly argument to the cc command. The source codes

```
main()
{
        return (yyparse());
}
```

and

```
# include <stdio.h>

yyerror(s)
        char *s;
{
        (void) fprintf(stderr, "%s\n", s);
}
```

show the triviality of these default programs. The argument to yyerror() is a string containing an error message, usually the string syntax error. The average application wants to do better than this. Ordinarily, the program should keep track of the input line number and print it along with the message when a syntax error is detected. The external integer variable yychar contains the lookahead token number at the time the error was detected. This may be of some interest in giving better diagnostics. Since the main() routine is probably supplied by the user (to read arguments, for instance), the yacc library is useful only in small projects or in the earliest stages of larger ones.

The external integer variable yydebug is normally set to 0. If it is set to a nonzero value, the parser will output a verbose description of its actions including a discussion of the input symbols read and what the parser actions are. It is possible to set this variable by using sdb(1).

Hints for Preparing Specifications

This part contains miscellaneous hints on preparing efficient, easy to change, and clear specifications. The individual subsections are more or less independent.

Input Style

It is difficult to provide rules with substantial actions and still have a readable specification file. The following are a few style hints.

1. Use all uppercase letters for token names and all lowercase letters for nonterminal names. This is useful in debugging.

2. Put grammar rules and actions on separate lines. It makes editing easier.

3. Put all rules with the same left-hand side together. Put the left-hand side in only once and let all following rules begin with a vertical bar.

4. Put a semicolon only after the last rule with a given left-hand side and put the semicolon on a separate line. This allows new rules to be easily added.

5. Indent rule bodies by one tab stop and action bodies by two tab stops.

6. Put complicated actions into subroutines defined in separate files.

Example 1 below is written following this style, as are the examples in this section (where space permits). The central problem is to make the rules visible through the morass of action code.

Left Recursion

The algorithm used by the yacc parser encourages so called left recursive grammar rules. Rules of the form

```
name    :    name   rest_of_rule   ;
```

match this algorithm. Rules such as

```
list    :    item
        |    list  ','   item
        ;
```

and

```
        seq    :    item
               |    seq  item
               ;
```

frequently arise when writing specifications of sequences and lists. In each of these cases, the first rule will be reduced for the first item only; and the second rule will be reduced for the second and all succeeding items.

With right recursive rules, such as

```
        seq    :    item
               |    item  seq
               ;
```

the parser is a bit bigger; and the items are seen and reduced from right to left. More seriously, an internal stack in the parser is in danger of overflowing if an extremely long sequence is read (although yacc can now process very large stacks). Thus, you should use left recursion wherever reasonable.

It is worth considering if a sequence with zero elements has any meaning, and if so, consider writing the sequence specification as

```
        seq    :    /* empty */
               |    seq  item
               ;
```

using an empty rule. Once again, the first rule would always be reduced exactly once before the first item was read, and then the second rule would be reduced once for each item read. Permitting empty sequences often leads to increased generality. However, conflicts might arise if yacc is asked to decide which empty sequence it has seen when it hasn't seen enough to know!

Lexical Tie-Ins

Some lexical decisions depend on context. For example, the lexical analyzer might want to delete blanks normally, but not within quoted strings, or names might be entered into a symbol table in declarations but not in expressions. One way of handling these situations is to create a global flag that is examined by the lexical analyzer and set by actions. For example,

```
%{
    int dflag;
%}
    ... other declarations ...

%%

prog    :    decls  stats
        ;

decls   :    /* empty */
        {
                dflag = 1;
        }
        |    decls  declaration
        ;

stats   :    /* empty */
        {
                dflag = 0;
        }
        |    stats  statement
        ;

        other rules
```

specifies a program that consists of zero or more declarations followed by zero
or more statements. The flag `dflag` is now 0 when reading statements and 1
when reading declarations, except for the first token in the first statement. This
token must be seen by the parser before it can tell that the declaration section
has ended and the statements have begun. In many cases, this single token
exception does not affect the lexical scan.

This kind of backdoor approach can be elaborated to a noxious degree.
Nevertheless, it represents a way of doing some things that are difficult, if not
impossible, to do otherwise.

Reserved Words

Some programming languages permit you to use words like if, which are normally reserved as label or variable names, provided that such use does not
conflict with the legal use of these names in the programming language. This is
extremely hard to do in the framework of yacc. It is difficult to pass information to the lexical analyzer telling it this instance of if is a keyword and that
instance is a variable. You can make a stab at it using the mechanism described
in the last subsection, but it is difficult.

Advanced Topics

This part discusses a number of advanced features of yacc.

Simulating error and accept in Actions

The parsing actions of error and accept can be simulated in an action by use of macros YYACCEPT and YYERROR. The YYACCEPT macro causes yyparse() to return the value 0; YYERROR causes the parser to behave as if the current input symbol had been a syntax error; yyerror() is called, and error recovery takes place. These mechanisms can be used to simulate parsers with multiple end-markers or context sensitive syntax checking.

Accessing Values in Enclosing Rules

An action may refer to values returned by actions to the left of the current rule. The mechanism is simply the same as with ordinary actions, $ followed by a digit.

```
sent    :    adj  noun  verb  adj  noun
        {
             look at the sentence ...
        }
        ;
adj     :    THE
        {
                 $$ = THE;
        }
        |  YOUNG
        {
                 $$ = YOUNG;
        }
        ...
        ;
noun    :    DOG
        {
             $$ = DOG;
        }
        |  CRONE
        {
             if( $0 == YOUNG )
             {
                  (void) printf( "what?\n" );
             }
             $$ = CRONE;
        }
        ;
        ...
```

In this case, the digit may be 0 or negative. In the action following the word
CRONE, a check is made that the preceding token shifted was not YOUNG. Obviously, this is only possible when a great deal is known about what might precede the symbol noun in the input. Nevertheless, at times this mechanism
prevents a great deal of trouble especially when a few combinations are to be
excluded from an otherwise regular structure.

Support for Arbitrary Value Types

By default, the values returned by actions and the lexical analyzer are integers. yacc can also support values of other types including structures. In addition, yacc keeps track of the types and inserts appropriate union member names so that the resulting parser is strictly type checked. The yacc value stack is declared to be a union of the various types of values desired. You declare the union and associate union member names with each token and nonterminal symbol having a value. When the value is referenced through a $$ or $n construction, yacc will automatically insert the appropriate union name so that no unwanted conversions take place.

There are three mechanisms used to provide for this typing. First, there is a way of defining the union. This must be done by the user since other subroutines, notably the lexical analyzer, must know about the union member names. Second, there is a way of associating a union member name with tokens and nonterminals. Finally, there is a mechanism for describing the type of those few values where yacc cannot easily determine the type.

To declare the union, you include

```
%union
{
    body of union
}
```

in the declaration section. This declares the yacc value stack and the external variables yylval and yyval to have type equal to this union. If yacc was invoked with the −d option, the union declaration is copied into the y.tab.h file as YYSTYPE.

Once YYSTYPE is defined, the union member names must be associated with the various terminal and nonterminal names. The construction

```
<name>
```

is used to indicate a union member name. If this follows one of the keywords %token, %left, %right, and %nonassoc, the union member name is associated with the tokens listed. Thus, saying

```
%left  <optype>  '+'  '-'
```

causes any reference to values returned by these two tokens to be tagged with the union member name optype. Another keyword, %type, is used to associate union member names with nonterminals. Thus, one might say

```
%type   <nodetype>  expr   stat
```

to associate the union member nodetype with the nonterminal symbols expr and stat.

There remain a couple of cases where these mechanisms are insufficient. If there is an action within a rule, the value returned by this action has no a priori type. Similarly, reference to left context values (such as $0) leaves yacc with no easy way of knowing the type. In this case, a type can be imposed on the reference by inserting a union member name between < and > immediately after the first $. The example below

```
rule    :   aaa
                {
                     $<intval>$ = 3;
                }
                bbb
        {
            fun( $<intval>2, $<other>0 );
        }
        ;
```

shows this usage. This syntax has little to recommend it, but the situation arises rarely.

A sample specification is given in Example 2 below. The facilities in this subsection are not triggered until they are used. In particular, the use of %type will turn on these mechanisms. When they are used, there is a fairly strict level of checking. For example, use of $n or $$ to refer to something with no defined type is diagnosed. If these facilities are not triggered, the yacc value stack is used to hold ints.

yacc Input Syntax

This section has a description of the yacc input syntax as a yacc specification.
Context dependencies and so forth are not considered. Ironically, although
yacc accepts an LALR(1) grammar, the yacc input specification language is
most naturally specified as an LR(2) grammar; the sticky part comes when an
identifier is seen in a rule immediately following an action. If this identifier is
followed by a colon, it is the start of the next rule; otherwise, it is a continuation
of the current rule, which just happens to have an action embedded in it. As
implemented, the lexical analyzer looks ahead after seeing an identifier and
decides whether the next token (skipping blanks, new-lines, comments, and so
on) is a colon. If so, it returns the token C_IDENTIFIER. Otherwise, it returns
IDENTIFIER. Literals (quoted strings) are also returned as IDENTIFIERs but
never as part of C_IDENTIFIERs.

```
        /* grammar for the input to yacc */

        /* basic entries */
%token      IDENTIFIER    /* includes identifiers and literals */
%token      C_IDENTIFIER  /* identifier (but not literal) followed by a : */
%token      NUMBER        /* [0-9]+ */

        /*    reserved words: %type=>TYPE %left=>LEFT,etc. */

%token      LEFT RIGHT NONASSOC TOKEN PREC TYPE START UNION

%token      MARK    /* the %% mark */
%token      LCURL   /* the %{ mark */
%token      RCURL   /* the %} mark */

        /* ASCII character literals stand for themselves */

%token      spec

%%

spec    :    defs MARK rules tail
        ;
tail    :    MARK
        {
                In this action, eat up the rest of the file
        }
```

(continued on next page)

```
             |    /* empty: the second MARK is optional */
             ;

defs    :    /* empty */
             |    defs def
             ;
def     :    START IDENTIFIER
             |    UNION
             {
                     Copy union definition to output
             }
             |    LCURL
             {
                        Copy C code to output file
             }
                  RCURL
             |    rword tag nlist
             ;

rword   :    TOKEN
             |    LEFT
             |    RIGHT
             |    NONASSOC
             |    TYPE
             ;

tag     :    /* empty: union tag is optional */
             |    '<' IDENTIFIER '>'
             ;

nlist   :    nmno
             |    nlist nmno
             |    nlist ',' nmno
             ;
nmno    :    IDENTIFIER          /* Note: literal illegal with % type */
             |    IDENTIFIER NUMBER   /* Note: illegal with % type */
             ;

   /* rule section */

rules   :    C_IDENTIFIER rbody prec
             |    rules rule
             ;
rule    :    C_IDENTIFIER rbody prec
             |    '|' rbody prec
             ;
```

(continued on next page)

```
rbody   :   /* empty */
        |   rbody IDENTIFIER
        |   rbody act
        ;

act     :   '{'
            {
                Copy action translate $$ etc.
            }
            '}'
        ;

prec    :   /* empty */
        |   PREC IDENTIFIER
        |   PREC IDENTIFIER act
        |   prec ';'
        ;
```

Examples

1. A Simple Example

This example gives the complete yacc applications for a small desk calculator; the calculator has 26 registers labeled a through z and accepts arithmetic expressions made up of the operators +, −, *, /, %, &, |, and the assignment operators.

If an expression at the top level is an assignment, only the assignment is done; otherwise, the expression is printed. As in the C language, an integer that begins with 0 is assumed to be octal; otherwise, it is assumed to be decimal.

As an example of a yacc specification, the desk calculator does a reasonable job of showing how precedence and ambiguities are used and demonstrates simple recovery. The major oversimplifications are that the lexical analyzer is much simpler than for most applications, and the output is produced immediately line by line. Note the way that decimal and octal integers are read in by grammar rules. This job is probably better done by the lexical analyzer.

```
%{
# include <stdio.h>
# include <ctype.h>

int regs[26];
int base;

%}

%start list

%token DIGIT LETTER

%left '|'
%left '&'
%left '+' '-'
%left '*' '/' '%'
%left UMINUS  /* supplies precedence for unary minus */

%%            /* beginning of rules section */

list    :  /* empty */
        |  list stat '\n'
        |  list error '\n'
        {
          yyerrok;
        }
        ;

stat    :  expr
        {
          (void) printf( "%d\n", $1 );
        }
        |  LETTER '=' expr
        {
          regs[$1] = $3;
        }
        ;

expr    :  '(' expr ')'
        {
            $$ = $2;
        }
        |  expr '+' expr
        {
            $$ = $1 + $3;
```

(continued on next page)

```
            }
            |   expr '-' expr
            {
                $$ = $1 - $3;
            }
            |   expr '*' expr
            {
                $$ = $1 * $3;
            }
            |   expr '/' expr
            {
                $$ = $1 / $3;
            }
            |   exp '%' expr
            {
                $$ = $1 % $3;
            }
            |   expr '&' expr
            {
                $$ = $1 & $3;
            }
            |   expr '|' expr
            {
                $$ = $1 | $3;
            }
            |   '-' expr  %prec UMINUS
            {
                $$ = -$2;
            }
            |   LETTER
            {
                $$ = reg[$1];
            }
            |   number
            ;

number      :   DIGIT
            {
                $$ = $1; base = ($1==0) ? 8 : 10;
            }
            |   number DIGIT
            {
                $$ = base * $1 + $2;
            }
            ;
```

(continued on next page)

ANSI C and Programming Support Tools

```
%%                    /* beginning of subroutines section */

int yylex( )    /* lexical analysis routine */
(               /* return LETTER for lowercase letter, */
                /* yylval - 0 through 25 */
                /* returns DIGIT for digit, yylval - 0 through 9 */
                /* all other characters are returned immediately */
        int c;
                /*skip blanks*/
        while ((c - getchar()) -- ' ')
                ;

                /* c is now nonblank */

        if (islower(c))
        (
                yylval - c - 'a';
                return (LETTER);
        )
        if (isdigit(c))
        )
                yylval - c - '0';
                return (DIGIT);

        )
        return (c);
)
```

2. An Advanced Example

This section gives an example of a grammar using some of the advanced features. The desk calculator in Example 1 is modified to provide a desk calculator that does floating point interval arithmetic. The calculator understands floating point constants, and the arithmetic operations +, −, *, /, and unary −. It uses the registers a through z. Moreover, it understands intervals written

        (X, Y)

where X is less than or equal to Y. There are 26 interval valued variables A through Z that may also be used. The usage is similar to that in Example 1;

yacc   **12-47**

assignments return no value and print nothing while expressions print the (floating or interval) value.

This example explores a number of interesting features of yacc and C. Intervals are represented by a structure consisting of the left and right endpoint values stored as doubles. This structure is given a type name, INTERVAL, by using typedef. The yacc value stack can also contain floating point scalars and integers (used to index into the arrays holding the variable values). Notice that the entire strategy depends strongly on being able to assign structures and unions in C language. In fact, many of the actions call functions that return structures as well.

It is also worth noting the use of YYERROR to handle error conditions — division by an interval containing 0 and an interval presented in the wrong order. The error recovery mechanism of yacc is used to throw away the rest of the offending line.

In addition to the mixing of types on the value stack, this grammar also demonstrates an interesting use of syntax to keep track of the type (for example, scalar or interval) of intermediate expressions. Note that scalar can be automatically promoted to an interval if the context demands an interval value. This causes a large number of conflicts when the grammar is run through yacc: 18 shift-reduce and 26 reduce-reduce. The problem can be seen by looking at the two input lines.

```
2.5 + (3.5 - 4.)
```

and

```
2.5 + (3.5, 4)
```

Notice that the 2.5 is to be used in an interval value expression in the second example, but this fact is not known until the comma is read. By this time, 2.5 is finished, and the parser cannot go back and change its mind. More generally, it might be necessary to look ahead an arbitrary number of tokens to decide whether to convert a scalar to an interval. This problem is evaded by having two rules for each binary interval valued operator — one when the left operand is a scalar and one when the left operand is an interval. In the second case, the right operand must be an interval, so the conversion will be applied automatically. Despite this evasion, there are still many cases where the conversion may be applied or not, leading to the above conflicts. They are resolved by listing the rules that yield scalars first in the specification file; in this way, the conflict will be resolved in the direction of keeping scalar valued expressions scalar valued until they are forced to become intervals.

This way of handling multiple types is instructive. If there were many kinds of expression types instead of just two, the number of rules needed would increase dramatically and the conflicts even more dramatically. Thus, while this example is instructive, it is better practice in a more normal programming language environment to keep the type information as part of the value and not as part of the grammar.

Finally, a word about the lexical analysis. The only unusual feature is the treatment of floating point constants. The C language library routine atof() is used to do the actual conversion from a character string to a double-precision value. If the lexical analyzer detects an error, it responds by returning a token that is illegal in the grammar, provoking a syntax error in the parser and thence error recovery.

```
%{

#include <stdio.h>
#include <ctype.h>

typedef struct interval
{
    double lo, hi;
} INTERVAL;

INTERVAL vmul(), vdiv();

double atof();

double dreg[26];

INTERVAL vreg[26];

%}

%start lines

%union
{
    int ival;
    double dval;
```

(continued on next page)

```
    INTERVAL vval;
}

%token <ival> DREG VREG    /* indices into dreg, vreg arrays */

%token <dval> CONST        /* floating point constant */

%type <dval> dexp          /* expression */

%type <vval> vexp          /* interval expression */

/* precedence information about the operators */

%left '+' '/-'
%left '*' '/'

%%      /* beginning of rules section */

lines  :   /* empty */
       |   lines line
       ;
line   :   dexp '\n'
       {
         (void)printf("%15.8f\n", $1);
       }
       |   vexp '\n'
       {
         (void)printf("(%15.8f, %15.8f)\n", $1.lo, $1.hi);
       }
       |   DREG '=' dexp '\n'
       {
         dreg[$1] = $3;
       }
       |   VREG '=' vexp '\n'
       {
         vreg[$1] = $3;
       }
       |   error '\n'
       {
         yyerrok;
       }
       ;
dexp   :   CONST
       |   DREG
       {
         $$ = dreg[$1];
```

(continued on next page)

```
        }
    |   dexp '+' dexp
        {
        $$ = $1 + $3;
        }
    |   dexp '-' dexp
        {
        $$ = $1 - $3;
        }
    |   dexp '*' dexp
        {
        $$ = $1 * $3;
        }
    |   dexp '/' dexp
        {
        $$ = $1 / $3;
        }
    |   '-' dexp
        {
        $$ = -$2;
        }
    |   '(' dexp ')'
        {
        $$ = $2;
        }
    ;
vexp    :   dexp
        {
        $$.hi = $$.lo = $1;
        }
    |   '(' dexp ',' dexp ')'
        {
        $$.lo = $2;
        $$.hi = $4;
        if($$.lo > $$.hi)
            {
            (void) printf("interval out of order\n");
            YYERROR;
            }
        }
    |   VREG
        {
        $$ = vreg[$1];
        }
    |   vexp '+' vexp
        {
```

(continued on next page)

```
        $$.hi = $1.hi + $3.hi;
        $$.lo = $1.lo + $3.lo;
    }
    |   dexp '+' vexp
    {
        $$.hi = $1 + $3.hi;
        $$.lo = $1 + $3.lo;
    }
    |   vexp '-' vexp
    {
        $$.hi = $1.hi - $3.lo;
        $$.lo = $1.lo - $3.hi;
    }
    |   dexp '-' vexp
    {
        $$.hi = $1 - $3.lo;
        $$.lo = $1 - $3.hi;
    }
    |   vexp '*' vexp
    {
        $$ = vmul($1.lo, $1.hi, $3);
    }
    |   dexp '*' vexp
    {
        $$ = vmul($1, $1, $3);
    }
    |   vexp '/' vexp
    {
        if (dcheck($3)) YYERROR;
        $$ = vdiv($1.lo, $1.hi, $3);
    }
    |   dexp '/' vexp
    {
        if (dcheck($3)) YYERROR;
        $$ = vdiv($1, $1, $3);
    }
    |   '-' vexp
    {
        $$.hi = -$2.lo; $$.lo = -$2.hi;
    }
    |   '(' vexp ')'
    {
        $$ = $2;
    }
    ;
```

(continued on next page)

ANSI C and Programming Support Tools

```
%%   /* beginning of subroutines section */

# define BSZ 50   /* buffer size for floating point number */

    /* lexical analysis */

int yylex()
{
    register int c;

        /* skip over blanks */

    while ((c=getchar()) == ' ')
        ;
    if (isupper(c))
    {
        yylval.ival = c - 'A';
        return(VREG);
    }
    if (islower(c))
    {
        yylval.ival = c - 'a';
        return(DREG);
    }

        /* gobble up digits, points, exponents */

    if (isdigit(c) || c == '.')
    {
        char buf[BSZ + 1], *cp = buf;
        int dot = 0, exp = 0;

        for (;(cp - buf) < BSZ; ++cp, c = getchar())
        {
            *cp = c;
            if (isdigit(c))
                continue;
            if (c == '.')
            {
                if (dot++ || exp)
                    return('.');   /* will cause
                        syntax error */
                continue;
            }
            if (c == 'e')
            {
```

(continued on next page)

yacc   **12-53**

```
            if (exp++)
                return ('e');    /* will cause
                        syntax error */
                continue;
        }
            /* end of number */
        break;
        }

    *cp = '\0';
    if (cp - buf >= BSZ)
        (void) printf ("constant too long -- truncated\n");
    else
        ungetc (c, stdin);    /* push back last char read */
    yylval.dval = atof (buf);
    return (CONST);
    }
    return (c);
}

INTERVAL
hilo (a, b, c, d)
    double a, b, c, d;
{
    /* returns the smallest interval containing a, b, c, and d
        used by vmul, vdiv routines */

    INTERVAL v;

    if (a > b)
    {
        v.hi = a;
        v.lo = b;
    }
    else
    {
        v.hi = b;
        v.lo = a;
    }
    if (c > d)
    {
        if (c > v.hi) v.hi = c;
        if (d < v.lo) v.lo = d;
    }
    else
    {
```

(continued on next page)

```
        if (d > v.hi) v.hi = d;
        if (c < v.lo) v.lo = c;
    }
    return(v);
}
INTERVAL
vmul(a, b, v)
    double a, b;
    INTERVAL v;
{
    return(hilo(a * v.hi, a * v.lo, b * v.hi, b * v.lo));
}

dcheck(v)
    INTERVAL v;
{
    if (v.hi >= 0. && v.lo <= 0.)
    {
        (void) printf("divisor interval contains 0.\n");
        return(1);
    }
    return(0);
}
INTERVAL
vdiv(a, b, v)
    double a, b;
    INTERVAL v;
{
    return(hilo(a / v.hi, a / v.lo, b / v.hi, b / v.lo));
}
```

13 Object Files

Table of Contents _____

ANSI C and Programming Support Tools

Introduction

This chapter describes the executable and linking format (ELF) of the object files produced by the C compilation system. The first section, "Program Linking," focuses on how the format pertains to building programs. The second section, "Program Execution," focuses on how the format pertains to loading programs. For background, see the "Link Editing" section in Chapter 2.

There are three main types of object files.

- A *relocatable file* holds code and data suitable for linking with other object files to create an executable or a shared object file.

- An *executable file* holds a program suitable for execution; the file specifies how exec() creates a program's process image.

- A *shared object file* holds code and data suitable for linking in two contexts. First, the link editor processes the shared object file with other relocatable and shared object files to create another object file. Second, the dynamic linker combines it with an executable file and other shared objects to create a process image.

Programs manipulate object files with the functions contained in the ELF access library, libelf. Subsection 3E of the *Programmer's Reference Manual* describes its contents.

File Format

As indicated, object files participate in program linking and program execution. For convenience and efficiency, the object file format provides parallel views of a file's contents, reflecting the differing needs of these activities. The figure below shows an object file's organization.

Figure 13-1: Object File Format

Linking View	Execution View
ELF header	ELF header
Program header table *optional*	Program header table
Section 1 . . .	Segment 1
Section *n* . . .	Segment 2
. . .	. . .
Section header table	Section header table *optional*

An *ELF header* resides at the beginning and holds a "road map" describing the file's organization. *Sections* hold the bulk of object file information for the linking view: instructions, data, symbol table, relocation information, and so on. Descriptions of special sections appear in the first part of this chapter. The second part of this chapter discusses *segments* and the program execution view of the file.

A *program header table*, if present, tells the system how to create a process image. Files used to build a process image (execute a program) must have a program header table; relocatable files do not need one. A *section header table* contains information describing the file's sections. Every section has an entry in the table; each entry gives information such as the section name, the section size, and so forth. Files used during linking must have a section header table; other object files may or may not have one.

NOTE Although the figure shows the program header table immediately after the ELF header, and the section header table following the sections, actual files may differ. Moreover, sections and segments have no specified order. Only the ELF header has a fixed position in the file.

Data Representation

As described here, the object file *format* supports various processors with 8-bit bytes and 32-bit architectures. Nevertheless, it is intended to be extensible to larger (or smaller) architectures. Object files therefore represent some control data with a machine-independent format, making it possible to identify object files and interpret their contents in a common way. Remaining data in an object file use the encoding of the target processor, regardless of the machine on which the file was created.

Figure 13-2: 32-Bit Data Types

Name	Size	Alignment	Purpose
Elf32_Addr	4	4	Unsigned program address
Elf32_Half	2	2	Unsigned medium integer
Elf32_Off	4	4	Unsigned file offset
Elf32_Sword	4	4	Signed large integer
Elf32_Word	4	4	Unsigned large integer
unsigned char	1	1	Unsigned small integer

All data structures that the object file format defines follow the "natural" size and alignment guidelines for the relevant class. If necessary, data structures contain explicit padding to ensure 4-byte alignment for 4-byte objects, to force structure sizes to a multiple of 4, and so forth. Data also have suitable alignment from the beginning of the file. Thus, for example, a structure containing an Elf32_Addr member will be aligned on a 4-byte boundary within the file. For portability reasons, ELF uses no bit-fields.

Program Linking

This section describes the object file information and system actions that create static program representations from relocatable files and shared objects.

ELF Header

Some object file control structures can grow, because the ELF header contains their actual sizes. If the object file format changes, a program may encounter control structures that are larger or smaller than expected. Programs might therefore ignore "extra" information. The treatment of "missing" information depends on context and will be specified when and if extensions are defined.

Figure 13-3: ELF Header

```
#define EI_NIDENT        16

typedef struct {
          unsigned char   e_ident[EI_NIDENT];
          Elf32_Half      e_type;
          Elf32_Half      e_machine;
          Elf32_Word      e_version;
          Elf32_Addr      e_entry;
          Elf32_Off       e_phoff;
          Elf32_Off       e_shoff;
          Elf32_Word      e_flags;
          Elf32_Half      e_ehsize;
          Elf32_Half      e_phentsize;
          Elf32_Half      e_phnum;
          Elf32_Half      e_shentsize;
          Elf32_Half      e_shnum;
          Elf32_Half      e_shstrndx;
} Elf32_Ehdr;
```

e_ident   The initial bytes mark the file as an object file and provide machine-independent data with which to decode and interpret the file's contents. Complete descriptions appear below, in "ELF Identification."

e_type   This member identifies the object file type.

Name	Value	Meaning
ET_NONE	0	No file type
ET_REL	1	Relocatable file
ET_EXEC	2	Executable file
ET_DYN	3	Shared object file
ET_CORE	4	Core file
ET_LOPROC	0xff00	Processor-specific
ET_HIPROC	0xffff	Processor-specific

Although the core file contents are unspecified, type ET_CORE is reserved to mark the file. Values from ET_LOPROC through ET_HIPROC (inclusive) are reserved for processor-specific semantics. Other values are reserved and will be assigned to new object file types as necessary.

e_machine   This member's value specifies the required architecture for an individual file.

Name	Value	Meaning
EM_NONE	0	No machine
EM_M32	1	AT&T WE 32100
EM_SPARC	2	SPARC
EM_386	3	Intel 80386
EM_68K	4	Motorola 68000
EM_88K	5	Motorola 88000
EM_860	7	Intel 80860

Other values are reserved and will be assigned to new machines as necessary. Processor-specific ELF names use the machine name to distinguish them. For example, the flags mentioned below use the prefix EF_; a flag named WIDGET for the EM_XYZ machine would be called EF_XYZ_WIDGET.

e_version   This member identifies the object file version.

Name	Value	Meaning
EV_NONE	0	Invalid version
EV_CURRENT	1	Current version

The value 1 signifies the original file format; extensions will create new versions with higher numbers. The value of EV_CURRENT, though given as 1 above, will change as necessary to reflect the current version number.

e_entry   This member gives the virtual address to which the system first transfers control, thus starting the process. If the file has no associated entry point, this member holds zero.

e_phoff   This member holds the program header table's file offset in bytes. If the file has no program header table, this member holds zero.

e_shoff   This member holds the section header table's file offset in bytes. If the file has no section header table, this member holds zero.

e_flags   This member holds processor-specific flags associated with the file. Flag names take the form EF_*machine_flag*. See "ELF Header Flags" for flag definitions.

e_ehsize   This member holds the ELF header's size in bytes.

e_phentsize This member holds the size in bytes of one entry in the file's program header table; all entries are the same size.

e_phnum   This member holds the number of entries in the program header table. Thus the product of e_phentsize and e_phnum gives the table's size in bytes. If a file has no program header table, e_phnum holds the value zero.

e_shentsize This member holds a section header's size in bytes. A section header is one entry in the section header table; all entries are the same size.

e_shnum

This member holds the number of entries in the section header table. Thus the product of e_shentsize and e_shnum gives the section header table's size in bytes. If a file has no section header table, e_shnum holds the value zero.

e_shstrndx

This member holds the section header table index of the entry associated with the section name string table. If the file has no section name string table, this member holds the value SHN_UNDEF. See "Section Header" and "String Table" below for more information.

ELF Identification

As mentioned above, ELF provides an object file framework to support multiple processors, multiple data encodings, and multiple classes of machines. To support this object file family, the initial bytes of the file specify how to interpret the file, independent of the processor on which the inquiry is made and independent of the file's remaining contents.

The initial bytes of an ELF header (and an object file) correspond to the e_ident member.

Figure 13-4: e_ident[ ] Identification Indexes

Name	Value	Purpose
EI_MAG0	0	File identification
EI_MAG1	1	File identification
EI_MAG2	2	File identification
EI_MAG3	3	File identification
EI_CLASS	4	File class
EI_DATA	5	Data encoding
EI_VERSION	6	File version
EI_PAD	7	Start of padding bytes
EI_NIDENT	16	Size of e_ident[]

These indexes access bytes that hold the following values.

EI_MAG0 to EI_MAG3

> A file's first 4 bytes hold a "magic number," identifying the file as an ELF object file.

Name	Value	Position
ELFMAG0	0x7f	e_ident[EI_MAG0]
ELFMAG1	'E'	e_ident[EI_MAG1]
ELFMAG2	'L'	e_ident[EI_MAG2]
ELFMAG3	'F'	e_ident[EI_MAG3]

EI_CLASS

The next byte, e_ident[EI_CLASS], identifies the file's class, or capacity.

Name	Value	Meaning
ELFCLASSNONE	0	Invalid class
ELFCLASS32	1	32-bit objects
ELFCLASS64	2	64-bit objects

The file format is designed to be portable among machines of various sizes, without imposing the sizes of the largest machine on the smallest. Class ELFCLASS32 supports machines with files and virtual address spaces up to 4 gigabytes; it uses the basic types defined above.

Class ELFCLASS64 is reserved for 64-bit architectures. Its appearance here shows how the object file may change, but the 64-bit format is otherwise unspecified. Other classes will be defined as necessary, with different basic types and sizes for object file data.

EI_DATA

Byte e_ident[EI_DATA] specifies the data encoding of the processor-specific data in the object file. The following encodings are currently defined.

Name	Value	Meaning
ELFDATANONE	0	Invalid data encoding
ELFDATA2LSB	1	See below
ELFDATA2MSB	2	See below

More information on these encodings appears below. Other values are reserved and will be assigned to new encodings as necessary.

EI_VERSION   Byte e_ident[EI_VERSION] specifies the ELF header version number. Currently, this value must be EV_CURRENT, as explained above for e_version.

EI_PAD   This value marks the beginning of the unused bytes in e_ident. These bytes are reserved and set to zero; programs that read object files should ignore them. The value of EI_PAD will change in the future if currently unused bytes are given meanings.

A file's data encoding specifies how to interpret the basic objects in a file. As described above, class ELFCLASS32 files use objects that occupy 1, 2, and 4 bytes. Under the defined encodings, objects are represented as shown below. Byte numbers appear in the upper left corners.

Encoding ELFDATA2LSB specifies 2's complement values, with the least significant byte occupying the lowest address.

Figure 13-5: Data Encoding ELFDATA2LSB

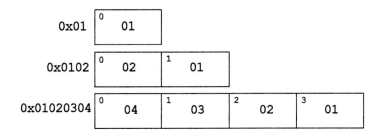

Encoding ELFDATA2MSB specifies 2's complement values, with the most significant byte occupying the lowest address.

Figure 13-6: Data Encoding ELFDATA2MSB

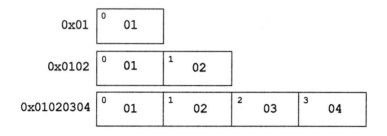

ELF Header Flags (3B2 Computer-Specific)

For file identification in e_ident, the WE 32100 requires the following values.

Figure 13-7: WE 32100 Identification, e_ident

Position	Value
e_ident[EI_CLASS]	ELFCLASS32
e_ident[EI_DATA]	ELFDATA2MSB

Processor identification resides in the ELF header's e_machine member and must have the value 1, defined as the name EM_M32.

The ELF header's e_flags member holds bit flags associated with the file.

Figure 13-8: Processor-Specific Flags, e_flags

Name	Value
EF_M32_MAU	0x1

EF_M32_MAU   If this bit is asserted, the program in the file must execute on a machine with a Math Acceleration Unit. Otherwise, the program will execute on a machine with or without a MAU.

ELF Header Flags (6386 Computer-Specific)

For file identification in e_ident, the 6386 computer requires the following values.

Figure 13-9: 6386 Computer Identification, e_ident

Position	Value
e_ident[EI_CLASS]	ELFCLASS32
e_ident[EI_DATA]	ELFDATA2LSB

Processor identification resides in the ELF header's e_machine member and must have the value 3, defined as the name EM_386.

The ELF header's e_flags member holds bit flags associated with the file. The 6386 computer defines no flags; so this member contains zero.

Section Header

An object file's section header table lets one locate all the file's sections. The section header table is an array of Elf32_Shdr structures as described below. A section header table index is a subscript into this array. The ELF header's e_shoff member gives the byte offset from the beginning of the file to the section header table; e_shnum tells how many entries the section header table contains; e_shentsize gives the size in bytes of each entry.

Some section header table indexes are reserved; an object file will not have sections for these special indexes.

Figure 13-10: Special Section Indexes

Name	Value
SHN_UNDEF	0
SHN_LORESERVE	0xff00
SHN_LOPROC	0xff00
SHN_HIPROC	0xff1f
SHN_ABS	0xfff1
SHN_COMMON	0xfff2
SHN_HIRESERVE	0xffff

SHN_UNDEF   This value marks an undefined, missing, irrelevant, or otherwise meaningless section reference. For example, a symbol "defined" relative to section number SHN_UNDEF is an undefined symbol.

NOTE   Although index 0 is reserved as the undefined value, the section header table contains an entry for index 0. That is, if the e_shnum member of the ELF header says a file has 6 entries in the section header table, they have the indexes 0 through 5. The contents of the initial entry are specified later in this section.

SHN_LORESERVE   This value specifies the lower bound of the range of
                    reserved indexes.

SHN_LOPROC through SHN_HIPROC
                    Values in this inclusive range are reserved for processor-
                    specific semantics.

SHN_ABS   This value specifies absolute values for the corresponding
                    reference. For example, symbols defined relative to section
                    number SHN_ABS have absolute values and are not affected
                    by relocation.

SHN_COMMON   Symbols defined relative to this section are common sym-
                    bols, such as FORTRAN COMMON or unallocated C external
                    variables.

SHN_HIRESERVE   This value specifies the upper bound of the range of
                    reserved indexes. The system reserves indexes between
                    SHN_LORESERVE and SHN_HIRESERVE, inclusive; the values
                    do not reference the section header table. That is, the sec-
                    tion header table does *not* contain entries for the reserved
                    indexes.

Sections contain all information in an object file except the ELF header, the program header table, and the section header table. Moreover, object files' sections
satisfy several conditions.

■ Every section in an object file has exactly one section header describing it.
  Section headers may exist that do not have a section.

■ Each section occupies one contiguous (possibly empty) sequence of bytes
  within a file.

■ Sections in a file may not overlap. No byte in a file resides in more than
  one section.

■ An object file may have inactive space. The various headers and the sections might not "cover" every byte in an object file. The contents of the
  inactive data are unspecified.

A section header has the following structure.

Figure 13-11: Section Header

```
typedef struct {
        Elf32_Word      sh_name;
        Elf32_Word      sh_type;
        Elf32_Word      sh_flags;
        Elf32_Addr      sh_addr;
        Elf32_Off       sh_offset;
        Elf32_Word      sh_size;
        Elf32_Word      sh_link;
        Elf32_Word      sh_info;
        Elf32_Word      sh_addralign;
        Elf32_Word      sh_entsize;
} Elf32_Shdr;
```

sh_name   This member specifies the name of the section. Its value is an
              index into the section header string table section (see "String
              Table" below), giving the location of a null-terminated string.

sh_type   This member categorizes the section's contents and semantics.
              Section types and their descriptions appear below.

sh_flags   Sections support 1-bit flags that describe miscellaneous attri-
              butes. Flag definitions appear below.

sh_addr   If the section will appear in the memory image of a process,
              this member gives the address at which the section's first byte
              should reside. Otherwise, the member contains 0.

sh_offset   This member's value gives the byte offset from the beginning
              of the file to the first byte in the section. One section type,
              SHT_NOBITS described below, occupies no space in the file,
              and its sh_offset member locates the conceptual placement
              in the file.

sh_size   This member gives the section's size in bytes. Unless the sec-
                 tion type is SHT_NOBITS, the section occupies sh_size bytes
                 in the file. A section of type SHT_NOBITS may have a non-
                 zero size, but it occupies no space in the file.

sh_link   This member holds a section header table index link, whose
                 interpretation depends on the section type. A table below
                 describes the values.

sh_info   This member holds extra information, whose interpretation
                 depends on the section type. A table below describes the
                 values.

sh_addralign   Some sections have address alignment constraints. For exam-
                 ple, if a section holds a doubleword, the system must ensure
                 doubleword alignment for the entire section. That is, the
                 value of sh_addr must be congruent to 0, modulo the value
                 of sh_addralign. Currently, only 0 and positive integral
                 powers of two are allowed. Values 0 and 1 mean the section
                 has no alignment constraints.

sh_entsize   Some sections hold a table of fixed-size entries, such as a sym-
                 bol table. For such a section, this member gives the size in
                 bytes of each entry. The member contains 0 if the section does
                 not hold a table of fixed-size entries.

A section header's sh_type member specifies the section's semantics.

Figure 13-12: Section Types, sh_type

Name	Value
SHT_NULL	0
SHT_PROGBITS	1
SHT_SYMTAB	2
SHT_STRTAB	3
SHT_RELA	4
SHT_HASH	5
SHT_DYNAMIC	6
SHT_NOTE	7
SHT_NOBITS	8

Figure 13-12: Section Types, sh_type (continued)

Name	Value
SHT_REL	9
SHT_SHLIB	10
SHT_DYNSYM	11
SHT_LOPROC	0x70000000
SHT_HIPROC	0x7fffffff
SHT_LOUSER	0x80000000
SHT_HIUSER	0xffffffff

SHT_NULL

This value marks the section header as inactive; it does not have an associated section. Other members of the section header have undefined values.

SHT_PROGBITS

The section holds information defined by the program, whose format and meaning are determined solely by the program.

SHT_SYMTAB and SHT_DYNSYM

These sections hold a symbol table. Currently, an object file may have only one section of each type, but this restriction may be relaxed in the future. Typically, SHT_SYMTAB provides symbols for link editing, though it may also be used for dynamic linking. As a complete symbol table, it may contain many symbols unnecessary for dynamic linking. Consequently, an object file may also contain a SHT_DYNSYM section, which holds a minimal set of dynamic linking symbols, to save space. See "Symbol Table" below for details.

SHT_STRTAB

The section holds a string table. An object file may have multiple string table sections. See "String Table" below for details.

SHT_RELA

The section holds relocation entries with explicit addends, such as type Elf32_Rela for the 32-bit class of object files. An object file may have multiple relocation sections. See "Relocation" below for details.

SHT_HASH
The section holds a symbol hash table. Currently, an object file may have only one hash table, but this restriction may be relaxed in the future. See "Hash Table" in the second part of this chapter for details.

SHT_DYNAMIC
The section holds information for dynamic linking. Currently, an object file may have only one dynamic section, but this restriction may be relaxed in the future. See "Dynamic Section" in the second part of this chapter for details.

SHT_NOTE
The section holds information that marks the file in some way. See "Note Section" in the second part of this chapter for details.

SHT_NOBITS
A section of this type occupies no space in the file but otherwise resembles SHT_PROGBITS. Although this section contains no bytes, the sh_offset member contains the conceptual file offset.

SHT_REL
The section holds relocation entries without explicit addends, such as type Elf32_Rel for the 32-bit class of object files. An object file may have multiple relocation sections. See "Relocation" below for details.

SHT_SHLIB
This section type is reserved but has unspecified semantics.

SHT_LOPROC through SHT_HIPROC
Values in this inclusive range are reserved for processor-specific semantics.

SHT_LOUSER
This value specifies the lower bound of the range of indexes reserved for application programs.

SHT_HIUSER
This value specifies the upper bound of the range of indexes reserved for application programs. Section types between SHT_LOUSER and SHT_HIUSER may be used by the application, without conflicting with current or future system-defined section types.

Other section type values are reserved. As mentioned before, the section header for index 0 (SHN_UNDEF) exists, even though the index marks undefined section references. This entry holds the following.

Figure 13-13: Section Header Table Entry: Index 0

Name	Value	Note
sh_name	0	No name
sh_type	SHT_NULL	Inactive
sh_flags	0	No flags
sh_addr	0	No address
sh_offset	0	No file offset
sh_size	0	No size
sh_link	SHN_UNDEF	No link information
sh_info	0	No auxiliary information
sh_addralign	0	No alignment
sh_entsize	0	No entries

A section header's sh_flags member holds 1-bit flags that describe the section's attributes. Defined values appear below; other values are reserved.

Figure 13-14: Section Attribute Flags, sh_flags

Name	Value
SHF_WRITE	0x1
SHF_ALLOC	0x2
SHF_EXECINSTR	0x4
SHF_MASKPROC	0xf0000000

If a flag bit is set in sh_flags, the attribute is "on" for the section. Otherwise, the attribute is "off" or does not apply. Undefined attributes are set to zero.

SHF_WRITE   The section contains data that should be writable during process execution.

SHF_ALLOC   The section occupies memory during process execution. Some control sections do not reside in the memory image of an object file; this attribute is off for those sections.

SHF_EXECINSTR   The section contains executable machine instructions.

SHF_MASKPROC   All bits included in this mask are reserved for processor-specific semantics.

Two members in the section header, sh_link and sh_info, hold special information, depending on section type.

Figure 13-15: sh_link and sh_info Interpretation

sh_type	sh_link	sh_info
SHT_DYNAMIC	The section header index of the string table used by entries in the section.	0
SHT_HASH	The section header index of the symbol table to which the hash table applies.	0
SHT_REL SHT_RELA	The section header index of the associated symbol table.	The section header index of the section to which the relocation applies.
SHT_SYMTAB SHT_DYNSYM	The section header index of the associated string table.	One greater than the symbol table index of the last local symbol (binding STB_LOCAL).
other	SHN_UNDEF	0

Special Sections

Various sections hold program and control information. Sections in the list below are used by the system and have the indicated types and attributes.

Figure 13-16: Special Sections

Name	Type	Attributes
.bss	SHT_NOBITS	SHF_ALLOC + SHF_WRITE
.comment	SHT_PROGBITS	none
.data	SHT_PROGBITS	SHF_ALLOC + SHF_WRITE
.data1	SHT_PROGBITS	SHF_ALLOC + SHF_WRITE
.debug	SHT_PROGBITS	none
.dynamic	SHT_DYNAMIC	SHF_ALLOC + SHF_WRITE
.dynstr	SHT_STRTAB	SHF_ALLOC
.dynsym	SHT_DYNSYM	SHF_ALLOC
.fini	SHT_PROGBITS	SHF_ALLOC + SHF_EXECINSTR
.got	SHT_PROGBITS	see below
.hash	SHT_HASH	SHF_ALLOC
.init	SHT_PROGBITS	SHF_ALLOC + SHF_EXECINSTR
.interp	SHT_PROGBITS	none
.line	SHT_PROGBITS	none
.note	SHT_NOTE	none
.plt	SHT_PROGBITS	see below
.rel*name*	SHT_REL	see below
.rela*name*	SHT_RELA	see below
.rodata	SHT_PROGBITS	SHF_ALLOC
.rodata1	SHT_PROGBITS	SHF_ALLOC
.shstrtab	SHT_STRTAB	none
.strtab	SHT_STRTAB	see below
.symtab	SHT_SYMTAB	see below
.text	SHT_PROGBITS	SHF_ALLOC + SHF_EXECINSTR

.bss   This section holds uninitialized data that contribute to the program's memory image. By definition, the system initializes the data with zeros when the program begins to run. The section occupies no file space, as indicated by the section type, SHT_NOBITS.

.comment   This section holds version control information.

.data and .data1
            These sections hold initialized data that contribute to the
            program's memory image.

.debug   This section holds information for symbolic debugging. The con-
            tents are unspecified.

.dynamic   This section holds dynamic linking information. See the second
            part of this chapter for more information.

.dynstr   This section holds strings needed for dynamic linking, most com-
            monly the strings that represent the names associated with sym-
            bol table entries. See the second part of this chapter for more
            information.

.dynsym   This section holds the dynamic linking symbol table, as "Symbol
            Table" describes. See the second part of this chapter for more
            information.

.fini   This section holds executable instructions that contribute to the
            process termination code. That is, when a program exits nor-
            mally, the system arranges to execute the code in this section.

.got   This section holds the global offset table. See "Global Offset
            Table" in the second part of this chapter for more information.

.hash   This section holds a symbol hash table. See "Hash Table" in the
            second part of this chapter for more information.

.init   This section holds executable instructions that contribute to the
            process initialization code. That is, when a program starts to run,
            the system arranges to execute the code in this section before cal-
            ling the main program entry point (called main for C programs).

.interp   This section holds the path name of a program interpreter. See
            "Program Interpreter" in the second part of this chapter for more
            information.

.line   This section holds line number information for symbolic debug-
            ging, which describes the correspondence between the source pro-
            gram and the machine code. The contents are unspecified.

.note   This section holds information in the format that "Note Section" in the second part of this chapter describes.

.plt   This section holds the procedure linkage table. See "Procedure Linkage Table" in the second part of this chapter for more information.

.rel*name* and .rela*name*
         These sections hold relocation information, as "Relocation" below describes. If the file has a loadable segment that includes relocation, the sections' attributes will include the SHF_ALLOC bit; otherwise, that bit will be off. Conventionally, *name* is supplied by the section to which the relocations apply. Thus a relocation section for .text normally would have the name .rel.text or .rela.text.

.rodata and .rodata1
         These sections hold read-only data that typically contribute to a non-writable segment in the process image. See "Program Header" in the second part of this chapter for more information.

.shstrtab This section holds section names.

.strtab   This section holds strings, most commonly the strings that represent the names associated with symbol table entries. If the file has a loadable segment that includes the symbol string table, the section's attributes will include the SHF_ALLOC bit; otherwise, that bit will be off.

.symtab   This section holds a symbol table, as "Symbol Table" below describes. If the file has a loadable segment that includes the symbol table, the section's attributes will include the SHF_ALLOC bit; otherwise, that bit will be off.

.text   This section holds the "text," or executable instructions, of a program.

Section names with a dot (.) prefix are reserved for the system, although applications may use these sections if their existing meanings are satisfactory. Applications may use names without the prefix to avoid conflicts with system sections. The object file format lets one define sections not in the list above. An object file may have more than one section with the same name.

Various sections hold program and control information. Both the 3B2 and the 6386 computers use the sections in the list below, with the indicated types and attributes.

Figure 13-17: Special Sections, .got and .plt

Name	Type	Attributes
.got	SHT_PROGBITS	SHF_ALLOC + SHF_WRITE
.plt	SHT_PROGBITS	SHF_ALLOC + SHF_EXECINSTR

.got   This section holds the global offset table. See "Global Offset Table" in the second part of the chapter for more information.

.plt   This section holds the procedure linkage table. See "Procedure Linkage Table" in the second part of this chapter for more information.

String Table

String table sections hold null-terminated character sequences, commonly called strings. The object file uses these strings to represent symbol and section names. One references a string as an index into the string table section. The first byte, which is index zero, is defined to hold a null character. Likewise, a string table's last byte is defined to hold a null character, ensuring null termination for all strings. A string whose index is zero specifies either no name or a null name, depending on the context. An empty string table section is permitted; its section header's sh_size member would contain zero. Non-zero indexes are invalid for an empty string table.

A section header's sh_name member holds an index into the section header string table section, as designated by the e_shstrndx member of the ELF header. The following figures show a string table with 25 bytes and the strings associated with various indexes.

Figure 13-18: String Table

Index	+0	+1	+2	+3	+4	+5	+6	+7	+8	+9
0	\0	n	a	m	e	.	\0	V	a	r
10	i	a	b	l	e	\0	a	b	l	e
20	\0	\0	x	x	\0					

Figure 13-19: String Table Indexes

Index	String
0	*none*
1	name.
7	Variable
11	able
16	able
24	*null string*

As the example shows, a string table index may refer to any byte in the section. A string may appear more than once; references to substrings may exist; and a single string may be referenced multiple times. Unreferenced strings also are allowed.

Symbol Table

An object file's symbol table holds information needed to locate and relocate a program's symbolic definitions and references. A symbol table index is a subscript into this array. Index 0 both designates the first entry in the table and serves as the undefined symbol index. The contents of the initial entry are specified later in this section.

Name	Value
STN_UNDEF	0

A symbol table entry has the following format.

Figure 13-20: Symbol Table Entry

```
typedef struct {
            Elf32_Word        st_name;
            Elf32_Addr        st_value;
            Elf32_Word        st_size;
            unsigned char     st_info;
            unsigned char     st_other;
            Elf32_Half        st_shndx;
} Elf32_Sym;
```

st_name   This member holds an index into the object file's symbol string
                 table, which holds the character representations of the symbol
                 names. If the value is non-zero, it represents a string table
                 index that gives the symbol name. Otherwise, the symbol table
                 entry has no name.

 NOTE External C symbols have the same names in C, assembly code, and object files' symbol tables.

st_value   This member gives the value of the associated symbol.
                 Depending on the context, this may be an absolute value, an
                 address, and so forth; details appear below.

st_size   Many symbols have associated sizes. For example, a data
                 object's size is the number of bytes contained in the object.
                 This member holds 0 if the symbol has no size or an unknown
                 size.

st_info   This member specifies the symbol's type and binding attributes.
             A list of the values and meanings appears below. The follow-
             ing code shows how to manipulate the values.

```
#define ELF32_ST_BIND(i)    ((i)>>4)
#define ELF32_ST_TYPE(i)    ((i)&0xf)
#define ELF32_ST_INFO(b,t)  (((b)<<4)+((t)&0xf))
```

st_other   This member currently holds 0 and has no defined meaning.

st_shndx   Every symbol table entry is "defined" in relation to some sec-
             tion; this member holds the relevant section header table index.
             Some section indexes indicate special meanings.

A symbol's binding determines the linkage visibility and behavior.

Figure 13-21: Symbol Binding, ELF32_ST_BIND

Name	Value
STB_LOCAL	0
STB_GLOBAL	1
STB_WEAK	2
STB_LOPROC	13
STB_HIPROC	15

STB_LOCAL   Local symbols are not visible outside the object file containing
             their definition. Local symbols of the same name may exist in
             multiple files without interfering with each other.

STB_GLOBAL   Global symbols are visible to all object files being combined.
             One file's definition of a global symbol will satisfy another file's
             undefined reference to the same global symbol.

STB_WEAK   Weak symbols resemble global symbols, but their definitions
             have lower precedence.

STB_LOPROC through STB_HIPROC
> Values in this inclusive range are reserved for processor-specific semantics.

Global and weak symbols differ in two major ways, as described in "Multiply Defined Symbols" in Chapter 2.

- When the link editor combines several relocatable object files, it does not allow multiple definitions of STB_GLOBAL symbols with the same name. On the other hand, if a defined global symbol exists, the appearance of a weak symbol with the same name will not cause an error. The link editor honors the global definition and ignores the weak ones.

- When the link editor searches archive libraries, it extracts archive members that contain definitions of undefined global symbols. The member's definition may be either a global or a weak symbol. The link editor does *not* extract archive members to resolve undefined weak symbols. Unresolved weak symbols have a zero value.

In each symbol table, all symbols with STB_LOCAL binding precede the weak and global symbols. As "Section Header" above describes, a symbol table section's sh_info section header member holds the symbol table index for the first non-local symbol.

A symbol's type provides a general classification for the associated entity.

Figure 13-22: Symbol Types, ELF32_ST_TYPE

Name	Value
STT_NOTYPE	0
STT_OBJECT	1
STT_FUNC	2
STT_SECTION	3
STT_FILE	4
STT_LOPROC	13
STT_HIPROC	15

STT_NOTYPE   The symbol's type is not specified.

STT_OBJECT   The symbol is associated with a data object, such as a variable, an array, and so forth.

STT_FUNC   The symbol is associated with a function or other executable code.

STT_SECTION   The symbol is associated with a section. Symbol table entries of this type exist primarily for relocation and normally have STB_LOCAL binding.

STT_FILE   Conventionally, the symbol's name gives the name of the source file associated with the object file. A file symbol has STB_LOCAL binding, its section index is SHN_ABS, and it precedes the other STB_LOCAL symbols for the file, if it is present.

STT_LOPROC through STT_HIPROC

Values in this inclusive range are reserved for processor-specific semantics.

Function symbols (those with type STT_FUNC) in shared object files have special significance. When another object file references a function from a shared object, the link editor automatically creates a procedure linkage table entry for the referenced symbol. Shared object symbols with types other than STT_FUNC will not be referenced automatically through the procedure linkage table.

If a symbol's value refers to a specific location within a section, its section index member, st_shndx, holds an index into the section header table. As the section moves during relocation, the symbol's value changes as well, and references to the symbol continue to "point" to the same location in the program. Some special section index values give other semantics.

SHN_ABS   The symbol has an absolute value that will not change because of relocation.

SHN_COMMON   The symbol labels a common block that has not yet been allocated. The symbol's value gives alignment constraints, similar to a section's sh_addralign member. That is, the link editor will allocate the storage for the symbol at an address that is a multiple of st_value. The symbol's size tells how many bytes are required.

SHN_UNDEF   This section table index means the symbol is undefined. When
             the link editor combines this object file with another that
             defines the indicated symbol, this file's references to the symbol
             will be linked to the actual definition.

As mentioned above, the symbol table entry for index 0 (STN_UNDEF) is
reserved; it holds the following.

Figure 13-23: Symbol Table Entry: Index 0

Name	Value	Note
st_name	0	No name
st_value	0	Zero value
st_size	0	No size
st_info	0	No type, local binding
st_other	0	
st_shndx	SHN_UNDEF	No section

Symbol Values

Symbol table entries for different object file types have slightly different
interpretations for the st_value member.

- In relocatable files, st_value holds alignment constraints for a symbol
  whose section index is SHN_COMMON.

- In relocatable files, st_value holds a section offset for a defined symbol.
  That is, st_value is an offset from the beginning of the section that
  st_shndx identifies.

- In executable and shared object files, st_value holds a virtual address.
  To make these files' symbols more useful for the dynamic linker, the section offset (file interpretation) gives way to a virtual address (memory
  interpretation) for which the section number is irrelevant.

Although the symbol table values have similar meanings for different object
files, the data allow efficient access by the appropriate programs.

Relocation

Relocation is the process of connecting symbolic references with symbolic
definitions. For example, when a program calls a function, the associated call
instruction must transfer control to the proper destination address at execution.
In other words, relocatable files must have information that describes how to
modify their section contents, thus allowing executable and shared object files to
hold the right information for a process's program image. *Relocation entries* are
these data.

Figure 13-24: Relocation Entries

```
typedef struct {
        Elf32_Addr      r_offset;
        Elf32_Word      r_info;
} Elf32_Rel;

typedef struct {
        Elf32_Addr      r_offset;
        Elf32_Word      r_info;
        Elf32_Sword     r_addend;
} Elf32_Rela;
```

r_offset   This member gives the location at which to apply the relocation
            action. For a relocatable file, the value is the byte offset from the
            beginning of the section to the storage unit affected by the reloca-
            tion. For an executable file or a shared object, the value is the vir-
            tual address of the storage unit affected by the relocation.

r_info   This member gives both the symbol table index with respect to
            which the relocation must be made, and the type of relocation to
            apply. For example, a call instruction's relocation entry would
            hold the symbol table index of the function being called. If the
            index is STN_UNDEF, the undefined symbol index, the relocation
            uses 0 as the "symbol value." Relocation types are processor-
            specific; descriptions of their behavior appear below. When the
            text below refers to a relocation entry's relocation type or symbol

ANSI C and Programming Support Tools

table index, it means the result of applying ELF32_R_TYPE or ELF32_R_SYM, respectively, to the entry's r_info member.

```
#define ELF32_R_SYM(i)      ((i)>>8)
#define ELF32_R_TYPE(i)     ((unsigned char)(i))
#define ELF32_R_INFO(s,t)   (((s)<<8)+(unsigned char)(t))
```

r_addend   This member specifies a constant addend used to compute the value to be stored into the relocatable field.

As shown above, only Elf32_Rela entries contain an explicit addend. Entries of type Elf32_Rel store an implicit addend in the location to be modified. Depending on the processor architecture, one form or the other might be necessary or more convenient. Consequently, an implementation for a particular machine may use one form exclusively or either form depending on context.

A relocation section references two other sections: a symbol table and a section to modify. The section header's sh_info and sh_link members, described in "Section Header" above, specify these relationships. Relocation entries for different object files have slightly different interpretations for the r_offset member.

- In relocatable files, r_offset holds a section offset. That is, the relocation section itself describes how to modify another section in the file; relocation offsets designate a storage unit within the second section.

- In executable and shared object files, r_offset holds a virtual address. To make these files' relocation entries more useful for the dynamic linker, the section offset (file interpretation) gives way to a virtual address (memory interpretation).

Although the interpretation of r_offset changes for different object files to allow efficient access by the relevant programs, the relocation types' meanings stay the same.

Relocation Types (3B2 Computer-Specific)

Relocation entries describe how to alter the following instruction and data fields (bit numbers appear in the lower box corners; byte numbers appear in the upper box corners).

Figure 13-25: 3B2 Computer Relocatable Fields

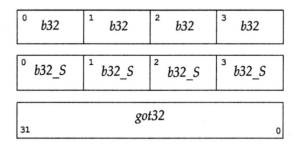

$b32$ This specifies a 32-bit field occupying 4 bytes with arbitrary alignment. These values use the byte order illustrated below.

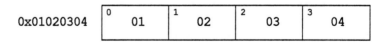

$b32\_S$ This specifies a 32-bit field occupying 4 bytes with arbitrary alignment. The "S" in the name indicates the bytes are "swapped." These values use the byte order illustrated below.

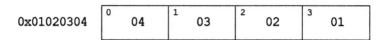

$got32$ This specifies a 32-bit field occupying 4 bytes with word alignment. These bytes represent values in the same byte order as $b32$.

Calculations below assume the actions are transforming a relocatable file into either an executable or a shared object file. Conceptually, the link editor merges one or more relocatable files to form the output. It first decides how to combine and locate the input files, then updates the symbol values, and finally performs the relocation. Relocations applied to executable or shared object files are similar and accomplish the same result. Descriptions below use the following notation.

A   This means the addend used to compute the value of the relocatable field.

B   This means the base address at which a shared object has been loaded into memory during execution. Generally, a shared object file is built with a 0 base virtual address, but the execution address will be different. See "Program Header" in the second part of this chapter for more information about the base address.

G   This means the offset into the global offset table at which the address of the relocation entry's symbol will reside during execution. See "Global Offset Table" in the second part of this chapter for more information.

L   This means the place (section offset or address) of the procedure linkage table entry for a symbol. A procedure linkage table entry redirects a function call to the proper destination. The link editor builds the initial procedure linkage table, and the dynamic linker modifies the entries during execution. See "Procedure Linkage Table" in the second part of this chapter for more information.

P   This means the place (section offset or address) of the storage unit being relocated (computed using `r_offset`).

S   This means the value of the symbol whose index resides in the relocation entry.

A relocation entry's `r_offset` value designates the offset or virtual address of the first byte of the affected storage unit. The relocation type specifies which bits to change and how to calculate their values. Because the WE 32100 uses only `Elf32_Rel` relocation entries, the field to be relocated holds the addend. In all cases, the addend and the computed result use the same byte order.

Figure 13-26: 3B2 Computer Relocation Types

Name	Value	Field	Calculation
R_M32_NONE	0	none	none
R_M32_32	1	*b32*	S + A
R_M32_32_S	2	*b32_S*	S + A
R_M32_PC32_S	3	*b32_S*	S + A − P
R_M32_GOT32_S	4	*b32_S*	G + A − P
R_M32_PLT32_S	5	*b32_S*	L + A − P
R_M32_COPY	6	none	none
R_M32_GLOB_DAT	7	*got32*	S
R_M32_JMP_SLOT	8	*got32*	S
R_M32_RELATIVE	9	*b32*	B + A
R_M32_RELATIVE_S	10	*b32_S*	B + A

Some relocation types have semantics beyond simple calculation.

R_M32_GOT32_S   This relocation type resembles R_M32_PC32_S, except it refers to the address of the symbol's global offset table entry and additionally instructs the link editor to build a global offset table.

R_M32_PLT32_S   This relocation type resembles R_M32_PC32_S, except it refers to the address of the symbol's procedure linkage table entry and additionally instructs the link editor to build a procedure linkage table.

R_M32_COPY   This relocation type assists dynamic linking. Its offset member refers to a location in a writable segment. The symbol table index specifies a symbol that should exist both in the current object file and in a shared object. During execution, the dynamic linker copies data associated with the shared object's symbol to the location specified by the offset.

R_M32_GLOB_DAT   This relocation type resembles R_M32_32, except it is used to set a global offset table entry to the specified symbol's value. The relocation type allows one to determine the correspondence between symbols and global offset table entries. The relocated field should be aligned on a word boundary. This relocation type does *not* extract the original value of the relocated field to use as an addend.

R_M32_JMP_SLOT   This relocation type resembles R_M32_GLOB_DAT, except it is used for global offset table entries associated with the procedure linkage table (see "Procedure Linkage Table" in the second part of this chapter). The relocated field should be aligned on a word boundary. This relocation type does *not* extract the original value of the relocated field to use as an addend.

R_M32_RELATIVE   This relocation type assists dynamic linking. Its offset member gives a location within a shared object that contains a value representing a relative address. The dynamic linker computes the corresponding virtual address by adding the virtual address at which the shared object was loaded to the relative address. Relocation entries for this type must specify 0 for the symbol table index.

R_M32_RELATIVE_S   This type is similar to R_M32_RELATIVE, except the byte order of the relocated field is different.

Relocation Types (6386 Computer-Specific)

Relocation entries describe how to alter the following instruction and data fields (bit numbers appear in the lower box corners).

Figure 13-27: 6386 Computer Relocatable Fields

word32
31   0

word32   This specifies a 32-bit field occupying 4 bytes with arbitrary byte
             alignment. These values use the same byte order as other word
             values in the Intel386 architecture.

	3		2		1		0	
0x01020304	01		02		03		04	
	31							

Calculations below assume the actions are transforming a relocatable file into
either an executable or a shared object file. Conceptually, the link editor merges
one or more relocatable files to form the output. It first decides how to combine
and locate the input files, then updates the symbol values, and finally performs
the relocation. Relocations applied to executable or shared object files are similar and accomplish the same result. Descriptions below use the following notation.

A   This means the addend used to compute the value of the relocatable
             field.

B   This means the base address at which a shared object has been
             loaded into memory during execution. Generally, a shared object file
             is built with a 0 base virtual address, but the execution address will
             be different. See "Program Header" in the second part of this
             chapter for more information about the base address.

G   This means the offset into the global offset table at which the address
             of the relocation entry's symbol will reside during execution. See
             "Global Offset Table" in the second part of this chapter for more
             information.

GOT   This means the address of the global offset table. See "Global Offset
             Table" in the second part of this chapter for more information.

L   This means the place (section offset or address) of the procedure link-
             age table entry for a symbol. A procedure linkage table entry
             redirects a function call to the proper destination. The link editor
             builds the initial procedure linkage table, and the dynamic linker
             modifies the entries during execution. See "Procedure Linkage
             Table" in the second part of this chapter for more information.

P   This means the place (section offset or address) of the storage unit being relocated (computed using r_offset).

S   This means the value of the symbol whose index resides in the relocation entry.

A relocation entry's r_offset value designates the offset or virtual address of the first byte of the affected storage unit. The relocation type specifies which bits to change and how to calculate their values. The 6386 computer uses only Elf32_Rel relocation entries, the field to be relocated holds the addend. In all cases, the addend and the computed result use the same byte order.

Figure 13-28: 6386 Computer Relocation Types

Name	Value	Field	Calculation
R_386_NONE	0	none	none
R_386_32	1	word32	S + A
R_386_PC32	2	word32	S + A − P
R_386_GOT32	3	word32	G + A − P
R_386_PLT32	4	word32	L + A − P
R_386_COPY	5	none	none
R_386_GLOB_DAT	6	word32	S
R_386_JMP_SLOT	7	word32	S
R_386_RELATIVE	8	word32	B + A
R_386_GOTOFF	9	word32	S + A − GOT
R_386_GOTPC	10	word32	GOT + A − P

Some relocation types have semantics beyond simple calculation.

R_386_GOT32   This relocation type computes the distance from the base of the global offset table to the symbol's global offset table entry. It additionally instructs the link editor to build a global offset table.

R_386_PLT32   This relocation type computes the address of the symbol's procedure linkage table entry and additionally instructs the link editor to build a procedure linkage table.

R_386_COPY

The link editor creates this relocation type for dynamic linking. Its offset member refers to a location in a writable segment. The symbol table index specifies a symbol that should exist both in the current object file and in a shared object. During execution, the dynamic linker copies data associated with the shared object's symbol to the location specified by the offset.

R_386_GLOB_DAT

This relocation type is used to set a global offset table entry to the address of the specified symbol. The special relocation type allows one to determine the correspondence between symbols and global offset table entries.

R_386_JMP_SLOT

The link editor creates this relocation type for dynamic linking. Its offset member gives the location of a procedure linkage table entry. The dynamic linker modifies the procedure linkage table entry to transfer control to the designated symbol's address (see "Procedure Linkage Table" in the second part of this chapter).

R_386_RELATIVE

The link editor creates this relocation type for dynamic linking. Its offset member gives a location within a shared object that contains a value representing a relative address. The dynamic linker computes the corresponding virtual address by adding the virtual address at which the shared object was loaded to the relative address. Relocation entries for this type must specify 0 for the symbol table index.

R_386_GOTOFF

This relocation type computes the difference between a symbol's value and the address of the global offset table. It additionally instructs the link editor to build the global offset table.

R_386_GOTPC

This relocation type resembles R_386_PC32, except it uses the address of the global offset table in its calculation. It additionally instructs the link editor to build the global offset table.

Program Execution

This section describes the object file information and system actions that create running programs. Some information here applies to all systems; information specific to one processor resides in sections marked accordingly.

Executable and shared object files statically represent programs. To execute such programs, the system uses the files to create dynamic program representations, or process images.

Program Header

An executable or shared object file's program header table is an array of structures, each describing a segment or other information the system needs to prepare the program for execution. An object file *segment* contains one or more *sections*, as "Segment Contents" describes below.

Program headers are meaningful only for executable and shared object files. A file specifies its own program header size with the ELF header's e_phentsize and e_phnum members (see "ELF Header" in the first part of this chapter).

Figure 13-29: Program Header

```
typedef struct {
        Elf32_Word      p_type;
        Elf32_Off       p_offset;
        Elf32_Addr      p_vaddr;
        Elf32_Addr      p_paddr;
        Elf32_Word      p_filesz;
        Elf32_Word      p_memsz;
        Elf32_Word      p_flags;
        Elf32_Word      p_align;
} Elf32_Phdr;
```

p_type   This member tells what kind of segment this array element
                describes or how to interpret the array element's information.
                Type values and their meanings appear below.

p_offset	This member gives the offset from the beginning of the file at which the first byte of the segment resides.
p_vaddr	This member gives the virtual address at which the first byte of the segment resides in memory.
p_paddr	On systems for which physical addressing is relevant, this member is reserved for the segment's physical address. Because UNIX System V ignores physical addressing for application programs, this member has unspecified contents for executable files and shared objects.
p_filesz	This member gives the number of bytes in the file image of the segment; it may be zero.
p_memsz	This member gives the number of bytes in the memory image of the segment; it may be zero.
p_flags	This member gives flags relevant to the segment. Defined flag values appear below.
p_align	As "Program Loading" describes later, loadable process segments must have congruent values for p_vaddr and p_offset, modulo the page size. This member gives the value to which the segments are aligned in memory and in the file. Values 0 and 1 mean no alignment is required. Otherwise, p_align should be a positive, integral power of 2, and p_vaddr should equal p_offset, modulo p_align.

Some entries describe process segments; others give supplementary information and do not contribute to the process image. Segment entries may appear in any order, except as explicitly noted below. Defined type values follow; other values are reserved for future use.

Figure 13-30: Segment Types, p_type

Name	Value
PT_NULL	0
PT_LOAD	1
PT_DYNAMIC	2
PT_INTERP	3

Figure 13-30: Segment Types, p_type (continued)

Name	Value
PT_NOTE	4
PT_SHLIB	5
PT_PHDR	6
PT_LOPROC	0x70000000
PT_HIPROC	0x7fffffff

PT_NULL   The array element is unused; other members' values are undefined. This type lets the program header table have ignored entries.

PT_LOAD   The array element specifies a loadable segment, described by p_filesz and p_memsz. The bytes from the file are mapped to the beginning of the memory segment. If the segment's memory size (p_memsz) is larger than the file size (p_filesz), the "extra" bytes are defined to hold the value 0 and to follow the segment's initialized area. The file size may not be larger than the memory size. Loadable segment entries in the program header table appear in ascending order, sorted on the p_vaddr member.

PT_DYNAMIC   The array element specifies dynamic linking information. See "Dynamic Section" below for more information.

PT_INTERP   The array element specifies the location and size of a null-terminated path name to invoke as an interpreter. This segment type is meaningful only for executable files (though it may occur for shared objects); it may not occur more than once in a file. If it is present, it must precede any loadable segment entry. See "Program Interpreter" below for further information.

PT_NOTE   The array element specifies the location and size of auxiliary information. See "Note Section" below for details.

PT_SHLIB   This segment type is reserved but has unspecified semantics.

PT_PHDR   The array element, if present, specifies the location and size of
                the program header table itself, both in the file and in the
                memory image of the program. This segment type may not
                occur more than once in a file. Moreover, it may occur only if
                the program header table is part of the memory image of the
                program. If it is present, it must precede any loadable segment
                entry. See "Program Interpreter" below for further informa-
                tion.

PT_LOPROC through PT_HIPROC
                Values in this inclusive range are reserved for processor-specific
                semantics.

NOTE   Unless specifically required elsewhere, all program header segment types
       are optional. That is, a file's program header table may contain only those
       elements relevant to its contents.

Base Address

Executable and shared object files have a *base address*, which is the lowest virtual
address associated with the memory image of the program's object file. One use
of the base address is to relocate the memory image of the program during
dynamic linking.

An executable or shared object file's base address is calculated during execution
from three values: the memory load address, the maximum page size, and the
lowest virtual address of a program's loadable segment. As "Program Loading"
later in this chapter describes, the virtual addresses in the program headers
might not represent the actual virtual addresses of the program's memory
image. To compute the base address, one determines the memory address associated with the lowest p_vaddr value for a PT_LOAD segment. One then
obtains the base address by truncating the memory address to the nearest multiple of the maximum page size. Depending on the kind of file being loaded into
memory, the memory address might or might not match the p_vaddr values.

Segment Permissions

A program to be loaded by the system must have at least one loadable segment (although this is not required by the file format). When the system creates loadable segments' memory images, it gives access permissions as specified in the p_flags member. All bits included in the PF_MASKPROC mask are reserved for processor-specific semantics.

Figure 13-31: Segment Flag Bits, p_flags

Name	Value	Meaning
PF_X	0x1	Execute
PF_W	0x2	Write
PF_R	0x4	Read
PF_MASKPROC	0xf0000000	Unspecified

If a permission bit is 0, that type of access is denied. Actual memory permissions depend on the memory management unit, which may vary from one system to another. Although all flag combinations are valid, the system may grant more access than requested. In no case, however, will a segment have write permission unless it is specified explicitly. The following table shows both the exact flag interpretation and the allowable flag interpretation.

Figure 13-32: Segment Permissions

Flags	Value	Exact	Allowable
none	0	All access denied	All access denied
PF_X	1	Execute only	Read, execute
PF_W	2	Write only	Read, write, execute
PF_W+PF_X	3	Write, execute	Read, write, execute
PF_R	4	Read only	Read, execute
PF_R+PF_X	5	Read, execute	Read, execute
PF_R+PF_W	6	Read, write	Read, write, execute
PF_R+PF_W+PF_X	7	Read, write, execute	Read, write, execute

For example, typical text segments have read and execute – but not write – permissions. Data segments normally have read, write, and execute permissions.

Segment Contents

An object file segment comprises one or more sections, though this fact is transparent to the program header. Whether the file segment holds one or many sections also is immaterial to program loading. Nonetheless, various data must be present for program execution, dynamic linking, and so on. The diagrams below illustrate segment contents in general terms. The order and membership of sections within a segment may vary; moreover, processor-specific constraints may alter the examples below.

Text segments contain read-only instructions and data, typically including the following sections described earlier in this chapter. Other sections may also reside in loadable segments; these examples are not meant to give complete and exclusive segment contents.

Figure 13-33: Text Segment

.text
.rodata
.hash
.dynsym
.dynstr
.plt
.rel.got

Data segments contain writable data and instructions, typically including the following sections.

Figure 13-34: Data Segment

.data
.dynamic
.got
.bss

A `PT_DYNAMIC` program header element points at the `.dynamic` section, explained in "Dynamic Section" below. The `.got` and `.plt` sections also hold information related to position-independent code and dynamic linking. Although the `.plt` appears in a text segment above, it may reside in a text or a data segment, depending on the processor. See "Global Offset Table" and "Procedure Linkage Table" later in this chapter for details.

As described in "Section Header" in the first part of this chapter, the `.bss` section has the type `SHT_NOBITS`. Although it occupies no space in the file, it contributes to the segment's memory image. Normally, these uninitialized data reside at the end of the segment, thereby making `p_memsz` larger than `p_filesz` in the associated program header element.

Note Section

Sometimes a vendor or system builder needs to mark an object file with special information that other programs will check for conformance, compatibility, and so forth. Sections of type `SHT_NOTE` and program header elements of type `PT_NOTE` can be used for this purpose. The note information in sections and program header elements holds any number of entries, each of which is an array of 4-byte words in the format of the target processor. Labels appear below to help explain note information organization, but they are not part of the specification.

Figure 13-35: Note Information

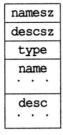

namesz and name

> The first namesz bytes in name contain a null-terminated character representation of the entry's owner or originator. There is no formal mechanism for avoiding name conflicts. By convention, vendors use

their own name, such as "XYZ Computer Company," as the identifier. If no name is present, `namesz` contains 0. Padding is present, if necessary, to ensure 4-byte alignment for the descriptor. Such padding is not included in `namesz`.

`descsz` and `desc`
: The first `descsz` bytes in `desc` hold the note descriptor. If no descriptor is present, `descsz` contains 0. Padding is present, if necessary, to ensure 4-byte alignment for the next note entry. Such padding is not included in `descsz`.

`type`
: This word gives the interpretation of the descriptor. Each originator controls its own types; multiple interpretations of a single type value may exist. Thus, a program must recognize both the name and the type to "understand" a descriptor. Types currently must be non-negative.

To illustrate, the following note segment holds two entries.

Figure 13-36: Example Note Segment

	+0	+1	+2	+3	
`namesz`	7				
`descsz`	0				No descriptor
`type`	1				
`name`	X	Y	Z		
	C	o	\0	*pad*	
`namesz`	7				
`descsz`	8				
`type`	3				
`name`	X	Y	Z		
	C	o	\0	*pad*	
`desc`	*word 0*				
	word 1				

NOTE The system reserves note information with no name (namesz==0) and with a zero-length name (name[0]=='\0') but currently defines no types. All other names must have at least one non-null character.

Program Loading (Processor-Specific)

As the system creates or augments a process image, it logically copies a file's segment to a virtual memory segment. When—and if—the system physically reads the file depends on the program's execution behavior, system load, and so forth. A process does not require a physical page unless it references the logical page during execution, and processes commonly leave many pages unreferenced. Therefore delaying physical reads frequently obviates them, improving system performance. To obtain this efficiency in practice, executable and shared object files must have segment images whose file offsets and virtual addresses are congruent, modulo the page size.

Virtual addresses and file offsets for segments are congruent modulo 8 K (0x2000) or larger powers of 2 for the 3B2 computer and 4 K (0x1000) for the 6386 computer. By aligning segments to the maximum page size, the files will be suitable for paging regardless of physical page size. The following examples show 8 K alignment. Although this works for both the 3B2 and the 6386 computers, it is more strict than necessary for the 6386 computer.

Figure 13-37: Executable File

File Offset	File	Virtual Address
0	ELF header	
	Program header table	
	Other information	
0x100	Text segment	0x80000100
	. . .	
	0x2be00 bytes	0x8002beff
0x2bf00	Data segment	0x8002df00
	. . .	
	0x4e00 bytes	0x80032cff
0x30d00	Other information	
	. . .	

Figure 13-38: Program Header Segments

Member	Text	Data
p_type	PT_LOAD	PT_LOAD
p_offset	0x100	0x2bf00
p_vaddr	0x80000100	0x8002df00
p_paddr	unspecified	unspecified
p_filesz	0x2be00	0x4e00
p_memsz	0x2be00	0x5e24
p_flags	PF_R+PF_X	PF_R+PF_W+PF_X
p_align	0x2000	0x2000

Although the example's file offsets and virtual addresses are congruent modulo the maximum page size for both text and data, up to four file pages hold impure text or data (depending on page size and file system block size).

- The first text page contains the ELF header, the program header table, and other information.

- The last text page holds a copy of the beginning of data.

- The first data page has a copy of the end of text.

- The last data page may contain file information not relevant to the running process.

Logically, the system enforces the memory permissions as if each segment were complete and separate; segments' addresses are adjusted to ensure each logical page in the address space has a single set of permissions. In the example above, the region of the file holding the end of text and the beginning of data will be mapped twice: at one virtual address for text and at a different virtual address for data.

The end of the data segment requires special handling for uninitialized data, which the system defines to begin with zero values. Thus if a file's last data page includes information not in the logical memory page, the extraneous data must be set to zero, not the unknown contents of the executable file. "Impurities" in the other three pages are not logically part of the process image; whether the system expunges them is unspecified. The memory image for this program follows, assuming 2 KB (0x800) pages. For simplicity, this example illustrates only one page size. A similar figure with 4 KB pages would be appropriate for 6386 computers.

Figure 13-39: Process Image Segments

Virtual Address	Contents	Segment
0x80000000	*Header padding* 0x100 bytes	
0x80000100	Text segment	
	. . .	Text
	0x2be00 bytes	
0x8002bf00	*Data padding* 0x100 bytes	
0x8002d800	*Text padding* 0x700 bytes	
0x8002df00	Data segment	
	. . .	Data
	0x4e00 bytes	
0x80032d00	Uninitialized data 0x1024 zero bytes	
0x80033d24	*Page padding* 0x2dc zero bytes	

One aspect of segment loading differs between executable files and shared objects. Executable file segments typically contain absolute code. To let the process execute correctly, the segments must reside at the virtual addresses used to build the executable file. Thus the system uses the p_vaddr values unchanged as virtual addresses.

On the other hand, shared object segments typically contain position-independent code. (For background, see "Link Editing" in Chapter 2.) This lets a segment's virtual address change from one process to another, without invalidating execution behavior. Though the system chooses virtual addresses for individual processes, it maintains the segments' *relative positions*. Because position-independent code uses relative addressing between segments, the difference between virtual addresses in memory must match the difference between virtual addresses in the file. The following table shows possible shared object virtual address assignments for several processes, illustrating constant relative positioning. The table also illustrates the base address computations. Once again, the maximum page size used below is 8 KB; for 6386 computers, the calculation would assume 4 KB pages.

Figure 13-40: Example Shared Object Segment Addresses

Source	Text	Data	Base Address
File	0x200	0x2a400	0x0
Process 1	0xc0080200	0xc00aa400	0xc0080000
Process 2	0xc0082200	0xc00ac400	0xc0082000
Process 3	0xd00c0200	0xd00ea400	0xd00c0000
Process 4	0xd00c6200	0xd00f0400	0xd00c6000

Program Interpreter

An executable file may have one PT_INTERP program header element. During exec(), the system retrieves a path name from the PT_INTERP segment and creates the initial process image from the interpreter file's segments. That is, instead of using the original executable file's segment images, the system composes a memory image for the interpreter. It then is the interpreter's responsibility to receive control from the system and provide an environment for the application program.

The interpreter receives control in one of two ways. First, it may receive a file descriptor to read the executable file, positioned at the beginning. It can use this file descriptor to read and/or map the executable file's segments into memory. Second, depending on the executable file format, the system may load the executable file into memory instead of giving the interpreter an open file descriptor. With the possible exception of the file descriptor, the interpreter's initial process state matches what the executable file would have received. The interpreter itself may not require a second interpreter. An interpreter may be either a shared object or an executable file.

■ A shared object (the normal case) is loaded as position-independent, with addresses that may vary from one process to another; the system creates its segments in the dynamic segment area used by mmap() and related services. Consequently, a shared object interpreter typically will not conflict with the original executable file's original segment addresses.

■ An executable file is loaded at fixed addresses; the system creates its segments using the virtual addresses from the program header table. Consequently, an executable file interpreter's virtual addresses may collide with the first executable file; the interpreter is responsible for resolving conflicts.

Dynamic Linker

When building an executable file that uses dynamic linking, the link editor adds a program header element of type PT_INTERP to an executable file, telling the system to invoke the dynamic linker as the program interpreter. exec() and the dynamic linker cooperate to create the process image for the program, which entails the following actions:

■ Adding the executable file's memory segments to the process image;

■ Adding shared object memory segments to the process image;

■ Performing relocations for the executable file and its shared objects;

■ Closing the file descriptor that was used to read the executable file, if one was given to the dynamic linker;

■ Transferring control to the program, making it look as if the program had received control directly from exec().

The link editor also constructs various data that assist the dynamic linker for executable and shared object files. As shown above in "Program Header," these data reside in loadable segments, making them available during execution. (Once again, recall the exact segment contents are processor-specific.)

■ A .dynamic section with type SHT_DYNAMIC holds various data. The structure residing at the beginning of the section holds the addresses of other dynamic linking information.

- The .hash section with type SHT_HASH holds a symbol hash table.

- The .got and .plt sections with type SHT_PROGBITS hold two separate tables: the global offset table and the procedure linkage table. Sections below explain how the dynamic linker uses and changes the tables to create memory images for object files.

As explained in "Program Loading" earlier, shared objects may occupy virtual memory addresses that are different from the addresses recorded in the file's program header table. The dynamic linker relocates the memory image, updating absolute addresses before the application gains control. Although the absolute address values would be correct if the library were loaded at the addresses specified in the program header table, this normally is not the case.

If the process environment contains a variable named LD_BIND_NOW with a non-null value (see "Checking for Run-Time Compatibility" in Chapter 2), the dynamic linker processes all relocations before transferring control to the program. For example, all the following environment entries would specify this behavior.

- LD_BIND_NOW=1

- LD_BIND_NOW=on

- LD_BIND_NOW=off

Otherwise, LD_BIND_NOW either does not occur in the environment or has a null value. The dynamic linker is permitted to evaluate procedure linkage table entries lazily, thus avoiding symbol resolution and relocation overhead for functions that are not called. See "Procedure Linkage Table" below for more information.

Dynamic Section

If an object file participates in dynamic linking, its program header table will have an element of type PT_DYNAMIC. This "segment" contains the .dynamic section. A special symbol, _DYNAMIC, labels the section, which contains an array of the following structures.

Figure 13-41: Dynamic Structure

```
typedef struct {
        Elf32_Sword        d_tag;
        union {
                Elf32_Word        d_val;
                Elf32_Addr        d_ptr;
        } d_un;
} Elf32_Dyn;

extern Elf32_Dyn        _DYNAMIC[];
```

For each object with this type, d_tag controls the interpretation of d_un.

d_val   These Elf32_Word objects represent integer values with various
           interpretations.

d_ptr   These Elf32_Addr objects represent program virtual addresses. As
           mentioned previously, a file's virtual addresses might not match the
           memory virtual addresses during execution. When interpreting
           addresses contained in the dynamic structure, the dynamic linker
           computes actual addresses, based on the original file value and the
           memory base address. For consistency, files do *not* contain relocation
           entries to "correct" addresses in the dynamic structure.

The following table summarizes the tag requirements for executable and shared
object files. If a tag is marked "mandatory," then the dynamic linking array
must have an entry of that type. Likewise, "optional" means an entry for the
tag may appear but is not required.

Figure 13-42: Dynamic Array Tags, d_tag

Name	Value	d_un	Executable	Shared Object
DT_NULL	0	ignored	mandatory	mandatory
DT_NEEDED	1	d_val	optional	optional
DT_PLTRELSZ	2	d_val	optional	optional
DT_PLTGOT	3	d_ptr	optional	optional
DT_HASH	4	d_ptr	mandatory	mandatory
DT_STRTAB	5	d_ptr	mandatory	mandatory
DT_SYMTAB	6	d_ptr	mandatory	mandatory
DT_RELA	7	d_ptr	mandatory	optional
DT_RELASZ	8	d_val	mandatory	optional
DT_RELAENT	9	d_val	mandatory	optional
DT_STRSZ	10	d_val	mandatory	mandatory
DT_SYMENT	11	d_val	mandatory	mandatory
DT_INIT	12	d_ptr	optional	optional
DT_FINI	13	d_ptr	optional	optional
DT_SONAME	14	d_val	ignored	optional
DT_RPATH	15	d_val	optional	ignored
DT_SYMBOLIC	16	ignored	ignored	optional
DT_REL	17	d_ptr	mandatory	optional
DT_RELSZ	18	d_val	mandatory	optional
DT_RELENT	19	d_val	mandatory	optional
DT_PLTREL	20	d_val	optional	optional
DT_DEBUG	21	d_ptr	optional	ignored
DT_TEXTREL	22	ignored	optional	optional
DT_JMPREL	23	d_ptr	optional	optional
DT_LOPROC	0x70000000	unspecified	unspecified	unspecified
DT_HIPROC	0x7fffffff	unspecified	unspecified	unspecified

DT_NULL
: An entry with a DT_NULL tag marks the end of the _DYNAMIC array.

DT_NEEDED
: This element holds the string table offset of a null-terminated string, giving the name of a needed library. The offset is an index into the table recorded in the DT_STRTAB entry. See "Shared Object Dependencies" below for more information

about these names. The dynamic array may contain multiple entries with this type. These entries' relative order is significant, though their relation to entries of other types is not.

DT_PLTRELSZ   This element holds the total size, in bytes, of the relocation entries associated with the procedure linkage table. If an entry of type DT_JMPREL is present, a DT_PLTRELSZ must accompany it.

DT_PLTGOT   This element holds an address associated with the procedure linkage table and/or the global offset table. On the 3B2 and 6386 computers, this entry's d_ptr member gives the address of the first entry in the global offset table. As mentioned below, the first three global offset table entries are reserved, and two are used to hold procedure linkage table information.

DT_HASH   This element holds the address of the symbol hash table, described in "Hash Table" below.

DT_STRTAB   This element holds the address of the string table, described in the first part of this chapter. Symbol names, library names, and other strings reside in this table.

DT_SYMTAB   This element holds the address of the symbol table, described in the first part of this chapter, with Elf32_Sym entries for the 32-bit class of files.

DT_RELA   This element holds the address of a relocation table, described in the first part of this chapter. Entries in the table have explicit addends, such as Elf32_Rela for the 32-bit file class. An object file may have multiple relocation sections. When building the relocation table for an executable or shared object file, the link editor catenates those sections to form a single table. Although the sections remain independent in the object file, the dynamic linker sees a single table. When the dynamic linker creates the process image for an executable file or adds a shared object to the process image, it reads the relocation table and performs the associated actions. If this element is present, the dynamic structure must also have DT_RELASZ and DT_RELAENT elements. When relocation is "mandatory" for a file, either DT_RELA or DT_REL may occur (both are permitted but not required).

DT_RELASZ	This element holds the total size, in bytes, of the DT_RELA relocation table.
DT_RELAENT	This element holds the size, in bytes, of the DT_RELA relocation entry.
DT_STRSZ	This element holds the size, in bytes, of the string table.
DT_SYMENT	This element holds the size, in bytes, of a symbol table entry.
DT_INIT	This element holds the address of the initialization function, discussed in "Initialization and Termination Functions" below.
DT_FINI	This element holds the address of the termination function, discussed in "Initialization and Termination Functions" below.
DT_SONAME	This element holds the string table offset of a null-terminated string, giving the name of the shared object. The offset is an index into the table recorded in the DT_STRTAB entry. See "Shared Object Dependencies" below for more information about these names.
DT_RPATH	This element holds the string table offset of a null-terminated search library search path string, discussed in "Shared Object Dependencies" below. The offset is an index into the table recorded in the DT_STRTAB entry.
DT_SYMBOLIC	This element's presence in a shared object library alters the dynamic linker's symbol resolution algorithm for references within the library. Instead of starting a symbol search with the executable file, the dynamic linker starts from the shared object itself. If the shared object fails to supply the referenced symbol, the dynamic linker then searches the executable file and other shared objects as usual.
DT_REL	This element is similar to DT_RELA, except its table has implicit addends, such as Elf32_Rel for the 32-bit file class. If this element is present, the dynamic structure must also have DT_RELSZ and DT_RELENT elements.
DT_RELSZ	This element holds the total size, in bytes, of the DT_REL relocation table.

DT_RELENT   This element holds the size, in bytes, of the DT_REL relocation
             entry.

DT_PLTREL   This member specifies the type of relocation entry to which the
             procedure linkage table refers. The d_val member holds
             DT_REL or DT_RELA, as appropriate. All relocations in a pro-
             cedure linkage table must use the same relocation.

DT_DEBUG   This member is used for debugging.

DT_TEXTREL   This member's absence signifies that no relocation entry should
             cause a modification to a non-writable segment, as specified by
             the segment permissions in the program header table. If this
             member is present, one or more relocation entries might request
             modifications to a non-writable segment, and the dynamic
             linker can prepare accordingly.

DT_JMPREL   If present, this entry's d_ptr member holds the address of relo-
             cation entries associated solely with the procedure linkage
             table. Separating these relocation entries lets the dynamic
             linker ignore them during process initialization, if lazy binding
             is enabled. If this entry is present, the related entries of types
             DT_PLTRELSZ and DT_PLTREL must also be present.

DT_LOPROC through DT_HIPROC
             Values in this inclusive range are reserved for processor-specific
             semantics.

Except for the DT_NULL element at the end of the array, and the relative order
of DT_NEEDED elements, entries may appear in any order. Tag values not
appearing in the table are reserved.

Shared Object Dependencies

When the link editor processes an archive library, it extracts library members
and copies them into the output object file. These statically linked services are
available during execution without involving the dynamic linker. Shared objects
also provide services, and the dynamic linker must attach the proper shared
object files to the process image for execution. Thus executable and shared
object files describe their specific dependencies. (For further background, see
"Link Editing" in Chapter 2.)

When the dynamic linker creates the memory segments for an object file, the dependencies (recorded in DT_NEEDED entries of the dynamic structure) tell what shared objects are needed to supply the program's services. By repeatedly connecting referenced shared objects and their dependencies, the dynamic linker builds a complete process image. When resolving symbolic references, the dynamic linker examines the symbol tables with a breadth-first search. That is, it first looks at the symbol table of the executable program itself, then at the symbol tables of the DT_NEEDED entries (in order), then at the second level DT_NEEDED entries, and so on.

 NOTE Even when a shared object is referenced multiple times in the dependency list, the dynamic linker will connect the object only once to the process.

Names in the dependency list are copies either of the DT_SONAME strings or the path names of the shared objects used to build the object file. For example, if the link editor builds an executable file using one shared object with a DT_SONAME entry of lib1 and another shared object library with the path name /usr/lib/lib2, the executable file will contain lib1 and /usr/lib/lib2 in its dependency list.

If a shared object name has one or more slash (/) characters anywhere in the name, such as /usr/lib/lib2 above or directory/file, the dynamic linker uses that string directly as the path name. If the name has no slashes, such as lib1 above, three facilities specify shared object path searching, with the following precedence.

- First, the dynamic array tag DT_RPATH may give a string that holds a list of directories, separated by colons (:). For example, the string /home/dir/usr/lib:/home/dir2/usr/lib: tells the dynamic linker to search first the directory /home/dir/lib, then /home/dir2/usr/lib, and then the current directory to find dependencies.

- Second, a variable called LD_LIBRARY_PATH in the process environment may hold a list of directories as above, optionally followed by a semicolon (;) and another directory list. The following values would be equivalent to the previous example:

    ❑ LD_LIBRARY_PATH=/home/dir/usr/lib:/home/dir2/usr/lib:

    ❑ LD_LIBRARY_PATH=/home/dir/usr/lib;/home/dir2/usr/lib:

    ❑ LD_LIBRARY_PATH=/home/dir/usr/lib:/home/dir2/usr/lib:;

All LD_LIBRARY_PATH directories are searched after those from
DT_RPATH. Although some programs (such as the link editor) treat the
lists before and after the semicolon differently, the dynamic linker does
not. Nevertheless, the dynamic linker accepts the semicolon notation,
with the semantics described above.

■ Finally, if the other two groups of directories fail to locate the desired
library, the dynamic linker searches /usr/lib.

NOTE   For security, the dynamic linker ignores environmental search specifications
(such as LD_LIBRARY_PATH) for set-user and set-group ID programs. It
does, however, search DT_RPATH directories and /usr/lib.

Global Offset Table (Processor-Specific)

Position-independent code cannot, in general, contain absolute virtual addresses.
Global offset tables hold absolute addresses in private data, thus making the
addresses available without compromising the position-independence and sharability of a program's text. A program references its global offset table using
position-independent addressing and extracts absolute values, thus redirecting
position-independent references to absolute locations.

Initially, the global offset table holds information as required by its relocation
entries (see "Relocation" in the first part of this chapter). After the system
creates memory segments for a loadable object file, the dynamic linker processes
the relocation entries, some of which will be type R_M32_GLOB_DAT or
R_386_GLOB_DAT referring to the global offset table. The dynamic linker determines the associated symbol values, calculates their absolute addresses, and sets
the appropriate memory table entries to the proper values. Although the absolute addresses are unknown when the link editor builds an object file, the
dynamic linker knows the addresses of all memory segments and can thus calculate the absolute addresses of the symbols contained therein.

If a program requires direct access to the absolute address of a symbol, that symbol will have a global offset table entry. Because the executable file and shared objects have separate global offset tables, a symbol's address may appear in several tables. The dynamic linker processes all the global offset table relocations before giving control to any code in the process image, thus ensuring the absolute addresses are available during execution.

The table's entry zero is reserved to hold the address of the dynamic structure, referenced with the symbol _DYNAMIC. This allows a program, such as the dynamic linker, to find its own dynamic structure without having yet processed its relocation entries. This is especially important for the dynamic linker, because it must initialize itself without relying on other programs to relocate its memory image. On the 3B2 and 6386 computers, entries one and two in the global offset table also are reserved. "Procedure Linkage Table" below describes them.

The system may choose different memory segment addresses for the same shared object in different programs; it may even choose different library addresses for different executions of the same program. Nonetheless, memory segments do not change addresses once the process image is established. As long as a process exists, its memory segments reside at fixed virtual addresses.

A global offset table's format and interpretation are processor-specific. For the WE 32100, an offset into the table is an *unsigned* value, allowing only non-negative "subscripts" into the array of addresses.

For the 6386 computer, the symbol _GLOBAL_OFFSET_TABLE_ may be used to access the table.

Figure 13-43: Global Offset Table

```
extern Elf32_Addr          _GLOBAL_OFFSET_TABLE_[];
```

The symbol _GLOBAL_OFFSET_TABLE_ may reside in the middle of the .got section, allowing both negative and non-negative "subscripts" into the array of addresses.

Procedure Linkage Table (Processor-Specific)

Much as the global offset table redirects position-independent address calculations to absolute locations, the procedure linkage table redirects position-independent function calls to absolute locations. The link editor cannot resolve execution transfers (such as function calls) from one executable or shared object to another. Consequently, the link editor arranges to have the program transfer control to entries in the procedure linkage table. On the 3B2 and 6386 computers, procedure linkage tables reside in shared text, but they use addresses in the private global offset table. The dynamic linker determines the destinations' absolute addresses and modifies the global offset table's memory image accordingly. The dynamic linker thus can redirect the entries without compromising the position-independence and sharability of the program's text. Executable files and shared object files have separate procedure linkage tables.

Procedure Linkage Table (3B2 Computer-Specific)

To illustrate the 3B2 computer procedure linkage table, consider the following example.

Figure 13-44: 3B2 Computer Procedure Linkage Table

```
.PLT0:   PUSHW    got_plus_4
         JMP      *got_plus_8
         NOP3
         NOP3
.PLT1:   JMP      *name1@GOT
         PUSHW    &offset
         JMP      .PLT0@PC
.PLT2:   JMP      *name2@GOT
         PUSHW    &offset
         JMP      .PLT0@PC
         . . .
```

Following the steps below, the dynamic linker and the program "cooperate" to resolve symbolic references through the procedure linkage table and the global offset table.

1. When first creating the memory image of the program, the dynamic linker sets the second and the third entries in the global offset table to special values. Steps below explain more about these values.

2. For illustration, assume the program calls name1, which transfers control to the label .PLT1.

3. The first instruction jumps to the address in the global offset table entry for name1. Initially, the global offset table holds the address of the following PUSHW instruction, not the real address of name1.

4. Consequently, the program pushes a relocation offset (*offset*) on the stack. The relocation offset is a 32-bit, non-negative byte offset into the relocation table. The designated relocation entry will have type R_M32_JMP_SLOT, and its offset will specify the global offset table entry used in the previous JMP instruction. The relocation entry also contains a symbol table index, thus telling the dynamic linker what symbol is being referenced, name1 in this case.

5. After pushing the relocation offset, the program then jumps to .PLT0, the first entry in the procedure linkage table. The PUSHW instruction places the value of the second global offset table entry (*got_plus_4*) on the stack, thus giving the dynamic linker one word of identifying information. The program then jumps to the address in the third global offset table entry (*got_plus_8*), which transfers control to the dynamic linker.

6. When the dynamic linker receives control, it unwinds the stack, looks at the designated relocation entry, finds the symbol's value, stores the "real" address for name1 in its global offset table entry, and transfers control to the desired destination.

7. Subsequent executions of the procedure linkage table entry will transfer directly to name1, without calling the dynamic linker a second time. That is, the JMP instruction at .PLT1 will transfer to name1, instead of "falling through" to the PUSHW instruction.

Procedure Linkage Table (6386 Computer-Specific)

To illustrate the 6386 computer's procedure linkage table, consider the following examples.

Figure 13-45: 6386 Computer Absolute Procedure Linkage Table

```
.PLT0:    pushl    got_plus_4
          jmp      *got_plus_8
          nop; nop
          nop; nop
.PLT1:    jmp      *name1_in_GOT
          pushl    $offset
          jmp      .PLT0@PC
.PLT2:    jmp      *name2_in_GOT
          pushl    $offset
          jmp      .PLT0@PC
          . . .
```

Figure 13-46: 6386 Computer Position-Independent Procedure Linkage Table

```
.PLT0:    pushl    4(%ebx)
          jmp      *8(%ebx)
          nop; nop
          nop; nop
.PLT1:    jmp      *name1@GOT(%ebx)
          pushl    $offset
          jmp      .PLT0@PC
.PLT2:    jmp      *name2@GOT(%ebx)
          pushl    $offset
          jmp      .PLT0@PC
          . . .
```

NOTE As the figures show, the procedure linkage table instructions use different operand addressing modes for absolute code and for position-independent code. Nonetheless, their interfaces to the dynamic linker are the same.

Following the steps below, the dynamic linker and the program "cooperate" to resolve symbolic references through the procedure linkage table and the global offset table.

1. When first creating the memory image of the program, the dynamic linker sets the second and the third entries in the global offset table to special values. Steps below explain more about these values.

2. If the procedure linkage table is position-independent, the address of the global offset table must reside in %ebx. Each shared object file in the process image has its own procedure linkage table, and control transfers to a procedure linkage table entry only from within the same object file. Consequently, the calling function is responsible for setting the global offset table base register before calling the procedure linkage table entry.

3. For illustration, assume the program calls name1, which transfers control to the label .PLT1.

4. The first instruction jumps to the address in the global offset table entry for name1. Initially, the global offset table holds the address of the following pushl instruction, not the real address of name1.

5. Consequently, the program pushes a relocation offset (*offset*) on the stack. The relocation offset is a 32-bit, non-negative byte offset into the relocation table. The designated relocation entry will have type R_386_JMP_SLOT, and its offset will specify the global offset table entry used in the previous jmp instruction. The relocation entry also contains a symbol table index, thus telling the dynamic linker what symbol is being referenced, name1 in this case.

6. After pushing the relocation offset, the program then jumps to .PLT0, the first entry in the procedure linkage table. The pushl instruction places the value of the second global offset table entry (*got_plus_4* or 4(%ebx)) on the stack, thus giving the dynamic linker one word of identifying information. The program then jumps to the address in the third global offset table entry (*got_plus_8* or 8(%ebx)), which transfers control to the dynamic linker.

7. When the dynamic linker receives control, it unwinds the stack, looks at the designated relocation entry, finds the symbol's value, stores the "real" address for name1 in its global offset table entry, and transfers control to the desired destination.

8. Subsequent executions of the procedure linkage table entry will transfer directly to name1, without calling the dynamic linker a second time. That is, the jmp instruction at .PLT1 will transfer to name1, instead of "falling through" to the pushl instruction.

Lazy Symbol Binding

The LD_BIND_NOW environment variable can change dynamic linking behavior. If its value is non-null, the dynamic linker evaluates procedure linkage table entries before transferring control to the program. That is, the dynamic linker processes relocation entries of type R_M32_JMP_SLOT or R_386_JMP_SLOT during process initialization. Otherwise, the dynamic linker evaluates procedure linkage table entries lazily, delaying symbol resolution and relocation until the first execution of a table entry.

 NOTE   Lazy binding generally improves overall application performance, because unused symbols do not incur the dynamic linking overhead. Nevertheless, two situations make lazy binding undesirable for some applications. First, the initial reference to a shared object function takes longer than subsequent calls, because the dynamic linker intercepts the call to resolve the symbol. Some applications cannot tolerate this unpredictability. Second, if an error occurs and the dynamic linker cannot resolve the symbol, the dynamic linker will terminate the program. Under lazy binding, this might occur at arbitrary times. Once again, some applications cannot tolerate this unpredictability. By turning off lazy binding, the dynamic linker forces the failure to occur during process initialization, before the application receives control.

Hash Table

A hash table of Elf32_Word objects supports symbol table access. Labels appear below to help explain the hash table organization, but they are not part of the specification.

Figure 13-47: Symbol Hash Table

nbucket
nchain
bucket[0]
. . .
bucket[nbucket − 1]
chain[0]
. . .
chain[nchain − 1]

The bucket array contains nbucket entries, and the chain array contains nchain entries; indexes start at 0. Both bucket and chain hold symbol table indexes. Chain table entries parallel the symbol table. The number of symbol table entries should equal nchain; so symbol table indexes also select chain table entries. A hashing function (shown below) accepts a symbol name and returns a value that may be used to compute a bucket index. Consequently, if the hashing function returns the value x for some name, bucket[x%nbucket] gives an index, y, into both the symbol table and the chain table. If the symbol table entry is not the one desired, chain[y] gives the next symbol table entry with the same hash value. One can follow the chain links until either the selected symbol table entry holds the desired name or the chain entry contains the value STN_UNDEF.

Figure 13-48: Hashing Function

```
unsigned long
elf_hash(const unsigned char *name)
{
        unsigned long   h = 0, g;

        while (*name)
        {
                h = (h << 4) + *name++;
                if (g = h & 0xf0000000)
                        h ^= g >> 24;
                h &= ~g;
        }
        return h;
}
```

Initialization and Termination Functions

After the dynamic linker has built the process image and performed the relocations, each shared object gets the opportunity to execute some initialization code. These initialization functions are called in no specified order, but all shared object initializations happen before the executable file gains control.

Similarly, shared objects may have termination functions, which are executed with the atexit() mechanism after the base process begins its termination sequence. (See atexit() in Section 3C of the *Programmer's Reference Manual*.) Once again, the order in which the dynamic linker calls termination functions is unspecified.

Shared objects designate their initialization and termination functions through the DT_INIT and DT_FINI entries in the dynamic structure, described in "Dynamic Section" above. Typically, the code for these functions resides in the .init and .fini sections, mentioned in "Section Header" in the first part of this chapter.

| | Although the atexit() termination processing normally will be done, it is not guaranteed to have executed upon process death. In particular, the process will not execute the termination processing if it calls _exit() or if the process dies because it received a signal that it neither caught nor ignored. |

14 Floating Point Operations

Introduction

The C compilation system supports the *IEEE Standard for Binary Floating Point Arithmetic* (ANSI/IEEE Standard 754-1985). To support floating point on a 3B2 computer, a math co-processor is required. A math co-processor is not required on the 6386 computer.

The C compiler uses the IEEE standard single- and double-precision data types, operations, and conversions. Library functions are provided for further IEEE support.

You will probably not need any special functions to use floating point operations in your programs. If you do, however, you can find information about floating point support in this chapter. (For more details on how the C compilation system supports the IEEE standard see "IEEE Requirements" in this chapter.)

This chapter contains sections on the following topics:

- the details of IEEE arithmetic

- floating point exception handling

- conversion between binary and decimal values

- single-precision floating point operations

- implicit precision of subexpressions

- IEEE requirements

 If your code depends on a side effect of a floating point operation (such as the setting of a trap), note that the optimizer may remove the floating point operation if the result of the operation is not used elsewhere. Therefore, your process may never see the side effect it depends on. For example, if your program depends on a trap resulting from the following operation:

```
x = a + b
```

and the operation is removed by the optimizer because the result is not used anywhere else, the trap never occurs.

IEEE Arithmetic

This section provides the details of floating point representation, the environment of the 3B2 computer and the 6386 computer, and exception handling. Most users need not be concerned with the details of the floating point environment.

NOTE Some programs that previously dumped core will now proceed using computations with diagnostic values or floating point "infinities."

NOTE The floating point subsystems of the 3B2 computer and the 6386 computer are based on the *Standard for Binary Floating-Point Arithmetic,* ANSI/IEEE Standard 754-1985. For more information about this standard, write to IEEE Service Center, 445 Hoes Lane, Piscataway, NJ, 08854, or call (201) 981-0060

Data Types and Formats

Single-Precision

Single-precision floating point numbers have the following format:

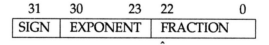

31	30	23	22	0
SIGN	EXPONENT		FRACTION	

binary point

Field	Position	Full Name
sign	31	sign bit (0==positive, 1==negative)
exponent	30-23	exponent (biased by 127)
fraction	22-0	fraction (bits to right of binary point)

Double-Precision

Double-precision floating point numbers have the following format:

63	62	52 51	0
SIGN	EXPONENT	FRACTION	

binary point

Field	Position	Full Name
sign	63	sign bit (0==positive, 1==negative)
exponent	62-52	exponent (biased by 1023)
fraction	51-0	fraction (bits to right of binary point)

NOTE For the 3B2 computer, the high-order word is at the low address; for the 6386 computer, the high-order word is at the high address:

Normalized Numbers

A number is normalized if the exponent field contains other than all 1's or all 0's.

The exponent field contains a biased exponent, where the bias is 127 in single-precision, and 1023 in double-precision. Thus, the exponent of a normalized floating point number is in the range -126 to 127 inclusive for single-precision, and in the range -1022 to 1023 inclusive for double-precision.

There is an implicit bit associated with both single- and double-precision formats. The implicit bit is not explicitly stored anywhere (thus its name). Logically, for normalized operands the implicit bit has a value of 1 and resides immediately to the left of the binary point (in the 2^0 position). Thus the implicit bit and fraction field together can represent values in the range 1 to $2-2^{-23}$ inclusive for single-precision, and in the range 1 to $2-2^{-52}$ inclusive for double-precision.

Thus normalized single-precision numbers can be in the range (plus or minus) 2^{-126} to $(2-2^{-23}) \times 2^{127}$ inclusive.

Normalized double-precision numbers can be in the range (plus or minus) 2^{-1022} to $(2-2^{-52}) \times 2^{1023}$ inclusive.

Denormalized Numbers

A number is denormalized if the exponent field contains all 0's and the fraction field does not contain all 0's.

Thus denormalized single-precision numbers can be in the range (plus or minus) $2^{-126} \times 2^{-22} = 2^{-148}$ to $(1-2^{-22}) \times 2^{-126}$ inclusive.

Denormalized double-precision numbers can be in the range (plus or minus) $2^{-1022} \times 2^{-51} = 2^{-1073}$ to $(1-2^{-51}) \times 2^{-1022}$ inclusive.

Both positive and negative zero values exist, but they are treated the same during floating point calculations.

Maximum and Minimum Representable Floating Point Values

The maximum and minimum representable values in floating point format are defined in the header file values.h:

```
#define MAXDOUBLE        1.79769313486231570e+308
#define MAXFLOAT         ((float)3.40282346638528860e+38)
#define MINDOUBLE        4.94065645841246544e-324
#define MINFLOAT         ((float)1.40129846432481707e-45)
```

Special-Case Values

The following table gives the names of special cases and how each is represented.

Value Name	Sign	Exponent	Fraction	
			MSB	Rest of Fraction
NaN (non-trapping)	X	Max	0	Nonzero
Trapping NaN	X	Max	1	X
Positive Infinity	0	Max	Min	
Negative Infinity	1	Max	Min	
Positive Zero	0	Min	Min	
Negative Zero	1	Min	Min	
Denormalized Number	X	Min	Nonzero	
Normalized Number	X	NotMM	X	

Key:

X	does not matter
Max	maximum value that can be stored in the field (all 1's)
Min	minimum value that can be stored in the field (all 0's)
NaN	not a number
NotMM	field is not equal to either Min or Max values
Nonzero	field contains at least one "1" bit
MSB	Most Significant Bit

The algorithm for classification of a value into special cases follows:

```
If (Exponent==Max)
    If (Fraction==Min)
        Then the number is Infinity (Positive or Negative
        as determined by the Sign bit).
    Else the number is NaN (Trapping if FractionMSB==0,
    non-Trapping if FractionMSB==1).

Else If (Exponent==Min)
    If (Fraction==Min)
```

>   Then the number is Zero (Positive or Negative
>   as determined by the Sign bit).
>   Else the number is Denormalized.
>   Else the number is Normalized.

NaNs and Infinities

The floating point system supports two special representations:

- Infinity –Positive infinity in a format compares greater than all other representable numbers in the same format. Arithmetic operations on infinities are quite intuitive. For example, adding any representable number to infinity is a valid operation the result of which is positive infinity. Subtracting positive infinity from itself is invalid. If some arithmetic operation overflows, and the overflow trap is disabled, in some rounding modes the result is infinity.

- Not-a-Number (NaN)– These floating point representations are not numbers. They can be used to carry diagnostic information. There are two kinds of NaNs: signaling NaNs and quiet NaNs. Signaling NaNs raise the invalid operation exception whenever they are used as operands in floating point operations. Quiet NaNs propagate through most operations without raising any exception. The result of these operations is the same quiet NaN. NaNs are sometimes produced by the arithmetic operations themselves. For example, 0.0 divided by 0.0, when the invalid operation trap is disabled, produces a quiet NaN.

The header file `ieeefp.h` defines the interface for the floating point exception and environment control. This header defines three interfaces:

- Rounding Control
- Exception Control
- Exception Handling

Rounding Control

The floating point arithmetic provides four rounding modes that affect the result of most floating point operations. (These modes are defined in the header ieeefp.h):

FP_RN	round to nearest representable number, tie -> even
FP_RP	round toward plus infinity
FP_RM	round toward minus infinity
FP_RZ	round toward zero (truncate)

You can check the current rounding mode with the function

```
fp_rnd fpgetround(void); /* return current rounding mode */
```

You can change the rounding mode for floating point operations with the function:

```
fp_rnd fpsetround(fp_rnd); /* set rounding mode, */
                           /* return previous */
```

(fp_rnd is an enumeration type with the enumeration constants listed and described above. The values for these constants are in ieeefp.h.)

NOTE The examples in this section, such as the one directly above, illustrate function prototypes. For information on function prototypes, see "Function Definitions" in Chapter 3 of this guide.

The default rounding mode is round-to-nearest. In C and FORTRAN (F77), floating point to integer conversions are always done by truncation, and the current rounding mode has no effect on these operations.

(For more information on fpgetround() and fpsetround(), see the fpgetround() manual page in the *Programmer's Reference Manual*.)

Exceptions, Sticky Bits, and Trap Bits

Floating point operations can lead to any of the following types of floating point exceptions:

- Divide by zero exception

  This exception happens when a non-zero number is divided by floating point zero.

- Invalid operation exception

  All operations on signaling NaNs raise an invalid operation exception. Zero divided by zero, infinity subtracted from infinity, infinity divided by infinity all raise this exception. When a quiet NaN is compared with the greater or lesser relational operators, an invalid operation exception is raised.

- Overflow exception

  This exception occurs when the result of any floating point operation is too large in magnitude to fit in the intended destination.

- Underflow exception

  When the underflow trap is enabled, an underflow exception is signaled when the result of some operation is a very tiny non-zero number that may cause some other exception later (such as overflow upon division). When the underflow trap is disabled, an underflow exception occurs only when both the result is very tiny (as explained above) and a loss of accuracy is detected.

- Inexact or imprecise exception

  This exception is signaled if the rounded result of an operation is not identical to the infinitely precise result. Inexact exceptions are quite common. 1.0 / 3.0 is an inexact operation. Inexact exceptions also occur when the operation overflows without an overflow trap.

The above examples for the exception types do not constitute an exhaustive list of the conditions when an exception can occur.

The floating point implementation on the 6386 computer includes another exception type called "Denormalization exception." This exception occurs when the result of an expression is a denormalized number.

Whenever an exception occurs, a corresponding sticky bit is set (=1) for that exception. The sticky bits are all cleared at the start of a process. Individual sticky bits are cleared when the corresponding trap is enabled using fpsetmask(). Otherwise, the bits are never cleared, but remain set to indicate that an exception occurred.

You can check the status of the sticky bits by using the function

```
fp_except fpgetsticky(void);   /* return logged exceptions */
```

fp_except is an integer type that can have any combination of the following constant values:

FP_X_DZ	divide-by-zero exception
FP_X_INV	invalid operation exception
FP_X_OFL	overflow exception
FP_X_UFL	underflow exception
FP_X_IMP	imprecise (loss of precision)
FP_X_DNML	denormalization exception (6386 computer only)

(The hexadecimal values for these constants are in ieeefp.h.)

You can change the sticky bits by using the function

```
fp_except fpsetsticky(fp_except);   /* set logged excep- */
                                    /* tions, return previous */
```

There is also a trap-enable bit (mask bit) associated with each exception. When an exception occurs, if the corresponding trap bit is enabled (=1), a trap occurs. When a trap occurs, the result of the operation is not written and a signal is sent to the user process. You can check the status of these mask bits by using the function

```
fp_except fpgetmask(void);    /* current exception mask */
```

You can also selectively enable or disable any of the exceptions by calling the
function

```
fp_except fpsetmask(fp_except);     /* set mask, */
                                    /* return previous */
```

with appropriate mask values.

All the exceptions are masked by default to conform to the IEEE requirements.

(For more information on fpgetsticky(), fpsetsticky(), fpgetmask(), and
fpsetmask(), see the fpgetround() manual page in the *Programmer's Reference
Manual*.)

Exception Handling on the 3B2 Computer

If a floating point trap is enabled, your process is signaled when the
corresponding floating point exception occurs. The UNIX system signals your
process by sending SIGFPE. If you intend to handle the exception, you must
include the file ieeefp.h in at least one module of the program and specify a
handler for SIGFPE. You can specify the handler by calling the signal() routine as follows:

```
#include <signal.h>

extern void myhandler ();

foo ()
{
    (void) signal (SIGFPE, myhandler);
}
```

When a trap takes place, the state of the co-processor is saved and the co-
processor is re-initialized. This method allows floating point operations within
a signal handler.

On the 3B2 computer, when a floating point exception handler is entered, two
global variables are set:

_fpftype   floating point fault type

                  _fpftype identifies the primary exception type. Possible
                  values for _fpftype are FP_UFLW, FP_DIVZ, INT_DIVZ, etc.
                  (See the header file ieeefp.h.)

_fpfault   pointer to floating point exception structure

                  _fpfault points to a structure that provides all other infor-
                  mation about the floating point operation. The information
                  that _fpfault points to includes the type of operation being
                  performed, the types and values of the operands, the type of
                  a trapped value (if any), and the desired type of the result:

```
struct fp_fault {
    fp_op   operation;
    fp_dunion   operand[2];
    fp_dunion   t_value;
    fp_dunion   result;
};

extern struct fp_fault * _fpfault;
```

The operation field identifies the floating point operation that raised the exception. The possible values are included in ieeefp.h. fp_dunion is a discrim-
inated union that contains information about the type and format of the
operands or result. (For example, fp_dunion contains information on whether
the operand is in single-precision or double-precision). It also contains the actual
values. See ieeefp.h for exact definitions of fp_op and fp_dunion.

A user handler has the information about the floating point operation, the
operands, the computed result, and the format in which the result is to be
returned. The user handler can supply a result (by assignment to
_fpfault->result) in the right format, and when the handler returns, this
result is used to complete the floating point operation. If no result is assigned
by the user handler, a default result of 0.0 is used.

Exception Handling on the 6386 Computer

 NOTE You cannot perform exception handling on the 6386 computer unless it is equipped with a math co-processor.

If a floating point trap is enabled, your process is signaled when the corresponding floating point exception occurs. The UNIX system signals your process by sending SIGFPE. If you intend to handle the exception, you must include the file ieeefp.h in at least one module of the program and specify a handler for SIGFPE. You can specify the handler by calling the signal() routine as follows:

```
#include <signal.h>

extern void myhandler ();

foo ()
{
    (void) signal (SIGFPE, myhandler);
}
```

When a trap takes place, the state of the co-processor is saved and the co-processor is re-initialized. This method allows floating point operations within a signal handler.

The signal handler receives a single argument of type struct _fpstackframe (defined in ieeefp.h) that contains the following information on the co-processor state at the time of the exception: program counter, general and floating point registers, data address if the floating point operation involved a memory location, co-processor status and control registers. This state information is restored when the signal handler returns, so you can control the state of the co-processor by modifying the data contained in the _fpstackframe structure.

Conversion Between Binary and Decimal Values

 NOTE The functionality for conversion between binary and decimal values is not available on the 6386 computer.

There are four functions in the C library that allow the programmer to convert binary values to binary coded decimal (BCD) values, and vice versa. These functions are _s2dec(), _d2dec(), _dec2s(), and _dec2d(). They are described in this chapter and on the decconv() manual page in the *Programmer's Reference Manual*.

All of the conversion functions use the following structure found in ieeefp.h:

```
typedef struct decimal { /* ascii-decimal floating point    */
        char *i;            /* significand ascii digit string */
        char *e;            /* exponent ascii digit string    */
        char sign;          /* sign of number                 */
                            /*    0    +                       */
                            /*    1    -                       */
        char esign;         /* sign of exponent               */
                            /*    0    +                       */
                            /*    1    -                       */
                            /*    2    NaN                     */
                            /*    3    infinity                */
        int ilen;           /* # digits in significand        */
        int elen;           /* # digits in exponent           */
        } decimal;
```

The _s2dec() function returns a decimal floating point value, given a pointer to a single-precision binary floating point number (float *x) and a precision specification (int p).

```
void _s2dec (float *x, decimal *d, int p);
```

On input, you should set the value of the ilen field (for rounding purposes) in the decimal structure to the number of decimal digits to output in the significand. If the ilen field is not in the range of 1 to 9, a NaN is returned in the esign field. If the input binary value pointed to by x is a NaN or infinity, the value returned in d is a NaN or infinity with the appropriate sign. The exponential component of the returned decimal value is always two digits.

The parameter p ($0 \leq p \leq$ ilen) specifies how many of the digits in the output decimal significand string are to the right of the implicit decimal point. If p is out of range, a NaN is returned.

The _d2dec() function works like the _s2dec() function except that it takes a pointer to a double-precision value for x. The ilen field must be in the range from 1 to 17, and the exponential component of the returned decimal is always three digits (elen = 3).

```
void _d2dec (double *x, decimal *d, int p);
```

The _dec2s() function returns a single-precision binary floating point value, given a decimal value and a precision specification.

```
void _dec2s (decimal *d, float *x, int p);
```

The parameter p ($0 \leq p \leq$ ilen) tells how many of the digits in the significand string are to the right of an implicit decimal point.

Because the decimal format can represent a larger range of numbers than the binary formats, this conversion may overflow or underflow. Upon overflow or underflow, a signed infinity (signed zero) is returned, and the appropriate sticky bit is set.

The significand and exponent strings may contain leading zero characters. But, once all leading 0 characters are removed, the significand string should have a length between 1 and 9 digits. The exponent string should have a length (specified by elen) between 1 and 2 digits.

The _dec2d() function is analogous to the _dec2s() function except that it returns a double-precision value. After leading zero characters are removed, the significand string should have a length of no more than 17 digits and the exponent string should have a length (specified by elen) of no more than three digits.

```
void _dec2d (decimal *d, double *x, int p);
```

The conversion library functions use the round control, mask, and sticky bits just like any other floating point operation. Rounding is performed according to the current rounding mode. The default mode is round-to-nearest.

The conversion functions will set the following sticky bits, if appropriate:

- overflow

- underflow

- inexact result

- invalid operation

If a trap occurs, the usual trap handling conventions are used. Thus, a trap handler that the user may have specified via signal() will also catch exceptions encountered during conversions between binary and decimal values. When a trap occurs, the following happens:

- the global variable _fpftype will be set to FP_CONV

- the global variable _fpfault will point to the floating point exception structure

- the user's trap handler will be called

If the conversion was to decimal, the source operand will be either single- or double-precision and the intermediate result (the t_value field) will be decimal.

If the conversion was from decimal, the source operand will be decimal and the result type will indicate the size of the expected result (i.e., single or double). The t_value field will be the same size as the result size unless an overflow or underflow occurred. In the case of an overflow or an underflow, an extended precision value will be returned with the exponent adjusted by 192 for single-precision or 1536 for double-precision.

If the trap handler does not supply a return value when a trap occurs, the default zero value will be returned.

Single-Precision Floating Point Operations

The ANSI standard for C has a provision that allows expressions to be evaluated in single-precision arithmetic if there is no double (or long double) operand in the expression. The C compiler supports this provision.

Floating point constants are double-precision, unless explicitly stated to be float. For example, in the statements

```
float a,b;
    ...
a = b + 1.0;
```

because the constant 1.0 has type double, b is promoted to double before the addition and the result is converted back to float. However, the constant can be made explicitly a float:

```
a = b + 1.0f;
    or
a = b + (float) 1.0;
```

In this case, the statement can potentially be compiled to a single instruction. Single-precision operations tend to be faster than double-precision operations.

Whether a computation can be done in single-precision is decided based on the operands of each operator. Consider the following:

```
float s;
double d;

d = d + s * s;
```

s * s is computed to produce a single-precision result, which is promoted to double-precision and added to d.

 NOTE The IEEE P854 task force responsible for format independent floating point environment issues may disallow the multiplication to be carried in single-precision in this context; a future release of the C compilation system may be modified to take that into account.

Note that using single-precision (as versus double-precision) arithmetic can result in loss of precision, as illustrated in the following example.

```
float f  = 8191.f * 8191.f;     /* evaluate as a float  */
double d = 8191.  * 8191. ;     /* evaluate as a double */
printf ("As float:  %f\nAs double: %f\n", f, d);
```

The result is:

```
As float:   67092480.000000
As double:  67092481.000000
```

Also, long int variables (same as int) have more precision than float variables. Consider the following example:

```
int i,j;
i = 0x7ffffff;
j = i * 1.0;
printf("j = %x\n", j);
j = i * 1.0f;
printf("j = %x\n", j);
```

The first printf() statement outputs 7ffffff, while the second prints 0. The second printf() prints 0 because the nearest float to 0x7fffffff has a value of 0x80000000. When the value is converted to an integer, the result is 0, and a floating point imprecise result exception occurs. A trap occurs if this exception was enabled.

A function that is declared to return a float may actually return either a float or a double. If the function declaration is a prototype declaration in which at least one of the parameters is float, the function returns a float. Otherwise, it returns a double with precision limited to that of a float. (All of this is transparent.) For example:

```
float retflt(float);    /* actually returns a float  */
float retdbl1();        /* actually returns a double */
float retdbl2(int);     /* actually returns a double */
```

Arguments work as follows:

```
double takeflt(float x);    /* takes a float  */

double takedbl(x)
float x;                    /* takes a double */
```

Single-Precision Functions

The math library (libm) contains single-precision versions of several functions. These floating point functions all have names that end in f, take and return floats, and do most internal computations in single-precision arithmetic. For a complete list of floating point functions in the math library, see "Math Library" in Chapter 2 of this guide.

Floating point functions in a separate library, libsfm, are also available. This special-purpose, single-precision assembly source math library contains the functions sinf(), cosf(), tanf(), asinf(), acosf(), atanf(), expf(), logf(), log10f(), powf(), and sqrtf(). The routines in this source library are in-line expanded by the optimizer to provide faster execution by reducing the overhead of argument passing, function calling and returning, and return value passing. The source library is designed for applications that desire an increase in speed at the potential cost of size.

 libsfm should be used only when necessary and with extreme caution. This library is a special purpose library that does not do domain reduction or error checking. In other words, these functions never call matherr(), and arguments are not reduced to be within a finite range.

 libsfm is not available on the 6386 computer.

In libsfm, inputs to sinf() and cosf() must be in the range: $-\dfrac{\pi}{2} \leq x \leq \dfrac{\pi}{2}$; for tanf(), the range is $-\dfrac{\pi}{2} < x < \dfrac{\pi}{2}$; for sqrtf(), logf(), and log10f(), inputs must be greater than 0.

Double-Extended-Precision

The C compiler does not produce code that uses IEEE double-extended-precision arithmetic, either for intermediate or final results. All results are computed with the precision implicit in their type.

The proposed ANSI standard for C (X3J11/88-090) includes a new data type called long double, which could possibly map to the IEEE double-extended-precision format. ANSI C does not require a long double to be wider than a double.

The C compilation system handles long double in a limited fashion. When you use the −Xc option to the cc command, the compiler treats a long double as computationally equivalent to a double. When you use the −Xt or −Xa options, the compiler treats a long double as an error.

 NOTE AT&T intends to fully support long double in the future. However, because of compatibility constraints, we recommend that you do not use long double as of this issue of C.

IEEE Requirements

All arithmetic computations generated by the C compiler strictly conform to IEEE requirements. The following is a discussion of some topics where the C compilation system falls short of completely meeting the ANSI/IEEE Standard 754-1985 requirements or the spirit of the requirements.

Conversion of Floating Point Formats to Integer

IEEE requires floating point to integer format conversions to be affected by the current rounding mode. However, the C language requires these conversions to be done by truncation (which is the same as round-to-zero). In the C compilation system floating point to integer conversions are done by truncation.

Conversion of floating point numbers to integers should signal integer overflow or invalid operation for an overflow condition. In the current implementation the integer overflow flag is set, but there is no way to enable the overflow trap. Enabling the integer overflow trap would result in a substantial performance penalty due to stalled pipeline effects.

The C compilation system provides the rint() function for IEEE- style conversion from floating point to integers. For information on the rint() function, see the floor() manual page in the *Programmer's Reference Manual*.

Square Root

IEEE requires the square root of a negative non-zero number to raise invalid operation, whereas UNIX system compatibility requires square root to return 0.0 with errno set to EDOM. When you use the –Xt option to the cc command, the sqrt() routine in the C compilation system returns 0.0 for negative non-zero inputs. Otherwise, the –Xt option operation conforms to IEEE requirements. When you use the –Xa or –Xc option, the square root of a negative non-zero number raises invalid operation and returns a NaN, in strict conformance with the IEEE standard.

Compares and Unordered Condition

In addition to the usual relationships between floating point values (less than, equal, greater than), there is a fourth relationship: unordered. The unordered case arises when at least one operand is a NaN. Every NaN compares unordered with any value, including itself.

The C compilation system provides the following predicates required by IEEE between floating point operands:

$$
\begin{array}{ll}
== & >= \\
!= & < \\
> & <=
\end{array}
$$

While there is no predicate to test for unordered, you can use isnand() or isnanf() to test whether an argument is a NaN. For information on isnand() and isnanf(), see the isnan() manual page in the *Programmer's Reference Manual*.

The relations >, >=, <, and <= raise invalid operation for unordered operands. The compiler generated code does not guard against the unordered outcome of a comparison. If the trap is masked, the path taken for unordered conditions is the same as if the conditional were true, which may result in incorrect behavior.

For the predicates == and !=, unordered condition does not lead to invalid operation. The path taken for unordered condition is the same as when the operands are non-equal, which is correct.

(a > b) is not the same as (!(a <= b)) in IEEE floating point arithmetic. The difference occurs when b or a compares unordered. The C compiler generates the same code for both cases.

NaNs and Infinities in Input/Output

The printf() family of functions prints NaNs or infinities. NaNs are printed with their diagnostic values.

Ideally, whatever printf() outputs, scanf() should be able to read using the same format. However, scanf() does not recognize NaNs and infinities for floating point formats. However, since these special cases serve mostly as diagnostics for erroneous floating point computation, outputting these cases was considered more important than being able to read them.

Conversion to and from Decimal

 NOTE The functionality for conversion between binary and decimal values is not available on the 6386 computer.

While IEEE requires functions for converting to and from decimal, it does not specify the format of decimal numbers. The routines on the decconv() manual page provide a common form of binary coded decimal (BCD).

For C programmers, the printf() and scanf() routines are probably more useful. The accuracy of conversion in these routines meets the IEEE requirements. However, these routines always work in the round-to-nearest mode. The current rounding mode has no effect on them.

15 m4 Macro Processor

Overview

m4 is a general purpose macro processor that can be used to preprocess C and assembly language programs, among other things. Besides the straightforward replacement of one string of text by another, m4 lets you perform

- integer arithmetic
- file inclusion
- conditional macro expansion
- string and substring manipulation

You can use built-in macros to perform these tasks or define your own macros. Built-in and user-defined macros work exactly the same way except that some of the built-in macros have side effects on the state of the process. A list of built-in macros appears on the m4 page in Section 1 of the *Programmer's Reference Manual*.

The basic operation of m4 is to read every alphanumeric token (string of letters and digits) and determine if the token is the name of a macro. The name of the macro is replaced by its defining text, and the resulting string is pushed back onto the input to be rescanned. Macros may be called with arguments. The arguments are collected and substituted into the right places in the defining text before the defining text is rescanned.

Macro calls have the general form

      name (*arg1*, *arg2*, ..., *argn*)

If a macro name is not immediately followed by a left parenthesis, it is assumed to have no arguments. Leading unquoted blanks, tabs, and new-lines are ignored while collecting arguments. Left and right single quotes are used to quote strings. The value of a quoted string is the string stripped of the quotes.

When a macro name is recognized, its arguments are collected by searching for a matching right parenthesis. If fewer arguments are supplied than are in the macro definition, the trailing arguments are taken to be null. Macro evaluation proceeds normally during the collection of the arguments, and any commas or right parentheses that appear in the value of a nested call are as effective as those in the original input text. After argument collection, the value of the macro is pushed back onto the input stream and rescanned. We'll explain all this in more detail below.

You invoke m4 with a command of the form

> $ m4 *file file file*

Each argument file is processed in order. If there are no arguments or if an argument is a hyphen, the standard input is read. If you are eventually going to compile the m4 output, you could use a command something like this:

> $ m4 file1.m4 > file1.c

You can use the −D option to define a macro on the m4 command line. Suppose you have two similar versions of a program. You might have a single m4 input file capable of generating the two output files. That is, file1.m4 could contain lines such as

> if(VER, 1, *do_something*)
> if(VER, 2, *do_something*)

Your makefile for the program might look like this:

```
file1.1.c : file1.m4
            m4 -DVER=1 file1.m4 > file1.1.c
            . . .

file1.2.c : file1.m4
            m4 -DVER=2 file1.m4 > file1.2.c
            . . .
```

You can use the −U option to "undefine" VER. If file1.m4 contains

> if(VER, 1, *do_something*)
> if(VER, 2, *do_something*)
> ifndef(VER, *do_something*)

then your makefile would contain

```
file0.0.c : file1.m4
             m4 -UVER file1.m4 > file1.0.c
             ...

file1.1.c : file1.m4
             m4 -DVER=1 file1.m4 > file1.1.c
             ...

file1.2.c : file1.m4
             m4 -DVER=2 file1.m4 > file1.2.c
             ...
```

m4 Macros

Defining Macros

The primary built-in m4 macro is define(), which is used to define new macros. The following input

        define (*name, stuff*)

causes the string *name* to be defined as *stuff*. All subsequent occurrences of *name* will be replaced by *stuff*. The defined string must be alphanumeric and must begin with a letter (underscore counts as a letter). The defining string is any text that contains balanced parentheses; it may stretch over multiple lines. As a typical example

        define (N, 100)
        . . .
        if (i > N)

defines N to be 100 and uses the "symbolic constant" N in a later if statement. As noted, the left parenthesis must immediately follow the word define to signal that define() has arguments. If the macro name is not immediately followed by a left parenthesis, it is assumed to have no arguments. In the previous example, then, N is a macro with no arguments.

A macro name is only recognized as such if it appears surrounded by non-alphanumeric characters. In the following example

        define (N, 100)
        . . .
        if (NNN > 100)

the variable NNN is unrelated to the defined macro N even though the variable contains Ns.

m4 expands macro names into their defining text as soon as possible. So

        define (N, 100)
        define (M, N)

defines M to be 100 because the string N is immediately replaced by 100 as the arguments of define (M, N) are collected. To put this another way, if N is redefined, M keeps the value 100.

There are two ways to avoid this behavior. The first, which is specific to the situation described here, is to interchange the order of the definitions:

```
define(M, N)
define(N, 100)
```

Now M is defined to be the string N, so when the value of M is requested later, the result will always be the value of N at that time (because the M will be replaced by N which will be replaced by 100).

Quoting

The more general solution is to delay the expansion of the arguments of define() by quoting them. Any text surrounded by left and right single quotes is not expanded immediately, but has the quotes stripped off as the arguments are collected. The value of the quoted string is the string stripped of the quotes. So

```
define(N, 100)
define(M, `N')
```

defines M as the string N, not 100.

The general rule is that m4 always strips off one level of single quotes whenever it evaluates something. This is true even outside of macros. If the word define is to appear in the output, the word must be quoted in the input:

```
`define' = 1;
```

It's usually best to quote the arguments of a macro to assure that what you are assigning to the macro name actually gets assigned. To redefine N, for example, you delay its evaluation by quoting:

```
define(N, 100)
  ...
define(`N', 200)
```

Otherwise

```
define(N, 100)
  ...
define(N, 200)
```

the N in the second definition is immediately replaced by 100. The effect is the same as saying

        define(100, 200)

Note that this statement will be ignored by m4 since only things that look like names can be defined.

If left and right single quotes are not convenient for some reason, the quote characters can be changed with the built-in macro changequote():

        changequote([,])

In this example the macro makes the "quote" characters the left and right brackets instead of the left and right single quotes. The quote symbols can be up to five characters long. The original characters can be restored by using changequote() without arguments:

        changequote

undefine() removes the definition of a macro or built-in:

        undefine('N')

Here the macro removes the definition of N. Be sure to quote the argument to undefine(). Built-ins can be removed with undefine() as well:

        undefine('define')

Note that once a built-in is removed or redefined, its original definition cannot be reused.

Macros can be renamed with defn(). Suppose you want the built-in define() to be called XYZ(). You specify

        define(XYZ, defn('define'))
        undefine('define')

After this, XYZ() takes on the original meaning of define(). So

        XYZ(A, 100)

defines A to be 100.

The built-in `ifdef()` provides a way to determine if a macro is currently defined. Depending on the system, a definition appropriate for the particular machine can be made as follows:

```
ifdef('pdp11', 'define(wordsize,16)')
ifdef('u3b', 'define(wordsize,32)')
```

The `ifdef()` macro permits three arguments. If the first argument is defined, the value of `ifdef()` is the second argument. If the first argument is not defined, the value of `ifdef()` is the third argument:

```
ifdef('unix', on UNIX, not on UNIX)
```

If there is no third argument, the value of `ifdef()` is null.

Arguments

So far we have discussed the simplest form of macro processing — replacing one string with another (fixed) string. Macros can also be defined so that different invocations have different results. In the replacement text for a macro (the second argument of its `define()`), any occurrence of $n is replaced by the nth argument when the macro is actually used. So the macro `bump()`, defined as

```
define(bump, $1 = $1 + 1)
```

is equivalent to `x = x + 1` for `bump(x)`.

A macro can have as many arguments as you want, but only the first nine are accessible individually, $1 through $9. $0 refers to the macro name itself. As noted, arguments that are not supplied are replaced by null strings, so a macro can be defined that simply concatenates its arguments:

```
define(cat, $1$2$3$4$5$6$7$8$9)
```

That is, `cat(x, y, z)` is equivalent to `xyz`. Arguments $4 through $9 are null since no corresponding arguments were provided.

Leading unquoted blanks, tabs, or new-lines that occur during argument collection are discarded. All other white space is retained, so

```
define(a,    b    c)
```

defines `a` to be `b    c`.

Arguments are separated by commas. A comma "protected" by parentheses does not terminate an argument:

```
define(a,  (b,c))
```

has two arguments, a and (b,c). You can specify a comma or parenthesis as an argument by quoting it.

$* is replaced by a list of the arguments given to the macro in a subsequent invocation. The listed arguments are separated by commas. So

```
define(a,  1)
define(b,  2)
define(star,  '$*')
star(a,  b)
```

gives the result 1,2. So does

```
star('a',  'b')
```

because m4 strips the quotes from a and b as it collects the arguments of star(), then expands a and b when it evaluates star().

$@ is identical to $* except that each argument in the subsequent invocation is quoted. That is,

```
define(a,  1)
define(b,  2)
define(at,  '$@')
at('a',  'b')
```

gives the result a,b because the quotes are put back on the arguments when at() is evaluated.

$# is replaced by the number of arguments in the subsequent invocation. So

```
define(sharp,  '$#')
sharp(1,  2,  3)
```

gives the result 3,

```
sharp()
```

gives the result 1, and

```
sharp
```

gives the result 0.

The built-in shift () returns all but its first argument. The other arguments
are quoted and pushed back onto the input with commas in between. The simplest case

```
shift (1, 2, 3)
```

gives 2,3. As with $@, you can delay the expansion of the arguments by quot-
ing them, so

```
define (a, 100)
define (b, 200)
shift ('a', 'b')
```

gives the result b because the quotes are put back on the arguments when
shift () is evaluated.

Arithmetic Built-Ins

m4 provides three built-in macros for doing integer arithmetic. incr () increments its numeric argument by 1. decr () decrements by 1. So to handle the
common programming situation in which a variable is to be defined as "one
more than N" you would use

```
define (N, 100)
define (N1, 'incr (N) ')
```

That is, N1 is defined as one more than the current value of N.

The more general mechanism for arithmetic is a built-in called eval (), which is
capable of arbitrary arithmetic on integers. Its operators in decreasing order of
precedence are

```
+  -  (unary)
**
*  /  %
+  -
==  !=  <  <=  >  >=
!  ~
&
|  ^
&&
||
```

Parentheses may be used to group operations where needed. All the operands of an expression given to eval() must ultimately be numeric. The numeric value of a true relation (like 1 > 0) is 1, and false is 0. The precision in eval() is 32 bits on the UNIX system.

As a simple example, you can define M to be 2**N+1 with

```
define(M, `eval(2**N+1)')
```

Then the sequence

```
define(N, 3)
M(2)
```

gives 9 as the result.

File Inclusion

A new file can be included in the input at any time with the built-in macro include():

```
include(filename)
```

inserts the contents of *filename* in place of the macro and its argument. The value of include() (its replacement text) is the contents of the file. If needed, the contents can be captured in definitions and so on.

A fatal error occurs if the file named in include() cannot be accessed. To get some control over this situation, the alternate form sinclude() ("silent include") can be used. This built-in says nothing and continues if the file named cannot be accessed.

Diversions

m4 output can be diverted to temporary files during processing, and the collected material can be output on command. m4 maintains nine of these diversions, numbered 1 through 9. If the built-in macro divert (*n*) is used, all subsequent output is put onto the end of a temporary file referred to as *n*. Diverting to this file is stopped by the divert () or divert (0) macros, which resume the normal output process.

Diverted text is normally output at the end of processing in numerical order. Diversions can be brought back at any time by appending the new diversion to the current diversion. Output diverted to a stream other than 0 through 9 is discarded. The built-in undivert () brings back all diversions in numerical order; undivert () with arguments brings back the selected diversions in the order given. Undiverting discards the diverted text (as does diverting) into a diversion whose number is not between 0 and 9, inclusive.

The value of undivert () is *not* the diverted text. Furthermore, the diverted material is *not* rescanned for macros. The built-in divnum () returns the number of the currently active diversion. The current output stream is 0 during normal processing.

System Command

Any program can be run by using the syscmd () built-in:

        syscmd (date)

invokes the UNIX system date command. Normally, syscmd () would be used to create a file for a subsequent include ().

To make it easy to name files uniquely, the built-in maketemp () replaces a string of XXXXX in the argument with the process ID of the current process.

Conditionals

Arbitrary conditional testing is performed with the built-in ifelse(). In its simplest form

>   ifelse(a, b, c, d)

compares the two strings *a* and *b*. If *a* and *b* are identical, ifelse() returns the string *c*. Otherwise, string *d* is returned. Thus, a macro called compare() can be defined as one that compares two strings and returns yes or no, respectively, if they are the same or different:

>   define(compare, 'ifelse($1, $2, yes, no)')

Note the quotes, which prevent evaluation of ifelse() from occurring too early. If the final argument is omitted, the result is null, so

>   ifelse(a, b, c)

is *c* if *a* matches *b*, and null otherwise.

ifelse() can actually have any number of arguments and provides a limited form of multiway decision capability. In the input

>   ifelse(a, b, c, d, e, f, g)

if the string *a* matches the string *b*, the result is *c*. Otherwise, if *d* is the same as *e*, the result is *f*. Otherwise, the result is *g*.

String Manipulation

The len() macro returns the length of the string (number of characters) in its argument. So

>   len(abcdef)

is 6, and

>   len((a,b))

is 5.

The `substr()` macro can be used to produce substrings of strings. So

>   substr(s, i, n)

returns the substring of s that starts at the *i*th position (origin 0) and is *n* characters long. If *n* is omitted, the rest of the string is returned. Inputting

>   substr('now is the time',1)

returns the following string:

>   ow is the time

If *i* or *n* are out of range, various sensible things happen.

The `index(s1, s2)` macro returns the index (position) in s1 where the string s2
occurs, −1 if it does not occur. As with `substr()`, the origin for strings is 0.

`translit()` performs character transliteration and has the general form

>   translit(s, f, t)

which modifies s by replacing any character in *f* by the corresponding character
in *t*. Using input

>   translit(s, aeiou, 12345)

replaces the vowels by the corresponding digits. If *t* is shorter than *f*, characters
that do not have an entry in *t* are deleted. As a limiting case, if *t* is not present
at all, characters from *f* are deleted from s. So

>   translit(s, aeiou)

would delete vowels from s.

The macro `dnl()` deletes all characters that follow it up to and including the
next new-line. It is useful mainly for throwing away empty lines that otherwise
would clutter up m4 output. Using input

>   define(N, 100)
>   define(M, 200)
>   define(L, 300)

results in a new-line at the end of each line that is not part of the definition. So
the new-line is copied into the output where it may not be wanted. When you
add `dnl()` to each of these lines, the new-lines will disappear. Another method
of achieving the same result is to input

```
divert (–1)
define (...)
   ...
divert
```

Printing

The built-in errprint () writes its arguments out on the standard error file.
An example would be

```
errprint ('fatal error')
```

dumpdef () is a debugging aid that dumps the current names and definitions of
items specified as arguments. If no arguments are given, then all current names
and definitions are printed.

A Appendix A: Enhanced asm Facility

Introduction

Although the ability to write portable code is one reason for using the C
language, sometimes it is necessary to introduce machine-specific assembly
language instructions into C code. This need arises most often within operating
system code that must deal with hardware registers that would otherwise be
inaccessible from C. The asm facility makes it possible to introduce this assembly code.

In earlier versions of C the asm facility was primitive. You included a line that
looked like a call on the function asm, which took one argument, a string:

```
asm("assembly instruction here");
```

Unfortunately this technique has shortcomings when the assembly instruction
needs to reference C language operands. You have to guess the register or stack
location into which the compiler would put the operand and encode that location into the instruction. If the compiler's allocation scheme changed, or, more
likely, if the C code surrounding the asm changed, the correct location for the
operand in the asm would also change. That is, you would have to be aware
that the C code would affect the asm and change it accordingly.

The new facility is upwardly compatible with old code, since it retains the old
capability. In addition, it allows you to define asm macros that describe how
machine instructions should be generated when their operands take particular
forms that the compiler knows about, such as register or stack variables.

 NOTE Although this enhanced asm facility is easier to use than before, you are still
strongly discouraged from using it for routine applications because those
applications will not be portable to different machines. The primary intended
use of the asm facility is to help implement operating systems in a clean way.

The optimizer (cc −O) may work incorrectly on C programs that use the asm
facility, particularly when the asm macros contain instructions or labels that are
unlike those that the C compiler generates. Furthermore, you may need to
rewrite asm code in the future to maximize its benefits as new optimization
technology is introduced into the compilation system.

Example

Before we get into the details of the asm facility, let us consider a hypothetical example. Imagine a machine with an spl instruction for setting machine interrupt priority levels. spl takes one operand, which must be in a register. Nevertheless, it would be convenient to have a function that produces in-line code to set priority levels, uses the spl instruction, and works with register variables or constants.

Our example consists of two parts, the *definition* of the asm macro, and its *use*.

Definition

We define an asm macro, which we'll call SPL, like this:

```
asm void SPL(newpri)
{
%       reg newpri;
        spl newpri
%       con newpri;
        movw newpri,%r0
        spl %r0
}
```

The lines that begin with % are patterns. If the arguments at the time the macro is called match the *storage modes* in a pattern, the code that follows the pattern line will be expanded.

Use

The table below shows the (assembly) code that the compiler would generate with two different uses of SPL. Imagine the following introductory code (along with the above definition):

```
f() {
        register int i;
```

code...	matches...	generates...
SPL(i);	% reg	spl %r8
SPL(3);	% con	movw &3,%r0 spl %r0

The first use of SPL has a register variable as its argument (assuming that i
actually gets allocated to a register). This argument has a storage mode that
matches reg, the storage mode in the first pattern. Therefore the compiler
expands the first code body. Note that newpri, the formal parameter in the
definition, has been replaced in the expanded code by the compiler's idea of the
assembly time name for the variable i, namely %r8. Similarly, the second use
of SPL has a constant as its argument, which leads to the compiler's choosing
the second pattern. Here again newpri has been replaced by the assembly time
form for the constant, &3.

Definition Of Terms

The example above introduced several terms that will be used in the description that follows. We will define them here.

asm macro

An *asm macro* is the mechanism by which programs use the enhanced asm facility. asm macros have a *definition* and *uses*. The definition includes a set of pattern/body pairs. Each *pattern* describes the *storage modes* that the actual arguments must match for the *asm macro body* to be expanded. The *uses* resemble C function calls.

storage mode

The *storage mode*, or *mode*, of an asm macro argument is the compiler's idea of where the argument can be found at run time. Examples are "in a register" or "in memory."

pattern

A *pattern* specifies the modes for each of the arguments of an asm macro. When the modes in the pattern all match those of the use, the corresponding body is expanded.

asm macro body

The *asm macro body*, or *body*, is the portion of code that will be expanded by the compiler when the corresponding pattern matches. The body may contain references to the formal parameters, in which case the compiler substitutes the corresponding assembly language code.

Detailed Description

Using asm Macros

The enhanced asm facility allows you to define constructs that behave syntactically like static C functions. Each asm macro has one definition and zero or more uses per source file. The definition must appear in the same file with the uses (or be #included), and the same asm macro may be defined multiply (and differently) in several files.

The asm macro definition declares a return type for the macro code, specifies patterns for the formal parameters, and provides bodies of code to expand when the patterns match. When it encounters an asm macro call, the compiler replaces uses of the formal parameters by its idea of the assembly language locations of the actual arguments as it expands the code body. This constitutes an important difference between C functions and asm macros. An asm macro can thus have the effect of changing the value of its arguments, whereas a C function can only change a copy of its argument values.

The uses of an asm macro look exactly like normal C function calls. They may be used in expressions and they may return values. The arguments to an asm macro may be arbitrary expressions, except that they may not contain uses of the same or other asm macros.

When the argument to an asm macro is a function name or structure, the compiler generates code to compute a pointer to the structure or function, and the resulting pointer is used as the actual argument of the macro.

Definition

The syntactic descriptions that follow are presented in the style used in Chapter 3, "C Language." The syntactic classes *type-specifier*, *identifier*, and *parameter-list* have the same form as in that chapter. A syntactic description enclosed in square brackets ([ ]) is optional, unless the right bracket is followed by +. A + means "one or more repetitions" of a description. Similarly, * means "zero or more repetitions."

asm macro:
>   asm [_type-specifier_] _identifier_ ([_parameter-list_])
>   {
>   [_storage-mode-specification-line_
>   _asm-body_] *
>   }

That is, an asm macro consists of the keyword asm, followed by what looks like a C function declaration. Inside the macro body there are one or more pairs of _storage-mode-specification-line(s)_ (patterns) and corresponding _asm-body(ies)_. If the _type-specifier_ is other than void, the asm macro should return a value of the declared type.

storage-mode-specification-line:
>   % [_storage-mode_ [_identifier_ [, _identifier_]*] ;]+

That is, a _storage-mode-specification-line_ consists of a single line (no continuation with \) that begins with % and contains the names (_identifier(s)_) and _storage mode(s)_ of the formal parameters. Modes for all formal parameters must be given in each _storage-mode-specification-line_ (except for error). The % must be the first character on a line. If an asm macro has no _parameter-list_, the _storage-mode-specification-line_ may be omitted.

Storage

These are the storage modes that the compiler recognizes in asm macros.

treg
: A compiler-selected temporary register.

ureg
: A C register variable that the compiler has allocated in a machine register.

reg
: A treg or ureg.

con
: A compile time constant.

mem
: A mem operand matches any allowed machine addressing mode, including reg and con.

lab
: A compiler-generated unique label. The _identifier(s)_ that are specified as being of mode lab do not appear as formal parameters in the asm macro definition, unlike the preceding modes. Such identifiers must be unique.

error   Generate a compiler error. This mode exists to allow you to flag errors at compile time if no appropriate pattern exists for a set of actual arguments.

asm Body

The asm body represents (presumed) assembly code that the compiler will generate when the modes for all of the formal parameters match the associated pattern. Syntactically, the asm body consists of the text between two pattern lines (that begin with %) or between the last pattern line and the } that ends the asm macro. C language comment lines are not recognized as such in the asm body. Instead they are simply considered part of the text to be expanded.

Formal parameter names may appear in any context in the asm body, delimited by non-alphanumeric characters. For each instance of a formal parameter in the asm body the compiler substitutes the appropriate assembly language operand syntax that will access the actual argument at run time. As an example, if one of the actual arguments to an asm macro is x, an automatic variable, a string like 4(%fp) would be substituted for occurrences of the corresponding formal parameter. An important consequence of this macro substitution behavior is that asm macros can change the value of their arguments. Note that this is different from standard C semantics!

For lab parameters a unique label is chosen for each new expansion.

If an asm macro is declared to return a value, it must be coded to return a value of the proper type in the machine register that is appropriate for the implementation.

An implementation restriction requires that no line in the asm body may start with %.

Writing asm Macros

Here are some guidelines for writing asm macros.

1. Know the implementation. You must be familiar with the C compiler and assembly language with which you are working. You can consult the *Application Binary Interface* for your machine for the details of function calling and register usage conventions.

2. Observe register conventions. You should be aware of which registers the C compiler normally uses for scratch registers or register variables. An asm macro may alter scratch registers at will, but the values in register variables must be preserved. You must know in which register(s) the compiler returns function results.

3. Handle return values. asm macros may "return" values. That means they behave as if they were actually functions that had been called via the usual function call mechanism. asm macros must therefore mimic C's behavior in that respect, passing return values in the same place as normal C functions. Note that float and double results sometimes get returned in different registers from integer-type results. On some machine architectures, C functions return pointers in different registers from those used for scalars. Finally, structs may be returned in a variety of implementation-dependent ways.

4. Cover all cases. The asm macro patterns should cover all combinations of storage modes of the parameters. The compiler attempts to match patterns in the order of their appearance in the asm macro definition.

   There are two escape mechanisms for the matching process. If the compiler encounters a storage mode of error while attempting to find a matching pattern, it generates a compile time error for that particular asm macro call. If the asm macro definition lacks an error storage mode and no pattern matches, the compiler generates a normal function call for a function having the same name as the asm macro. Note that such a function would have to be defined in a different source file, since its name would conflict with that of the asm macro.

5. Beware of argument handling. asm macro arguments are used for macro substitution. Thus, unlike normal C functions, asm macros can alter the underlying values that their arguments refer to. Altering argument values is discouraged, however, because doing so would make it impossible to substitute an equivalent C function call for the asm macro call.

6. Try it and see. asm macros are inherently nonportable and implementation-dependent. Although they make it easier to introduce assembly code reliably into C code, the process cannot be made foolproof. You will always need to verify correct behavior by inspection.

7. Debuggers like sdb will generally have difficulty with asm macros. It may be impossible to set breakpoints within the in-line code that the compiler generates.

8. Because optimizers are highly tuned to the normal code generation sequences of the compiler, using asm macros may cause optimizers to produce incorrect code. Generally speaking, any asm macro that can be directly replaced by a comparable C function may be optimized safely. However, the sensitivity of an optimizer to asm macros varies among implementations and may change with new software releases.

B Appendix B: Mapfile Option

Introduction

The ELF linker (ld) automatically and intelligently maps input sections from object files (.o files) to output segments in executable files (a.out files). The mapfile option to the ld command allows you to change the default mapping provided by the ELF linker.

In particular, the mapfile option allows you to:

- declare segments and specify values for segment attributes such as segment type, permissions, addresses, length, and alignment

- control mapping of input sections to segments by specifying the attribute values necessary in a section to map to a specific segment (the attributes are section name, section type, and permissions) and by specifying which object file(s) the input sections should be taken from, if necessary

- declare a global-absolute symbol that is assigned a value equal to the size of a specified segment (by the linker) and that can be referenced from object files

 NOTE The major purpose of the mapfile option is to allow users of *ifiles* (an option previously available to ld that used link editor command language directives) to convert to mapfiles. All other facilities previously available for *ifiles*, other than those mentioned above, are not available with the mapfile option.

 CAUTION When using the mapfile option, be aware that you can easily create a.out files that do not execute. Therefore, the use of the mapfile option is strongly discouraged. ld knows how to produce a correct a.out without the use of the mapfile option. The mapfile option is intended for system programming use, not application programming use.

This appendix describes the structure and syntax of a mapfile and the use of the –M option to the ld command.

Using the Mapfile Option

To use the mapfile option, you must:

1. enter mapfile directives into a file (this is your "mapfile")

2. enter the following option on the ld command line:

    −M *mapfile*

    mapfile is the file name of the file you produced in step 1. If the *mapfile* is not in your current directory, you must include the full path name; no default search path exists. (See the ld manual page for information on operation of the ld command.)

 The mapfile option can only by used in static mode. The −dn option must accompany the −M option on the ld command line or ld returns a fatal error.

Mapfile Structure and Syntax

You can enter three types of directives into a mapfile:

- segment declarations
- mapping directives
- size-symbol declarations

Each directive can span more than one line and can have any amount of white space (including new-lines) as long as it is followed by a semicolon. You can enter 0 (zero) or more directives in a mapfile. (Entering 0 directives causes ld to ignore the mapfile and use its own defaults.) Typically, segment declarations are followed by mapping directives, i.e., you would declare a segment and then define the criteria by which a section becomes part of that segment. If you enter a mapping directive or size-symbol declaration without first declaring the segment to which you are mapping (except for built-in segments, explained later), the segment is given default attributes as explained below. This segment is then an "implicitly declared segment."

Size-symbol declarations can appear anywhere in a mapfile.

The following sections describe each directive type. For all syntax discussions, the following apply:

- All entries in constant width, all colons, semicolons, equal signs, and at (@) signs are typed in literally.

- All entries in italics are substitutables.

- { ... }* means "zero or more."

- { ... }+ means "one or more."

- [...] means "optional."

- *section_names* and *segment_names* follow the same rules as C identifiers where a period (.) is treated as a letter (e.g., .bss is a legal name).

- *section_names*, *segment_names*, *file_names*, and *symbol_names* are case sensitive; everything else is not case sensitive.

- Spaces (or new-lines) may appear anywhere except before a *number* or in the middle of a name or value.

■ Comments beginning with # and ending at a new-line may appear any-where that a space may appear.

Segment Declarations

A segment declaration creates a new segment in the a.out or changes the attri-bute values of an existing segment. (An existing segment is one that you previ-ously defined or one of the three built-in segments described below.)

A segment declaration has the following syntax:

segment_name = {*segment_attribute_value*}* ;

For each *segment_name*, you can specify any number of *segment_attribute_values* in any order, each separated by a space. (Only one attribute value is allowed for each segment attribute.) The segment attributes and their valid values are as follows:

segment_type:	LOAD
	NOTE
segment flags:	?[R][W][X]
virtual_address:	V*number*
physical_address:	P*number*
length:	L*number*
alignment:	A*number*

There are three built-in segments with the following default attribute values:

■ text (LOAD, ?RX, no *virtual_address*, *physical_address*, or *length* specified, *alignment* values set to defaults per CPU type)

■ data (LOAD, ?RWX, no *virtual_address*, *physical_address*, or *length* specified, *alignment* values set to defaults per CPU type)

■ note (NOTE)

ld behaves as if these segments had been declared before your mapfile is read in. See the "Mapfile Option Defaults" section below for more information.

Note the following when entering segment declarations:

- A *number* can be hexadecimal, decimal, or octal, following the same rules as in the C language.

- No space is allowed between the V, P, L, or A and the *number*.

- The *segment_type* value can be either LOAD or NOTE.

- The *segment_type* value defaults to LOAD.

- The *segment_flags* values are R for readable, W for writable, and X for executable. No spaces are allowed between the question mark and the individual flags that make up the *segment_flags* value.

- The *segment_flags* value for a LOAD segment defaults to RWX.

- NOTE segments cannot by assigned any segment attribute value other than a *segment_type*.

- Implicitly declared segments default to *segment_type* value LOAD, *segment_flags* value RWX, a default *virtual_address*, *physical_address*, and *alignment* value, and have no *length* limit.

 ld calculates the addresses and length of the current segment based on the previous segment's attribute values. Also, even though implicitly declared segments default to "no length limit," any machine memory limitations still apply.

- LOAD segments can have an explicitly specified *virtual_address* value and/or *physical_address* value, as well as a maximum segment *length* value.

- If a segment has a *segment_flags* value of ? with nothing following, the value defaults to not readable, not writable and not executable.

- The *alignment* value is used in calculating the virtual address of the beginning of the segment. This alignment only affects the segment for which it is specified; other segments still have the default alignment unless their alignments are also changed.

- If any of the *virtual_address*, *physical_address*, or *length* attribute values are not set, ld calculates these values as it builds the a.out.

■ If an *alignment* value is not specified for a segment, it is set to the built-in default. (The default differs from one CPU to another and may even differ between kernel versions. You should check the appropriate documentation for these numbers).

■ If both a *virtual_address* and an *alignment* value are specified for a segment, the *virtual_address* value takes priority.

■ If a *virtual_address* value is specified for a segment, the alignment field in the program header contains the default *alignment* value.

 If a *virtual_address* value is specified, the segment is placed at that virtual address. For the UNIX system kernel this creates a correct result. For files that start via exec(), this method creates an incorrect a.out file because the segments do not have correct offsets relative to their page boundaries.

Mapping Directives

A mapping directive tells ld how to map input sections to segments. Basically, you name the segment that you are mapping to and indicate what the attributes of a section must be in order to map into the named segment. The set of *section_attribute_value*s that a section must have to map into a specific segment is called the entrance criteria for that segment. In order to be placed in a specified segment of the a.out, a section must meet the entrance criteria for a segment exactly.

A mapping directive has the following syntax:

segment_name : {*section_attribute_value*}* [: {*file_name*}+];

For a *segment_name*, you specify any number of *section_attribute_value*s in any order, each separated by a space. (At most one section attribute value is allowed for each section attribute.) You can also specify that the section must come from a certain .o file(s) via the *file_name* substitutable. The section attributes and their valid values are as follows:

section_name:	any valid section name
section_type:	$PROGBITS
	$SYMTAB
	$STRTAB
	$REL
	$RELA
	$NOTE
	$NOBITS
section_flags:	?[[!]A][[!]W][[!]X]

Note the following when entering mapping directives:

- You must choose at most one *section_type* from the *section_types* listed above. The *section_types* listed above are built-in types. For more information on *section_types*, see Chapter 13, "Object Files."

- The *section_flags* values are A for allocatable, W for writable, or X for executable. If an individual flag is preceded by an exclamation mark (!), the linker checks to make sure that the flag is not set. No spaces are allowed between the question mark, exclamation point(s), and the individual flags that make up the *section_flags* value.

- *file_name* may be any legal file name and can be of the form *archive_name(component_name)*, e.g., /usr/lib/usr/libc.a(printf.o). A file name may be of the form *file_name* (see next bullet item). Note that ld does not check the syntax of file names.

- If a *file_name* is of the form *file_name*, ld simulates a basename (see basename in the *User's Manual*) on the file name from the command line and uses that to match against the mapfile *file_name*. In other words, the *file_name* from the mapfile only needs to match the last part of the file name from the command line. (See "Mapping Example" below.)

- If you use the −l option on the cc or ld command line, and the library after the −l option is in the current directory, you must precede the library with ./ (or the entire path name) in the mapfile in order to create a match.

■ More than one directive line may appear for a particular output segment, e.g., the following set of directives is legal:

```
S1 : $PROGBITS;
S1 : $NOBITS;
```

Entering more than one mapping directive line for a segment is the only way to specify multiple values of a section attribute.

■ A section can match more than one entrance criteria. In this case, the first segment encountered in the mapfile with that entrance criteria is used, e.g., if a mapfile reads:

```
S1 : $PROGBITS;
S2 : $PROGBITS;
```

the $PROGBITS sections are mapped to segment S1.

Size-Symbol Declarations

Size-symbol declarations let you define a new global-absolute symbol that represents the size, in bytes, of the specified segment. This symbol can be referenced in your object files. A size-symbol declaration has the following syntax:

segment_name @ *symbol_name*

symbol_name can be any legal C identifier, although the ld command does not check the syntax of the *symbol_name*.

Mapping Example

Figure B-1 is an example of a user-defined mapfile. The numbers on the left are included in the example for tutorial purposes. Only the information to the right of the numbers would actually appear in the mapfile.

Figure B-1: User-Defined Mapfile

```
1.      elephant : .bss : peanuts.o *popcorn.o;

2.      monkey : $PROGBITS ?AX;
3.      monkey : .bss;
4.      monkey = LOAD V0x80000000 L0x4000;

5.      donkey : .bss;
6.      donkey = ?RX A0x1000;

7.      text = V0x80008000;
```

Four separate segments are manipulated in this example. The implicitly declared segment elephant (line 1) receives all of the .bss sections from the files peanuts.o and popcorn.o. Note that *popcorn.o matches any popcorn.o file that may have been entered on the ld command line; the file need not be in the current directory. On the other hand, if /var/tmp/peanuts.o were entered on the ld command line, it would not match peanuts.o because it is not preceded by a *.

The implicitly declared segment monkey (line 2) receives all sections that are both $PROGBITS and allocatable-executable (?AX), as well as all sections (not already in the segment elephant) with the name .bss (line 3). The .bss sections entering the monkey segment need not be $PROGBITS or allocatable-executable because the *section_type* and *section_flags* values were entered on a separate line from the *section_name* value. (An "and" relationship exists between attributes on the same line as illustrated by $PROGBITS "and" ?AX on line 2. An "or" relationship exists between attributes for the same segment that span more than one line as illustrated by $PROGBITS ?AX on line 2 "or" .bss on line 3.)

The monkey segment is implicitly declared in line 2 with *segment_type* value LOAD, *segment_flags* value RWX, and no *virtual_address, physical_address, length* or *alignment* values specified (defaults are used). In line 4 the *segment_type* value of monkey is set to LOAD (since the *segment_type* attribute value does not change, no warning is issued), *virtual_address* value to 0x80000000 and maximum *length* value to 0x4000 (since the *length* attribute value changed, a warning is issued).

Line 5 implicitly declares the donkey segment. The entrance criteria is designed to route all .bss sections to this segment. Actually, no sections fall into this segment because the entrance criteria for monkey in line 3 capture all of these sections. In line 6, the *segment_flags* value is set to ?RX and the *alignment* value is set to 0x1000 (since both of these attribute values changed, a warning is issued).

Line 7 sets the *virtual_address* value of the text segment to 0x80008000 (no warning is issued here).

The example user-defined mapfile in Figure B-1 is designed to cause warnings for illustration purposes. If you wanted to change the order of the directives to avoid warnings, the example would appear as follows:

```
1.      elephant : .bss : peanuts.o *popcorn.o;

4.      monkey = LOAD V0x80000000 L0x4000;
2.      monkey : $PROGBITS ?AX;
3.      monkey : .bss;

6.      donkey = ?RX A0x1000;
5.      donkey : .bss;

7.      text = V0x80008000;
```

This order eliminates all warnings.

Mapfile Option Defaults

The ld command has three built-in segments (text, data, and note) with
default *segment_attribute_values* and corresponding default mapping directives as
described under "Segment Declarations." Even though the ld command does
not use an actual "mapfile" to store the defaults, the model of a "default
mapfile" helps to illustrate what happens when the ld command encounters
your mapfile.

Figure B-2 shows how a mapfile would appear for the ld command defaults.
The ld command begins execution behaving as if the mapfile in Figure B-2 has
already been read in. Then ld reads your mapfile and either augments or
makes changes to the defaults.

 The interp segment, which precedes all others, and the dynamic segment, which follows the data segment, are not shown in Figure B-2 and
Figure B-3 because you cannot manipulate them.

Figure B-2: Default Mapfile

```
text = LOAD ?RX;
text : $PROGBITS ?A!W;

data = LOAD ?RWX;
data : $PROGBITS ?AW;
data : $NOBITS ?AW;

note = NOTE;
note : $NOTE;
```

As each segment declaration in your mapfile is read in, it is compared to the
existing list of segment declarations as follows:

1. If the segment does not already exist in the mapfile, but another with the
   same *segment-type* value exists, the segment is added before all of the
   existing segments of the same *segment_type*.

2. If none of the segments in the existing mapfile has the same *segment_type*
   value as the segment just read in, then the segment is added by
   segment_type value to maintain the following order:

          1. INTERP
          2. LOAD
          3. DYNAMIC
          4. NOTE

3. If the segment is of *segment_type* LOAD and you have defined a *virtual_address* value for this LOADable segment, the segment is placed before any LOADable segments without a defined *virtual_address* value or with a higher `virtual_address` value, but after any segments with a *virtual_address* value that is lower.

As each mapping directive in your mapfile is read in, the directive is added after any other mapping directives that you already specified for the same segment but before the default mapping directives for that segment.

Internal Map Structure

One of the most important data structures in the ELF-based ld is the map structure. A default map structure, corresponding to the model default mapfile mentioned above, is used by ld when the command is executed. Then, if the mapfile option is used, ld parses the mapfile to augment and/or override certain values in the default map structure.

A typical (although somewhat simplified) map structure is illustrated in Figure B-3. The "Entrance Criteria" boxes correspond to the information in the default mapping directives and the "Segment Attribute Descriptors" boxes correspond to the information in the default segment declarations. The "Output Section Descriptors" boxes give the detailed attributes of the sections that fall under each segment. The sections themselves are in circles.

Figure B-3: Simple Map Structure

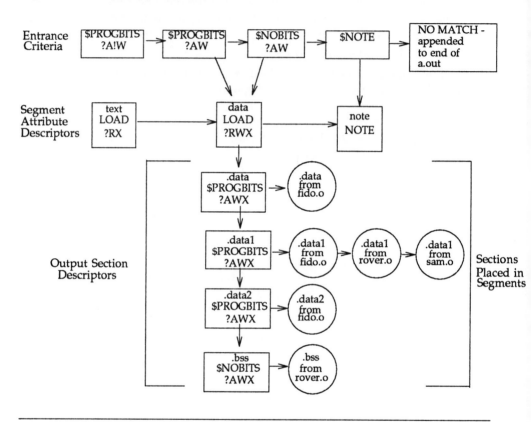

ld performs the following steps when mapping sections to segments:

1. When a section is read in, ld checks the list of Entrance Criteria looking for a match. (All specified criteria must match):

   ■ In Figure B-3, for a section to fall into the text segment it must have a *section_type* value of $PROGBITS and have a *section_flags* value of ?A!W. It need not have the name .text since no name is specified in the Entrance Criteria. The section may be either X or !X (in the *section_flags* value) since nothing was specified for the execute bit in the Entrance Criteria.

■ If no Entrance Criteria match is found, the section is placed at the end of the a.out file after all other segments. (No program header entry is created for this information. See Chapter 13 for information on program headers.)

2. When the section falls into a segment, ld checks the list of existing Output Section Descriptors in that segment as follows:

■ If the section attribute values match those of an existing Output Section Descriptor exactly, the section is placed at the end of the list of sections associated with that Output Section Descriptor.

For instance, a section with a *section_name* value of .data1, a *section_type* value of $PROGBITS, and a *section_flags* value of ?AWX falls into the second Entrance Criteria box in Figure B-3, placing it in the data segment. The section matches the second Output Section Descriptor box exactly (.data1, $PROGBITS, ?AWX) and is added to the end of the list associated with that box. The .data1 sections from fido.o, rover.o, and sam.o illustrate this point.

■ If no matching Output Section Descriptor is found, but other Output Section Descriptors of the same *section_type* exist, a new Output Section Descriptor is created with the same attribute values as the section and that section is associated with the new Output Section Descriptor. The Output Section Descriptor (and the section) are placed after the last Output Section Descriptor of the same *section_type*. The .data2 section in Figure B-3 was placed in this manner.

■ If no other Output Section Descriptors of the indicated
section_type exist, a new Output Section Descriptor is created and
the section is placed so as to maintain the following *section_type*
order:

$DYNAMIC

$PROGBITS

$SYMTAB

$STRTAB

$RELA

$REL

$HASH

$NOTE

$NOBITS

The .bss section in Figure B-3 illustrates this point.

NOTE If the input section has a user-defined *section_type* value
(i.e. between SHT_LOUSER and SHT_HIUSER, see the "Section Header" section of Chapter 13 of this guide) it is
treated as a $PROGBITS section. Note that no method
exists for naming this *section_type* value in the mapfile, but
these sections can be redirected using the other attribute
value specifications (*section_flags*, *section_name*) in the
entrance criteria.

3. If a segment contains no sections after all of the command line object files
and libraries have been read in, no program header entry is produced for
that segment.

NOTE Note that input sections of type $SYMTAB, $STRTAB, $REL, and $RELA are
used internally by ld. Directives that refer to these *section_type*s can only
map output sections produced by ld to segments.

Error Messages

When using the mapfile option, ld can return the following types of error messages:

Warnings   do not stop execution of the linker nor prevent the linker from producing a viable a.out

Fatal Errors   stop execution of the linker at the point at which the fatal error occurred

Either warning: or fatal: appears at the beginning of each error message. Error messages are not numbered.

Warnings

The following conditions produce warnings:

- a *physical_address* or a *virtual_address* value or a *length* value appears for any segment other than a LOAD segment (the directive is ignored)

- a second declaration line exists for the same segment that changes an attribute value(s) (the second declaration overrides the original)

- an attribute value(s) (*segment_type* and/or *segment_flags* for text and data; *segment_type* for note) was changed for one of the built-in segments

- an attribute value(s) (*segment_type*, *segment_flags*, *length* and/or *alignment*) was changed for a segment created by an implicit declaration

Fatal Errors

The following conditions produce fatal errors:

- specifying more than one –M option on the command line

- specifying both the –r and the –M option on the same command line

- specifying the –M option without the –dn option on the command line (–dy is the default; you must specify –dn with the –M option)

- a mapfile cannot be opened or read
- a syntax error is found in the mapfile

 NOTE ld does not return an error if a *file_name, section_name, segment_name* or *symbol_name* does not conform to the rules under the "Mapfile Structure and Syntax" section unless this condition produces a syntax error. For instance, if a name begins with a special character and this name is at the beginning of a directive line, ld returns an error. If the name is a *section_name* (appearing within the directive) ld does not return an error.

- more than one *segment_type, segment_flags, virtual_address, physical_address, length,* or *alignment* value appears on a single declaration line
- you attempt to manipulate either the interp segment or dynamic segment in a mapfile

 CAUTION The interp and dynamic segments are special built-in segments that you cannot change in any way.

- a segment grows larger than the size specified by a your *length* attribute value
- a user-defined *virtual_address* value causes a segment to overlap the previous segment
- more than one *section_name, section_type,* or *section_flags* value appears on a single directive line
- a flag and its complement (e.g., A and !A) appear on a single directive line

Glossary

ANSI
: ANSI is an acronym for the American National Standards Institute. ANSI establishes standards in the computing industry from the definition of ASCII (see below) to the measurement of overall datacom system performance. ANSI standards have been established for the Ada, FORTRAN, and C programming languages.

a.out
: a.out, historically for "assembler output," is the default file name for an executable program produced by the C compilation system.

application
: An application program is a working program in a given operating system, that is, an application of that system. When the source code for an application program is portable to another operating system, the program is an application of that system as well.

archive
: An archive, or statically linked library, is a collection of object files each of which contains the code for a function or a group of related functions in the library. When you call a library function in your program, and specify a static linking option on the cc command line, a copy of the object file that contains the function is incorporated in your executable at link time. For a discussion, see "Link Editing" in Chapter 2, and compare "shared object."

argument
: You use an argument to pass information to a command or a function. A command instructs the operating system to execute a program. The command is the name of the file containing the program. Command line arguments are character strings or numbers that follow the command, separated from it by a space, or that follow another command line argument, separated from it by a space. There are two types of command line arguments: options and operands. Options, which are immediately preceded by a minus sign (–), change the behavior of the program. Some options can themselves take arguments. Options are also called flags. Operands specify files or directories to be operated on by the program. So in the command line

```
$ cc -o hello hello.c
```

all the elements after the cc command are arguments.
cc is the name of the file containing the C compiler program. The C source file hello.c is its operand. -o is
an option that tells the compilation system to generate
an executable program with a name other than a.out.
hello is an argument to -o that specifies the name of
the executable program to be created. For a discussion
of how command line arguments are passed to C programs, see "Passing Command Line Arguments" in
Chapter 2.

Function arguments are enclosed in a pair of
parentheses immediately following the function name.
The number of arguments can be zero or more; if two or
more are given, they must be separated by commas and
the whole list enclosed by parentheses. The formal
definition of a function describes the number and data
type of arguments expected by the function. You can
find formal definitions of the functions supplied with
the C compilation system in Sections 2 and 3 of the
Programmer's Reference Manual.

ASCII
ASCII is an acronym for the American Standard Code
for Information Interchange, the standard for data
representation followed in the UNIX system. ASCII code
represents 128 upper- and lowercase letters, numerals,
and special characters as binary numbers. Each
alphanumeric and special character has an ASCII
equivalent that is one byte long.

assembler
Assembly language is a programming language that
uses symbolic names to represent the machine instructions of a given computer. An assembler is a program
that accepts instructions written in the assembly
language of the computer and translates them into a
binary representation of the corresponding machine
instructions. Because each assembly language instruction usually has a one-to-one correspondence with a

machine instruction, programs written in assembly
language are not portable to different machines.

buffer

A buffer is a space in computer memory where data are
stored temporarily in convenient units for system operations. Buffers are often used by programs such as editors that access and alter text or data frequently. When
you edit a file, for instance, a copy of its contents are
read into a buffer; the copy is what you change. For
your changes to become part of the permanent file, you
must write the buffer's contents back into the permanent
file. This replaces the contents of the file with the contents of the buffer. When you quit the editor, the contents of the buffer are flushed.

child process

See "fork()."

command

A command instructs the operating system to execute a
program. On the UNIX system, an executable program
is a compiled and linked program or a shell program.
The command to execute either is the name of the file
containing the program. A command line consists of
the command followed by its arguments, so

```
$ cc file1.c file2.c
```

instructs the operating system to execute the C compiler
program, which is stored in the file cc, and to use the
source files file1.c and file2.c as input. A command line can extend over multiple terminal lines.

compiler

A compiler is a program that translates a source program written in a higher-level language into the assembly language of the computer the program is to run on.
An assembler translates the assembly language code into
the machine instructions of the computer. On the C
compilation system, these instructions are stored in
object files that correspond to each of your source files.
That is, each object file contains a binary representation
of the C language code in the corresponding source file.
Source file names must end with the characters .c;
object files take the name of the source file with .o in
place of .c. The link editor links these object files with

each other, and with any library functions you have used in your source code, to produce an executable program called a.out by default. The preprocessor component of the C compiler performs macro expansion, conditional compilation, and file inclusion before the compiler proper translates C source code into assembly language. For a discussion, see "Compiling and Linking" in Chapter 2.

core image

A core image is a a copy of the memory image of a process. A file named core is created in your current directory when the UNIX system aborts an executing program. The file contains the core image of the process at the time of the failure. For a discussion, see Chapter 6, "sdb."

data symbol

A data symbol names a variable that may or may not be initialized. Normally, these variables reside in read/write memory during execution. Compare "text symbol."

debugging

Debugging is the process of locating and correcting errors in executable programs. For a discussion, see Chapter 6, "sdb."

default

A default is the way a program will perform a task in the absence of other instructions, that is, in default of your specifying something else.

directory

A directory is a type of file used to group and organize other files or directories. A subdirectory is a directory that is pointed to by a directory one level above it in the file system. A directory name is a string of characters that identifies the directory. It can be a simple directory name, a relative path name, or a full path name. For a discussion, see the *User's Guide*, Chapter 3, "Using the File System."

dynamic linking

Dynamic linking refers to the process in which external references in a program are linked with their definitions when the program is executed. For a discussion, see "Link Editing" in Chapter 2, and compare "static linking."

ELF	ELF is an acronym for the executable and linking format of the object files produced by the C compilation system. For a discussion, see Chapter 13, "Object Files."
environment	An environment is a collection of resources used to support a function. On the UNIX system, the shell environment consists of variables whose values define the way you interact with the operating system. The shell environment variable $HOME, for example, stands for your login directory; $PATH is a list of directories the shell will search for executable programs. When you log in, the system executes programs that create most of the environment variables you need to do your work. These variables are stored in /etc/profile, a file that defines a common environment for users when they log in to the system. You can tailor your environment to your own needs by defining and setting variables in the file .profile in your login directory. You can also temporarily set variables at the shell level. For a discussion, see the *User's Guide*, Chapter 7, "Shell Tutorial."
executable program	On the UNIX system, an executable program is a compiled and linked program or a shell program. The command to execute either is the name of the file containing the program. A compiled and linked program is called an executable object file. Compare "object file."
exit ()	The exit () function causes a process to terminate. exit () closes any open files and cleans up most other information and memory used by the process. An exit status, or return code, is an integer value that your program returns to the operating system to say whether it completed successfully or not. For a discussion, see "How C Programs Communicate with the Shell" in Chapter 1.
expression	An expression is a mathematical or logical symbol or meaningful combination of symbols.

file	A file is a potential source of input or a potential destination for output; at some point, then, an identifiable collection of information. A file is known to the UNIX system as an inode plus the information the inode contains that tells whether the file is a plain file, a special file, or a directory. A plain file contains text, data, programs, or other information that forms a coherent unit. A special file is a hardware device or portion thereof, such as a disk partition. A directory is a type of file that contains the names and inode addresses of other plain, special, or directory files. For a discussion, see the *User's Guide*, Chapter 3, "Using the File System."
file descriptor	A file descriptor is an integer value assigned by the operating system to a file when the file is opened by a process.
file system	A UNIX file system is a hierarchical collection of directories and other files that are organized in a tree structure. The base of the structure is the root (/) directory; other directories, all subordinate to root, are branches. The collection of files can be mounted on a block special file. Each file of a file system appears exactly once in the inode list of the file system and is accessible via a single, unique path from the root directory of the file system. For a discussion, see the *User's Guide*, Chapter 3, "Using the File System."
filter	A filter is a program that reads information from the standard input, acts on it in some way, and sends its result to the standard output. It is called a filter because it can be used in a pipeline (see "pipe") to transform the output of another program. Filters are different from editors in that they do not change the contents of a file. Examples of UNIX system filters are sort, which sorts the input, and wc, which counts the number of words, characters, and lines in the input. sort, wc, and other UNIX system filters are described in Section 1 of the *User's Reference Manual*.

flag	See "argument."
fork ()	fork () is a system call that splits one process into two, the parent process and the child process, with separate, but initially identical, text, data, and stack segments. fork () is described in Section 2 of the *Programmer's Reference Manual.*
header file	A header file is a file that usually contains shared data declarations that are to be copied into source files by the compiler. Header file names conventionally end with the characters .h. Header files are also called include files, for the C language #include directive by which they are made available to source files. For a discussion, see Chapter 2, "C Compilation System."
include file	See "header file."
interrupt	An interrupt is a break in the normal flow of a system or program. Interrupts are initiated by signals generated by a hardware condition or a peripheral device to indicate the occurrence of a specified event. When the interrupt is recognized by the hardware, an interrupt handling routine is executed. An interrupt character is a character (normally ASCII) that, when typed on a terminal, causes an interrupt. You can usually interrupt UNIX system programs by pressing the delete or break keys, or by pressing the CTRL and d keys simultaneously.
I/O	I/O stands for input/output, the process by which information enters (input) and leaves (output) a computer system. For a discussion, see "Standard I/O" in Chapter 2.
kernel	The kernel is the basic resident software of the UNIX system. The kernel is responsible for most system operations: scheduling and managing the work done by the computer, maintaining the file system, and so forth. The kernel has its own text, data, and stack areas.

lexical analysis	Lexical analysis is the process by which a stream of characters (often comprising a source program) is broken up into its elementary words and symbols, called tokens. The tokens can include the reserved words of a programming language, its identifiers and constants, and special symbols such as =, :=, and ;. Lexical analysis enables you to recognize, for instance, that the stream of characters `printf("hello, world\n");` is a series of tokens beginning with `printf` and not with, say, `printf("h`. In compilers, a lexical analyzer is often called by a syntactic analyzer, or parser, that analyzes the grammatical form of tokens passed to it by the lexical analyzer. For discussions, see Chapter 11, "`lex`," and Chapter 12, "`yacc`."
library	A library is a file that contains object code for a group of commonly used functions. Rather than write the functions yourself, you arrange for the functions to be linked with your program when an executable is created (see "archive"), or when it is run (see "shared object").
link editing	Link editing refers to the process in which a symbol referenced in one module of a program is connected with its definition in another. On the C compilation system, programs are linked statically, when an executable is created, or dynamically, when it is run. For a discussion, see "Link Editing" in Chapter 2.
makefile	A `makefile` is a file that is used with the program `make` to keep track of the dependencies between modules of a program, so that when one module is changed, dependent ones are brought up to date. For a discussion, see Chapter 9, "`make`."
module	A module is a program component that typically contains a function or a group of related functions. Source files and libraries are modules.
null pointer	A null pointer is a C pointer with a value of 0.

object file	An object file contains a binary representation of programming language code. A relocatable object file contains references to symbols that have not yet been linked with their definitions. An executable object file is a linked program. Compare "source file."
optimizer	An optimizer improves the efficiency of the assembly language code generated by a compiler. That, in turn, will speed the execution time of your object code. For a discussion, see "Commonly Used cc Command Line Options" in Chapter 2.
option	See "argument."
parent process	See "fork()."
parser	A parser, or syntactic analyzer, analyzes the grammatical form of tokens passed to it by a lexical analyzer (see "lexical analysis"). For discussions, see Chapter 11, "lex," and Chapter 12, "yacc."
path name	A path name designates the location of a file in the file system. It is made up of a series of directory names that proceed down the hierarchical path of the file system. The directory names are separated by a slash character (/). The last name in the path is the file. If the path name begins with a slash, it is called an absolute, or full, path name; the initial slash means that the path begins at the root directory. A path name that does not begin with a slash is known as a relative path name, meaning relative to your current directory. For a discussion, see the *User's Guide*, Chapter 3, "Using the File System."
permissions	Permissions define a right to access a file in the file system. Permissions are granted separately to you, your group, and all others. There are three basic permissions: read, write, and execute. For a discussion, see the *User's Guide*, Chapter 3, "Using the File System."
pipe	A pipe causes the output of one program to be used as the input to another program, so that the programs run in sequence. You create a pipeline by preceding each command after the first command with the pipe symbol

(|), which indicates that the output from the process on the left should be routed to the process on the right. So

```
$ who | wc -l
```

causes the output of the who command, which lists the users who are logged in to the system, to be used as the input of the wc, or word count, command with the −1 option. The result is the number of users logged in to the system. The who and wc commands are described in Section 1 of the *User's Reference Manual*.

portability
: Portability refers to the degree of ease with which a program can be moved, or ported, to a different operating system or machine.

preprocessor
: A preprocessor is a a program that prepares an input file for another program. The preprocessor component of the C compiler performs macro expansion, conditional compilation, and file inclusion.

process
: A process is an executing program. Every time you enter the name of a file that contains an executable program you initiate a new process. A process ID is a unique system-wide number that identifies an active process. You can use the ps command, described in Section 1 of the *User's Reference Manual*, to determine the process ID of any process currently active on your system.

regular expression
: A regular expression is a string of alphanumeric characters and special characters that describes, in a shorthand way, a pattern to be searched for in a file. For a discussion, see Chapter 11, "lex."

routine
: A routine is another name for a function.

shared object
: A shared object, or dynamically linked library, is a single object file that contains the code for every function in the library. When you call a library function in your program, and specify a dynamic linking option on the cc command line, the entire contents of the shared object are mapped into the virtual address space of your process at run time. As its name implies, a shared

object contains code that can be used simultaneously by different programs at run time. For a discussion, see "Link Editing" in Chapter 2, and compare "archive."

shell
The shell is the UNIX system program that handles communication between you and the system. The shell is known as a command interpreter because it translates your commands into a language understandable by the system. A shell normally is started for you when you log in to the system. A shell program calls the shell to read and execute commands contained in an executable file. For discussions, see the *User's Guide*, Chapter 7, "Shell Tutorial," and the sh page in Section 1 of the *User's Reference Manual*.

signal
A signal is a message you send to a process or that processes send to one another. You might use a signal, for example, to initiate an interrupt (see above). A signal sent by a running process is usually a sign of an exceptional occurrence that has caused the process to terminate or divert from the normal flow of control.

source file
Source files contain the programming language version of a program. Before a computer can execute the program, the source code must be translated by a compiler and assembler into the machine language of the computer. Compare "object file."

standard error
Standard error is an output stream from a program that normally is used to convey error messages. On the UNIX system, the default case is to associate standard error with the user's terminal.

standard input
Standard input is an input stream to a program. On the UNIX system, the default case is to associate standard input with the user's terminal.

standard output
Standard output is an output stream from a program. On the UNIX system, the default case is to associate standard output with the user's terminal.

static linking	Static linking refers to the process in which external references in a program are linked with their definitions when an executable is created. For a discussion, see "Link Editing" in Chapter 2, and compare "dynamic linking."
stream	A stream is an open file with its associated buffering. For a discussion, see "Standard I/O" in Chapter 2. Stream also refers to a full duplex processing and data transfer path in the kernel that implements a connection between a driver in kernel space and a process in user space, providing a general input/output interface for user processes.
string	A string is a contiguous sequence of characters treated as a unit. In C, a character string is an array of characters terminated by the null character, \0.
syntax	Command syntax is the order in which commands and their arguments must be put together. The command always comes first. The order of arguments varies from command to command. Language syntax is the set of rules that describes how the elements of a programming language may legally be used.
system call	A system call is a request from a program for an action to be performed by the UNIX system kernel. For a discussion, see "System Calls" in Chapter 2.
text symbol	A text symbol names a program instruction. Instructions reside in read-only memory during execution. Compare "data symbol."
user ID	A user ID is an integer value, usually associated with a login name, that the system uses to identify owners of files and directories. The user ID of a process becomes the owner of files created by the process and by descendent processes (see "fork ()").
variable	In a program, a variable is an object whose value may change during the execution of the program or from one execution to the next. A variable in the shell is a name representing a string of characters.

white space   White space is one or more spaces, tabs, or new-line
                     characters. White space is normally used to separate
                     strings of characters, and is required to separate the
                     command from its arguments on a command line.

INDEX

Index

ANSI C and Programming Support Tools

M